Dillinger's Wild Ride

Also by Elliott J. Gorn

The Manly Art: Bare-Knuckle Prize Fighting in America

Constructing the American Past (with Randy Roberts and Terry Bilhartz)

A Brief History of American Sports (with Warren Goldstein)

The McGuffey Readers

Muhammad Ali: The People's Champ

The Encyclopedia of American Social History (with Peter Williams and Mary Kupiec Cayton)

Mother Jones: The Most Dangerous Woman in America

Chicago Sports

ELLIOTT J. GORN

Dillinger's Wild Ride

The Year That Made America's Public Enemy Number One

OXFORD

UNIVERSITY PRESS

2009

OXFORD
UNIVERSITY PRESS

Oxford University Press, Inc., publishes works that further
Oxford University's objective of excellence
in research, scholarship, and education.

Oxford   New York
Auckland   Cape Town   Dar es Salaam   Hong Kong   Karachi
Kuala Lumpur   Madrid   Melbourne   Mexico City   Nairobi
New Delhi   Shanghai   Taipei   Toronto

With offices in
Argentina   Austria   Brazil   Chile   Czech Republic   France   Greece
Guatemala   Hungary   Italy   Japan   Poland   Portugal   Singapore
South Korea   Switzerland   Thailand   Turkey   Ukraine   Vietnam

Published by Oxford University Press, Inc.
198 Madison Avenue, New York, NY 10016

www.oup.com

Oxford is a registered trademark of Oxford University Press

Library of Congress Cataloging-in-Publication Data
Gorn, Elliott J., 1951–
Dillinger's wild ride : the year that made America's
public enemy number one / Elliott J. Gorn.
p. cm.
ISBN 978-0-19-530483-1
1. Dillinger, John, 1903–1934.
2. Criminals—Middle West—Biography.
I. Title.
HV6248.D5G67 2009
364.152'3092—dc22   [B]
2008048150

9 8 7 6 5 4 3 2 1

Printed in the United States of America
on acid-free paper

For Jade.
I'm so proud of you, Kid.

Contents

Chronology

The Year That Made America's Public Enemy Number One

June 1933   A month after his release from the Indiana State
                     Penitentiary, John Dillinger and accomplices take
                     $10,000 from the New Carlisle National Bank in
                     Ohio. Through the summer Dillinger works with
                     Sam Goldstein, Hilton Crouch, Harry Copeland,
                     William Shaw, and others.

July 1933   Dillinger and Copeland rob the Commercial Bank
                     in Daleville, Indiana, of $3,500.

August 1933   Dillinger and accomplices steal $12,000 from the
                     First National Bank of Montpelier, Indiana.

                     Dillinger, Copeland, and Goldstein steal $2,000
                     from the Citizens National Bank in Bluffton,
                     Ohio.

September 1933   Dillinger, Copeland, and Crouch rob State Bank of
                     Massachusetts Avenue, Indianapolis, of $25,000.

Dillinger arrested in Dayton, Ohio, at the home of his girlfriend, Mary Longnaker, the sister of one of his old prison mates. Officials transfer Dillinger to the Lima jail.

Harry Pierpont, Charles Makley, John "Red" Hamilton, Russell Clark, and six others break out of Indiana State Penitentiary with guns smuggled in by Dillinger just before his arrest.

October 1933   Pierpont, Makley, Hamilton, and Clark steal $11,000 from the First National Bank in St. Mary's, Ohio.

Pierpont, Makley, Hamilton, Clark, and Copeland free Dillinger from the Lima jail, killing Sheriff Jess Sarber.

Dillinger and two accomplices raid Auburn, Indiana, police station. A week later they do the same in Peru, Indiana.

Dillinger, Pierpont, Makley, Clark, Hamilton, and Copeland—now called the "Dillinger gang" in the newspapers—rob the Central National Bank of Greencastle, Indiana, of $75,000 in cash and bonds.

November 1933   Car chase and shoot-out with police on Irving Park Boulevard in Chicago as Dillinger and his new girlfriend, Evelyn "Billie" Frechette, leave his doctor's office.

Dillinger gang robs the American Bank and Trust Company in Racine, Wisconsin, of $28,000, wounding two and briefly taking the bank president and a policeman hostage.

December 1933   Hamilton kills Chicago police officer William Shanley.

Chicago Police Department organizes forty-man "Dillinger Squad" under Captain John Stege.

Chicago police raid apartment on Farwell Avenue, killing three men they wrongly believe are part of the Dillinger gang.

Dillinger and several accomplices top the Chicago Police's "Public Enemies" list. Before the month ends, the gang drives south to Florida.

January 1934 The Dillinger gang spends New Year's in Daytona Beach.

Dillinger and John Hamilton rob First National Bank of East Chicago, Indiana, of $20,000. Dillinger accused of killing officer William O'Malley; Hamilton wounded.

Dillinger, Makley, Clark, and Pierpont captured in Tucson, Arizona. Girlfriends Mary Kinder, Opal Long, and Billie Frechette arrested as accomplices.

Pierpont, Makley, and Clark sent back to Ohio to stand trial for Sheriff Sarber's murder; Dillinger flown to Indiana for the O'Malley killing.

Dillinger photographed with prosecutor Robert Estill and Sheriff Lillian Holley in Crown Point, Indiana.

February 1934 Dillinger indicted for murder; spends the month in the Crown Point jail, preparing for his trial on March 12. Chicago attorney Louis Piquett represents Dillinger.

March 1934 Using a wooden gun, Dillinger breaks out of Crown Point Jail. He and prisoner Herbert Youngblood drive to Chicago in Sheriff Holley's car.

The second Dillinger gang, including Baby Face Nelson, Homer Van Meter, Tommy Carroll, and Harry "Eddie" Green, rob the Security

National Bank in Sioux Falls, South Dakota, of almost $50,000.

Dillinger named in a federal complaint for violating the Dyer Act, transporting a stolen vehicle across state lines. The FBI is now actively pursuing the case.

Dillinger gang robs First National Bank in Mason City, Iowa, of more than $50,000; Dillinger and Hamilton wounded.

Youngblood killed in gun battle in Port Huron, Michigan.

Pierpont and Makley sentenced to death in Lima; Russell Clark receives life sentence.

Dillinger and Billie Frechette escape an FBI shoot-out in St. Paul, Minnesota; Dillinger again wounded.

April 1934

Gang member Eddie Green killed in ambush by the FBI, St. Paul.

Dillinger and Billie Frechette spend long weekend with Dillinger family in Mooresville, Indiana.

Billie Frechette captured by FBI in a State Street tavern in Chicago; Dillinger escapes unnoticed.

Dillinger and Van Meter raid police arsenal in Warsaw, Indiana.

Dillinger gang shoots its way out of the Little Bohemia lodge in Northern Wisconsin. Nelson kills one federal agent and wounds two peace officers; the FBI shoots three bystanders, one fatally. Feds capture three women running with the gang.

Dillinger, Van Meter, and Hamilton shoot it out in a car chase with St. Paul police. The three return to Chicago; Hamilton dies of his wounds four days later in Aurora, Illinois.

May 1934 Dillinger and Van Meter rob the First National Bank in Fostoria, Ohio, of $17,000.

United States Congress passes ten new laws, the "New Deal on Crime," endorsed by the president and the attorney general, who cite Dillinger as a reason such legislation is necessary.

Billie Frechette convicted of harboring Dillinger; sentenced to two years in federal prison and fined $1,000.

Officers Martin O'Brien and Lloyd Mulvihill of the East Chicago Police slain on a deserted highway; Dillinger and Van Meter suspected.

Dillinger and Van Meter undergo plastic surgery while hiding out in the Chicago home of bar owner and underworld figure Jimmy Probasco.

June 1934 Dillinger meets Polly Hamilton, who becomes his new girlfriend.

Dillinger and Polly celebrate his 31st birthday in Chicago, the very day he is named America's "Public Enemy Number One."

Dillinger gang robs the Merchant's National Bank in South Bend, Indiana, of $30,000, killing one policeman and wounding several civilians.

July 1934 Dillinger—sporting glasses, dyed hair, a mustache, and a surgically reconstructed face—and Polly are frequently out on the town in Chicago.

Dillinger and Van Meter plot a train robbery and talk about making a movie of their experiences.

Martin Zarkovich and Anna Sage meet with Melvin Purvis regarding Dillinger's plans to attend a film the next night.

Dillinger killed by federal agents as he leaves the Biograph theater on Lincoln Avenue in Chicago. He, Polly Hamilton, and Anna Sage had just watched the movie *Manhattan Melodrama*, starring Clark Gable, William Powell, and Myrna Loy.

Dillinger's death is headline news across America; tens of thousands come to the morgue, the funeral home, and the cemetery to view his body.

Preface

At 10:20 p.m. on July 22, 1934, John Dillinger was gunned down by federal agents as he left Chicago's Biograph theater. Thousands of people turned out on Lincoln Avenue where he fell, at the city morgue to view the body, at his grave in Indianapolis's Crown Hill Cemetery. For the next several days the newspaper headlines were filled with little else aside from Dillinger's death. Someone scrawled a bit of doggerel on the Lincoln Avenue sidewalk:

> Stranger, stop and wish me well,
>> Just say a prayer for my soul in hell.
> I was a good fellow, most people said,
>> Betrayed by a woman all dressed in red.

Over and over, reporters reprised Dillinger's wild year of bank robberies, jailbreaks, and shoot-outs. They framed it as a story of big money, senseless violence, fast women, and faster cars as the gang members and their molls went on a months-long road trip across the heartland, down to Florida then all the way to Arizona. And it all took place against a backdrop of Depression-era America, with ten thousand banks closed, a quarter of the population unemployed, and homeless people everywhere.

Born and raised in Indiana, Dillinger spent nine years, most of his adulthood, in prison for a botched stickup, his first felony. Released at age twenty-nine in the spring of 1933, at the nadir of the Great

Depression, by the end of summer he had pulled several heists, broken his friends out of the Indiana state penitentiary, gotten arrested, then was sprung by his newly freed cronies, who killed the local sheriff in the process. For the next several months "the Dillinger gang" took it on the lam: bank robberies across the Midwest, shoot-outs with local police, staying one step ahead of the law. They were all arrested in Tucson in January 1934 and shipped back to the Midwest to stand trial.

But the story wasn't over. Once again Dillinger escaped, formed a new gang, and, with machine guns blazing, commenced a cycle of increasingly bloody bank jobs. Meanwhile J. Edgar Hoover, head of the Justice Department's Division of Investigation—soon to be renamed the Federal Bureau of Investigation—staked his personal and his agency's reputation on bringing down Dillinger. Again and again the Hoosier outlaw humiliated authorities, going home to his father's farm for a chicken dinner under the G-men's noses in March, escaping in April from the feds in a dramatic shoot-out at a resort in northern Wisconsin, disappearing without a trace in May. Before Dillinger's year-long rampage was over, a dozen policemen, gang members, and civilians were dead, hundreds of thousands of dollars had been stolen, and public faith in law enforcement was shaken. It was one bloody road trip, one wild ride, and it haunted America's imagination.

The violence notwithstanding, there was something deeply appealing about John Dillinger, his nerve, his coolness, his élan. Some said that of all the famous Americans of this era only Franklin Roosevelt and Charles Lindbergh were better known. Dillinger's charisma was especially compelling against the Depression's breakdown of social and economic institutions, the bank runs, foreclosures, plant closings, strikes, unemployed marches, breadlines, Hoovervilles—in a word, the collapse of Americans' confidence in the future.

Dillinger's ghost still haunts us today, in ways large and small. Early on in this project I drove around Ohio, Indiana, and Illinois with my friend Tom Silfen, checking out Dillinger sites. We found one of the banks that he robbed at the very beginning of his crime spree still standing. The building had become a candle shop, its vault a storage locker. No one had died in the robbery, but the owner of the store was convinced it was haunted. She once saw a lit candle rise off a table, move through the air, then crash to the floor. And later, a spectral young man dressed in overalls startled her husband in the basement. They still refer to the vanishing stranger as John. Dillinger's ghost was an Indiana farm boy.

On Sheridan Road in Uptown Chicago the building still stands that housed McCready's Funeral Home, where Dillinger's body was laid out for burial in 1934. In the wake of World War II, after the neighborhood had absorbed an influx of newcomers, St. Augustine's Episcopal Parish took over the structure and converted it to a social services center, catering to the needs of Chicago's large new Native American population. Whatever spirits inhabited the building would not be still. To continue their work undisturbed, the leaders of St. Augustine's held not one but two exorcisms, the first by an Episcopal priest, the second by a Native holy man. The place quieted down.

Beginning a few years ago and continuing to this day, an annual memorial service in Chicago has honored Dillinger. A few dozen gather at a tavern on Lincoln Avenue on the anniversary of his death, drink up, chat, then, a little after 10 p.m., line up outside to follow a bagpiper across the street to the Biograph theater. There they observe a moment of silence as 10:20 approaches, listen to a few words about the fallen outlaw, toast him, and sing "Amazing Grace" accompanied by the bagpipes. Inevitably something is said about lights flickering and cool breezes blowing at the instant of his passing.

Legends cling to John Dillinger: stories about the gang lying low after a bank job, aided by townsfolk in some Indiana village; Dillinger picking up a hitchhiker by the highway; Dillinger gassing up his car at the local filling station; chance meetings with the outlaw, even after his death. Near Crown Point, Indiana, where Dillinger broke out of prison in early March 1934, locals referred to a road that ran by a desolate farm as "the Big Mary Road." Dillinger hid out at that farm, people said, harbored by a lover named Mary. Cops who drove by at night maintained they sometimes saw Big Mary's ghost glaring at them.

There has always been something uncanny about Dillinger. In 1934 people reported seeing him everywhere; literally tens of thousands of sightings of him poured into police stations and newspaper offices. Dillinger has been ubiquitous for me too. From the living-room window in my apartment on Farwell Avenue in Chicago I can see the building where police believed the gang was holed up late in 1933. The cops came in blasting, killing three obscure Jewish hoodlums, but Dillinger was nowhere to be found. My old apartment in the Lakeview section of town was half a block from where Dillinger's girlfriend lived and a block and a half from the flat on Halsted Street where he spent his first night after the Crown Point breakout.

Others stole larger amounts of money than Dillinger, robbed more banks, killed more people, yet *his* name became a household word. Some have said he wasn't even the leader of his own gang, that his accomplice Harry Pierpont was the real brains of the outfit. In truth the Dillinger gang was really more like a constantly shifting band of brothers, making decisions by consensus. But Dillinger was the charismatic center of the action.

Three-quarters of a century after his death he remains famous. The reason, of course, is that popular culture has kept his memory alive. Newspapers note the anniversary of his death each year, and several feature-length films have told his story. There were radio programs after he died and television documentaries in more recent years. He has been the subject of novels, short stories, and poems. Not one but two Dillinger museums displayed the artifacts of his days on earth. Websites testify to a continuing fascination with his life and times, and even musicians—such as the rapper Daz Dillinger and the punk band Dillinger Escape Plan—use his name as an emblem of gangster life. Now Hollywood is at it again, adding to Dillinger's filmic legacy with a new blockbuster movie by a distinguished director, featuring one of America's best-known actors.

His words have appeared in compilations of famous quotations. "They're giving bank robbery a bad name," Dillinger supposedly said about Bonnie and Clyde, a reference to their violent carelessness in contrast to his craftsmanship. "I won't cause you any trouble, except to escape," he once told his jailers. "I guess my only bad habit is robbing banks; I smoke very little and don't drink much." Such homespun understatement, whether or not he ever made these remarks, underscored his charisma and charm, which arose out of his seeming nonchalance. Dillinger was a regular guy—funny, easy-going, loyal to his friends—yet he pulled off the most hair-raising deeds.

Much of the Dillinger story has been told: by the journalists John Tolland, Ellen Poulsen, and Brian Burrough, academics such as Claire Bond Potter, and the writers Dary Matera, William Helmer, Rick Mattix, William Cromie, and Joe Pinkston. They disagree over details, and larger issues too. Was young Johnnie Dillinger a budding criminal just waiting to bloom, or did prison make him a hardened felon?

Were some banks complicit in their own robberies in order to cover malfeasance and collect insurance money? Did Dillinger himself carve the wooden gun he used in a jailbreak, or was it smuggled to him, and if so, by whom? For that matter, might it have been a real gun? Mostly the differences are matters of emphasis. Potter, for example, argues that Dillinger became a useful tool in the Justice Department's drive to expand federal authority over crime and thereby enhance the power of the state; Poulsen tells the story from the point of view of the working-class women associated with the gang; Burrough puts the story in the context of the 1930s crime wave; Tolland offers a psychological profile of Dillinger; Matera's book is closest to a comprehensive biography.

I take a little different tack here. Like the others I tell the story of Dillinger's wild year. Using government documents and newspapers I describe the activities of the gang and the efforts of law enforcement agencies to stop them. More than that, however, I seek to explain how the Dillinger story was created, interpreted, and reworked, how Americans felt about his exploits, and how we have come to remember him. This often means paying attention to the language of those who first told the story, law enforcement officials, politicians, and journalists. I rely heavily on news items from the wire services, like the Associated Press, so that while I might cite a particular article in a footnote, the same or a similar story appeared simultaneously in several newspapers. Given the integrated nature of print culture by the 1930s, the Dillinger story was told with considerable uniformity.

Dillinger's chroniclers often called him the last American outlaw, and newspapers in the 1930s compared him more often to Jesse James than Al Capone. The immigrant Capone was usually referred to as a "gangster" (as are black and Latino kids in the drug trade today), but the native-born Dillinger was as likely to be called an "outlaw." "Gangster" implies the city; "outlaw" resonates with open spaces. The former has valances of darker races and ethnicities, the latter with white, heartland bandits. Gangsters operate illegal businesses in drugs, gambling, and bootleg liquor; outlaws more often assault legitimate institutions, such as banks. "Outlaw" is a term from the West of the imagination, and though outlaws are the "bad guys" they are also part of America's deepest hero myths.

Outlaws were literally beyond the law, outside of society, and that was part of Dillinger's appeal, then and now. There was nothing consciously political or ideological about him, but he expressed with his deeds the rage that many Americans felt in 1933 and 1934. Dillinger was not admired because he aided the poor but because he attacked the rich, symbolically anyway. His victims were banks, bastions of capitalism that were deeply unpopular in the 1930s. He came in blasting at a moment when many Americans felt betrayed. He assaulted his targets frontally, brazenly, in acts that at once appalled and thrilled his countrymen. To read about his gang's exploits in the papers or see his image in the newsreels was to feel both the fear and the excitement of men taking matters into their own hands. There was also an edgy working-class bohemianism to gang life. Men and women on the lam lived fugitive lives, ducking in and out of the daily flow of the city, changing apartments and neighborhoods often, living together out of wedlock, stealing or buying cars, then heading back out into the countryside, resisting settled and respectable ways. Much of the power of this story comes from Americans' romance with the road.

One final note: I am writing this preface in the midst of the financial crisis of 2008. Having lived with this book for several years I am surprised at how much our current banking meltdown deepens the emotional resonance of Dillinger's story. Now when I think back on those 1934 letters from Americans to their leaders expressing sympathy for Dillinger as he robbed banks; on those citizens criticized by newspapers and politicians for saying openly that they admired the man; on the people who asked why, during the Depression, a few profited handsomely while others suffered, I understand them all a little better. As our own day's story of stupid policies and lax regulations, of greedy moneymen, free-market hucksters, white-collar thieves, and self-serving politicians unfolds, and as banks foreclose on millions of families' homes, workers lose their jobs, and life savings disappear, it becomes clear why Dillinger's wild ride so fascinated America during the 1930s.

Dillinger's Wild Ride

ONE

"He Would Try Hard
to Be a Man"

THE GAS-STATION ATTENDANT AT INDIANAPOLIS TOLD ME I'D miss Mooresville at night. 'It's just a wide place in the road,' he said." So the *New Yorker* columnist James Finan began his May 1934 article about John Dillinger, the notorious Indiana bandit who, just days before, had shot it out with federal agents, escaped their clutches, and was once again at large, somewhere in the American heartland. Finan went back to where the story began, back to Dillinger's home-town: "Four concrete corners, and a traffic light in the centre. A row of shops, a post office, and avenues of maple-lined streets leading back into the countryside again. Seventeen hundred and seventy-four fairly good citizens and one very bad citizen call it home."[1]

Finan interviewed townsmen who knew Johnnie Dillinger, includ-ing Pastor Huston of the First Christian Church. "On the end seat there," the minister pointed to the back row of pews in his small wooden church, "Johnnie used to sit at Sunday school." There must have been a lot of good in Johnnie, the pastor told Finan, otherwise those who knew him would not speak so well of him. "It is not for us to judge," Huston added; "Saul of Tarsus was a murderer, you remember—and he later became St. Paul." Still, Huston mused, "these recent newspaper reports of Dillinger going around with all these women didn't do him any good. People don't take to that sort of thing very kindly." Johnnie's old Sunday school teacher, Mrs. Willis Richardson, remembered him only as an inattentive boy who wore his cap to the side, the bill pulled down over one eye, just like that boy who led him astray, Ed Singleton, and just like, she might have added, all the tough little felons in the motion pictures.[2]

The *New Yorker* did not have to say out loud what American readers implicitly understood: that to know Mooresville was to know John Dillinger. More precisely, to know the little Hoosier town was to trace how far Dillinger, and maybe America itself, had fallen. Finan even interviewed Frank Morgan, the local grocer whom Dillinger assaulted back in 1924, a crime for which he received a ten- to twenty-year prison sentence. Morgan signed the petition that helped parole Johnnie nine years later, and a chastened Dillinger, newly released from the Indiana State Penitentiary, sought out Morgan and apologized, pledging to "go straight." Morgan promised to help him any way he could. Within a few months, however, Dillinger started his year-long spree of bank robberies. "Johnnie has the wrong idea of what it takes to make a man, that's all," Morgan sadly told Finan.[3]

The *New Yorker* article portrayed Dillinger's father as much like Frank Morgan, a simple man of the soil, a man of honest toil. He came to the door of his modest farmhouse to greet the reporter from New York wearing clean overalls and a patched denim shirt. Johnnie was a good boy who got a raw deal from a harsh judge, Old John said. With Finan looking on, Dillinger Senior patiently answered mail from around the country, much of it offering words of encouragement for his hunted son, America's Public Enemy Number One. Old John apologized that only Sundays allowed him time away from his farm chores for such tasks, and added in his sad, laconic way, "Christian people write me letters saying John should make his peace with the Lord and then give himself up. If they take his life after that, his soul will be saved anyway. Maybe that would be the best way."[4]

Mooresville, Indiana, the heart of the heart of the country, was not just a place, it was a metaphor by which Americans understood Dillinger's saga. Dillinger's Hoosier boyhood, followed by his descent into crime, was an age-old American story: rural virtue and small-town honesty succumbing to urban vice. Two months after the *New Yorker* article appeared, Dillinger's life ended, appropriately enough, on the streets of Chicago, long regarded as America's most corrupt city.[5]

It was an old American story, but just then an especially poignant one. In 1934 little over a decade had passed since the Census Bureau reported that for the first time more Americans lived in cities than in small towns or on farms. The 1920s had been tough years in the heartland, and now the Great Depression, grinding down toward its lowest depths in the early 1930s, devastated farms and villages. The fall from grace of this son of the soil paralleled America's.[6]

The problem was that little of the Dillinger story—this version of it, anyway—was true. John Dillinger did not grow up in Mooresville, the memories of his teacher and preacher notwithstanding. The Dillingers moved there in 1920, when he was almost seventeen years old. Dillinger spent his youth in a midsize metropolis, Indianapolis, a center of automobile manufacturing about fifteen miles east of Mooresville. Even after the family's move out to the country, young Dillinger split his time between Mooresville and Indianapolis. The Dillinger family had deep connections to the soil, going back a couple of generations, but Johnnie was a city boy. The trope of a rural lad losing his way was inaccurate, though that did not stop magazines like the *New Yorker* from glossing the story as a parable of America's declension from country virtues to city vices.[7]

BORN IN APRIL 1831, Matthias Dillinger, a French-speaking immigrant from Alsace, founded the family line in America. It is unclear how or why he ended up in Hancock County, Indiana, but there, in September 1863, he wed Mary E. Brown, nine years his junior and a native of North Carolina. Their first child, John Wilson Dillinger (Johnnie's father), was born ten months later, in July 1864. Matthias and Mary next had a daughter, Gennie, then three more sons, James, Early, and Everett. Until late in the nineteenth century the Dillingers lived on the land, and the surviving records reveal that they were not terribly successful. Each federal census found them in a new county, first Hancock, then Shelby immediately to the south, then Marion to the northwest. Mary kept house and the children went to school, but when the boys reached their teens they worked the soil alongside their father. As of 1870 Matthias did not own a farm but rented land, and the family's total personal property was valued at two hundred dollars. By 1880 things had picked up enough that Matthias

employed a laborer, who lived with the family. At best, however, the Dillingers remained small-scale family farmers, tenants at the mercy not only of the elements but of a highly competitive boom-and-bust economy.[8]

Maybe it was because of hard times on the land as a farmer's rebellion began to sweep through the heartland. Or maybe it was new opportunities in the city. But rather suddenly the Dillinger family moved on once again. In 1887 twenty-three-year-old John W. Dillinger, who had lived on Indiana farms all of his life, married Mary Ellen "Mollie" Lancaster, a farmer's daughter from nearby Cumberland. Within months they began life anew in Indianapolis. In 1889 and 1890 Dillinger was listed as a laborer in city directories. A few years later, the entire Dillinger clan had come to town. By 1892 the Indianapolis directory listed John W. as a foreman, brother James as a carpenter, brother Early as a machinist, pater familias Matthias as a laborer; a few years later brother Everett showed up as a carpenter. They seem to have been a tight-knit bunch, living near each other in a section of town known as Oak Hill, perhaps best described as a working-class neighborhood, with small wood-frame houses along narrow streets. Then came one more change. A little before 1900 John W. went into the grocery business, and he kept a store for the next twenty years, occasionally moving his business or his residence, but always within a radius of a few blocks in Oak Hill. The family was certainly not poor as Johnnie grew up. Hard-working and respectable, they enjoyed a few of life's luxuries and avoided its worst indignities.[9]

John and Mollie's first child was a daughter named Audrey, born in 1889. She became a talented musician, and though the family was far from rich she studied at the Indianapolis Conservatory of Music, then for years gave lessons and played piano in local churches. Fourteen years passed before a second child arrived on June 22, 1903. They named him John Herbert Dillinger. John Dillinger Sr. remembered the birth of his son as a grand day for the family. "I was just a small-time, hard-working grocer with no illusions of any future grandeur but that night as I leaned over Mollie to kiss her good night I saw in her eyes dreams of a great destiny for our boy. Like every proud mother, Mollie already was weaving a fanciful grand future for Johnnie."[10]

Mollie Dillinger did not die as a result of John's birth, but according to her husband it made her an invalid. Three years after her son was born she entered the hospital and never came out. "It wrung my

heart in those days to see Johnnie's bewilderment at his mother's continued absence. He toddled around hunting Mollie and crying for her. He was so young, however, that in a few weeks he forgot his loss." Months before Mollie's death in 1906 Johnnie's sister Audrey, just seventeen years old, married a local man, Emmett Hancock. The newlyweds moved into the Dillinger household and Audrey became Johnnie's surrogate mother, raising him along with her own children as they came along. Dillinger Senior described their home of the next several years as a typically American one: "We were all hard-working, God-fearing people. We never sat down to a meal without saying grace. All of us went to church and the children attended Sunday school."[11]

Johnnie's boyhood was unexceptional. He was energetic, adventurous, maybe a bit headstrong. He attended local public schools for eight years in Indianapolis and was an indifferent student. One of his teachers later remembered that he was good with things mechanical and that he liked reading better than math. She characterized him as a "nice, clean, and industrious boy." He played well with other children, was interested in marbles and baseball, learned to hunt and fish, and got into some fights (which he usually won), but not many. Johnnie's father remembered him as a natural leader among other boys: "He had a verve about him that was contagious. His self-reliance was assuring. He had a quick wit. He always had a ready retort when it was needed." Boyhood friends interviewed by Dillinger's biographers Robert Cromie and Joe Pinkston thirty years after the outlaw's death remembered a pretty average kid, not particularly mean or troublesome, who occasionally played hooky from school or joined with friends to steal fruit from some local garden. Dillinger Senior, who had become a teetotaler and joined a church on the death of his wife, said that his son was also a churchgoer while they lived in Indianapolis but that he fell away from any sort of observance after the family moved to Mooresville.[12]

The interior life of the Dillinger family will remain forever opaque. Writers and biographers have speculated that the death of Johnnie's mother explains the man he became. Certainly the loss of a parent must have had an impact on him, though countless children lose their mother or father and don't become criminals. Others have said that Dillinger Senior was inconsistent in his child rearing, first unreasonably strict, then unconscionably lenient. Not only is there

no evidence for this, but there is no reason to believe that such a pattern explains his son's adult behavior. There were, of course, plenty
of childhood events that might have had a deep effect on Johnnie: the
tragic loss of his aunt and cousin in a freak river accident in 1909, the
death of his grandfather Matthias early in 1912, the remarriage of his
father to Elizabeth Fields a few months later. But if such events made
Johnnie sullen or caused him to act out there is no record of it. His
sister remembered a sweet-tempered boy who had a mostly pleasant
childhood.[13]

Perhaps more than any other book, John Toland's *The Dillinger
Days*, first published in 1963, sought the origins of who Dillinger
became in childhood traumas. Toland touches all the pop-psychology
bases. He suggests that the elder Dillinger was alternately indulgent and brutal; that Johnnie never got along with his stepmother
and resented her as a rival for his father's affection (causing Johnnie
to develop "a sarcastic, lopsided smile"); that the birth of his half-
brother, Hubert, only created more resentment. Out of these early
difficulties came a series of antisocial acts. By the beginning of his second decade, according to Toland, Dillinger had organized a gang called
the Dirty Dozen, which stole and then sold tons of coal from railroad
yards; when they were caught and hauled into court everyone was
frightened but young Dillinger: "He stood arms folded, slouch cap
over one eye, staring at the judge—and chewing gum." In another
incident Dillinger and a friend tied up a third boy inside an abandoned
sawmill and sent him toward the blade, sparing the terrified child
only at the last minute. Worse still, Dillinger led a group of boys in
a gang rape, teaching the uninitiated all they needed to know. As the
brutal behaviors escalated, so did the punishments; Dillinger Senior
beat his son with barrel staves and chained him up in the back of the
grocery store, all to no avail. Finally the old man decided that only
moving out of Indianapolis and into the country could save his son;
thus the relocation to Mooresville.[14]

It is a fine story, and it would explain a lot if there was substantial
proof for any of it. The picture of youths tying one of their companions to a rail, the buzz saw about to slice open his head, has a filmic
quality; so does the image of young Dillinger as a gum-popping street
tough, cap pulled low over his brow. They give us a comforting sense of
uncomplicated evil, of black-heartedness pure and simple, unleashed
in childhood and sent out into the world. But, again, there is no real

evidence. Those who knew Johnnie best—his older sister, his ex-wife, his young half-sisters, his niece—describe a very different boy and man. Journalists from the 1930s through the 1960s interviewed relatives and neighbors who knew Dillinger as a child, and though a few reliable informants remembered one or another troubled moment of his early life, mostly they described a genial, high-spirited kid given, at worst, to occasional fights and pranks.[15]

Dillinger's father told reporters that his son was a good worker and that the high wages offered by companies during World War I enticed Johnnie to quit school after the eighth grade and work in a wood veneer factory, then as a messenger at the Board of Trade in downtown Indianapolis. Johnnie also worked for an upholsterer and later still as a machinist. He apparently was good at the latter, fast and accurate, but though he kept at it for a few years his record was spotty. He would show up for a couple of months, disappear for a while, then return.[16]

It was early in 1920 that Dillinger Senior decided to move his family out of Indianapolis. He was nearing sixty, had survived wartime shortages and then postwar inflation, and now wished to return to the land. After he sold his grocery store he bought a small farm just outside his wife Lizzie's hometown of Mooresville. There they joined the Quaker congregation and quickly established themselves as respected members of the community. Farm labor, however, never appealed to Johnnie, especially as he suffered from hay fever. Between 1920 and 1923 he seems to have split his time between Mooresville, the larger nearby town of Martinsville, and Indianapolis, taking the interurban car or driving a motorcycle to the city to work. His sister later recalled that he spent more time living with her than in Mooresville with his father. Johnnie also dated local women and in 1923, at age twenty, fell deeply in love with a farm girl from nearby Rockville. Her father prevented them from getting married, perhaps because she was too young, perhaps because he considered Johnnie a poor prospect for a son-in-law.[17]

Broken-hearted, young Dillinger grew increasingly sullen. One Sunday in July he stole a car out of the parking lot of the Friends' Meeting House and drove to Indianapolis. The police found him, but he gave them the slip, hid out all night, then the very next morning panicked and enlisted in the U.S. Navy. He joined up in Indianapolis (falsely declaring St. Louis as his hometown) and was sent to the

Great Lakes Naval Station north of Chicago for basic training. The Navy transferred him in early October to the USS *Utah*, docked in Boston Harbor, as a fireman, third-class. Later that month Dillinger failed to return from shore leave and was declared AWOL. When he showed up twenty-four hours later he was given ten days of solitary confinement on bread and water and fined eighteen dollars. The next month he disobeyed orders, left his post on the *Utah*, and received another five days in solitary. Granted shore liberty in December he took off for good, leaving no personal effects. Two weeks later the Navy declared him a deserter and offered a fifty-dollar reward for news of his whereabouts. When Navy officials learned late in 1924 that he had been arrested by the state of Indiana they informed prison administrators that they had no desire to have him returned to naval jurisdiction and simply discharged him as undesirable.[18]

On his return to Mooresville Johnnie told his family that the Navy sent him home because of a heart murmur. His other heartache, the loss of his first love, apparently had abated, and he quickly became interested in another local farm girl, seventeen-year-old Beryl Hovious. They met at a party in Mooresville. Her family was quite poor, and shortly after meeting Johnnie, Beryl quit high school and worked as a waitress to help make ends meet. They grew close very quickly, dated for half a year, then married on April 12, 1924. The couple lived with Johnnie's parents first, then hers, before they rented a small house in Martinsville. Decades later Beryl's great-nephew interviewed her about her time with Dillinger. She was very old and in poor health, but she recalled him as polite and well-mannered, upbeat and with a good sense of humor. She described their time together as quiet and domestic. Occasionally the young couple went to the movies or visited with family; mostly they stayed home, ate the meals that Beryl cooked, read the newspapers, and played cards. Half a century after their marriage, and forty years after his death, she was still quite fond of him. Whatever hopes had attended their relationship, however, Johnnie could not make them last.[19]

So between 1920, when the family moved to Mooresville, and 1924, when he got married, Dillinger's life was a mixed bag of steadiness and volatility. We see a young man in his late teens seeking the trappings of stability—a job, marriage, the military—but too restless to behave entirely stably, stealing a car, going AWOL, falling head-over-heels in love. One constant in his life was baseball. He was good enough to pitch and play shortstop on a Martinsville semiprofessional team. No doubt he loved the local acclaim he received, and maybe it awakened in him a desire for fame, for some of the celebrity status lavished on a chosen few. As Dillinger entered his twenties he genuinely tried to cleave to a sheltering routine of work, marriage, and simple joys, but he could not quite pull it off.[20]

One can imagine young Johnnie Dillinger looking hard at what was unfolding for those around him. Reading the obituaries of his male cousins, for example, one gets a sense of life's limited possibilities in 1920s Indiana. They had been salesmen, clerks, and farmers, husbands, fathers, and churchgoers, men who had settled into their lives, some comfortably, others with nagging restlessness. Dillinger might have settled down too had fate not taken him in another direction—fate and something in his character that resisted settling. But we must take care not to read his future from his past, especially because we know little about that past. If John Dillinger's life seemed a little untidy as he approached his twenty-first birthday, he was no different from tens of thousands of other young American men. Nothing that he did or that happened to him as he grew into manhood portended what lay ahead.[21]

BERYL'S HAPPY VERSION of their married life was not the whole story. In addition to spending time with her, by the summer of 1924 Dillinger frequented pool halls in Mooresville and nearby Martinsville and hung around with some unsavory local characters. Edward Singleton was ten years older than Johnnie. He worked for the local power company, was married with two children, and spent some of his spare time umpiring local baseball games. He also had a police record. Singleton and Dillinger decided that a stickup was a quick way to earn some cash. Perhaps, as some have suggested, Johnnie was feeling the financial pressures of his marriage. The Dillinger family always maintained that the robbery was Singleton's idea, that he persuaded Johnnie to go along with the plan by plying him with "White Mule," the local home brew. Frank Morgan was an elderly grocer in Mooresville, a man whose store Johnnie frequented. Perhaps the similarities between Morgan and Dillinger's father were just coincidental; perhaps Johnnie subconsciously wished to strike at his father but found a surrogate instead. In any event, Morgan walked the same route on September 6 that he walked every Saturday night. The Mooresville *Times* reported the story:

AN ATTEMPTED HOLDUP

Frank Morgan, proprietor of the West Side Grocery Store, was badly hurt about the head and shoulders Saturday night between 10 and 11 o'clock. As he was returning from town a man stepped from behind the Christian Church and struck him twice on the side of the head with an iron bolt, which caused him to fall. He rose dazed, and the first thing he remembers he saw a revolver stuck in his face, and he was told to hold his hands up. He knocked the revolver out of the fellow's hand. It discharged as it struck the pavement. . . . The fellow evidently was frightened by the report of the revolver and fled east down Broad Alley. Soon the neighbors were on the scene and Mr. Morgan was carried home and a physician called. It required 11 stitches to sew up the two wounds. He was prostrated for two days, but is improving now.

Dillinger's confession to the court affirmed the newspaper account: "When [Morgan] came along I jumped out from behind the building and hit him twice on the head with a bolt which I had wrapped up in a handkerchief. He then turned and grabbed a revolver which I had in my hand. The gun was discharged when I jerked it away from him the bullet entering the ground. We then ran." One report claimed that Morgan gave the Masonic distress signal; others said he called for help with the secret whistle used by the Ku Klux Klan, an organization just then peaking in popularity in small Indiana towns and that based its appeal on a pledge to uphold traditional American morals.[22]

It is unclear whether Morgan recognized his assailants, but Dillinger gave his identity away when he asked around town if Old Man Morgan was all right before anyone even knew that a crime had been committed. The local peace officer, Marshall Greerson, came to the Dillinger home on Monday morning and hauled him off to the Martinsville jail. Members of Dillinger's family later claimed that the prosecutor led them to believe that Johnnie would get a break for cooperating. Dillinger Senior convinced his son that the best thing was to make a clean breast of it and throw himself on the mercy of the court, that there was no need to hire an attorney, that honesty and his boy's good record would be rewarded with a light sentence.[23]

Dillinger's father was forever after filled with remorse, for his advice proved terribly naïve. Old John later learned that the case against his son was weak, that the police had little evidence, and that the charges against Johnnie might well have been dropped were it not for his confession, which named Ed Singleton as his accomplice. Not only was Johnnie not given a break for confessing, but he made matters worse with Martinsville authorities by repeated attempts to slip out of custody. Judge Joseph Williams, known as the toughest in the area, decided to make an example of young Dillinger, perhaps because the local constable suspected Morgan's assailants had also recently held up two filling stations. Williams shocked the community by sentencing Johnnie to ten to twenty years at the Indiana State Reformatory at Pendleton for assault and battery and two to fourteen years on a charge of conspiracy to commit a felony. Dillinger Senior pled with Judge Williams for leniency, arguing that a suspended sentence or a year behind bars with strict supervision afterward would straighten Johnny out. Singleton, by contrast, retained an attorney, pleaded innocent, and was granted a change of venue. A month after Dillinger's case ended a jury sentenced the ex-con to two to fourteen years at Pendleton. Much to the chagrin of the Dillinger family he served the minimum term. Years later Dillinger Senior continued to maintain that Singleton's liquor and evil ideas had made a criminal of his son.[24]

Dillinger entered the Indiana State Reformatory on September 16, 1924, as inmate #14395. Prison intake records offer plenty of detailed information about him. Twenty-one years old now, he stood five feet, seven and one quarter inches tall and weighed 157 pounds, had gray eyes, a small scar above his lip, and a medium-size nose. He described himself as a smoker but not a drinker, a member of the Christian Church who had attended twelve years of Sunday school. Prison officials found that he could read and write "readily," that he solved arithmetic problems, including percentages, and that he demonstrated good penmanship. He had only one previous arrest (prison officials failed to note his military record), a 1920 conviction for speeding in Indianapolis; he had paid the eleven-dollar fine. Dillinger told prison officials that he was a screw machinist, though unemployed at the time of his arrest, and perhaps for that reason prison officials ranked his work habits as "fair." Only fair too, they believed, were his disposition and his mental condition. They described Dillinger's physical state as "good," despite their diagnosis that he had gonorrhea. On his record too was a notation, unexplained, that he had been married for five months but had been separated from his wife for three weeks before his arrest.[25]

One thing not mentioned by prison officials: Dillinger liked to read. He held a subscription to *Argosy All-Story*, a weekly compendium of pulp writing—cowboy fiction, romance and adventure stories, biographical sketches, humorous pieces—most of it long on action, short on character development, and all of it cranked out through time-honored formulas. He enjoyed reading about things technical, so *Popular Mechanics* often found its way into his hands, as well as storybook magazines like *Munsey's*. He also read the Mooresville newspaper, in addition to the Chicago *Herald* for its sports coverage. However, prisoners were not allowed access to anything that encouraged crime or revealed its techniques, so Dillinger's request for *Flynn's* detective magazine was denied.[26]

Pendleton requested that incoming prisoners provide the names of persons who might write on their behalf and sent out letters asking whether new inmates were "sober, honest industrious and trustworthy, or otherwise." James P. Burcham, the co-owner of Reliance Specialty Company in Indianapolis, wrote the most generous letter. Dillinger, he said, worked as a screw machine operator for Reliance for four or five years, "but not in any one time for more than three or four months." Burcham declared that Dillinger was so fast and skilled at his job that the company rehired him several times. "He was sober, honest and very industrious," and he added, "We liked Johnny very much personally." The problem was that he just would not stay long. Burcham asked prison officials to convey his good wishes and speculated that the boy had just "gotten into bad company" in the past year.[27]

Dillinger's other references were less positive. E. F. Hadley, president of the Farmer's State Bank, wrote that he hardly knew Dillinger, that the bank had recently turned him down for a loan, and that shortly thereafter the young man had committed his "brutal" holdup. T. H. Greeson of the Mooresville Civic Club wrote in praise of the elder Dillinger, but added that Johnnie wasn't around Mooresville much and that he had "been under suspicion" several times. Then Greeson repeated the story of the stolen car and the aborted naval career. He added that Dillinger allegedly made threats against people in Mooresville and concluded that he really could not say much good about the young man.[28]

Dillinger's prison years confirmed Greeson's impressions. His record was marred by numerous infractions for which he spent days and weeks in the guardhouse and, worse, had months added to his sentence. In October 1924 he hid out from the guards. Right before Christmas he and two other prisoners sawed their way out of their cells. The assistant superintendent noted in his report that the prisoners could have used the bars to assault unsuspecting guards but had refrained from doing so. "These boys had no murderous intentions when they attempted their escape," he concluded. Dillinger was also caught gambling, fighting, wearing nonregulation clothing, and destroying prison property. Once he was found in bed with another inmate. Officials repeatedly fined him, put him in solitary confinement, and sent him to the guardhouse for violations. Prison authorities noted not just his deeds, but his attitude, his "disrespect" for them. Hauled before a prison court for cutting up his mattress to hide a pen and some ink, Dillinger "talked very indifferent when asked about his conduct saying that a court report did not worry him in the least." Pendleton's assistant superintendent concluded, "Dillinger's record has been anything but good since he entered this institution."[29]

Dillinger's family pleaded with prison officials for clemency, arguing that his petty infractions were proof that he chafed under the injustice of his long incarceration. His stepmother wrote to Superintendent A. F. Miles in 1926 that other men had received shorter terms for murder and that the long sentence was demoralizing to her stepson. She acknowledged that Johnnie had not been a model prisoner but argued that if he could only be released and remain free based on his continued good conduct "he would try hard to be a man." Thinking back on Johnnie in prison, John Dillinger Sr. later mused, "While wishing to be a good Christian, I believe that I made the greatest mistake of my life when I persuaded him to confess for the reason that up to that time, my boy was a good boy—a good Christian boy, went to church, worked in a machine shop and was always good to his folks and never been in any kind of trouble. I feel sure that if it were not for the two drinks that he took, he would not have been in that trouble at that particular time." Dillinger's sister Audrey also wrote to Miles and addressed her brother's behavior: "John at heart is not a bad boy, and is doing time some one else ought to be doing, that is why he has been so dissatisfied and as we all know, has not been as obedient as he might of been." Miles was polite but firm: "Before the boy can hope to secure favorable consideration it will be necessary that he keep his record clear," thereby proving "that he will be able to obey the law on the outside."[30]

In the spring of 1929 Beryl sued Johnnie for divorce. She had dutifully made her trips to Pendleton to visit her husband, though less frequently as time passed. As they had not been married half a year before Johnnie began serving his sentence, and had not seen each other for weeks before the assault on Frank Morgan, it is not surprising that the marriage fell apart. Why Beryl waited so long to seek a dissolution is more puzzling. Perhaps her family pressured her now. Maybe she detected some sort of change in Dillinger's character. Certainly for a young woman who already had given her man five years, the new infractions that kept adding time to his sentence were hard to bear. John Dillinger Sr. suggested that his son may have made one too many fond remarks about the girlfriend who preceded Beryl. Whatever drove the case, the court quickly granted the divorce.[31]

SHORTLY AFTER DILLINGER ABSORBED the blow of Beryl's leaving him, Pendleton's parole board turned down his plea for freedom. The decision was made doubly painful by the fact that Ed Singleton had been back on the streets for two years now. Now too, Dillinger was transferred to the Indiana State Prison in Michigan City.[32]

One story has it that the Michigan City facility had an excellent baseball team and that prison officials wanted Dillinger to play shortstop. A letter home after his transfer gave credence to this notion. He wrote his niece Mary that he was not interested in playing for his new institution: "If I hadn't played on the team at the reformatory I don't think I would have been sent up here; and I am sure I would have made a parole there this winter, so you can understand why I am not enthusiastic about making this team." The explanation is self-serving, absolving Dillinger from any responsibility for his own fate. Given his record it was unrealistic for him to expect parole from the state reformatory, and the tone of his remarks seems both petulant and silly. Besides, there is reason to believe that Dillinger wanted the transfer. Several of his friends from Pendleton had already been sent over to the tougher facility, and he wished to be with them. Although it seems unlikely that Dillinger already had made a decision to become a big-time criminal, as Robert Cromie and Joseph Pinkston speculate, it was clear that those were the sorts of people he wanted to be around. Pendleton authorities may not have been willing to grant him parole, but they hesitated not at all to ship him out with the hard cases.[33]

Dillinger's problems with discipline continued at Michigan City. Again he was guilty mostly of minor infractions: gambling, using shop equipment inappropriately (he worked in the shirt factory), stealing produce from the prison stores, hiding a razor blade in his cell, smuggling cigarettes and a lighter. The most serious accusation was that he and another inmate had attempted to saw their way out of confinement. In his letters home he indicated that he was fully aware that these violations kept him behind bars, and he apologized to his family for them. But that did not keep him from continuing to challenge his captors, all the while playing the victim.[34]

Dillinger had many visits from his family throughout the nine years he served, and according to prison records, dozens of letters went back and forth. From the beginning of his confinement through the end these letters, the few that survive, do not reveal him as a hardened criminal. On the contrary, they exhibit a goofy cheerfulness. Years later Nellie Daly, a prison guard's daughter who got to know Dillinger in Michigan City, said of him, "Oh, he was a spoiled boy. He wasn't vicious at all. The Newspapers, the press, made him a villain. . . . He was a kid that liked attention and [robbing banks] was the only way he found out that he could get it."[35]

Dillinger was well into his twenties, but this notion of him as a "kid" and a "boy" persisted. Certainly his family embraced it, helping him to deflect blame and to reinforce his already formidable powers of denial. His niece Mary remembered him more as a brother than an uncle: "We used to go to the little grocery store in Maywood and buy chewing gum at a penny a pack," she recalled years later. "I remember lying flat on the floor, our heads together, trying to see who could chew the most gum. And I remember Johnnie's constant love of baseball. We used to play catch when I was seven or eight, because I was a tomboy." In long letters throughout his prison years Mary confided in him: "He knew when I had my first lipstick and went to my first party and had my first date." She told him she hoped to open a beauty shop some day, and he told her he'd be her best customer, that she would trim his fingernails and cut his hair. Years later she still lamented his fate: "I don't think he ever had any intention of living the kind of life he did. If only some one person had cared enough to say, 'I'll take him into business with me,' or had given him a chance—given him a feeling he would be useful!"[36]

If others thought of Dillinger as a kid, it might be because his personality encouraged it. His letters home, for example, reveal a strong streak of adolescent romanticism. Four years into his term, as his marriage unraveled, he wrote Beryl, "Gee honey I would like to see you," and later, as he anticipated a parole interview, he added, "We will be so happy when I can come home to you and chase your sorrows away." Though he must have known that she was close to filing for divorce, Dillinger kept up his sweet talk, telling her, "I am dying to see you," and asking her for recent pictures of herself. Maybe he thought his letters could persuade Beryl to keep loving him, or maybe he was refusing to face the fact that the marriage was over. His words cut both ways: "You can imagine what a disappointment it was to me when you didn't come on your birthday I've been cross as a bear ever since." He ended the same letter, "Lots of love and kisses to the sweetest little wife in the world." "Gee, honey," "chase your sorrows away," "cross as a bear," "sweetest little wife in the world"—his phrases sound like they came straight from Tin Pan Alley.[37]

When he wrote home from Pendleton on Mother's Day in 1929 he talked about baseball ("We had our second game today and won 12–9"), about taking classes in the prison school ("It won't do a bit of harm to go over some of the studies. . . . I wish I had listened to Dad and went to Tech"), and about upcoming visits from his family ("If Sis can't come this week or next, maybe Dad will have a chance to come and Bring Doris or Frances [his young half-sisters]"). He did not mention that Beryl was suing him for divorce. Perhaps he wanted to give his family hope as he applied for parole: "I am trying hard to make my time clear so I can come home," he assured them, and he added that next year he might be out and helping his father around the farm. He was turned down for parole the following month and then transferred to Michigan City.[38]

From the state prison too his letters were upbeat. Outgoing mail was read by prison officials, and it seems likely his cheerful tone and his professions of good behavior were tactical attempts to persuade his captors of his worthiness for parole. But given that he remained close to his niece Mary and his sisters Frances and Doris after he left prison, it seems impossible to read his letters to them as cynical. He joked that he might buy them a box of candy if he could find one on sale; he commented on Mooresville High School's basketball team; he even told Mary that he went to church every Sunday, adding, "Of course I have to go that explains it ha! ha!" Responding to a letter Mary had written him, he wrote her on Christmas Day 1929 saying how pleased he was that she enjoyed school and was making good grades. He wished everyone back home a happy holiday, and added, "Wouldn't it be swell if I was spending Christmas with you? But don't worry I will be out sometime and believe me I am going to stay out." He reassured Mary that he and his fellow prisoners were treated to a Christmas show and a big dinner.[39]

On a more introspective note he mentioned that Mary's mother, his sister Audrey, had not been feeling well, that she had asked him to pray for her. He explained that he believed it would take more than prayer to heal the sick, more than prayer for him to get out of prison. "Now don't think I am an atheist for I am not," he wrote. "I do believe in God, but his ways seem strange to me sometimes; for if anyone deserves health and happiness it is your dear mother who is the best and sweetest woman in the world." God or no God, Dillinger insisted that he knew right from wrong and intended to do only right when he got out. He added that just thinking about his sister Audrey often prevented him from doing things in prison that might get him into trouble and keep him longer behind bars.[40]

If Dillinger thought that it would be easier to make parole from Michigan City than from Pendleton, he was wrong. His acts of petty defiance often kept him in solitary confinement and under close watch. He wrote his brother Hubert at the beginning of 1932 that he had been out of touch for months because he had been in the guard-house a lot and in no mood to write. "It seems like I can't keep out of trouble here. . . . I guess I am just incorrigible. I wish I was back at the reformatory, for I know I could get out in six months there." He must have written this letter at a particularly low moment. He apologized for not sending Christmas presents, explained that prisoners' allow-ances had been cut so that they barely covered such things as tooth-paste, soap, and newspapers, and he mentioned that he was pretty sure he was going back to solitary again. Above all, he sounded lonely and bored. He twice asked Hubert to come visit and to bring his folks and wrote that he longed for the baseball season to hurry up and come. Even at a low moment like this, however, his manic optimism briefly burst through. He assured his brother that if his father and sister could get him transferred back to Pendleton, he would behave there: "I'll sure watch my step so I can get out next fall."[41]

In fact, there was cause for hope. By the early 1930s the Indiana state penal system was bursting at the seams. In 1920 the average daily population stood a little below three thousand; a decade later that number more than doubled to almost sixty-five hundred. Worse, in the first full year of the Great Depression new admissions totaled eighty-six hundred, four times the number in 1920. A combination of hard-line Republican administrations in the 1920s and hard times in the state economy sped the wheels of crime and punishment, and overcrowding made prisoners' lives increasingly difficult in the early 1930s. Now, to cut expenses, the State of Indiana moved toward releasing some inmates. To take advantage of the state's newfound willingness to parole prisoners, Dillinger straightened out, or at least he appeared to straighten out.[42]

He wrote a letter to Audrey in March 1933 with explicit instructions to his family. A new parole board was about to convene and he wanted his father and sister to go to Indianapolis to plead his case. The Dillingers circulated a petition in Mooresville in February and collected nearly two hundred signatures. A local doctor, J. E. Comer, wrote a strong letter to Governor McNutt and the parole board, arguing that young Dillinger had paid his debt: "I believe that this young man has had his lesson and that if permitted parole would go to his father's home, manage his farm and be a useful citizen in the community. He is a bright man and so far as I know was never in trouble until this unfortunate circumstance placed him in the condition he is now in. . . . I believe the community at large would sanction his release and think all would help him to become the man he should, should your Honorable Board decide to release him." Even Frank Morgan signed the petition, and Dillinger urged his father to ask Morgan to write the parole board too. Johnnie expressed his frustration to Audrey when he felt his father was not being aggressive enough: "I have asked Dad several times why he doesn't see Howard Phillips and Reverend Fillmore and get there help. But he doesn't say anything about them and I am sure they would help me out. People like them are the ones that count and we can't afford to miss any opportunity." Still he was hopeful, and he told Audrey to keep in practice making coconut cream pies in preparation for his return. J. W. Williams, the judge who sentenced Dillinger, also wrote a sympathetic letter to the parole board, pleading for clemency, praising Dillinger Senior as a "fine, substantial citizen," and noting that the petition had been signed by "very substantial citizens, business and professional men, and taxpayers," including the township's presiding judge and prosecuting attorney, as well as Morgan County's clerk, sheriff, treasurer and auditor, as well as the assessor and recorder.[43]

In rendering its decision the parole board specifically cited Williams's long letter urging that Dillinger be released to his father's custody so he could run the old man's farm. With the trial judge, the victim, and the Indiana Commission on Clemency all recommending the prisoner's release, Governor McNutt signed executive order #7723, granting Dillinger his parole. The boilerplate at the bottom of the declaration stipulated, "This parole will be revoked for any violation hereof, and may be revoked at any time the good of the prisoner and interests of society so warrant."[44]

Just before the parole papers came through, stepmother Lizzie Dillinger suffered a severe stroke. With some haste, then, Hubert drove up to Michigan City, accompanied by Audrey's oldest child, Fred, to bring their kinsman home. Bureaucratic delays kept Dillinger in the lockup for a few extra days. Officials failed to inform him of his stepmother's illness, nor did they tell him that his brother was waiting for him. The paperwork dragged on. Finally Dillinger received his requisite ten dollars and a new suit of clothes. The three men set out for Mooresville, but they had engine trouble around South Bend, then a blowout in Indianapolis. They made it back home a little after midnight on Monday, May 23, twenty minutes after Lizzie passed away. Dillinger's father later recalled that as Johnnie and Hubert sat beside their mother's body the whole family cried and rejoiced at the same time.[45]

JOHN DILLINGER WAS THEN nearly thirty years old and had spent almost a third of his life behind bars. A spotty work record and a failed marriage did not inspire confidence in his chances for a productive civilian life. Neither the Navy nor prison had enhanced his sense of discipline; quite the contrary. He was a felon with a serious crime to his name, an armed attack on an old man. In prison Dillinger engaged in steady, mostly petty, though occasionally serious infractions; he seemed unable to restrain himself. His professions of reform notwithstanding, he had changed over the course of the decade, and not for the better. He told his sister Audrey shortly after he got out, "When you're in a place like that, with not a kind word from anyone, how could you help from being sore toward everybody." He got a "bum rap," he said, and he swore never to go back to Michigan City alive.[46]

America also had changed, and the Dillingers, senior and junior, were emblematic of those changes. Old John had retreated to Mooresville at least in part to escape the forces that were overtaking cities like Indianapolis. Small-town Indiana in the 1920s was a bastion of conservatism. While most of the country prospered, rural areas like Morgan County, where Dillinger Senior worked his land, remained in a deep recession. The 1920s straddled the old America and the new: cities versus countryside; native-born versus immigrants and their children; modernism in art, literature, and science versus older religious views; the life of quiet toil and self-reliance versus the new urban world of glamour, fame, and celebrity. One detects these cultural tensions now between Johnnie and Old John, the former with his sharp suits and rakish good looks rushing outward toward the new world, the latter with his weathered face and overalls going back to the land.[47]

One of the great cultural divides of the decade was Prohibition. Dillinger Senior claimed that liquor had poisoned his son's brain when he attacked Frank Morgan. Dillinger Junior had no problem taking a glass. He had been a young man at the edge of adulthood in the early 1920s, craving everything that was exciting and new. With the economy strong, demand for labor high, and wages good, America more than ever was a consumer culture. Automobiles, radios, and phonographs were becoming part of middle-class life. The allure of fashion and glamour reached deeper and deeper into the social structure and into individual psyches. Hollywood studios released hundreds of films in thousands of theaters for millions of fans. A world of material goods, made more available than ever with the expansion of credit, raised expectations. Glossy magazines glamorized objects of desire, nightly radio programs dramatized the good life, advertising taught Americans about the things they needed to make their lives complete, as the twentieth century increasingly celebrated the trappings of fame, fortune, and celebrity. In 1924, then, many Americans believed that acquiring gleaming new objects was the high road to happiness, and before he robbed Frank Morgan and landed in prison for nearly a decade, young Dillinger had been eager to join the party.[48]

Then came the stock market crash in October 1929, followed by a downward economic spiral. When John Dillinger stepped out of prison in May 1933 America was in the trough of its deepest depression. Roughly a quarter of the American workforce was unemployed; those lucky enough to keep their jobs suffered pay cuts, shortened hours, and the constant threat of being laid off. Institutions that normally helped stanch the bleeding—welfare agencies, parish charities, unions—also found themselves broke. The Great Depression jarred Americans' confidence. The promise of an ever-improving life for those who worked hard, lived upright lives, and kept the faith seemed more tenuous than ever before. The problem was especially acute for men because earning a living for their loved ones always had been their responsibility. Fathers who had brought a taste of the good life to their families, politicians who thrived on 1920s prosperity, clergymen who tended big prosperous flocks, businessmen who waxed poetic on the endless bounty of American capitalism, all found their confidence shaken. The old consensus of masculine morality—hard work, steady habits, providing for a family, defending community and country—was still alive, but the ties between virtue and prosperity had frayed.[49]

Timing is important here. Just months before Dillinger emerged from the Indiana State Penitentiary, America's financial system underwent its greatest crisis yet. Since 1929, the economy had drifted downward, with the Hoover administration unable to stem the tide. For three years, surges of monetary panic had swept over America, as terrified citizens withdrew their savings from local banks, convinced the alternative was to lose everything. On the eve of Franklin Roosevelt's inauguration as president on March 4, 1933, a new wave of fear struck, larger than any before. Depositors swarmed into banks to grab their money, state governors declared "bank holidays" to forestall a total meltdown, panic selling forced the New York Stock Exchange and the Chicago Board of Trade to suspend operations on inauguration day itself. Roosevelt managed to stabilize the system in his first hundred days, but not before the crisis had drained away much of what remained of the economy's productive capacity, of Americans' trust in banks and bankers, and above all, of the ability of millions of citizens to make a living.[50]

Beginning from the low plateau of the 1920s, agricultural recession, the nation's heartland plummeted in the early 30s. An Indiana farmer wrote Franklin Roosevelt in October 1933 that he had abandoned all hope for the New Deal: "Henceforward I am swearing eternal vengeance on the financial barons and will do every single thing I can to bring about communism." His conversion to radical politics was still uncommon, but not the pain he saw all around him. Journalist Lorena Hickok toured the Midwest, the South, and the Plains, reporting back to Washington on horrifying scenes of poverty. South Dakota, she wrote, was the most hopeless place she had ever seen; half the farmers were scared to death, the other half shocked into apathy. In Georgia, she found half-starved tenant farmers, black and white, competing for less food than she fed her dog. In Texas, Oklahoma, Kansas, and Arkansas, over-cultivation and drought brought on the "dust bowl," where the wind kicked up enormous clouds of bone-dry silt. Black blizzards floated east, dropping tons of soil, while tens of thousands of "Oakies" drifted west to keep themselves alive. In the Midwest, banks foreclosed family farms, then auctioned the properties. Farmers sometimes gathered to intimidate buyers and purchase the properties for their original owners. In April 1933, masked men in Le Mars, Iowa, abducted a foreclosure judge, stripped, beat, and threatened to lynch him. By harvest time in '33, midwestern farmers organized a strike, refusing to ship their produce for less than the cost of production. Some of them blocked delivery of cattle, overturned vats of milk, and blocked roadways.[51]

It was not just on the farms that the pressures of four years of failure were building. Thirteen million workers were unemployed in 1933. Industrial production that year was half of its 1929 total, according to the Federal Reserve. Gross national product also had been cut in half, Detroit produced one third the number of automobiles, and stocks had lost three quarters of their value. House foreclosures came at an accelerating pace—150,000 in 1930, 200,000 in 1931, 250,000 in 1932—destroying not only families' homes but their savings, destroying too the tax base of states and cities. One gets a sense of the downward spiral, for example, from the fact that in the winter of 1933, Chicago ceased paying its teachers altogether. Perhaps the beginnings of the New Deal released unfulfilled hopes at this nadir of the crisis, but even as Roosevelt's policies began to have some effect, anger and the desire to act boiled over in many citizens. In 1934, a million and a half workers took part in eighteen hundred strikes. Most notably, in two cities, Minneapolis and San Francisco, general strikes of hundreds of thousands of workers and the unemployed in spring and summer of 1934 virtually shut those towns down, and more, the protests spread to other cities. The strikes brought to the fore powerful worker-leaders who explicitly spoke the language of class conflict.[52]

One last point about the America into which Dillinger reemerged in 1933: crime offered opportunities that the straight world denied. Prohibition had allowed Al Capone to attain fabulous wealth by systematizing vice; before he was imprisoned on tax-evasion charges late in 1931 he had built an urban, multiethnic syndicate, a multimillion-dollar business that organized alcohol distribution and gambling. During the 1920s several other imaginative midwestern criminals, especially bank robbers, found creative ways to prosper. With police departments preoccupied with the liquor trade, Baron Lamm, Eddie Bentz, and Harvey Bailey put together groups of men for raids on banks and payrolls. They updated the old outlaw techniques of Jesse and Frank James and of the Dalton gang by taking advantage of modern technology like automobiles and automatic weapons. They scouted, planned, and timed their heists carefully and skipped back and forth between towns and states, muddling police jurisdiction. These outlaws of the 1920s pulled off more robberies, pilfered more money, and served less prison time than felons before or since. They made theft into a science.[53]

When Dillinger re-entered the world in 1933 a new generation of criminals was gaining notoriety. Bonnie and Clyde were Texans, lovers, and stickup artists who robbed banks, filling stations, grocery stores, and murdered a dozen people along the way, mostly in the Southwest and lower Midwest. Machine Gun Kelly, a Chicagoan who briefly attended the University of Mississippi, was involved in rural bank robberies and at least one major kidnapping. Pretty Boy Floyd, a Georgian who settled in Oklahoma, committed highway robbery, perhaps ten murders, and dozens of bank holdups and participated in the Kansas City Massacre, in which four police officers were ambushed and killed. The Barker family was from Missouri; "Ma" Barker was the called the "mother of criminals," and though she probably was not directly involved, her four sons committed dozens of robberies, kidnappings, and murders in the Midwest and Great Plains. All had begun to dominate headlines in the newspapers, breathless coverage on radio, newsreels in movie houses. Like the bandits of the 1920s these were independent operators, working with small and shifting groups of accomplices; they were mostly native-born, heartland American thieves.[54]

Though the newspapers and the Justice Department's Division of Investigation tried to depict these criminal gangs as interlocking, highly structured organizations like the Capone syndicate, they were actually loosely assembled bands, raiding parties that occasionally shared personnel. To give just one example, Lester Gillis, better known as Baby Face Nelson, worked at different times with the Barkers, Pretty Boy Floyd, and John Dillinger. They all depended on a demimonde of fences, safe houses, hangouts, medical professionals, bail bondsmen, corrupt cops, politicians on the take, dealers of illegal weapons, and dodgy attorneys. Sometimes family ties knit criminals together, as in the case of brothers Clyde and Buck Barrow. Men tended to do the actual stealing, but wives and lovers were very much part of these operations, procuring housing and vehicles, taking care of domestic chores, sometimes also handling weapons and driving getaway cars.[55]

John Dillinger left Michigan City with a handful of underworld contacts from his prison mates, bleak prospects for success in the straight world, and the belief that wealth, fame, and excitement awaited the skilled bandit. He promised everyone in Mooresville that he had learned his lesson in prison. Indeed he had.

TWO

"The Farmer Turns Gangster"

THREE DAYS BEFORE DILLINGER'S RELEASE FROM THE INDIANA State Prison, *Commonweal* magazine ran an article called "The Farmer Turns Gangster." The piece told the story of fifty-one-year-old Kansan Russ Mundell, who robbed his local bank of nearly two thousand dollars. "I'm sorry, but I'm desperate," Mundell apologized as he pointed his gun at the teller. "I'll pay this back when times get good." The Great Depression brought a level of hopelessness to the farm belt worse than anything seen in America since the Populist era forty years earlier, back when the Dillinger family left the land. And not just farmers suffered. America's river of plenty was flowing backward; declining employment meant slack demand for goods, which in turn caused companies to lay off more workers who, in an era without a social welfare system, could not afford the necessities of life. But farmers were hit particularly hard. Falling demand meant dwindling prices for farm products, and because they could not pay their debts, banks foreclosed on hundreds of thousands of mortgages.[1]

"The Farmer Turns Gangster" told of countless heartland families cast "empty-handed and hungry into the road." Still, not everyone responded passively. Many farmers began to organize strikes and boycotts; some even joined vigilance societies aimed at preventing foreclosures. From the Alleghenies to the Rockies farm families banded together and intervened, sometimes violently, to stop banks from seizing their property. "The Farmer Turns Gangster" concluded,

"There probably is no essential difference between the action of these groups and the action of Russ Mundell, the Kansas farmer who held up the Garden City Bank. Call it agricultural gangsterism or what you will, the same spirit of hopeless desperation is behind the foreclosure sale strong-arm methods of these 'farmer's defense' organizations and the gun the apologetic farmer pointed at the bank cashier."[2]

John Dillinger may not have been a farm boy, but the Great Depression affected the way Americans viewed his exploits, for it colored their age-old assumptions about the goodness of capitalism and the inevitability of the American Dream. Hard times forced Americans to rethink their outlaws. Like the *Commonweal* article, a tone of condemnation against "agricultural gangsterism" often mingled with something like sympathy. Pretty Boy Floyd, Bonnie Parker, Clyde Barrow, Baby Face Nelson, Machine Gun Kelly, and their like elicited powerful and contradictory emotions. But for the moment Dillinger was just another ex-con back on the streets.[3]

ONE CAN IMAGINE the conflicted emotions Dillinger must have felt as he readjusted to civilian life and contemplated his future. When Reverend Filmore, an old family friend, came to preach Lizzie's funeral sermon, Dillinger allegedly told him, "I've learned my lesson. I expect to go straight from now on." The following Sunday he attended services with his father at the Friends' Meeting House in Mooresville. Pastor Gertrude Reinier, who promised prison officials that she would keep an eye out for Johnnie, chose as her text "The Return of the Prodigal Son." According to Dillinger Senior, both father and son wept, as did most of those at the meeting. After the service Dillinger went up to Reinier, shook her hand, and said, "You don't know how much good your sermon has done me." During these days he also sought out old Frank Morgan and apologized.[4]

A month later three men robbed the New Carlisle National Bank in Ohio of ten thousand dollars. They waited inside overnight, bound two employees at gunpoint the next morning, and forced a third to open the safe for them. As they sped away the robbers tossed roofing nails on the highway to stop pursuers. A week later three men attempted to rob the payroll of a Monticello, Indiana, thread mill; shots were fired, the company's manager was wounded, and the bandits escaped with nothing. Then came a series of stickups, at a restaurant, a grocery store, and a bank in Gravel Switch, Kentucky. According to Dillinger Senior, Johnnie's parole officer believed that his client was guilty of these offenses, and brother Hubert claimed that the lawman who had staked out their Mooresville home was ready to pick up Johnnie and send him back to prison. Years later William Shaw, one of Dillinger's accomplices in these early crimes, fingered his partner and reminisced about their wild times in the summer of 1933.[5]

Dillinger never confessed to these crimes and was not indicted for them, so there is no solid documentary evidence linking him to them or, for that matter, to countless other robberies he is alleged to have committed. As with so much of the Dillinger chronicle, there is lots of information, but much of it is unreliable. Once Dillinger became famous people came forward to offer stories. Witnesses all over America swore they saw him; others claimed to have been part of his life. In a celebrity-obsessed world people gain a bit of notoriety by cozying up to the famous and infamous. Dillinger's biographers have repeated and embellished the stories of men such as William Shaw because they fill in the gaps in the Dillinger story and add juicy details. It is impossible to sort out what is true from what is exaggerated, made up, or misremembered.[6]

A convicted felon when he ran with Dillinger while still in his teens, Shaw was not the most reliable witness. Dillinger was Shaw's one link with fame, and he made the most of it. As decades passed and interviewers kept coming to Shaw, he added new material, some of it implausible or detailed beyond reasonable human memory or sounding suspiciously like the movies. Those on the other side of the law too, officials such as Matt Leach, the chief of the Indiana state police who helped interrogate Shaw, had their own reasons for promulgating wild stories, from craving publicity to justifying more law enforcement expenditures by the state. Everyone had a vested interest in selling the most exciting story possible, so they made up conversations, added facts, repeated dubious material. Dillinger invited such treatment; gilding his already remarkable story came easily.[7]

Nonetheless we can be pretty certain that on July 17, not two months after his release from prison, Dillinger and another man robbed the Commercial Bank of Daleville, Indiana. According to a newspaper account, they walked in at noon. One of the robbers leveled his gun at the sole teller present and said coolly, "This is a stick-up, get me the money, honey." She froze, so he leaped over the counter (this became a Dillinger trademark) and began gathering cash while his accomplice herded customers into a corner. They unhurriedly picked up the loot, locked everyone in the vault, then escaped to their waiting Chevrolet coupe. Their take was thirty-five hundred dollars and four diamond rings. Local officials were impressed with how well prepared the robbers had been. Apparently they had spent a considerable amount of time in town, familiarizing themselves with the streets. The bank teller identified Dillinger from a photo and described the scar on his upper lip. It was right after this job that his parole officer came looking for him in Mooresville.[8]

Had Dillinger simply been disingenuous in the spring when he told family, friends, even preachers of his good intentions? It is impossible to know. Maybe it was true, as he reported to his father in May and June, that he went daily to Indianapolis in search of work and grew frustrated with failure. To outward appearances he was trying to go straight. Two weeks before the Daleville robbery Dillinger's parole officer reported that the ex-convict had spent his first month working the farm, that he also passed the time fishing, swimming, and going to movies, and that he had spent twenty-eight dollars on clothes, $1.80 on shoes, and $1.75 on toothpaste, quotidian details of a prosaic civilian life.[9]

But a thirty-year-old ex-convict with an uneven work record and a dishonorable discharge from the military did not stand much of a chance in the labor market, particularly as hard times ground on. The farm was too small for both men to work, especially with agricultural prices so deeply depressed. Dillinger Senior later described how his son faced the shame that convicts confronted in an era when the poor were already perceived as potential criminals. "I can see how the daily disappointment of being unable to get a decent job shattered Johnnie's good intentions and deepened his conviction that society had not done right by him," he mused. "Is it any wonder that such men slapped repeatedly in the face by the world that cannot forget a past misstep, seek in each other's company the contacts and understanding denied them elsewhere. . . ? That is the most damning experience of every ex-prisoner, that the smug world at large repulses him, while his old pals, who wore the same stripes with him, beckon to him." If Old John's words reflected the stilted cadences of a ghostwriting journalist, their meaning seemed heartfelt.[10]

Heartfelt but not quite satisfying. What if hard times had never come, if jobs had been plentiful, if the Dillinger farm was large and prosperous? Or what if Johnnie had gotten his old machinist job back? Might he have found a new woman, settled down, raised a family? Would he have lived the life of his kin and friends, small-town clerks, Indianapolis salesmen, prairie farmers? Certainly his letters from prison expressed longing for the domestic ideal of home, wife, and kids, but it is all more than a little hard to believe. There was an edge to Dillinger's personality, something more than mischievous, less than sociopathic. After nine years in prison, virtually his entire adult life spent playing jailhouse politics, testing the guards, seeing how much he might get away with, impressing his friends with his defiant attitude, it is hard to imagine Dillinger simply rejoining the straight world. He emerged from Michigan City deeply conflicted, angry at his unjust sentence yet motivated to prove his worthiness to his family. Most of all he must have felt a need to move around after so much confinement. If we think of his life in the abstract, even as a statistic, the fact that he returned to crime comes as no surprise. Recidivism was common enough, and the Depression only strengthened the tide. The one certain thing Dillinger had coming out of prison was solid knowledge of the underworld, and that knowledge included good contacts. He might not have known exactly what he would do as he left Michigan City, but by midsummer 1933 his course was set. By then the difficulties of the straight life—social, financial, emotional—were clear, as was the fact that Dillinger enjoyed crime. And he was good at it.[11]

On August 5 he and two others robbed the First National Bank of Montpelier, Indiana. Once again one man waited outside in a getaway car while two went in. Dillinger pointed his gun at a cashier, who loaded money from the vault into sacks; the other robber, Harry Copeland, a parolee who became a regular member of the Dillinger gang, held onlookers at gunpoint. The job was efficient and professional. According to local newspapers, they left only forty cents behind in the bank, their getaway was unhurried, they were long gone by the time police arrived, and they made off with twelve thousand dollars. The Fort Wayne *News Sentinel* concluded, "The robbers resembled those who raided the Daleville bank recently."[12]

They struck again not ten days later. On August 14, at midday, the gang hit the Citizens National Bank in Bluffton, Ohio. The Lima

News described them as well dressed and well organized, and local papers noted that one of the robbers made a stylish leap over the grill-work and into a teller's cage. The bank, however, had been robbed once before, and its security was much tighter than that of other institutions. Not only was there less money here—they got away with only two thousand dollars—but the gang's escape was hastened when an alarm went off, prompting them to fire shots across the street that broke plate glass windows. "The bandits vanished as quickly as they came," concluded the Bluffton *News*, "and only bullet-shattered windows together with empty .45-caliber shells scattered along the street in front of the bank remained as mute evidence of Bluffton's first gunplay in years."[13]

The gang's big score came three weeks later, when they took almost twenty-five thousand dollars from the State Bank of Massachusetts Avenue in Indianapolis. Again two men entered the building while one remained outside in the car. Again Dillinger leaped over a railing and forced a teller to fill sacks of money at gunpoint. Again the robbers made off with only ineffectual pursuit by authorities. Though the evidence is sketchy, Dillinger probably was involved in additional jobs during the summer of 1933.[14]

Dillinger worked his way into the criminal underworld with impressive ease. In a mere three or four months he had found partners, identified targets, acquired vehicles (often they were stolen, sometimes repainted, and always adorned with recycled license plates), and procured weapons. More, he transformed himself from an inexperienced felon into a poised professional thief, the perpetrator of several major armed robberies netting tens of thousands of dollars. From the time Dillinger left Michigan City he moved in a widening circle of crime. His prison buddies had given him the names of underworld bars and brothels, where contacts could be made, goods fenced, guns purchased or borrowed. Dillinger drove hundreds of miles to cultivate his contacts. His friends also supplied him with the locations of likely banks to rob (though bankruptcies had rendered much of the list obsolete). If we don't know for sure everyone with whom he worked during the summer of 1933, we do know that nineteen-year-old William Shaw was one accomplice (he soon ended up in the State Reformatory), that the seasoned veteran Sam Goldstein of Fort Wayne was another (until he was arrested in Gary, Indiana, for parole violations), that Dillinger recruited Homer Van Meter (who had been paroled from

Michigan City just four days before Dillinger, on May 19, 1933) in St. Paul, and that a fourth, Harry Copeland, was another Michigan City alum, paroled in late June 1933.[15]

The early 1930s were a good time to be robbing banks in the Midwest, especially in Indiana. Robberies doubled in the Hoosier state during the 1920s, and the number rose higher with the onset of the Depression. Officials blamed indulgent parents, lax discipline in schools, the erosion of public morality induced by motion pictures, and new technology that produced cars, highways, and machine guns. Robbers' success rate mattered too; crimes against banks usually went unpunished, encouraging new robberies. During the 1920s parsimonious Republican administrations in Indiana had stunted law enforcement. Heartland constabularies literally could not keep pace with criminals' new mobility. Back east, state police forces were equipped with high-speed vehicles, automatic weapons, and two-way radios. Not in the Midwest. As a stopgap measure Indiana bankers organized vigilance committees that deputized hundreds of local men to help stop the spread of crime. These irregulars were scarcely ready for the complexities of modern law enforcement, though not much less so than professional Indiana police and sheriffs, who were, by national standards, poorly paid, educated, and equipped. In fact, Indiana's State Police Department had only recently been organized when Dillinger walked out of Michigan City. Badly underfunded, it was very much a creature of politics. Dillinger began his new career at an opportune moment.[16]

Dillinger not only moved fast in the world of crime, but he managed to acquire a girlfriend within a few months of leaving prison. Houses of prostitution were important underworld meeting grounds, and he spent his share of time in them. But he also seems to have desired romantic attachments. His expressions of love, as in his letters to Beryl, continued to have an adolescent ardor about them. Women liked Dillinger, and he formed bonds with them easily. Sometime in early summer 1933, roughly two months after his release, he began keeping company with Mary Longnaker of Dayton, Ohio, whom he met through her brother, James Jenkins (rumors circulated that James was Dillinger's lover, his "old lady" or his "punk," in Michigan City). A year before Dillinger got out of prison Mary had broken up with her husband, who now had de facto custody of their two children.[17]

Dillinger's letters to Mary, written from midwestern towns where he and his friends plotted their robberies or hid out after them, were filled with pop-culture clichés: "Honey, I miss you like nobody's business, and I don't mean maybe," he wrote on July 25. "I hope I can get fixed so I can spend more time with you, for baby, I fell for you in a big way, and if you'll be on the level I'll give everybody the go by for you and that isn't a lot of hooey either. I know you like me dear but that isn't enough for me when I'm as crazy as I am about you." He pressed Mary for professions of love, told her it would be best not to see each other if she didn't love him the way he loved her, asked for a photograph of her wearing a dress he had bought her. He ended another letter, "You've sure got me tied up in a knot but don't leave me dangling for I want to know something when I see you again."[18]

We know from the detectives who tailed him that even as he pursued Mary, Dillinger spent considerable time with prostitutes. After nine years of confinement he craved sex, but love was important to him too, and so was a notion of committed domestic bliss: "I only wish I had you and two or three sweet kids and was in South America," he wrote Mary. His desire for a family was not disingenuous; he deeply loved his nieces and little sisters. After nine long years in prison he wanted to try out every kind of life. South America was not only a safe haven from the law, it was a place to fantasize a whole new identity. In the very next sentence, however, Dillinger's family idyll was broken by an ugly threat against Mary's spouse: "If that lousy husband of yours bothers you any more just let me know and he will never bother you again." Dillinger not only contacted a lawyer and paid the costs of Mary's divorce, specifying that he wanted the proceedings done quickly, but he appears to have had at least one physical confrontation with her husband, a fight that was quickly broken up.[19]

In any event, Mary fell for Johnnie. A good-looking man, well-dressed and with plenty of money in his pockets, Dillinger cut quite a figure. He began visiting her in Dayton, and they traveled together. In July he drove her west to Mooresville to meet his family, then north to Chicago for the Century of Progress World's Fair. On the way back home they stopped in Michigan City. While Dillinger stayed outside the penitentiary, Mary went in and managed to bribe a guard to bring a fruit basket stuffed with money to her brother. Mary was not only taken with Johnnie; for months after they stopped keeping company she still hoped to marry him, if FBI informants can be believed.[20]

During these first months after his release from prison Dillinger remained unknown to the public. His name was never mentioned in the newspapers, and his mini crime wave was of no more than local note. He was, however, becoming known to law enforcement officials. Parole Officer Frank Hope was not the only person looking for Dillinger. After the Montpelier job the American Surety Company, which stood to lose thousands of insurance dollars, hired Forrest Huntington, a private detective and veteran of the Pinkerton Agency, to find the culprits. Huntington stayed on the case for months, tracking his prey from Michigan to Kentucky and from Ohio to Minnesota, talking to bartenders and prostitutes, turning up all kinds of leads on Dillinger and his accomplices. Matt Leach, of the Indiana state police, was also deeply involved in the search for Dillinger, authorizing payoffs to snitches, cutting deals with prisoners, deploying men in stakeouts, piecing together bits of local information until a larger picture began to emerge.[21]

Detective work had uncovered the gang's hideouts in Gary and East Chicago and the garages where they housed their vehicles. After the Massachusetts Avenue bank job in Indianapolis police knew enough about the gang to stake out their haunts. By mid-September Dillinger had moved to Chicago, but Dayton police, acting on information supplied by the Pinkerton Agency, finally took him at gunpoint when he visited the boardinghouse where Mary Longnaker resided. They brought him to the county jail in Dayton and confiscated five pistols, detailed road maps, boxes of roofing nails (for throwing at the tires of pursuing police cars), and twenty-six hundred dollars as evidence. A parade of officials passed before Dillinger's cell, attempting to identify him as the man responsible for the crimes in their communities during the past three months.[22]

It was unclear where Dillinger would stand trial first. Governor Paul McNutt, for example, who had signed parole papers just four months earlier, rescinded his clemency order and requested Dillinger's rendition back to Indiana for the Massachusetts Avenue bank robbery. Dillinger surprised his captors and had his attorney plead guilty to the Bluffton job, though the evidence against him there was not strong. As a result he was taken to the old Allen County jail in Lima. Dillinger did not supply his captors with much information, but he was not a difficult prisoner. He seemed to be biding his time. His name was now in the news; along with a scattering of stories in small midwestern papers, some of them taken from the Associated Press wire, the Indianapolis *Star* gave Dillinger's capture in Dayton page-one headlines. They even referred to him as "Jack Rabbit" because of the way he vaulted into bank tellers' cages during holdups.[23]

As he had in Pendleton and Michigan City, Dillinger wrote to his family. "I know I have been a big disappointment to you," he began a letter to his farther. He absolved them all of responsibility, declaring of his upbringing, "My environment was the best." He blamed his plight on his prison experience: "I went in a carefree boy I came out bitter toward everything in general. . . . If I had gotten off more leniently when I made my first mistake this never would have happened." Dillinger repeated the family's official version of the story, that a cold-hearted criminal justice system had robbed him of his innocence. Still, Johnnie asked his father not to believe everything he read in the newspapers: "I am not guilty of half of the things I am charged with and I've never hurt anyone." He closed by saying that Lima officials were treating him well. Of course he knew that his letters were being censored, and it couldn't hurt to have the local sheriff and his deputies feel at ease around their prisoner.[24]

A week later he wrote to his niece Mary, told her how much he would love to see her before they shipped him off to the state facility in Columbus, and suggested she try coming on a Sunday: "The Sheriff has treated me just fine and if you explain to him you are working and going to school I am sure he will let you see me for a few minutes." Facing another long haul behind bars, there was wistfulness in Dillinger's remark to Mary that just before the police captured him, he had been planning to drive to New York City, then to Washington, D.C., for the World Series between the Giants and the Senators. Driving hundreds of miles to watch baseball must have seemed like the very definition of freedom for a man doing time. He signed off, "Lots of love, Uncle Johnnie."[25]

A week later the sheriff he had praised for his kind treatment, Jess Sarber, lay dying on the jailhouse floor as Dillinger's friends led their man out of his cell, across Sarber's body, and into the Ohio night.[26]

DILLINGER HAD MADE SEVERAL GOOD FRIENDS in the Indiana State Prison. They were of roughly the same age and background, sons of the Midwest. They too had done time in the State Reformatory before being transferred. Crime united them, and most of them knew from experience how to rob a bank. Above all they shared a hatred for the system that confined them, for the guards who watched them, and for the hierarchy that disciplined and punished them. Prisons are schools of crime. Or, to shift the metaphor to the business world, prisoners network with each other, sharing information, contacts, and techniques. They pass the time discussing case studies of dramatic heists, noted felons, and big scores, as well as their own exploits and missed opportunities. Dillinger had had nine years to learn about the underworld from men with far more experience than he. The Gordon East Coast Shirt Factory, the for-profit company for which Dillinger and his friends became a cheap labor source, contracted out by the state of Indiana, provided them all an ongoing crime seminar.[27]

Homer Van Meter, who was involved with some of the earliest Dillinger heists, was representative. He ran away from Fort Wayne to Chicago after the sixth grade, and from the age of fourteen worked as a salesman, bellhop, and waiter. After a few petty crimes Van Meter and an accomplice boarded a Pullman observation car on a New York Central train passing through Gary, Indiana, and held up the passengers. Police in Chicago picked him up and sent him back to Lake County, Indiana, where he was sentenced to ten to twenty years for highway robbery. He went first to Pendleton in 1925, where he met Dillinger, then to the Indiana State Prison. Van Meter was in constant trouble with prison officials, who saw a deeply sinister man behind the jokester façade. Early in Van Meter's prison career one Pendleton official wrote of him, "This fellow is a criminal of the most dangerous type. . . . He is a murderer at heart, and if society is to be safe-guarded, his type must be confined throughout their natural lives."[28]

If the letters Van Meter wrote to his relatives are any indication, he was also intelligent and articulate. He certainly impressed the clemency board in 1933, writing to them, "This is the age of the new deal. I place my destiny in your hands. You can restore a sterling citizen and a sound matured man to freedom." The board no doubt was equally impressed with a glowing letter written on his behalf by the Reverend Robert Hall, chaplain at Michigan City. Van Meter, he declared, had made the transition from a wild youth to a conscientious man: "About one and a half years ago he was given a position of trust as an attendant in the hospital, and glory be, he has not had any trouble since." Hall went on to quote Van Meter's own words: "Chaplain, I want a chance to live, to work, to go out into the world and make good. I'm not bad now. Please tell the 'Board' to weigh the good I am doing, and tell them also that if 'reformation' is the main end in view of prison, I am reformed—and ready to play the game and be a man." Although his record at Michigan City was far from spotless, Van Meter was paroled in May 1933, just ahead of John Dillinger.[29]

Another friend of Dillinger's was singularly charismatic and had been a leader in prison. Harry Pierpont from Leipsic, Ohio, an auto mechanic and hoisting engineer by trade, was more than six feet tall, slender, handsome, with piercing pale blue eyes. Pierpont first got into serious trouble at age nineteen; he stole a car, and when its owner confronted him Pierpont pulled a gun and fired four shots at the man. Later Indiana indicted him for a bank job in Kokomo and for assault and battery with intent to commit murder. Pierpont's prison evaluation, recommending a transfer from Pendleton to Michigan City, described him as a natural leader "along criminal lines" and called for rigid discipline to keep him from interfering with other inmates' reformation. He staged several escape attempts, and guards considered him a very dangerous man. As with Van Meter, Dillinger knew Pierpont in Pendleton and followed him to Michigan City. Only weeks after Dillinger's parole Pierpont was turned down by the clemency board, and it was then, most likely, that Dillinger went forward with a plan to free his pals.[30]

Van Meter, Pierpont, and Dillinger were part of a larger circle of friends, most of them repeat offenders: John "Red" Hamilton, a carpenter, age thirty-four, serving twenty-five years for auto theft; Charles Makley, a salesman, older than the others at age forty-four, in for robbery; Russell Clark, thirty-five, a tailor, doing twenty years for bank robbery. These men became the core of the Dillinger gang. Others among the Michigan City circle of friends included Edward Shouse, a miner, serving twenty-five years for auto theft and grand larceny; Joseph Fox, a glass worker in for life for sticking up banks; Walter Dietrich, a plumber and steamfitter, serving a life sentence for the 1930 Citizens Bank robbery in Clinton, Indiana; James Clark, Dietrich's accomplice, formerly a farmer, also a lifer for the 1930 Citizens Bank robbery; Joseph Burns of Kosciusko County, in his twelfth year of a life sentence for first-degree murder; and James Jenkins, Mary Longnaker's brother, also serving a life sentence for killing a man during a holdup. And of course there was Harry Copeland, another veteran of Michigan City, paroled in the spring, who had first worked with Dillinger on the Daleville robbery.[31]

Dillinger learned from these men, liked them, felt beholden to them, and was determined to help them break out. No doubt they had started scheming before Dillinger's parole came through, and afterward they found ways to convey messages to each other, through visitors and guards, across prison walls. Harry Pierpont is usually considered the scheme's mastermind, and though that is certainly plausible the evidence is too scanty to know with any certainty. On September 12 Dillinger allegedly threw several guns over the wall into the Michigan City facility; they were discovered by authorities and confiscated. Nonetheless security apparently remained lax, and the real plan unfolded two weeks later. A few days before his arrest in Dayton, Dillinger managed to have three.38-caliber guns smuggled into the prison. The story later given to the FBI was that a local Muncie theater owner, ostensibly a respectable businessman but with deep ties to Indiana hoodlums, helped Dillinger repackage the guns inside a box filled with spools from the East Coast Thread Company. Dillinger somehow tipped Pierpont to be on the lookout for the box and shipped it to the shirt-making plant inside the prison. Then Dillinger drove to Indianapolis to tell a woman named Mary Kinder that several Michigan City inmates would be coming to stay with her soon, including her brother (who in fact did not get out) and her lover, Harry Pierpont.[32]

On the cool rainy afternoon of September 26 the prisoners, led by Pierpont, gathered in the shirt shop. Using the guns Dillinger smuggled in, they took the superintendent and an assistant warden hostage. With these two in front and the ten convicts falling in behind, pistols and iron bars hidden under piles of shirts, they walked through the grounds, past a series of checkpoints. The caravan was invisible in its ordinariness, just prisoners delivering the shirts they had made. Suspecting nothing, guards opened the gates for them. Only when they got to the administration building, steps away from the outside world, did anyone challenge them. The convicts shot one guard, beat two others, and herded the remaining prison employees into an office vault. Then they unlocked the main entrance, kidnapped a visiting sheriff, Charles Neal, who had come to Michigan City from Harrison County to deliver a prisoner, and stole two cars, initially making a clean getaway.[33]

The cars quickly split up, one heading west, the other south. The first group promptly drove their vehicle into a ditch, stole another, ran out of gas, then wandered for two days and nights on foot in the northern Indiana woods. Dietrich, Burns, and Fox eventually got away, but James Clark was captured and returned to Michigan City. The car with the other six men—Pierpont, Shouse, Makley, Hamilton, Russell Clark, and James Jenkins—headed to Indianapolis, to Mary Kinder's home. She sheltered them briefly, went out and bought clothes to replace their prison garb, and found them another safe house. Three days after the jailbreak, however, the Indiana State Police picked up their trail and gave chase. Although state and local officials as well as vigilante groups were out in force, the convicts managed to outrun the squad cars. James Jenkins, however, became separated from the larger group. He stole a car at gunpoint and forced the driver to head south toward Bloomington, but the car soon ran out of gas. Continuing on foot Jenkins was finally cornered by armed civilians in Bean Blossom; they killed him in the ensuing struggle. The remaining corps of five escapees found refuge first with Pierpont's father and mother near Leipsic, Ohio, then in Hamilton, Ohio. A week after their prison break they robbed the First National Bank of St. Mary's, Ohio, of ten thousand dollars. Bank patrons and employees recognized Charles Makley as a fellow townsman and neighbor who had lived among them.[34]

The jailbreak was major news across America, and it captured banner headlines in the Midwest: "Sheriff Kidnapped, Three Wounded in Desperate Flight," "10 Fugitives Called Worst of Bad Men," and "Escaped Indiana Convicts Members of John Dillinger Gang." That last phrase may not even have crossed Dillinger's mind yet; Harry Pierpont was the more experienced and more notorious criminal. Still, a few newspapers had already made the connection between the obscure convict sitting in a Dayton cell and this larger story. Thus the lead paragraph at the top of page one in the Gary *Post-Tribune* described him as "John Dillinger, alleged leader of a gang of bank bandits who have robbed 27 banks in the last 60 days and said to be the 'brains' behind the prison break at Michigan City Tuesday which resulted in the escape of 10 desperate men."[35]

The Chicago *Tribune*'s headline story noted that hundreds of lawmen and civilians had taken to the field: "Ten desperate convicts who yesterday afternoon slugged and shot their way out of the Indiana state prison here were being hunted early today, principally in farming districts near here, by posses comprising more than 500 vigilantes, police and deputy sheriffs." The reports of "man-hunters" tracking the "desperados" with "shoot to kill orders" took a surreal turn when the Columbia Broadcasting System staged a radio drama and aired it as a real shootout between the convicts and troopers. Matt Leach was so incensed he threatened to file charges of news falsification with the Federal Radio Commission in Washington, and five CBS employees were brought in for questioning. But the radio play was a sign that news agencies sensed a big story here, a developing drama. The wire services, United Press, Associated Press, and International News Service, carried reports into markets large and small. However, as September ended coverage shrank back into northern Indiana, and the main focus became name-calling by Democrats and Republicans over who was to blame, since prison officials, including wardens, were political appointments.[36]

Meanwhile Dillinger had been transferred from Dayton to Lima. In retrospect Allen County authorities ignored the obvious security problems this posed. When Dillinger was first arrested in Dayton the police had found among his possessions a crude map of the Indiana State Prison; local officials expressed alarm, and after the Michigan City breakout they added guards both inside and outside their prisoner's jail. But in Lima security remained lax. Sheriff Sarber was apparently not overly worried that the Michigan City escapees might attempt to free his prisoner; he did not take seriously warnings from other law enforcement agencies or newspaper reports of a connection between Dillinger and the Michigan City breakout. Indeed, when a large party of heavily armed guards transferred Dillinger from Dayton to a midway point in Piqua, Ohio, where the handoff of the prisoner was to be made, the Dayton police were so astonished at the meagerness of their counterpart from Lima that they refused to give their captive over until Sarber sent more men and guns.[37]

The night of October 12 was a typically relaxed one in the Allen County Jail. Sheriff Sarber sat at his desk in the office, reading the newspaper, while his wife sat nearby doing a crossword puzzle and Deputy Wilbur Sharp lay napping on the sofa. Six men (five Michigan City escapees plus Harry Copeland) gathered at the courthouse; Copeland, Shouse, and Hamilton took up positions outside, then Pierpont, Makley, and Russell Clark went in. They did not have a clear plan but apparently agreed that Pierpont would do the talking and that they would try to avoid gunfire if possible. When they approached Sheriff Sarber, he asked how he might help them. Pierpont replied they were officers from Michigan City, come to question Dillinger. Sarber asked to see their credentials. Pierpont pulled a gun, said, "Here are our credentials," and fired twice, one fatal bullet ripping through Sarber's abdomen (later reports claimed that Pierpont fired only after Sarber reached for his gun). The sheriff tried to rise but was pistol-whipped by Makley and Pierpont as they demanded the keys to the cells. Mrs. Sarber screamed, begged them to stop beating her husband, and gave them the keys. They freed Dillinger, then locked Mrs. Sarber and Deputy Sharp in the cells. Now seven strong, the gang escaped in two waiting cars and headed back to Hamilton.[38]

DILLINGER'S RESCUE WAS COVERED in local midwestern papers with daily headlines, and the closer to the epicenter, the longer the page-one coverage lasted. Building on the Michigan City coverage, the national wire services devoted considerable resources to the story. Even the New York *Times* gave it several inches of copy. The Chicago *Tribune*'s lead story began, "Three gunmen, one of whom has been identified as a member of the group of ten convicts who escaped from the Michigan City, Ind., penitentiary on Sept. 26, walked boldly into the county jail here this evening. Drawing revolvers, they killed Sheriff Jess Sarber when he barred the way and then effected the delivery of John Dillinger, bank robber and desperado, who was the 'outside man' of the Indiana jail break." Dillinger was becoming good copy, and the *Tribune* included his prison photograph.[39]

Never averse to publicity, Indiana State police chief Matt Leach further burnished Dillinger's reputation for reporters. He claimed that there was no parallel in American history to the Dillinger gang's twenty-four successful bank robberies in sixty days (how he came up with this wild figure is a mystery). Leach called Dillinger the most dangerous outlaw in America, "more deadly than 'Machine Gun' Kelly ever dreamed of being." He added that Ohio officials had been gulled by Dillinger's innocent looks when they took him for a common thief. Indiana law enforcement had dealt with the man and knew better: "When all the known facts about Dillinger are once dragged into publicity, it will be found that no desperado in America can approach this Indiana bad man's record." Leach pledged to put aside all of his other obligations to bring in Dillinger. What he did not say, of course, was that the more dangerous the criminal, the more heroic his captor.[40]

In Marion County, Indiana, by contrast, the outlaw's salt-of-the-earth background continued to get play. The local Mooresville paper asked Dillinger Senior about his son. The lean old man in overalls looked like a Grant Wood figure come to life. Whenever he was interviewed, then and in future months, it was always while doing a round of chores, in this case cutting poplar trees for the oncoming winter. Dillinger Senior talked about his son as a good boy victimized by the criminal justice system, using much the same language for the local paper as he would for the national media a few months later. If not for that severe sentence back in 1924 Johnnie never would have embarked on a life of crime. Then the old man returned to his work, "for he says that despite all the trouble that can come to a family, he realizes that corn must be shucked and wood must be cut."[41]

Two nights after Dillinger's liberation, as Lima prepared to bury Sheriff Sarber, three nattily dressed men approached the police station in Auburn, Indiana. Dillinger, Pierpont, and Dietrich leveled guns at the two officers on duty, disarmed them, locked them in a cell, and walked out with several pistols, two automatic rifles, one Thompson machine gun, three bulletproof vests, and hundreds of rounds of ammunition. A week later, on October 21, the three struck again at a police station in Peru, Indiana; this time they herded officers into the basement at the point of the machine gun they had stolen earlier. They came away with two more Thompsons, two sawed-off shotguns, six bulletproof vests, and assorted rifles and pistols. The real prizes, of course, were the machine guns and the bulletproof vests, still rare items among small-town police departments. The gang had taken the battle to the law, and in response Indiana officials demanded more powerful guns, armored cars, and better communications equipment. The state chapter of the American Legion offered to put thirty thousand armed vigilantes on the roads, and the National Guard contemplated using tanks, poison gas, and airplanes.[42]

But for now the gang committed robberies of small-town banks with better weapons, faster cars, and more body-armor than the police. On Monday, October 23, a little before 3 p.m., four men parked their Studebaker sedan outside the Central National Bank and Trust Company of Greencastle, Indiana. One stood guard at the door while the other three entered the bank. Pierpont handed a cashier a twenty-dollar bill and asked if it was genuine. As the banker studied it, the bandits drew their weapons, including machine guns hidden under their overcoats. Dillinger leaped over a railing into a teller's cage—as he became famous, other robbers imitated this trademark—and began emptying drawers full of money into a sack. Calmly, methodically, the men kept the dozen employees and customers covered, forced the bank cashier to open the vault, and helped themselves to stacks of money. They left town with approximately twenty-five thousand dollars in cash and fifty thousand in bonds. No alarms sounded until they were well on the road, and eyewitnesses later identified Dillinger, Pierpont, Makley, and Copeland as the stickup men.[43]

The Chicago *Tribune's* coverage of the Greencastle heist can only be described as hysterical. It reported that eight robbers, not four, had pulled off the job with frightening efficiency: "Almost with the precision of military squads they alighted, entered the bank and revealed their guns." It was one thing for armed men to rob banks; the *Tribune* story gave them a capacity for evil far beyond holding tellers at gunpoint and stealing cash: "The terrorists, it is certain, have formed a marauding band of guerrillas, willing and powerful enough to inflict their outlaw enterprises wherever they go."[44]

It was the vagueness of the threat that was most frightening, and the *Tribune's* tone soon became the norm. The day after Greencastle, four men robbed a South Bend bank of three thousand dollars; although they were apprehended eventually, newspapers leaped to the conclusion that it was the Dillinger gang, or the "Terror Gang," as some now called them. A day later two more banks were hit, this time in the Indiana towns of Modoc and Fillmore. Newspapers reported that nearly a quarter of a million dollars had been stolen in more than thirty bank robberies since the first of the year. These "depredations" were the work of "desperados" hiding out in the "badlands" of northern Indiana, a "gang of outlaws" that was "bound by oath never to be captured alive," a "band of fugitive convicts preying upon banks and citizens" and spreading "terror" throughout the region. Chief Matt Leach, master of the press conference, gave the "facts": the Dillinger gang had carried out eighteen robberies in sixty days (his numbers kept changing); they now had sixty-four connections with other gangs in the Midwest; they possessed eleven machine guns and eighteen bulletproof vests, plus shotguns and pistols.[45]

It was no big leap from Leach's "statistics" to imagining dozens of armed men, organized, invincible, and bloodthirsty. State and local officials were forced to act, lest they appear to be losing control of the situation. Federal agents were brought in to consult on October 24, and two days later Governor McNutt, the man who had signed John Dillinger's parole papers, called out the National Guard. More than seventy officers and five hundred soldiers were deputized, armed with machine guns, rifles, and shotguns, and deployed in small squads at strategic points throughout the state. The American Legion once again offered the assistance of a vigilante "shotgun army," and local officials deputized countless men into posses manning improvised roadblocks.[46]

The ongoing economic depression was the backdrop for these actions, and it made banditry especially frightening. Indiana courts, for example, were trying to deal with the problem of thousands of families unable to pay their mortgages and threatened with eviction from their homes. Hobo "jungles" at the edge of every town where the homeless gathered bore witness to the crisis; "Hoovervilles," the unemployed called them, in honor of the former president. Just a year earlier fifty thousand citizens had gathered in Washington to demand early payment of the bonuses promised World War I veterans; so terrifying was the threat that the army forcibly dispersed them. The image of armed, desperate men grew doubly terrifying under the specter of genuine want abroad in the land and the government apparently powerless to do much about it. The Chicago *Tribune* spoke for many when it declared that civil authorities could no longer cope with the situation, for the Dillinger gang was "as dangerous as the one headed by Jesse James many years ago." The newspaper wrote approvingly of new military measures being taken to "wipe out banditry" and to "halt the depredations."[47]

Another note, equally discordant, occasionally sounded in this chorus. Some banks, it was rumored, welcomed the robberies. They were so mismanaged or so overextended by the Depression—or, some argued, so baldly plundered by their owners—that a raid by the likes of Dillinger helped cover their misfeasance or malfeasance. Before long it was whispered that banks arranged robberies in order to collect insurance money and thereby bail themselves out of insolvency.[48]

Nor was the public's response to the "Terror Gang" entirely negative. "I am for John Dillinger," wrote one citizen to the "Voice of the Reader" column in the Indianapolis *Star*. The writer went on to explain that he was not excusing crime, though he questioned whether Dillinger was really guilty of all that the newspapers alleged. Why single out Dillinger, he asked, since "he wasn't any worse than the bankers or politicians who took the poor people's money." Even more pointedly the writer declared, "Dillinger did not rob poor people. He robbed those who became rich by robbing the poor. I am for Johnnie." Another writer likewise defended Dillinger, arguing that bandits gave bankers more of a chance to protect themselves than bankers gave the common people, whose life savings they stole or squandered.[49]

With Indiana policed so heavily, the gang decided to move on, and they disappeared from public view for the next few weeks. Dillinger had enjoyed his time in Chicago with Mary Longnaker the previous summer, and no doubt other members of the gang, newly released from years of confinement with thousands of dollars of Greencastle money in their pockets, longed for the action of the city. Besides, in a town like Chicago, with its long-standing traditions of crime and corruption, with lawyers who specialized in underworld cases, doctors willing to treat the victims of firearms mishaps without reporting to the police, fences who brokered stolen goods, taverns where felons could find each other and exchange information, the gang's money could buy protection. They slipped into North Side apartments and quietly blended in. Girlfriends, old and new, joined them. Mary Kinder shared an apartment with Harry Pierpont; Charlie Makley kept company with Patricia Long (who also called herself Pat Cherrington); Russell Clark dated her sister, Opal Long; Homer Van Meter spent his time with Marie Conforti. And Dillinger met a new woman, a hatcheck girl named Evelyn Sparks. "Billie," as she was known, was married to a man named Welton Sparks, who had recently been sent to the federal prison at Leavenworth for robbing the U.S. mail. She went back to using her French Canadian maiden name, Frechette. Billie's mother was a Menomonee Indian, and she raised her daughter on the reservation in northern Wisconsin.[50]

There is a striking hominess to the descriptions of gang life by Mary Kinder, who gave interviews to the newspapers after it was all over. There were always clothes hanging on the line and meals being cooked. Two couples often shared an apartment, yet in Kinder's telling very little tension arose between the gang members. Everyone made their own decisions about where to live. They came and went from each other's lives casually, easily. Business decisions—which bank to rob and when—were reached through discussion and consensus. Mostly the gang members and their women lived quietly.

Working-class folks who suddenly had money in their pockets, they now took care of long-delayed tasks like going to the dentist to get their teeth fixed. Not just necessities, though; there were good times to be had. The men bought expensive gifts for their lovers. They often went clothes shopping together. All frequented restaurants, bars, ball-games, and nightclubs. Dillinger loved the movies, and he constantly tried to persuade his friends to go along with him. The men had freedom, female companionship, and money. The women, working-class girls all, had men who could protect them, both physically and financially, from what had been hard lives. And all of them flaunted middle class morality. They cohabited out of wedlock, let the banks' money dispel their material deprivations, enjoyed plenty of leisure time, and had some thrilling adventures together. The gang was far from care-free, but it beat the straight life.[51]

Nonetheless the fear of being captured was very real, and gang members stayed only briefly in any one apartment. The Chicago police were vigilant, and though they never had solid information about the whereabouts of individuals they staked out suspicious places and raided several flats. The gang rented mostly on the North Side and moved often from location to location, sometimes just ahead of the police. For a while Dillinger and friends rented at 154 North Parkside, then at 4310 Clarendon, then a little farther north at 5510 Winthrop, then a few blocks south and west at 1343 Argyle. At least one of the apartments, Billie Frechette later told a friend, was quite elegant, six rooms with cut glass and lush furnishings, including a complete silver service. Through November and into December the gang led an oddly bifurcated life, settling into a comfortable daily routine yet never able to completely forget that they were on the lam.[52]

Their caution was well-founded, for officials were closing in. The former Pinkerton detective Forrest Huntington had cultivated Arthur McGinnis, an underworld figure who had served time with Dillinger and now acted as a paid informant. McGinnis wormed his way into the company of Dillinger and Pierpont, offering to fence the bonds stolen in the St. Mary's and Massachusetts Avenue robberies that were difficult to exchange. McGinnis told Huntington that Dillinger had developed a skin condition for which he had an appointment with a dermatologist on the evening of November 15. Rather than wait for an opportunity to nab the whole gang, Matt Leach and the Indiana state police chose to act.[53]

Leach later claimed that they had no intention of taking Dillinger alive. Assisted by Chicago police officers, they staked out the doctor's office on West Irving Park at Keeler. The plan was to get their man as he left. Billie drove with Johnnie, then waited outside in the car. She watched as three vehicles pulled up on Keeler and parked ahead of Dillinger's auto. The police hoped to cut him off as he pulled forward, then block him from behind with another car. Billie must have figured out the trap and told Dillinger as he stepped in, because he immediately gunned his engine, threw his car into reverse, careened backward onto Irving Park, then sped east toward Lake Michigan. According to newspapers the police gave chase, and both sides exchanged gunshots while bystanders ran for cover. Some stories had the police pulling alongside Dillinger's elegant Essex Terraplane and firing at close range, only to find that it was equipped with bulletproof glass and that its sides were armored. Newspapers said that Dillinger returned fire as he steered and that the woman sitting at his side got off a few rounds as well; "Gun Girl Helps Desperado Flee," one headline put it. Still, the police might have captured their man had not a secret portal opened in his speeding car and a mysterious machine-gunner fired away. Dillinger and his accomplices escaped. Police later raided apartments on Montrose and Clarendon and found nothing.[54]

Dillinger's father once suggested that American newspaper publishers raise a monument to his son with the inscription "In memory of the greatest circulation builder in history!" It was not a foolish idea. The Chicago *Tribune* opened its story on the North Side shootout by calling Dillinger the "desperate leader of a band of outlaws which has been terrorizing northern and central Indiana for weeks." Dillinger was great copy, and reporters were more than willing to sensationalize events and fabricate facts. Criminals on the lam, after all, rarely gave interviews, so the subject invited creative journalism. Stories about Dillinger's armored car came up repeatedly during the next several months. No such vehicle ever existed. Writers did not even bother to reconcile their descriptions of a bulletproof car with the discovery the next day of Dillinger's abandoned, bullet-drilled auto on a North Side street. The notion of an armored car helped explain police failures even as it titillated the public imagination by underscoring the gang's apparent invincibility.[55]

Police reports later revealed that there was no secret portal, no machine-gunner; in fact no shots at all were fired from Dillinger's car.

Newspapers also erred in naming the woman sitting next to Dillinger. They identified her as Mary Jenkins, the sister of deceased Michigan City escapee James Jenkins (they meant, of course, Mary Longnaker, the woman at whose Dayton home Dillinger had been captured in September). But Mary Longnaker was long gone from Dillinger's side. Dillinger, it turned out, was both lucky and skillful when he made the unexpected move backing up onto Irving Park: lucky that only two cars followed him, lucky that one of them suffered brake failure, skillful at handling a speeding vehicle under fire (he was driving perhaps seventy-five miles per hour), and lucky one more time when he ducked unseen into an alley. And now he knew that Arthur McGinnis had ratted on him.[56]

This near-miss did not prevent the gang from quickly pulling another bank job. Their final robbery of the year, though successful monetarily, was more chaotic and bloody than previous ones. On November 20 they held up the American Bank and Trust Company in Racine, Wisconsin. Though they cased the town and the bank well and drew up careful getaway maps ("gits," as pros called them), this was not a textbook robbery. Makley, Dillinger, Pierpont, and Clark entered the bank, followed by their driver, Leslie Homer. A recently paroled friend of the Michigan City escapees, Homer had made himself useful to Dillinger and Pierpont, meeting with fences, driving to remote towns to post money to family members, moving stolen goods in and out of lockers. While Pierpont and Dillinger went back to the vault, Makley turned his gun on Harold Graham, the head teller, who was counting cash. Graham either did not hear the command "Hands up" or thought it was a joke, and when he turned away Makley shot him. The bullet pierced his arm and entered his hip, but he managed to hit an alarm button as he went down, setting off a ceaseless clanging. Unfazed, Makley and Clark cleaned out the tellers' cages, while Dillinger and Pierpont got the bank president, Grover Weyland, to open the vault. Meanwhile the alarm bell attracted a crowd, and police began to gather outside. Officer Wilbur Hansen sauntered in, apparently thinking this was another false alarm; Clark shot him. Makley picked up Hansen's machine gun and fired a burst through the front window, probably at another policeman. Glass shattered and onlookers screamed and ran.[57]

Their sacks loaded with twenty-eight thousand dollars in bills, the bandits now moved toward the front door. They grabbed several hostages, and using them as a human shield pushed their way outside. Dillinger drove the getaway car, a Buick, with three hostages held at gunpoint on the running boards. Several officers had the car in their sights as it drove along, but the hostages kept them from firing. Police followed the getaway Buick, but a fortuitously timed train at a crossing separated the gang from their pursuers. Once they were clear, the hostages crammed into the car, and Dillinger took to small rural roads. As evening fell they refueled with gasoline they had deposited along the roadside the night before. Then the gang let the hostages out and tied them up, though not terribly well, as they quickly freed themselves and walked to a nearby farm. Newspapers later reported that before dropping off their captives Dillinger asked Charles Makley to stop his swearing because one of the hostages was a lady and Pierpont gave her his coat when she shivered in the November cold.[58]

It had been a thrilling autumn. Men who only months before had nothing but time to ruminate on the bad luck that put them under the thumb of every prison guard with an attitude were now free and rich. Still, they had served enough prison time to know that luck turned on a dime. The way newspapers reported Dillinger's escape from the dermatologist's office and the gang's getaway from Racine added to their reputation for slickness, but these episodes might just as easily have resulted in capture or death. Events over the next few weeks helped dispel the notion that the gang was indomitable.

On November 19, the day before the Racine heist, Harry Copeland was arrested in Chicago. Copeland had a drinking problem and was unreliable, so the gang had marginalized him. He apparently got into an altercation with a woman, a prostitute, it was alleged, who had lifted cash from his wallet after he fell asleep. Copeland brandished a gun and police were called. When fingerprints revealed whom they had in custody, Matt Leach and his men rushed to interrogate Copeland. Detectives questioned him under threat of return to prison and, worse, death row back in Ohio. Through it all the gaunt, rubber-faced felon gave up nothing and kept his laconic sense of humor. He smiled for photographers and blamed his arrest on whiskey, taken purely for medicinal purposes: "It was supposed to be good stuff too—prescription liquor, right out of a drug store. . . . I got it for a cold." He told newspapermen that everything was kind of hazy: "I took a few drinks and about the next thing I knew the cops had me." Asked whether he helped free the Michigan City fugitives, he said no, the prisoners were a "pretty crummy bunch—bad characters." Did he commit the recent bank robberies? "Wasn't in any of the places. . . . Would have had to have wings to be at all of them." In a few days he was on his way back to Indiana, then to Ohio to stand trial for the murder of Sheriff Sarber.[59]

Then on December 14 John "Red" Hamilton, the quiet, older ex-con, easily identifiable because he was missing two fingers on his right hand from a childhood sledding accident, went to a North Side auto mechanic to pick up his car. Along with Dillinger, Makley, Pierpont, Van Meter, and Clark, Hamilton was a core member of the gang, and because they all were suspects in a spectacular bank robbery that had occurred the day before (it turned out to be the work of another outfit), the police were on high alert. Hamilton's car was identified from a previous heist, so when they spotted it on the lot they staked out the mechanic's shop. Hamilton showed up with his current girlfriend, Elaine DeKant Dent. Sergeant William Shanley, a decorated World War I veteran, winner of the Chicago *Tribune's* "Hero" award, father of four daughters, member of his parish church, approached the two and asked if it was their car. When they said yes, he told them to keep their hands visible. Shanley began to search Hamilton, who pulled a gun from his shoulder holster and shot the officer twice, fatally. Hamilton barely managed to get away on foot, leaving Ms. Dent behind. He then made his way back to his apartment and his comrades.[60]

Two days after Shanley's death, Chicago's thirteenth police fatality in 1933, the city started its own Dillinger Squad, made up of forty marksmen under the command of Captain John Stege. With newspapers' help, the Chicago police department now laid crime after crime at the feet of the Dillinger gang. At the same time the young special agent in charge of the Bureau of Investigation's Chicago office, Melvin Purvis, wrote to his boss, J. Edgar Hoover, that he had just attended an excellent conference put together by the Cook County state's attorney to coordinate various agencies' efforts to break up the Dillinger gang. Purvis took heart that police and politicians all declared their determination to eradicate the scourge.[61]

A week after the Shanley killing the lawmen picked up Hilton Crouch. Crouch had worked with Dillinger before the Michigan City breakout. He had become a partner in a tavern and had not been active with the gang in recent months, but his arrest got plenty of attention. He confessed to the Massachusetts Avenue robbery, told police that his share of the take was more than eight thousand dollars, following the group's rule of splitting all earnings equally. As with Copeland, the police shipped him back to Indiana. Three days later local police captured Edward Shouse in Paris, Illinois, after a shootout in which one officer was killed. Shouse too had become marginal to the gang; the others found him untrustworthy, and when he was caught planning to pull a bank job on his own they cut him loose. After his arrest, Shouse denounced his former colleagues, and newspaper reporters had a field day with his comments: "They are all kill-crazy and that's why I left them. . . . If you policemen are married men with families I warn you to be careful about trying to take the other boys. . . . They'll shoot it out to the last bullet and they have plenty of guns and bullets." Then, just after the first of the year, another Michigan City escapee, Walter Dietrich, was captured in a Chicago suburb during a bloody shootout between police and gang leader Theodore Klutas.[62]

So the cops had some success picking off members of Dillinger's "invincible" band, albeit marginal ones. Though Shouse called the gang "kill-crazy," police violence also bloodied these days. Shortly before 1933 ended, Chicago cops raided an apartment on Farwell Avenue in Rogers Park, believing they had cornered members of the Dillinger gang; the three men turned out to be small-time Jewish hoods who had no connection to the Hoosier outlaw, but that discovery came only after the cops had shot them all down. In word and deed, the police made plain their intention to shoot first and ask questions later.[63]

Dillinger, Pierpont, and the others recognized that Chicago, like Indiana, was too hot for them, especially after the Shanley killing. With winter coming on they headed south. Johnnie and Billie arrived first in Daytona Beach. On December 19 they rented a large home on Ocean Avenue, facing the Atlantic, for one hundred dollars a month. Billie later referred to the place as a mansion, with four fireplaces. Using the alias Frank Kirtley, Dillinger told the building manager, Edwin Utter, that he planned to stay several months. A day or two later three more cars arrived, carrying Harry Pierpont and Mary Kinder, Russell Clark and Opal Long, Homer Van Meter and Charles Makley. Interviewed by the FBI months later, Utter said that all of them stayed together in the beach house. They said they were from Chicago, drove fancy new cars (a Buick, a Studebaker, an Essex Terraplane, a Ford V-8), and though Utter told the feds that they all appeared "to be of the gangster type," he had not asked any questions. He added that nothing out of the ordinary occurred during their stay; they drank a good bit, but they were not rowdy and no neighbors complained. They kept to themselves, got little mail, neither sent nor received phone calls or telegrams, had no apparent outside contacts, entertained no visitors. They swam and fished and lounged; they even went horseback riding. At one point they all took a brief trip to Miami and sampled the nightlife there. It was a vacation for all of them, right down to having most of their meals sent in.[64]

No doubt Florida was the farthest any of them ever had been from home. Everything—the ocean, the weather, the citrus trees—must have seemed terribly exotic, and their time in the sun, away from the midwestern winter, was the height of luxury. During the last days of 1933, however, shortly after having some dental work done, Billie Frechette decided to return to Wisconsin. Probably she merely wanted to visit her family for the holidays, though stories persisted for years that she and Dillinger had had a violent fight. A few days after Billie left, the gang threw a New Year's Eve party. As the story goes, Dillinger, who normally drank very little, just a beer or two, got very drunk, and as midnight approached he stepped out onto the balcony, machine gun in hand, and fired away at the moon.[65]

As the year ended back in Chicago, the Illinois state attorney general declared John Dillinger to be "Public Enemy No. 1," a phrase that had originated with the Chicago Crime Commission. Only two other men had held the distinction, one of them Al Capone. In fact the first ten on the list now were all Dillinger associates, including Harry Pierpont, John Hamilton, Charles Makley, and Russell Clark, as well as two of the gang's "molls"—the first time women had made the top ten—Mary Kinder and Pearl Elliott (Billie Frechette's name was still unknown to the officials). The state released a bulletin of these notorious criminals, complete with photographs, fingerprints, and thumbnail descriptions, and placed them in the hands of every officer in Cook County. So Dillinger was up there now with the likes of Al Capone. It had been a wild half-year, but nothing compared to what was coming.[66]

THREE

"John Dillinger, Houdini of the Outlaws"

Florida was a good place to get away from the Midwestern cold and the police heat. But playing tourist—swimming, fishing, lounging around, playing cards, eating, drinking, enjoying the sun—got old for this crowd. Maybe they felt suspicious eyes on them. Maybe they grew uncomfortable staying in one place. Maybe the intoxicant of new places, warmer climes, exotic settings—escaping working-class drudgery, living the life of the rich as imagined in movies and magazines—made them want more new experiences. Whatever the reason, the open road beckoned again, and about four weeks into their Florida stay the Dillinger gang packed up and left, giving no warning of their departure. By the middle of the month each car had commenced the long drive north off the Florida peninsula, then west along the panhandle, through the Deep South, across the Mississippi, into Arkansas, Oklahoma, and Texas, then finally into the Southwest, through New Mexico, into Arizona, and down to the sleepy town of Tucson. Nearly three thousand miles, all of it much harder than a modern tourist would experience in a climate-controlled car on carefully engineered highways with ubiquitous roadside services.[1]

Dillinger, however, did not take this drive, not yet. Though he later claimed he stayed in Florida and then accompanied the others to Arizona, in fact he headed north, back toward Chicago and Billie. The two intended to stay together now, since Billie went to the trouble of filing for a dissolution of her marriage to Welton Sparks on the grounds of desertion. In any event, they were on their way to Tucson together in late January.[2]

But first came the events of January 15. While the rest of the gang was either in Tucson or making their way there Dillinger and John Hamilton entered the First National Bank of East Chicago, an Indiana town just south and east of the Illinois metropolis. For the rest of his life Dillinger denied that he had been in East Chicago that day. Eyewitnesses said otherwise; so did the cash later found in his possession, with serial numbers from the East Chicago Bank. As in most of their other jobs they came in a bit before three o'clock, just shy of closing time, when deposits were at their height. The newspapers reported that Dillinger pulled a submachine gun from its case and yelled, "This is a stick up; put up your hands, everybody." Bank Vice President Edward Steck told reporters what happened next:

> "We were all electrified. . . . There were about a dozen employes of the bank at work and some fifteen or twenty customers at the windows. We all obeyed the command with alacrity. But another of our vice presidents, Walter Spencer, touched off the alarm that notified the police station a block and a half away of the robbery.
>
> "When we were all lined up the machine gunner called out to his companion: 'go in and get it.' The second man, who the police say is Hamilton, stepped behind the counter and scooped up all the money in the cages. While he was at his work Patrolman Hobart Wilgus, the first to arrive from the station, walked in with his pistol drawn. But the gunner bandit got the drop on him and forced him to drop the pistol and line up with the rest of us.
>
> "While Hamilton, the second man, was getting the money Dillinger glanced out the doorway and saw other policemen congregating. Instead of appearing frightened, he called out to the money-gatherer:
>
> "'There's been an alarm and the police are outside. But don't hurry. Get all that dough. We'll kill all these coppers and get away. Take your time.'"[3]

The two bandits finished bagging more than twenty thousand dollars, and, just as they did in Racine, they moved to the door with a human shield, in this case bank vice president Walter Spencer, and police officer Wilgus. Unlike the Wisconsin job, however, one of the policemen on the street, William O'Malley, thought he might get a clear shot. Wilgus later described what he saw:

> There were about thirty of us lined up before Dillinger's machine gun. When we got outside the door, O'Malley, who had put himself in front of a five-and-ten-cent store across from the bank, yelled, "Wilgus, Wilgus!" I knew he wanted me to jump to one side so that he could get a shot at Dillinger. I jumped and O'Malley opened fire. He and Dillinger shot about the same time. O'Malley shot Dillinger four times in the chest, but Dillinger was wearing a bullet-proof vest and the bullets just splashed off. When they picked up O'Malley afterward he had eight bullet holes in him. The bullets went right on through—not a bullet in his body.

Dillinger and Hamilton hustled to their waiting Plymouth, let the captives fall away, and sped off. But not before receiving a full fusillade from the officers on the street, with one bullet wounding Hamilton—his blood-stained gun was later found in the street—and forcing Dillinger to help his companion into their auto as shots continued to fly at them. Police speculated that the car was equipped with bullet-proof glass, an idea that once again proved false when the vehicle was found the next day on the streets of Chicago. Referring to the dead peace officers killed by the Dillinger gang over the previous months, the United Press reported grimly from Indianapolis that O'Malley's death "was marked on the wall of a state police headquarters office here today as the fourth score for the John Dillinger convict gang."[4]

Dillinger must have been shaken by Officer O'Malley's death. It was the first and only killing ever laid directly at his feet. He later insisted that he had still been in Florida in mid-January, though sometimes he added that he understood how, under the right circumstances, a man would have to return fire in self-defense. He also claimed that Red Hamilton had killed O'Malley and then died of his wounds.[5]

Dillinger now had a capital crime linked to his name. He headed back to Chicago after the robbery and found medical care for Hamilton. The underworld had its favorite doctors, men whose careers were already on the skids due to drug addiction, alcoholism, performing illegal procedures such as abortions, medical malpractice, or just a fascination with the seamy side of life. Dr. Joseph Moran, an alcoholic, pulled half a dozen slugs out of Hamilton's arm, shoulder, and pelvis.

By now Billie had come down from Wisconsin, and they found a safe house where their friend could recuperate, dumped the bullet-riddled getaway car on the North Side, and headed out of town in a 1932 Essex Terraplane, which Dillinger had bought for Billie months earlier. They stopped in Mooresville to spend a few minutes with Dillinger's father, then continued south to St. Louis. At the Hudson-Frampton showroom, using the name Frank Sullivan and giving a home address in Green Bay, Wisconsin, Dillinger traded in the Terraplane for a new Hudson Club Sedan, paying the thousand-dollar balance in twenty-dollar bills, pulled off a stack still bound in a bank wrapper. Billie and Johnnie stayed overnight at the Roosevelt Hotel, then on January 21 drove west to Arizona to meet up with the others.[6]

WHY TUCSON? Maybe they thought it was a good place to lie low, or perhaps Dillinger hoped for a final big score in the area before disappearing into Mexico. The gang did have a tenuous Arizona connection: Charles Makley knew a woman there, and he argued that the desert was the perfect place to be invisible for a while. Some newspapers later put words in the gangsters' mouths. Under his own byline Dillinger explained, "We had come to Arizona to quit the game and rest. We were through. None of us ever liked it anyway. We thought no one would know us way out here. Why, this is the end of the world. Just look at this dreary desert, if you don't believe it." The gang eluded some "brilliant sleuths" in the Midwest, Dillinger concluded; certainly they could evade a bunch of "desert detectives."[7]

Whatever drew them there, Arizona proved a bad idea. Before they even got to the Southwest the feds were sniffing around. In the weeks following the Michigan City breakout the gang had spent considerable time in Hamilton, Ohio, about twenty-five miles north of Cincinnati, and at a nearby "auto camp" on the Miami River. Not long after the murder of Sheriff Sarber, the Division of Investigation, making its first forays into the case, noted that the gang stole a car in Chicago and abandoned it in Hamilton, thus violating the National Motor Vehicle Theft Act.[8]*

*The Division of Investigation was renamed the Federal Bureau of Investigation in 1935. Because that name is so much better known, and because the organization's mission, structure, and leadership remained largely unchanged, I use Division of Investigation, Federal Bureau of Investigation, FBI, and "the feds" interchangeably.

By early January the feds had figured out that a Hamilton couple, Leroy and Naomi Hooten, had been assisting the Dillinger gang. Both had underworld ties, and they became part of the lifeline that secured food, shelter, clothes, and information to Dillinger's men. According to a field report from Cincinnati, Naomi was the "intimate friend" of several felons, including Harry Copeland; Leroy had been a bootlegger, a trade much less in demand since Prohibition ended. Another Hamilton couple, Walter and Edna Clark, friends of the Hootens, also had ties to the gang. Federal agents reported that before the Michigan City escapees showed up the Hootens had been strapped for money, but by October they were flashing lots of cash at known underworld hangouts. More important, the Hootens and Clarks took a trip together from Ohio to Arizona toward the end of 1933; they returned in a brand-new car with Arizona plates and even more money to impress their friends back in Hamilton. The agents suspected that the Hootens and Clarks were doing the gang's advance work, finding a safe town, checking out banks, scouting places to live, and looking into Mexico.[9]

The gang was in town only a few days before the Tucson police knew something was up. It is likely that federal agents tipped the locals about their investigation. But in a small western town this was a pretty flashy crowd anyway, with their big cars and city clothes. Russell Clark and Charles Makley arrived in Tucson perhaps as early as the second week in January. They explored the town's nightlife with a couple of local women (Opal Long, Clark's girlfriend, arrived days later). In alcohol-fueled banter with some traveling salesmen they apparently bragged about the weaponry in their possession and the easy money it could procure. The next day Makley and Clark's drinking companions reported these conversations to the police. Then, on January 22, a fire broke out at the Congress Hotel, where Makley and Clark were staying. They paid firemen to haul out the heavy trunks from their rooms, trunks filled with guns and money and bulletproof vests, and they gave as their new address a house at 927 North Second Avenue, which the gang had rented. Three days later firemen recognized Makley and Clark's photographs from the "Line Up," a regular feature in *True Detective Mysteries* that described America's most dangerous criminals. They too tipped off the cops.[10]

On January 25 four Tucson policemen staked out the house on Second Avenue. When Makley and an unidentified woman left and got in their car, the officers followed them to an electronics store. Makley was in the middle of purchasing a radio to monitor police activity when the four cops approached him, quietly placed him under arrest, and brought him in. They then returned to Second Avenue, and, using the ruse of attempting to deliver a letter, Officer Chester Sherman managed to pull a gun on Clark just inside the doorway. Clark, a much bigger man, grabbed for the gun, and the two began to wrestle through the house. Within seconds another cop, Dallas Ford, broke in past Opal Long and struck Clark on the head with his gun; Sherman, now free, added the knockout blow. Clark and Long were brought to the station to join Makley, and the police confiscated a cache of weapons and closetsful of new clothes.[11]

A few hours later Pierpont and Mary Kinder approached the house but left when they found no one home. Three officers tailed them, then pulled them over after they had driven a little ways. Pierpont and Kinder were not immediately arrested. Patrolman Frank Eyman casually asked them to come to the station to purchase an Arizona vehicle sticker, telling them that all out-of-state cars had to have one, and he sat in their backseat to guide them as two other officers drove behind in the squad car. Only at the station house did Pierpont recognize the trap; he went for his gun but was quickly and bloodlessly disarmed.[12]

About the time that police escorted Pierpont and Kinder to their cells, John Dillinger and Billie Frechette drove up Second Avenue. Dillinger got out of the car and walked up the steps. Two cops were waiting inside, and one approached from across the street. Dillinger explained that he must have the wrong house; pulling their guns, the officers assured him he'd come to the right place. Thus, without firing a shot, the Tucson police captured the entire Dillinger gang. They also confiscated several machine guns, rifles, and pistols, thousands of rounds of ammunition, jewelry valued at four thousand dollars, trunks full of new clothing, and more than twenty-five thousand dollars, most of it stashed in money belts and coat linings.[13]

Newspapers across America reprised the bloody history of the Dillinger gang and praised the work of the Tucson Police Department. Journalists painted the western landscape: "Hard riding, fast shooting men of the desert range country today flung down a challenge of death to the John Dillinger gang of hardened desperadoes," an International News Service story began. A New York *Times* editorial evoked "the great open spaces of Zane Grey and Hopalong Cassidy" to argue that the Tucson men merged modern detective work and "the old frontier style, with victory decided by the quickness of the 'draw.'" The *Times* implied that the cities spawned criminals, while virtuous rural America was their downfall: "It is a mistake on the part of the outlaws to abandon the security of their big-city hiding places. But the call of the open road after a successful raid is not to be resisted. They pack their machine guns, their women and their swag into big blue sedans and sooner or later get themselves recognized by a private citizen." Like many other newspapers, the Chicago *Daily News* supplemented its story with a page of photos of Stetson-wearing cops, of Dillinger staring sullenly at the camera, of Russell Clark covering his face, of Harry Pierpont manacled and manhandled, and of the whole lot of them arraigned in Tucson and averting their eyes.[14]

With the gang in custody the media circus began. Tucson awoke on January 26 to find itself the center of national attention. The Pima County courtroom was packed when the indictments were handed down, and two thousand more citizens milled around outside. Reporters poured into town by the hundreds, newsreel crews showed up to capture the faces of the gang for moviegoing audiences, and every lead story in America had Tucson as its dateline. "Gang Chieftain Is Trapped by Arizona Police," declared the Chicago *Tribune* headline, and the story told of the "desperate Indiana outlaw" who for months went from robbery to murder, evading the police and militia along the way. The *Tribune* noted that accompanying Dillinger "was a handsomely dressed blonde about 25 years old, who later identified herself as Anne Martin, his sweetheart." When Dillinger realized he was trapped, the *Tribune* declared, "his bravado deserted him," and he vented a stream of oaths and shook with rage and fear. "My God," the newspaper quoted him, "how did you know I was in town? I'll be the laughingstock of the country. How could a hick town police force ever suspect me?"[15]

Dillinger and the others had been gaining notoriety since the fall, but their voices were hardly heard, and even their faces were known mainly from old mug shots. With the Arizona arrests they became instant celebrities, and newspapers struggled to fill in the gaps. Reporters mostly depicted the gang as callous, even rabid. According to the New York *Times*, Dillinger led the others in defiance. He shook his fist at the guards outside his cell and yelled, "You can't keep me in any two-by-four jail like this; I'll get out and kill you all." Charles Makley added, "I've broken out of better Bastilles than this one." Harry Pierpont, disarmed after his futile attempt to pull a gun in the Tucson police station, sneered at his captors: "'I have a long memory and I won't forget this. I'll get you, and you, and you, and you,' he said, pointing his finger at each officer. 'A jail like you've got here can't hold me long.'" A few days later Pierpont raged and cursed when he spotted Matt Leach, whose state police had brought Pierpont's mother in for questioning and allegedly jailed her briefly: "I have just one regret, and that is that I didn't get back to Indiana to get you." Hauled into a packed courtroom the day after their capture, the men alternately shielded their faces and glared at photographers. When Dillinger's name was called he blurted out "I ain't Dillinger," scowled, refused to stand, and was pulled to his feet by the guards. Later he shouted at his captors, "You're framing me for crimes I never even read about." He told reporters, "They can't keep me penned up anywhere, here, Atlanta, Leavenworth, or Alcatraz Island." He swore, "None of these smart alec coppers have got a bit of evidence that I killed anybody or robbed any bank."[16]

Yet other accounts, sometimes in the same newspapers, even in the same stories, portrayed the men as funny, philosophical, sentimental, in a word, human. There was a trickster quality to Dillinger. He had a sense of humor, of irony, of theatricality, aspects of him that grew in importance as his story unfolded over the coming months. Reporters were allowed to interview the men in the Pima County Jail, and suddenly the stereotyped thugs had personalities. Some accounts depicted them as cool and easygoing, filled with self-confidence and aplomb. Dillinger was "quite affable" when he was brought in; he stepped "jauntily" into the police station, "conversing freely and politely." Though he had "got '12 cops' in his life of crime," the Tucson *Citizen* described him as "suave, soft-spoken, more like an academic professor than a hunted outlaw." The morning after his arrest Dillinger sent out for a breakfast of ham and eggs (prisoners were allowed to use their own money to order from local restaurants), then calmly reclined on his cot, reading newspaper accounts of his capture. The next day Sheriff John Belton opened the jail, allowing citizens to file through and view the prisoners. Dillinger urged folks to vote for Belton in the upcoming election, pointing out that his arrest was evidence of the sheriff's ability.[17]

Dillinger bantered easily, which made him very quotable. America had gotten used to seeing criminals in the movies; here were some real ones, not snarling and talking out of the sides of their mouths, but ad-libbing jokes as the authorities pondered their fates. "Oh, I guess we can beat the rap," Dillinger told reporters. "I've been in tougher spots than this. It's about ten to one we'll get out of this little mess." Told of his father's relief that no one was killed in the Tucson raids, he replied, "He's a good scout . . . and I wish for his sake I had taken up some other line of business." With his easy sense of irony, Dillinger told a United Press reporter, "I guess my only bad habit is robbing banks. I smoke very little and don't drink much." Other reporters quoted him making unlikely confessions: "In the prison I met a lot of good fellows. . . . There's no denying that I helped fix up the break at Michigan City last September. . . . Why not? I stick to my friends and they stick to me."[18]

Even "kill-crazy" Harry Pierpont took on a rough charm. He jokingly told his captors, "This is a great way to treat winter guests," pointing out that arresting tourists discouraged them from spending money. When he saw a wanted poster offering one hundred dollars for his capture, Pierpont was offended at the paltry sum and declared, "I'll ante another $100 for my captors." He praised the Tucson police in the parlance of the Old West: "These cops out here ain't like the kind they have in Indiana. They pull too fast for us." The Arizona *Star* expressed its surprise at the prisoners' gentlemanly demeanor: "Here are four men, above the average in intelligence, with steady nerves and considerable energy. . . . Any one of the four would pass on the streets as a respectable and honorable citizen. . . . Each of the four was immaculately, not flashily, dressed. They spoke good English in cultivated, cultured voices."[19]

Charles Makley too opened up to reporters. Told he was being investigated for a kidnapping in St. Paul, he said, "That's too low a business for a good gunman. I would never stoop to that. Bank robbery's my trade." Interviewed by J. F. Weadock, also a native son of St. Mary's, Ohio, Makley, the oldest and sometimes called the "hardest" convict of the Dillinger gang, grew introspective. Weadock remembered Makley as a young blacksmith working in his father's shop. Like Dillinger, Makley's only regret was embarrassing his family, whom he described as good people: "They were not like me; they were honest, at least, even if never rich." He spoke fondly of his homecoming during the St. Mary's heist, but added it was a tiny town with no room for a man who, as he put it, "wanted to live." He went on, "Look at my dad, he worked like the devil all his life and what did he get out of it? . . . I have lived as long in 40 minutes at times as my dad did in 40 years." Robbing banks brought big cars and fancy clothes, but equally important was the thrill of living by one's wits. It was life close to the ground, the excitement of the open road, the narcotic of sex and violence, freedom made all the more exhilarating by the constant danger of captivity or death.[20]

"Dillinger Gang Facing Death as States Act," declared a Chicago *Tribune* headline on January 27, and the story led with the disclosure by federal agents that several five-dollar bills found on Dillinger were part of the East Chicago loot, putting him at the scene of Officer O'Malley's killing. This meant that Indiana could execute Dillinger, while Ohio had capital cases against Pierpont, Makley, and Clark for Sheriff Sarber's death. Matt Leach of the Indiana State Police, Lake County Prosecutor Robert Estill, East Chicago Police Officer Hobart Wilgus, and Lake County Deputy Sheriff Carroll Holley all boarded a plane in Chicago for the grueling, multileg flight to Arizona. So did delegations from Ohio, Illinois, and Wisconsin. The gang retained the services of Tucson attorney John L. Van Buskirk, who attempted to secure writs of habeas corpus.[21]

Judge C. V. Budlong set bail at one hundred thousand dollars each for the men and five thousand dollars each for Mary Kinder, Opal Long, and Anne Martin (the court never learned Billie's real name), who were held as material witnesses and charged with resisting arrest and obstruction of justice. A rumor spread that the gang had buried $150,000 in the desert, that Dillinger's Chicago attorney was coordinating a plan for the women to make bail, dig up the money, and bail out Dillinger, who would then organize the remnants of his gang to break the others out of jail. Newspapers had so convinced their readers of the gang's invincibility that such a scheme seemed plausible, though in fact John Hamilton was still recovering from his East Chicago wounds and Joseph Burns and Joseph Fox had been marginal to the gang for months, leaving Homer Van Meter as the only one not in custody. Nonetheless Tucson police took no chances. Inside the prison and out twenty-four-hour armed guards patrolled with rifles and machine guns. More, Judge Budlong denied writs of habeas corpus, raised bail for the women to one hundred thousand dollars each, and froze the gang's assets. No one was going anywhere until the

Arizona governor and attorney general negotiated a rendition agreement with one or more of the four state delegations.[22]

Van Buskirk argued that his clients be sent to Wisconsin as no capital charges could be brought there. The Tucson police agreed. Even as reporters lavished praise on the valiant men who brought the gang down, they noted that Wisconsin offered the largest rewards for the fugitives' return, money the cops eagerly wished to share. But Indiana and Ohio prevailed upon Governor B. B. Moeur. Dillinger was forcibly removed from his cell on the evening of January 29. According to one newspaper account, five men hauled him out as he bellowed for his lawyer and demanded a hearing, while Pierpont yelled, "They're putting you on the spot, boy. They aren't taking you back to Indiana." Arizona officials manacled Dillinger and placed him on a chartered plane. To avoid any possibility of a rescue attempt—one newspaper story had three cars of gangsters driving to Tucson to liberate their comrades—flight plans were not revealed.[23]

Dillinger and the Indiana law enforcement officials flew to Douglass, Arizona, where they transferred to an American Airlines plane that carried them to Dallas, Fort Worth, Little Rock, Memphis, St. Louis, and Chicago, with growing crowds at each stop along the way. Three dozen Chicago officers, brandishing rifles and machine guns, met the airplane as it taxied in. A nearly equal number of Indiana troopers joined them, and a thirteen-car convoy headed for Crown Point. Dillinger arrived roughly twenty-four hours after leaving Tucson. Two days later the State of Arizona placed Pierpont, Makley, Clark, and Mary Kinder on a heavily guarded Southern Pacific train and, with fifteen hundred Tucson citizens looking on, shipped them back to Ohio to stand trial for Sheriff Sarber's murder.[24]

The capture of the Dillinger gang represented a triumph of law enforcement, as newspaper editorials were quick to point out. The Mansfield (Ohio) *News-Journal* acknowledged Dillinger's right to hire the best lawyers, but that should not be allowed to interfere with "the unpleasant task of legally exterminating a public menace." The Sheboygan (Wisconsin) *Press* called the Tucson episode "one of the most gratifying stories published in the newspapers for a long time." Capturing the Dillinger gang proved that a life of crime was not only futile; it was the coward's road. "These so-called hard-boiled criminals are only tough when they have an automatic gun trained on the other fellow," the *Press* declared; men like Dillinger "show their usual yellow stripe" when confronted by determined lawmen. Another popular editorial, reprinted from Helena, Montana, to Clearfield, Pennsylvania, heralded law enforcement's success at bringing to heel the likes of Dillinger, Machine Gun Kelly, and the Touhy gang. The job was not yet finished, but historians of the future might well declare 1933 and 1934 "the years in which the nation actually began to break the dominance of its big-shot criminals."[25]

The Arizona *Star* reached for even larger meanings. Dillinger and his accomplices were not degenerates but men out of place and time, outlaws who had outlived their age. In a previous era honors went to soldiers and robber barons for their blustering ways. Those heroic times had passed. Makley's desire, expressed on the *Star*'s pages just two days earlier, to live more in forty minutes than his father had in forty years was an anachronism. Today men must seek satisfaction in "the daily round of hum-drum, commonplace tasks well done and carefully planned as a life work." The writer argued that Makley simply did not understand the virtue of "doing the same job day after day, year after year, of finishing each day's job and trudging wearily to bed . . . , of finishing each life's work and taking the sunset trail to the grave."[26]

This exaltation of ennui is a little difficult to take seriously, yet there is no indication that the writer intended any irony. The emphasis on the virtues of steady work, indeed the boredom of steady work, in the midst of the Great Depression had perhaps a larger meaning. What seemed like mind-deadening labor in prosperous times became a poetic ideal during an era of deepening poverty and unemployment. By severing the connection between hard work and steady progress the Depression shook the very foundations of American ideals. But the *Star* editorial implicitly rejected this view. Quite the contrary, the social cataclysm had reinforced faith in capitalism. The editorial upheld a utopian vision of progress, of America as "an ordered land of smiling fields and busy factories, of deep mines and shining railroads." What made that vision work was private property, the habit of "measuring the boundaries of thine and mine to a hair." Buccaneers like Dillinger, who seized what they pleased, belonged to a bygone era, and Makley's ideal of living intensely had no place in the modern scheme of things. The "new organization rather than the old adventure" was the order of the day. An advanced capitalist society required that citizens bend to the dictates of specialized labor, of bureaucratic discipline, of administrative efficiency. Controlling the likes of Dillinger made the world safe for those "who stand for order, for routine, for work and hope and the future generations of manhood."[27]

The battle was indeed between competing ideals of manhood. New men who would make the world "better, happier, safer, more comfortable" must meet those who "live out of their age, out of their place," and conquer them with facts and reason. That failing, the editorialist implied, they must conquer them with guns and prisons.[28]

But for many Americans there was something deeply appealing about the outlaws, especially in this age of want and hunger, when the apostles of capitalism stood by helpless as their world came crumbling down. Yes, Dillinger and his men had fallen to the forces of law and reason. Nevertheless their resistance to "finishing each day's job and trudging wearily to bed," their refusal to measure "the boundaries of thine and mine to a hair" held deep and growing appeal.[29]

"SPEED DILLINGER EAST BY AIR," read the front-page banner of the January 30 Chicago *Tribune*. For days Dillinger's rendition to Indiana was the lead of a number of papers, and the tone of the coverage merged the nitty-gritty of crime reporting with the high seriousness of the search for justice. Describing Dillinger's arrival at the Crown Point jail, the Associated Press story recorded every detail: "Armed deputies swarmed about the car and deputies even stood atop the jail as the prisoner, handcuffed [to one of the officers], climbed out." "Every light in the Lake county jail gleamed as Dillinger took the few steps from his automobile to the inside of the jail." "Mrs. Lillian Holley, sheriff, typically feminine in appearance, without a weapon on her, expressed every confidence she would be able to keep the prisoner safe until after the trial." Newsreel footage showed rifle-toting peace officers pacing the front of the Crown Point jail, ready to put down any attempted breakout. A Chicago *Tribune* editorial warned sternly that because Indiana had allowed Dillinger and his men out of prison, the state and its criminal justice system were on trial.[30]

The emphasis on crime and punishment, on wickedness and retribution, coexisted with something much lighter. As in Tucson, officials allowed journalists access to their prisoner. Dillinger arrived in good spirits, joking with reporters and guards and answering questions affably. He denied being in East Chicago and repeated that Red Hamilton killed Officer O'Malley and then died of wounds suffered during the robbery. He added that the person who told him this gave him seven thousand dollars for Hamilton's children, money confiscated by Tucson authorities. Dillinger said that they all left Chicago for Florida because police had been getting close and that the gang hid out in as many as twenty different places. He estimated that he had driven 150,000 miles in the past few months and gone through half a dozen automobiles. He admitted with a laugh that he had indeed anonymously sent a copy of a book called *How to Be a Detective* to the chief of the Indiana State Police, Matt Leach. Dillinger's smile and easy manner charmed them all. One reporter summed him up with the word "swashbuckling."[31]

Despite spending the month of February under heavy guard in Crown Point while the state pondered how most expeditiously to execute him, Dillinger's good humor and upbeat attitude rarely failed him. He assured his fourteen-year-old sister Doris in a chatty note that his case was progressing well. He told her to bring the family for a visit and requested that she ask their father to send him ten dollars right away. He asked how his niece Frances liked her classes, whether his brother Hubert was feeling better, and if Dad let them all go to the movies "as much as I used to take you?" Johnnie played the brotherly role, thanking his sister Audrey for being such a big help to their father, advising Hubert to reconsider quitting work, "as scarce as jobs are now." He apologized for not taking them all to the World's Fair in Chicago but urged them to go when summer came. A wistful note crept into his letter when he told young Doris, "I wish you kids could see the country I've seen the last few months it would sure have been a treat to you." But mostly his tone was expansive. Just being on the move, seeing new sights, experiencing fresh places was joy enough.[32]

This side of Dillinger—upbeat, confident, even a little cocky—is unmistakable in a photograph that appeared in newspapers across America when he first arrived at Crown Point and that captures his persona perfectly. Actually, there were several different versions of this picture, and even newsreel footage, taken at what can only be called a celebrity photo shoot. Dillinger stands on the right side of the image, Lake County Sheriff Lillian Holley on the left, and between them is prosecutor Robert G. Estill. All are smiling for the camera. Dillinger's elbow rests on the shoulder of the man who would try to send him to the electric chair, and Estill has his arm wrapped around Dillinger's waist "in a pally sort of way," as the New York *Times* put it. The *Times* story noted that twenty-two witnesses already had identified Dillinger as the slayer of Officer Patrick O'Malley. Most interesting was how the *Times* described the prisoner: "The suave, slim, 30-year-old Dillinger, Indiana's public enemy No. 1 and confessed raider of half a dozen banks, kept his aplomb and only murmured that the witnesses surely were mistaken, as he was in Florida when bandits leaving the bank killed the policeman." The following day a *Times* editorial heaped scorn on Lake County officials, noting that the photo might have been captioned "'the prodigal son's return,' with its sturdy and winsome youth, arm in arm with a middle-aged man smiling paternally, and on the left, a motherly woman, casting an approving eye."[33]

Estill and Holley's imprudence notwithstanding, the gang was safely behind bars. All that remained now was the slow grinding of the legal machinery, leading inexorably to trials, sentencing, and execution. Dillinger and his men did not disappear from the newspapers, but they were relegated to inside pages, as prosaic stories about arraignments, legal maneuvers, trial dates, and jury selections trickled in. Journalists raised the possibility of an escape attempt, either at Lima or Crown Point, then noted the dozens of heavily armed officers guarding the prisoners. Newsreel footage in thousands of theaters underscored the point, showing grim-faced men with powerful weapons pacing in front of jails. Harry Pierpont uttered an occasional oath of defiance, but the fact that he spoke from behind bars made his words seem more pathetic than threatening. The Chicago Police Department reassigned its forty-man "Dillinger Squad" to break up rogue labor unions under the new antiracketeering laws. The fact that Sheriff Holley was a woman (she took over the job after her husband's death just months before) raised a few eyebrows. As one Associated Press story noted, however, she might belong to a bridge club, paint pictures, and attend missionary society meetings, yet she was a crack shot at the target range. The Gary (Indiana) *Post-Tribune* summed it up: "The worst bad man in the country is a meek prisoner of Lake County's woman sheriff."[34]

After much legal wrangling the trial was set for March 12. Dillinger's attorney, Sheriff Holley, Prosecutor Estill, and Judge Murray all agreed not to send the prisoner back to Michigan City for safekeeping or to change the trial's venue. The local jail was secure enough. This was their show, and they wanted it to stay in Crown Point.[35]

"JOHN DILLINGER ESCAPES!" read the block-letter headline of the afternoon issue of the Gary *Post-Tribune* on Saturday, March 3: "Uses Wooden Gun in Jail Delivery." Like most other newspapers, the *Post-Tribune* illustrated its story with that photo of Dillinger, Estill, and Holley, taken a month earlier. The wise-cracking Chicago *Daily News* now captioned the picture, "They Smiled—When He Said He'd Escape." The International News Service ran a version of the photo with Estill cut out and Holley smiling at Dillinger, and the headline read, "He Escapes, Jailer in Hysterics." "Notorious Gangster Escapes from County Jail" the Hammond (Indiana) *Times* declared that same day, followed by "Getaway Is Effected by Colored Man Who Cowed Many Guards and Locked Them in Cell."[36]

All over America newspapers were filled with the news that Dillinger was at large once again. "Three States Hunting Dillinger," read the Chicago *Tribune* banner on March 4, and below that, "Locks Up Deputies and Flees in Sherif's [sic] Car." The Arizona *Star* led with "Dillinger Coolest Criminal Alive, Declares His Hostage," and the Sheboygan *Press* said, "Dillinger's Record Is Unprecedented." The New York *Times* ran a series of headlines down a column on page 1: "Dillinger Escapes Jail Using a Wooden Pistol," "Flees with Negro Killer," "Armed with Machine Guns They Are Hunted Near Chicago," "And Drive Off from Crown Point, Ind., in Woman Sheriff's Car." The *Times* summed up by calling the events of March 3 "a daring escape that rivals the exploits of the heroes of Wild West Thrillers."[37]

By the time Americans went back to work on Monday, the media had given them a spectacular story to discuss, one with just enough detail to invite speculation. Dillinger escaped, as the Chicago *Tribune* put it, "aided only by his own desperate courage and a little toy pistol he had made himself." Reporters described how he carved the fake gun in his cell over the previous month, then blackened it with shoe polish to make it look real. Saturday morning, momentarily left to himself in the exercise room, he saw his chance. First he called to Sam Cahoon, a prison trustee, stuck the wooden gun in the man's back, then locked him in a cell. Dillinger then called in Deputy Sheriff (and fingerprint expert) Ernest Blunk, and at "gun-point" forced him to call in more guards, then locked them up. Dillinger quickly garnered the assistance of another inmate, Herbert Youngblood, a "giant negro," as the Chicago *Tribune* called him (an FBI report a few days later described Youngblood as five feet, nine inches tall, weighing 150 pounds). Youngblood was in for murder and facing execution. Dillinger and Youngblood, who had armed himself with a plunger handle, lured in more than two dozen unarmed prison personnel, including Warden Lewis Baker, and locked them all up.[38]

With Blunk as their hostage the pair headed downstairs, where they found Baker's wife and two other women. Dillinger told them to "be good girls" and no one would get hurt, then he locked them in the laundry room. Now Dillinger and Youngblood helped themselves to weapons held in a prison locker. Then they walked across the street to the city garage, Blunk held at gunpoint in front of them, where they asked for the fastest car available. The mechanic, Edward Saager, pointed to Sheriff Holley's Ford, an irony that Dillinger found especially amusing. The four men—Saager was forced to join them—got in and drove north and west. "Take your time," Dillinger kept telling Blunk, who drove with a machine gun pointed at him. "Thirty miles an hour is enough." As they headed toward Chicago Dillinger boasted, "I did it all with my little toy pistol." He sang "The Last Roundup" as they drove through northern Indiana, belting out the words "Git along, little doggies, git along, git along." In Peotone he let Blunk and Saager out, gave them four dollars for carfare, and drove away.[39]

Chicago police radio repeated the same message over and over: "Dillinger and the Negro are in the front seat. Both armed with machine guns. . . . Be on your guard. These men are desperate." That night Sheriff Holley's car was found abandoned on the North Side. By then it was clear to the public that all of the highway blockades and police raids on underworld haunts and "shoot on sight" orders had produced nothing, despite the fact that as many as twenty thousand men were out searching for Dillinger. The Associated Press reported that Pierpont, Makley, and Clark now were confident their old pal would liberate them and had donned their best clothes in anticipation of his arrival.[40]

And no wonder. Dillinger seemed capable of the impossible. Reporters focused not just on his acts, but on his demeanor, his coolness. According to the New York *Times*, during his month in Crown

Point the other prisoners had taken to calling him "John the Whittler" because of his habit of always playing with a knife and a piece of wood. No one suspected that his hobby was part of an escape plan. The *Times* noted that "the bravado of this latest escape" by the "Indiana farm boy" was "typical of his career," and added, "He is accused by the police of having robbed more than 100 banks."[41]

The *Times* wasn't the only venue turning Dillinger into a legend. Hostage Edwin Saager appeared on newsreels describing his adventure, and he told the Associated Press in a widely reprinted story that his captor never seemed to be in a hurry: "The whole escape plot appeared to be only a lark to Dillinger." As they drove away from Crown Point, Deputy Blunk asked for the wooden gun, but "Dillinger laughed and said he wanted to keep it as a souvenir of the trial that won't be held on March 12." Back in Crown Point Sheriff Holley called the breakout "too ridiculous for words" and said she would lead the search for Dillinger and personally shoot him. A disgusted Prosecutor Estill, who well knew the outlaw's ingratiating ways, commented that the escape was a "beautiful comedy," and added, "From what I hear it seems strange that Dillinger didn't serve tea to the guards before he went away."[42]

Newspaper coverage again seemed divided about Dillinger. The Chicago *Tribune,* for example, pictured him as bloodthirsty and ready to die with guns blazing. Yet the paper also called him "the calm, humorously cynical bandit" and noted that he insisted on punctuating his exploits with laughter. The *Tribune* returned to the old theme of the disparity between Dillinger's rural origins and where he had gone, how he "began life on a small Indiana farm," how "his early days were not unlike those of thousands of youths," how, rather than make his way "from such wholesome surroundings to respected positions," Dillinger became "the country's most notorious criminal."[43]

A remarkable phenomenon began in the hours and days after Crown Point, and it lasted for months: Dillinger was everywhere. Four days after his escape a blue sedan with Illinois plates crashed into a post on 149th Street and Jackson Avenue in New York City. When the driver walked hurriedly away from the accident, "some residents of the Bronx made what seemed the obvious deductions and a manhunt was soon under way." The next day E. H. Deacon, a gas station attendant on Chicago's South Side, was sure it was Dillinger who drove up in a gray-colored car. As Deacon stared at him, the outlaw allegedly said, "You can tell your friends that I gave those Indiana coppers a good fooling." Later other witnesses claimed to see Dillinger speeding along near Deacon's service station, this time with a woman by his side. That very day police radios urged officers to keep a lookout for Dillinger, who had just been spotted in Dunellen, New Jersey. Soon Baltimore police were looking for him, and an eyewitness was sure he had spotted Dillinger in Annapolis. A few days after the Crown Point escape a Chicago chauffeur claimed that Dillinger and the gang had stolen his car, and Chicago police felt it must have been Dillinger who opened up with a machine gun on one of their squad cars.[44]

Sightings poured into Indiana State Police headquarters at the rate of one every five minutes. The tips came from inside and outside the state, by phone and telegraph, by mail and in person. Citizens described the desperado masquerading as an Army officer and as a coal miner, as a farmer and even as a woman. Concluded a United Press story, "John Dillinger, Houdini of the outlaws, continued his game of hide-and-seek with police of a dozen states today as armed posses raced up and down the country in response to frantic calls that 'Dillinger's here.'"[45]

These stories were told without much sense of terror; the brushes with Dillinger were more like celebrity sightings. Beginning in the Midwest, then spreading outward, newspapers burnished his legend. For example, Gary, Indiana, is a few miles up the road from Crown Point, and the *Post-Tribune* took the man-on-the-street angle: "'Dillinger's escaped!' cried a breathless, hatless patron as he burst into a downtown saloon. . . . 'He walked right out of the county jail after locking up all his guards!' 'More power to him!' remarked the bartender, polishing glasses." This article, entitled "Dillinger a Robin Hood to Boys in Backroom; They're Glad He's Loose," described the public's open contempt for Lake County law enforcement officials and the widespread admiration for Dillinger's ability to show them up as "just a big bunch of yokels." The consensus, according to the author, was that "any guy with nerve like Dillinger's deserves all he can get." Another story noted that the day after Dillinger's getaway thousands of people came to Crown Point, hundreds of them from out of state, just to see the prison where he broke out and walk the path to the garage where he stole Sheriff Holley's car. Still another piece quoted Mary Kinder, Harry Pierpont's girlfriend, whom an Indiana court had released just the week before: "Of course I'm glad

Johnnie got away. . . . I am tickled to death. The whole United States is glad. Everybody was for him." Most citizens' feelings were more complicated than that, but Kinder was on to something. Dillinger might be a hardened criminal, but the man had style. "Hard and implacable to his enemies," one *Post-Tribune* writer observed, "the killer is a bit of a gallant and a debonair to those who cross his path casually." He described Dillinger as "a carefree devil with many like-able traits."[46]

Editorials mused on the significance of Dillinger's escape. They condemned Indiana politicians, chummy prosecutors, the "woman sheriff," and slack prison guards. The Sheboygan *Press* added to the list of miscreants the legal officials who coddled criminals, the crooked judges and politically minded parole boards that released them, as well as the attorneys who misled juries, bribed judges, and manipulated witnesses. The *Press* suggested a week later that capital punishment was the answer; the Dillingers of the world deserved "a speedy trial and an equally speedy execution." The editor concluded, "They don't break out of jail after they have sat in the electric chair." The Arizona *Citizen* interpreted the story in overtly sexist terms. "Certainly no woman, no matter how capable, has any business being a sheriff," the editor wrote, because law enforcement demanded manly stoicism: "It is the sacred duty of police officers to fight and never surrender even when covered by a real gun, and even though it means the loss of their lives."[47]

Other editors took a lighter view. The Nevada *State Journal* argued that despite the setback to law enforcement "any man with a drop of sporting blood in his veins got a kick out of the almost absurd situation." Dillinger, like other very successful criminals, was obviously a "misguided genius," one who could have profited mightily on Wall Street or Madison Avenue (had investing and advertising, the author might have noted, not been devastated by the Depression). The writer added, "Like most men who read of his daring and cunning, we wish there were some way for him to end up in Borneo, Siam, Guatemala or Iceland, so he wouldn't harass our peace officers any more." A Wellsboro (Pennsylvania) *Gazette* editorial acknowledged that although an angry public wanted Dillinger and his ilk caught, the gangster's bravado had earned many citizens' admiration. The Mansfield (Ohio) *News-Journal* stated flatly that, so far, Dillinger had simply outsmarted his pursuers.[48]

The story looked different when viewed through the prism of race. According to his brother-in-law Emmett Hancock in an interview given several months after the escape, Dillinger first subdued the guards, then turned to Youngblood. "The nigger was right behind him and he said: 'Mr. John, what do you want me to do?' John said: 'Smoky, just trail along behind.' The nigger said: 'Yes sa, Mr. John, I's coming.'" The language is pure minstrelsy, and Youngblood is reduced from a participant to a tagalong.[49]

The Chicago *Defender*, America's foremost African American newspaper, also viewed Crown Point through a racial lens and devoted considerable copy to it. But the *Defender* turned the gutter racism on its head by reworking the story into a fictionalized parable on the absurdities of American segregation. Dillinger, according to the *Defender*, said to his jailer, "It injures my pride . . . to have a Negro in the same cell with me. In all prisons where I've been they never insulted me by making a Negro my bedfellow, and I resent it. No white man sleeps with a Negro in prison, and I don't see why you want to force it on me here." But Dillinger gets his revenge in the *Defender's* story, jailing his jailer, then telling him, "Since you made this Negro my cellmate, I'll take him along with me." The *Defender* poked fun at America's obsession with race, declaring that Dillinger's breakout might have been kept secret "had he not violated the long-established custom of America's social scheme and insisted on taking with him Herbert Youngblood, a gentleman of darker hue." Given the white press's attention to "the negro Youngblood," the *Defender's* declaration that the "social commingling between Mr. Youngblood and Mr. Dillinger may ultimately be the undoing of them both" seemed not entirely unreasonable. Certainly, the *Defender* observed, Dillinger's taking Youngblood along got African Americans' attention. The paper concluded on an ironic note, pointing out that Youngblood added to the list of Negro accomplishments. Blacks were rising in industry, the arts, science, technology, and athletics; it was only fitting that they should make their mark in jailbreaks too.[50]

HOW DID DILLINGER REALLY DO IT? According to his father, as recorded by reporter John Cejnar, Johnnie said of the wooden pistol during a family visit in April, "I carved it out of the top brace off a washboard. . . . I used a safety razor blade. . . . It was slow work and I raised several blisters before I got it done." Dillinger explained that as soon as he got to Crown Point he realized that his only way out was to gull his captors. He simply charmed everyone, convincing officials that he was a good guy: "I fed them a lot of soft talk and tried to make them think I wasn't half as smart as they were, and did they fall for it." His words ring true with what we know of the man. Especially as he grew famous, Dillinger's smiling good looks and easy manner gave him tremendous charisma, and he knew how to turn it on: "I played the good fellow with all the guards at the jail. I joked and wisecracked with them. I patted them on the back and told them what fine fellows they were. I volunteered for all the distasteful odd jobs that had to be done. . . . All jailers like soft talk. It puffs them up. The Crown Point jailers were no exception." He said that carrying the "slop jars" of human waste every day made it impossible for the guards to see him as a celebrity or a "public enemy." Then, when he pulled his wooden gun, the guards were most vulnerable: "I'm telling you that once I changed from a docile prisoner into a supposedly armed desperado, they were all like sheep." Dillinger added that he had read the newspaper coverage of the Crown Point escape and that Will Rogers's observation tickled him most: "You can't blame that woman sheriff so much after all because she thought she was depending on MEN!"[51]

Dillinger no doubt worked his captors, but this was only part of the story. What happened at Crown Point was considerably more complex, though the facts remain murky. Almost immediately after the breakout Sam Cahoon and Ernest Blunk came under suspicion. One of them may have passed Dillinger the wooden gun and, more important, provided the intelligence he needed—the jail's floor plan, the location of weapons, the numbers of guards, where they congregated—to make his getaway. Newspapers quickly raised suspicions that Cahoon and Blunk were too obliging while Dillinger made his escape, and Blunk invited more scrutiny by changing his story, first claiming that Dillinger had only a wooden gun, then declaring it was a real one (the weight of the evidence from interviews the FBI conducted later strongly suggests that it was fake). They were questioned repeatedly, but nothing ever came of it. Suspicions fell also on Judge William Murray, who had refused to send Dillinger to Michigan City for safekeeping, and on Edward Saager for being too cooperative with the desperado.[52]

Another source of information on Crown Point was Dillinger's attorney. Lawyers for big-time criminals in this era were minor celebrities, if also looked on as a bit shady, Chicago lawyers most of all. Dillinger hired himself one of the flashiest. Louis Piquett arrived in Chicago in 1908, already married and in his twenties. He worked as a dishwasher, waiter, and bartender, then became involved in local politics, rising rapidly from precinct captain through ward committeeman and finally ward boss. His legal training was strictly informal, but he received a license to practice in 1918, represented the bartenders union, then became city prosecutor during Republican mayor William Hale Thompson's administration. When the Democrats swept into power early in the 1920s, Piquett went into private practice. His theatricality and prematurely white mane of hair gave him a real courtroom presence, and he quickly became famous as a criminal attorney.[53]

Piquett realized that becoming Dillinger's mouthpiece would bring him tremendous publicity, and during the month between the Tucson arrest and the Crown Point escape he managed to win Dillinger's confidence over other attorneys. His emotional defense of American civil liberties in the Crown Point courtroom persuaded Judge Murray to remove Dillinger's shackles and to clear the courtroom of machine-gun-toting guards. As he gathered evidence, got to know Dillinger, and sized up the case Piquett became convinced he could get an acquittal. There was already some confusion among witnesses as to who had shot Officer O'Malley, whether Dillinger, Hamilton, or someone else, confusion that a good trial lawyer might transform into reasonable doubt for jurors. Piquett also had witnesses who swore they had seen Dillinger in Daytona the night before the robbery, and the attorney planned on dramatizing the impossibility of getting from Florida to Chicago in less than twenty-four hours by hiring a race car driver to try, fail, and then testify.[54]

Long after Dillinger's death Piquett cooperated on a series of newspaper articles, then on a book that was not published until decades later. Apparently Dillinger had been quite open about scheming to escape, and Piquett, along with his assistant, a private investigator named Arthur O'Leary, were deeply involved. Dillinger had Piquett get in touch with Red Hamilton, who was still recovering from the wounds he received in East Chicago. Hamilton in turn contacted Homer Van Meter, who of course had known Dillinger in Michigan City and run with him in the summer of 1933, and Lester Gillis, better known as

Baby Face Nelson. According to Piquett, Dillinger hoped his friends could spring him by blowing out the back wall of the Crown Point jail. Hamilton preferred coming in the front door, as the gang did in Lima, but Dillinger believed that Hamilton was in no shape for such a job. What was clear was that if his friends failed to get him out soon and he then lost in court, he would be sent back to Michigan City and the electric chair. Piquett thought the idea of a jailbreak was insane and persuaded Billie Frechette, visiting Crown Point posing as "Mrs. Dillinger," to dissuade his client. Then came the idea of the wooden pistol. Dillinger's friends agreed to advance him money out of his share of a future bank job they had been planning and sent Tommy Carroll to Indiana with the cash. G. Russell Girardin, who took down Piquett's story, quotes Dillinger as saying, "After East Chicago got the fix in, it made it much easier." But what did that mean? Who paid bribes to whom, and for what?[55]

Immediately after the Crown Point escape, Indiana Attorney General Philip Lutz appointed a special investigator, Attorney J. Edward Barce, to look into the case. Months later Barce wrote a confidential memo addressed to Lutz and to Governor Paul McNutt in which he alleged an elaborate conspiracy in Lake County to free Dillinger. Barce, however, failed to make specific charges; what he had gathered was mostly a series of connections and associations. His main source of information was Meyer Bogue, an old acquaintance of Dillinger's from Michigan City. Barce's allegations involved payoffs from Piquett and Arthur O'Leary to Warden Louis Baker, to presiding Judge William Murray, and to Murray's business partner, East Chicago attorney Hymie Cohen, a local political fixer as well as an indicted bootlegger and brothel owner. Also allegedly cooperating for a price were members of the notoriously corrupt East Chicago Police Department. Bogue, Barce believed, was the one who got the gun (wooden or otherwise) into Dillinger's hands, and payoffs to the others enabled him to carry out his plan. As addenda to his memo, Barce included carbon copies of letters written by Arthur O'Leary. One read "Dear Jimmy [James Regan, former East Chicago chief of police] Per your phone request of this morning I am enclosing another cashier's check in the sum of $500. . . . Kindest regards from Lou [Piquett] and also myself and with best of wishes to [Hymie] Cohen & Zark [Martin Zarkovich, an East Chicago detective previously convicted on corruption charges, who later figured prominently in the Dillinger story]."[56]

Barce's memo was vague and lacked substance. He relied primarily on Bogue, who was an ex-convict paid on a per diem basis by the state for his assistance, hardly a reliable witness. And since when do bagmen, O'Leary in this case, enclose thank-you notes with payoffs, even taking the trouble to make carbon copies? It is hardly credible that an experienced private detective would commit to paper the names of accomplices who craved anonymity. O'Leary's letters to the various participants probably were forgeries, perhaps written by Bogue to keep his fifteen-dollar-a-day fee coming in. Barce's investigation came crashing down toward the end of 1934. The assistant attorney general, apparently with the governor's blessing, ordered state police to detain without warrants eight "witnesses," including Blunk, Cahoon, and Warden Baker. They were held incommunicado in a hotel in Monticello, Indiana, then moved to a secret location to avoid writs of habeas corpus. Barce claimed that Dillinger had bought jail floor plans for eighteen hundred dollars and that his "witnesses" would reveal exactly who was involved. More accurately, lacking solid evidence, he hoped to coerce confessions. But anti-McNutt Republicans loudly condemned the special investigator's tactics, and amid charges of kidnapping and violating American civil liberties Barce released his witnesses and dropped his investigation.[57]

Barce's methods were suspect, his evidence thin, yet some of his conclusions might well have been right, and rumors continued to spread as the Dillinger story unfolded. It is hard to believe that Dillinger carved the pistol himself, and of course he denied that bribes were involved since, as we will see, he continued to depend on his East Chicago contacts.[58]

Louis Piquett and Arthur O'Leary gave an account of events whose details varied from Barce's but that nonetheless underscored East Chicago's influence. Money was the key. In prison Dillinger had none; even Piquett had been living on promises, and he knew that the East Chicago power brokers were interested only in cold cash. Smuggling a real gun into Crown Point was as risky and expensive as having Dillinger's friends break him out. O'Leary, however, remembered that a Wisconsin man attempted the previous autumn to bluff his way from jail with a wooden gun. Lake County insiders drew the line with a real gun. However, they were willing to help smuggle in a fake, which Dillinger would claim he carved himself. O'Leary had the gun made in a Chicago woodshop, then brought it to East Chicago on

Friday, March 2. He and Meyer Bogue apparently also delivered five thousand dollars, money Piquett procured from a friend and lover, a woman named Ada Martin, who ran an abortion clinic he represented. Blunk allegedly received two thousand dollars to pass the wooden gun to Dillinger, Saager one thousand dollars to prepare the car. Who else was paid and how far up the chain of East Chicago the bribes went is unclear, though O'Leary later claimed to have distributed eleven thousand dollars. Dillinger no sooner received the wooden gun on Saturday morning than he began rounding up the guards, procuring real weapons, then heading to Chicago.[59]

We will never know the full or real story of the Crown Point breakout. The exact parts played by people like Blunk, Saager, Murray, Cohen, Zarkovich, Bogue, Piquett, O'Leary, and possibly others were never inscribed in court records or revealed by authoritative witnesses. Suffice it to say that to gain his freedom Dillinger dove deep into the shadow world of East Chicago cops and politicians. And East Chicago would continue to be part of his story right up to the very end.[60]

THE CHARGES OF CORRUPTION and incompetence enveloping the Dillinger story remained a journalistic staple for months. The *Literary Digest*, a popular review of the week's news, summarized scores of editorials that lambasted both the "worst outlaw since Jesse James" and his captors. The *Digest* declared, "This tragic farce of a wooden pistol and wooden-headed jail keepers has blown up a national storm of shame and indignation." Newspaper columns from coast to coast condemned the sleaziness and ineptitude of northern Indiana officials. Dillinger, "that detestable human hyena," escaped so smoothly, so effortlessly, under such absurd circumstances, that the story was "made for laughter, but it was the painful, strained laughter of national humiliation, with a gritting of the teeth to follow." The *Digest* quoted a Chicago *Tribune* article that questioned the integrity of state government when killer and prosecutor posed arm in arm, "the law and crime just pals together."[61]

Dillinger's escape briefly became a big issue in Indiana politics; as one reporter put it, Dillinger's wooden gun was loaded with political dynamite, and it exploded all over the state. Republicans invoked Dillinger to attack Governor McNutt's "New Deal" for Indiana. A meeting of the Indiana Republican Editors' Association began with a speech by Congressman James Beck of Pennsylvania that focused on Dillinger, and "everywhere in the hall were wooden pistols bearing the words: 'Yours for the broom that swept the statehouse clean, John Dillinger'" (the reference was to Governor McNutt's 1932 campaign pledge to clean out the capitol). A mock telegram was read from Dillinger to McNutt, inviting the governor to a Morgan County reunion; then an actor dressed as the bandit and carrying a large wooden gun snaked his way through the hall. "We are the laughing stock of the United States," thundered Republican State Party Chairman Don Irwin in a speech titled "The Dillinger Disgrace" to the Indianapolis Press Club. He urged Republicans to "salvage the state's good name from this debris of political plunder before it is too late!" Even Dillinger's parole the previous spring looked suspicious in light of recent events: How did a man with such a poor prison record win his freedom? Dillinger was good political theater, and it looked for a moment as if Indiana's Democratic victory, ushered in with Franklin Roosevelt's landslide in 1932, might not survive November's elections. Meanwhile in Crown Point Sheriff Holley stepped down in April, and Prosecutor Estill was voted out in May.[62]

The feds also got into the act. Attorney General Homer Cummings lambasted Lake County officials, though he trod carefully around prominent Democrats. With Blunk and Cahoon detained for questioning (they would soon be released, and though new rumors circulated for months no evidence strong enough for indictments ever turned up against them or anyone else), he ordered eight federal prisoners moved from the Crown Point jail to "more secure" facilities. Cummings took aim at Holley and Estill. Their photograph with Dillinger had become iconic, and the attorney general told reporters, "If they had been Federal officials when the picture was taken they would not be now. I would remove them in ten minutes. Such disgraceful conduct, such negligence, violated all canons of common sense and made law enforcement doubly hard." Of course Cummings's criticism deflected attention from the slack work of his own Justice Department. Soon Cummings and others began invoking Dillinger's name as they advocated a "New Deal on Crime." More precisely, the Dillinger story was deployed to make the case for concentrating federal law enforcement power in J. Edgar Hoover's Division of Investigation.[63]

Beyond issues of criminal justice and politics, Dillinger was becoming part of American culture itself. A month after the Crown Point escape the Indianapolis Council of Women urged the state legislature to pass a law prohibiting the manufacture or sale of wooden pistols, and the group also urged Congress to ban the interstate shipment of all fake weapons. Such toys, the women argued, were unwholesome, causing children to play at being gunmen and gangsters.[64]

The women were not the only ones worried that the Dillinger story dangerously blurred the line between artifice and reality. In the days immediately following the escape the New York *Times* noted that Dillinger's jailbreak lived up to the dramatic standards set by popular fiction. The *Times* mused that the outlaw's raw audaciousness characterized much of American life. The Lake County *Star* echoed the *Times*, arguing that Dillinger surpassed in real life the hairbreadth escapes of the old dime novels such as *Deadwood Dick*, and an Associated Press report referred to recent events as Dillinger's "movie escape."[65]

Art was about to imitate life too. Just days after the Crown Point fiasco, Paramount Studios announced its intention to produce a film based on Dillinger's life, and a Hollywood writer gave notice in a trade publication that he was finishing a screenplay on the outlaw entitled "A Man without a City." Such notices were not lost on the new Hays Commission. Delegated to clean up Hollywood and make sure that American families entering the great cinema palaces would see only images worthy of a moral nation, the Hays Commission decreed that the Indiana bandit not be made a hero for impressionable young minds. "No motion picture based on the life or exploits of John Dillinger will be produced, distributed or exhibited by any company member," declared Will H. Hays, president of the Motion Picture Producers and Distributors of America. "This decision is based on the belief that such a picture would be detrimental to the best public interest." Any company that dared to make a Dillinger film would be frozen out of theaters. The Ohio *State Journal* applauded: "There are thousands of subjects yet untouched to form the basis of good pictures without going to a source so far below the sea level of decency as this." The *Journal* reminded readers of the "epidemic of gangster films" from the early 1930s that did nothing but glorify lawbreakers, and concluded, "After all the country isn't interested in the life story of Dillinger. It prefers to see him punished as he deserves."[66]

But why banish John Dillinger from the silver screen if all that Americans wanted was to see him punished? The Hays Commission's assertion of moral authority only mattered if something was at stake. As the furor over Crown Point settled down, there were more disturbing hints that Americans liked Dillinger. Shortly after the breakout the Gary *Post-Tribune* ran a brief editorial, "Not a Rob'n Hood." Several Indianapolis high school students declared the Hoosier outlaw their hero and said they hoped he would be neither caught nor prosecuted. The editors lectured readers that Dillinger preferred stealing to working, that he helped only himself and his cronies, that his acts had nothing to do with redressing grievances caused by hard times. "Law abiding citizens of all ages should sympathize with law enforcement because our social system and its improvement depend on it," they concluded. The editors protested too much. Most Americans did sympathize with the police, but many also admired John Dillinger, or at least were fascinated by him. And in the coming months he would give them much more to think about.[67]

FOUR

"Pulling That Off Was Worth Ten Years of My Life"

O N MARCH 6, 1934, JUST THREE DAYS AFTER DILLINGER'S now famous jailbreak, FBI Director J. Edgar Hoover wrote to Melvin Purvis, special agent in charge of the Chicago Office. In an agency staffed by the director's favorites, Purvis topped the list. He was young, good-looking, and independently wealthy, and Hoover kidded him often about being a ladies' man. But now the director was not in a joking mood. He noted the Chicago Office's lack of underworld contacts. More precisely, Hoover complained, Purvis had failed to cultivate the paid snitches that might reveal Dillinger's whereabouts. Hoover was convinced that the outlaw was hiding in Chicago, and he told Purvis to develop more "channels of information into underworld sources."[1]

On the very day that Hoover wrote Purvis, however, John Dillinger and five other men pulled up to the Security National Bank in Sioux Falls, South Dakota, five hundred miles from Chicago. Their driver, Tommy Carroll, waited on the sidewalk on this freezing morning, while Harry "Eddie" Green and Red Hamilton took up positions at the doors. Once inside the other three men opened their overcoats and pulled Thompson machine guns on the crowd. The smallest of the crew, Lester Gillis, better known as "Baby Face Nelson," shouted that a holdup was in progress and ordered everyone to drop to the floor.

Someone tripped an alarm, which began to ring loudly. Dillinger and his old jail buddy Homer Van Meter began raiding the tellers' cages, stuffing money into sacks. Then the two bandits took the bank president at gunpoint into the vault, where they helped themselves to more cash.[2]

A crowd gathered outside, attracted by the alarm. Nelson, watching the throng through the windows, grew increasingly agitated, paced back and forth, feinted with his gun. When a motorcycle cop pulled up Nelson shot him through the plate glass; luckily, the wounds were not fatal. By the time the robbers were ready to make their escape the crowd outside had grown substantially. The New York *Times* claimed that one thousand people milled around, while the Gary (Indiana) *Post-Tribune* reported that the gunmen held virtually the entire city at bay. Spectators watched from windows and rooftops, and a few cops joined them, hoping to get a clear shot at the men as they exited the bank. As in Racine, the gang grabbed half a dozen bank employees, mostly women, and used them as a human shield to get to their Packard, then forced the hostages to stand on the running boards as they headed out. One policeman managed to fire a shot into the car's radiator at the edge of town, which forced the gang to steal another vehicle at gunpoint from a passing citizen. That night, in St. Paul, Minnesota, Dillinger and his friends divided forty-six thousand dollars.[3]

But could it really have been Dillinger, reporters, the police, and the FBI asked? Bank president C. R. Clarke first said the leader of the group looked exactly like the famous outlaw, then changed his mind. Nonetheless in the hours following the raid eyewitness testimony was undeniable. Hoover was not eager for his agency to lead the difficult manhunt for Dillinger; he preferred continuing to quietly aid local law enforcement agencies. But with so much publicity the feds could no longer sit on the sidelines. Two days after the robbery, with Dillinger clearly back in the game, the Justice Department issued a warrant for his arrest for violating the Dyer Act, which was enacted in 1919 to impede the interstate trafficking of stolen vehicles by organized thieves. On March 12 the FBI issued its first wanted poster for Dillinger, which included two photographs of him taken in Tucson, fingerprints, a detailed physical description, and his full criminal record.[4]

A week after the Sioux Falls raid the same crew hit the First National Bank of Mason City, Iowa. This was a high-risk, high-reward job.

Green and Van Meter had studied the bank for several days and were convinced that as much as a quarter-million dollars lay in its vault. But the place was extremely well-protected. A guard armed with a teargas gun and a high-powered rifle perched above the lobby in a steel cage lined with bulletproof glass. This time Dillinger watched the front door and Nelson the back exit, while Hamilton, Green, and Van Meter entered. From the middle of the lobby one of them fired a blast into the ceiling, then ordered the two dozen customers to hit the floor as plaster dust rained down. The robbers worked the tellers' cages, then the vault, but the situation deteriorated rapidly. The guard in the steel cage shot a teargas canister into the lobby, making it difficult to see and breathe (he was unable to do anything more because his teargas gun jammed after its first blast, and his rifle was useless with so many bystanders in the building). Once again, Baby Face Nelson grew upset and began firing at cars, buildings, and finally at people.[5]

Meanwhile cops and citizens outside began taking up positions. An elderly judge, firing a pistol from a third-floor window, managed to wing Dillinger in the right shoulder. After a few minutes the gang knew that though they had only a fraction of the bank's money it was too dangerous to stay any longer. More shots were exchanged, Hamilton also took a bullet in the shoulder, and once again the outlaws surrounded themselves with hostages as they headed for their car. They ordered their captives to perch on the fenders and the running boards, then the getaway unfolded in slow motion. The chief of police trailed them for a while, Nelson fired away, and finally police gave up the chase. After an hour or so the gang released the last of the freezing hostages, abandoned their car for a waiting vehicle, then headed back to St. Paul. The take was fifty-two thousand dollars—good, but nowhere near as much as they had hoped. Newspapers speculated that Dillinger was building a stash to flee to Latin America.[6]

So just ten days after the Crown Point breakout, with most of his original gang behind bars in Ohio, John Dillinger had a new crew that stole more than one hundred thousand dollars. How did he do it? After Dillinger and Youngblood dropped off Blunk and Saager in Peotone they headed for Chicago. They dodged the police, who were out in force, and called Louis Piquett's office, where Billie Frechette and Arthur O'Leary waited to hear from the fugitive. Fearful of a wiretap they exchanged cryptic messages, then Dillinger drove to a North Side address to meet his mouthpiece and his girlfriend. Piquett handed Dillinger some money, one hundred dollars of which Dillinger gave to Youngblood, who boarded a train to Michigan. Billie and Johnnie stayed at her sister Patsy's apartment at 3512 North Halstead that night. Given the ardor they later publicly expressed for each other and the tense hours they had just passed through, it must have been a passionate reunion.[7]

The very next night, Sunday, March 4, they drove to St. Paul for a prearranged meeting. From his Crown Point cell Dillinger, using Billie and O'Leary as his intermediaries, had been in contact with Red Hamilton, who, having recovered from his wounds, hooked up with Homer Van Meter. Van Meter brought Hamilton into a new crew just then being assembled by Baby Face Nelson, a young thug rising in the criminal world on the strength of a bold but volatile temperament. Dillinger arrived just in time to join them for the Sioux Falls and Mason City jobs. Nelson (who hated the name "Baby Face" because he was sensitive about his small size and youthful looks) probably was happy to have Dillinger along, not only for his experience but because he gave the group instant fame. Though the twenty-four-year-old saw himself as boss, newspapers automatically referred to the group as the new Dillinger gang, a source of endless tension between the two men. More important, Dillinger's escape from Crown Point had been bankrolled out of future earnings, money that was made in the Sioux Falls and Mason City jobs.[8]

The group gathered in St. Paul because the town was remarkably hospitable to felons. Alvin Karpis, bank robber, kidnapper, jewel thief, leader of his own gang, and one of the most famous outlaws of the era, declared St. Paul to be a "crook's haven." "Every criminal of any importance in the 1930s," he wrote in his autobiography, "made his home at one time or another in St. Paul. If you were looking for a guy you hadn't seen for a few months, you usually thought of two places—prison or St. Paul. If he wasn't locked up in one, he was probably hanging out in the other." St. Paul was a thoroughly corrupt town during the Depression, with police and politicians reliably on the take. Establishments like the Green Lantern tavern and the Plantation nightclub on White Bear Lake were well-known meeting places for underworld figures. The former, in fact, was where the new Dillinger gang convened after the Mason City job and where they obtained the address of the man who treated their wounds, Dr. Nels Mortensen, a locally prominent physician, American Legion Post commander, St. Paul health commissioner, and president of the Minnesota State Board of Health. Through other underworld contacts Billie found nice accommodations where Dillinger could rest, first on Girard Avenue in Minneapolis, then on Lexington Parkway in St. Paul.[9]

Herbert Youngblood was less fortunate. Even as Dillinger and Hamilton were recovering from their wounds, Youngblood lay dying in Port Huron, Michigan. Local sheriffs had responded to a complaint of a black man, a stranger, causing a disturbance in a downtown shop. Newspapers later reported that an officer disarmed Youngblood, but the Crown Point escapee pulled a second weapon, killed one deputy, wounded another, and took seven bullets himself.[10]

There is an alternative and probably more accurate version of the story, though only the black press reported it. According to the Chicago *Defender*, the man who killed Youngblood was not a peace officer but a local resident, a white man named Eugene Fields. Other papers failed to stay with the story, but according to the *Defender* Fields was arraigned after Youngblood's death for carrying an unlicensed weapon. More, deputies were convinced that Fields and not Youngblood was the one who shot their comrades.[11]

Before he died Youngblood, perhaps boastfully connecting himself to the famous criminal, maybe returning a favor by throwing police off the scent of the man who had sprung him from jail, or possibly just delusional from shock, lied to officials that he had been with Dillinger just the night before. Now Michigan state police, Matt Leach's men from neighboring Indiana, and FBI agents swarmed over Michigan, concentrating especially along the Canadian border, where Dillinger, local folks claimed, crossed over by car, or by rowboat, or on foot. Some even speculated that Dillinger used burnt cork to disguise himself as a Negro.[12]

Of course Dillinger was nowhere near northern Michigan. His shoulder wound healed quickly, so he and Billie went on the road again. They drove to Chicago, where they met up with Arthur O'Leary. Dillinger told the detective that he and Billie intended to get married and asked him to arrange for Piquett, who was in Ohio consulting on the defense of Pierpont, Makley, and Clark, to secure Billie's divorce from her husband, Welton Sparks, still in Leavenworth.

Two days later O'Leary conveyed the attorney's answer: Piquett was not a divorce lawyer, Dillinger had brought him much aggravation, and he had received little compensation for his efforts. Dillinger dropped the idea. Still it was a remarkable request: in the middle of their daily gamble with death Billie and Johnnie sought the most lasting of human bonds. Of course the precariousness of their lives only underscored their longing for stability, for a future, for normality. To placate his mouthpiece, Dillinger gave O'Leary a package containing twenty-three hundred dollars. He specified that one thousand go to Piquett, another one thousand to his buddies' legal defense in Ohio, $250 to Meyer Bogue, and $100 to O'Leary. The next day Dillinger put Billie on an airplane to Indianapolis, then drove to Leipsic, Ohio, to visit Pierpont's parents. Remarkably, law enforcement officials had not yet fully staked out the homes of gang members' families.[13]

Billie found her way to Mooresville on March 19. She didn't stay long; Dillinger Senior later recalled that she "disappeared into the night as mysteriously as she had arrived." She brought some cash for Mr. Dillinger and his daughter Audrey. She also gave Emmett, Johnnie's brother-in-law, the famous wooden pistol for safekeeping. And she handed Audrey a letter from her brother. Johnnie told Audrey not to worry since it did no good anyway, that he was still "perculating" and still "having a lot of fun." He asked Emmet to take care of the wooden gun and declared that Deputy Blunk was lying, claiming now that Dillinger had pulled a real .45 in Crown Point. Dillinger reveled in the fact that his fake pistol had cowed the guards: "You should have seen their faces," he wrote. "Pulling that off was worth ten years of my life." He told Emmett to never part with the wooden gun for any amount of money: "For when you feel blue all you will have to do is look at the gun and laugh your blues away." He promised Audrey he would visit Mooresville when police vigilance in Indiana cooled off, and added, "Honey if any of you need any thing I wont forgive you if you don't let me know." Only in the last few months had he been in the position to play the family benefactor, but now he had the wherewithal to do it, and clearly he enjoyed the role. At the end of the letter he mentioned his wound, making light of it, saying he was just a little sore: "I bane one tough sweed Ha! Ha!" He signed off, "Lots of love from Johnnie." Billie flew back to Chicago, Dillinger drove in from Ohio to pick her up, and the following weekend the two lovers drove back to St. Paul, to their apartment at 93 South Lexington Parkway, just a block from elegant Grand Avenue, lined with homes belonging to the town's elite.[14]

For two weeks St. Paul sheltered them, but Daisy Coffee, manager of their apartment building, suspected something was up with Mr. and Mrs. Carl Hellman, her tenants in #303. They never used the front door, they kept their blinds shut all the time, and they came and went at all hours. More, there seemed to be other people coming and going too, even living in the apartment. Coffee reported her suspicions to the FBI. Although her fears must have seemed a little vague and no one had any idea who these mysterious Hellmans were, two agents visited the apartment on Saturday morning, March 31, and they brought a St. Paul cop with them. While Agent Rosser Nalls waited downstairs, Agent Rufus Coulter and Detective Henry Cummings went up to the third floor. The two knocked at #303 and asked for Mr. Hellman. Billie opened the door as far as the chain lock allowed; she told the men that Mr. Hellman was out and to come back in the afternoon. Coulter and Cummings asked to enter in order to speak with her. She insisted she wasn't yet dressed, but they said they would wait. She went back to tell Dillinger, still in bed, that the cops were outside. He immediately dressed and assembled a machine gun.[15]

Coincidentally, as Cummings and Coulter waited, Homer Van Meter came up the back stairs and realized something was up when he saw the two standing in front of Dillinger's door. When asked who he was, Van Meter claimed to be a soap salesman; asked for his samples he said they were down in his car; asked for identification he replied that it too was in his car, and he walked down the front stairs. Suspicious, Coulter followed a few moments later, but when he got to the building's entrance Van Meter was gone—until Coulter looked back and saw him crouching in the basement stairs, gun drawn. Van Meter fired and missed, Coulter bolted outside, and Nalls watched them run across the front of the building, Van Meter firing wildly. When Coulter pulled his gun and returned fire, Van Meter retreated back into the apartment building, escaped out the back, hijacked a garbage truck, and made his getaway.[16]

Hearing shots coming from outside, Dillinger aimed his machine gun and sprayed bullets through the front door. He then opened it a crack and fired down the hallway. Detective Cummings first pressed himself into an alcove, then bolted down the front stairs. With no return fire Dillinger and Billie walked out the door, down the back stairs, into the alley, and down to the garage. Coulter and Nalls were so preoccupied with Van Meter that they ignored the back stairwell. With Billie in the driver's seat the two fugitives made their casual getaway, backing down the alley and into the street.[17]

After they were gone police and the FBI searched the apartment and inventoried weapons, ammunition, airline ticket stubs, and maps. They found enormous amounts of new clothes, both men's and women's. They also found three photographs, one of a child, one of a youth, and one of a young man in a Navy uniform. Written across the back of the first was "John at the age of 3½. Return to Audrey Hancock." On the back of the second photo was "Dillinger in a Cherry tree. Return to Audrey." The third was taken by an Indianapolis studio and clearly was also the image of young John Dillinger. Fingerprints confirmed who had just escaped from the feds' grasp. One other thing the agents found in the apartment hallway: bloodstains. Dillinger was wounded again, by one of his own bullets, it so happened, that had ricocheted into his left calf.[18]

Billie drove from the South Lexington building to the apartment of Eddie Green, who knew the Twin Cities well. Green directed them to the office of Dr. Clayton May, who, in addition to his regular practice, performed abortions, treated venereal disease, and ministered to underworld figures on the side. May brought them to another apartment, outfitted as a private nursing home and run by a woman named Augusta Salt, with whom May had an arrangement for his less reputable patients. The doctor cleaned and bandaged Dillinger's wound, inoculated him against tetanus, and told him that rest was what he most needed.[19]

Between March 31 and April 4, as police scoured St. Paul and new sightings poured in from across the Midwest, Dillinger recuperated in Nurse Salt's quarters, aided by occasional visits from the good doctor. When the FBI captured May two weeks later and charged him with conspiracy to harbor a felon, he claimed that he had treated Dillinger only after the outlaw threatened him with violence. More precisely, brandishing a machine gun Dillinger allegedly warned the doctor, "I'll blow your brains out." Neither prosecutors nor the court believed it. More compelling to them was the evidence that Dillinger gave the highlife-loving May one thousand dollars for a few hours' work. "Dillinger's Doctor" ended up serving two years in Leavenworth and had his medical license revoked.[20]

Through it all, Dillinger's legend continued to grow. Most news stories focused on the necessity of bringing him to justice, but a number of them were quite sympathetic. The Central Press Association put out a long syndicated article by Francis F. Healy explaining Dillinger's transition from "callow youth" to "hardened criminal." Dillinger had been disappointed in love and bored to death when Ed Singleton got him drunk—and, according to Healy, drugged—back in 1924. Healy made up the dialogue: "'Gimme a cigarette, Johnny,' Ed asked. . . . 'I ain't got any more. And I haven't the price of another pack, Ed. I'm sick of this town, sick of being broke. I'd like to get my hands on a little dough and blow.'" Just when Johnnie was most vulnerable Singleton sprang his plan to rob Frank Morgan, and of course, Singleton turned on young Dillinger when they were caught. A simple farmer with his wife ill at home, John Senior could not afford the price of a lawyer, and when he told his son to do the honest thing and confess, the court handed down its draconian sentence. The Johnnie Dillinger Healy portrayed was as much a victim as anyone in this whole drama.[21]

Other articles depicted Dillinger as what later would be called an existential hero. "John 'The Killer' Dillinger, with a submachine gun in his hands and a big green sedan awaiting him, shot his way out of a police trap today and once more foiled the law," one Associated Press story began. An editorial titled "A Fast-Moving Life" ran in The Newark (Ohio) *Advocate*: "Life for the notorious gang leader is one of constant action. The price he is compelled to pay for what small freedom he enjoys is heavy. Night and day he is hunted by Uncle Sam's most expert trackers and local authorities in every part of the country. He cannot relax for a minute else the heavy hand of the law is clamped upon his shoulder." Even as the editorial assured readers that capture sooner or later awaited the desperado, the subtext was less about the wages of sin than the joy of the chase. Yes, the law would catch up with Dillinger, and probably he would die in the streets. But until then his story was about defying the humdrum of daily life. The Nevada *State Journal* emphasized how Dillinger's "laugh of defiance" taunted officers of the law. His ability to appear and disappear at will caused Chicago police to take seriously a witness who spotted him on the North Side driving down the street dressed as a nun. And the *Literary Digest* mentioned another idea just gaining currency: that Dillinger's own mother would no longer recognize her son because he had taken his shape-shifting to new heights with plastic surgery.

Dillinger was not just living his life, he was playing it like an actor on stage who improvised the script as he went along.[22]

While Billie and Johnnie lay low, J. Edgar Hoover, learning the details of the St. Paul escape, went from incredulity to fury. Dillinger not only fired at federal officers, he humiliated the Bureau. "In the twenty-odd years of the existence of this division," Hoover thundered, "no one has ever shot at any of our agents and got away with it. We run them to earth." Privately Hoover wanted to know why his office had not been informed before the intervention, why only two agents were sent to the scene, and why they were equipped with mere handguns. The presence of an officer from the notoriously corrupt St. Paul Police Department especially incensed him. Were his men afraid to act without bluecoats present? And how could federal agents allow the locals to do the all-important fingerprint analysis? Hoover avoided whenever possible sharing efforts with other law enforcement agencies, especially one with such a dubious reputation as the St. Paul police. Initially reluctant to take on the Dillinger case Hoover knew that his Bureau's reputation now depended on cracking it. He made Dillinger the top priority over all other matters, ordered four dozen more men to St. Paul, and told Melvin Purvis to concentrate all of his efforts there. Hoover urged his agents to question their underworld sources about Dillinger. He told them that the Bureau would pay as much as five thousand dollars for information leading to his capture, and if that didn't work his men were to intimidate snitches into cooperation.[23]

Hoover's determination to crack the case almost bore fruit. Suspecting that the gang would return to Chicago, federal agents kept at least ten potential apartments under surveillance. Back in St. Paul the feds broke into several hideouts, and they detained and questioned countless suspects. Officers searching the shoot-out scene found bank robbers' gear, including guns, ammunition, detailed maps and notes on getaway routes, license plates, even a dynamite fuse. They also turned up an address they believed to be that of the man who had traded bullets with Agent Coulter. Homer Van Meter was too smart to return home, but a cleaning lady came in while the feds were there. Eddie Green, using the name Stevens, had asked Lucy Jackson, an African American woman who occasionally did domestic work for underworld figures, to tidy up Van Meter's place and to pack some of his things in a suitcase, which Green would pick up later at her house.

(Green was a detail guy; he acted as "jug marker," the scout who gathered intelligence about prospective banks, including how secure they were, how big the take might be, and possible escape routes. Green also found safe houses and medical care for the gang and apparently even arranged housekeeping for them.) Under questioning by the feds, Jackson told them about Mr. Stevens's impending visit, so agents took up positions at the windows inside her home.[24]

Green drove up with his wife, Beth (Bessie, as she was more commonly known), who sat in their car while he walked up to the porch. Federal agents made no effort to confirm his identity or to arrest him; they assumed that he was the man who had shot at one of their own, and they now acted on orders from Inspector William Rorer. As Green picked up the suitcase Lucy Jackson had left for him on the front step, agents cut him down with a burst of machine-gun fire. Green did not die immediately. After the staff at St. Paul's Ancker Hospital stabilized him, they allowed the feds, posing as doctors, to question him. Green floated in and out of consciousness, rambled on about the gang, and eventually gave up a Minneapolis address, Nurse Salt's lying-in hospital, and told them that Dillinger was there. Eddie Green died a week later.[25]

The aftermath of Green's killing offers further insight into Hoover's methods. The St. Paul *Pioneer Press* did not criticize the Bureau over the Green affair but simply reprinted the information they were given. The St. Paul *Dispatch*, however, raised questions about the incident and called for a coroner's inquest. Hoover responded by shutting out the *Dispatch* from briefings and giving the rival *Pioneer Press* favorable treatment. Moreover the Bureau concealed the names of the agents involved in the shooting, shielding them from subpoenas. Internal memos were contradictory about what had really happened to Eddie Green. Initial reports simply said he had been shot. Later memos claimed that when agents called to him to halt he made a "suspicious" gesture. Later still, in another memo, the word "suspicious" was crossed out and "menacing" inserted. But the feds' most effective strategy regarding Green's death and many other troubling issues raised by the Dillinger case was simply to stonewall.[26]

Hoover's machinations worked. For the average citizen reading his or her daily newspaper, the story of the St. Paul shoot-out unfolded as a case of good police work. Dillinger got away—he was long gone from Augusta Salt's care when Eddie Green gave up her address—but this new efficient federal force was closing in on him. The wire services picked up Bureau press releases describing scores of new agents pouring into St. Paul, many of them sleeping in their offices, waking up in the morning, and going right to work. One Associated Press story on Eddie Green began, "The federal government flung down the gauntlet to John Dillinger, outlaw killer today, as it ferreted out two more of his mob's crime nests here, captured a red-headed woman, and wounded a henchman."[27]

The feds were indeed making progress on the case. Under relentless questioning Bessie Green became an important FBI informant, giving up lots of information on the makeup of the new Dillinger gang as well as some of the history of other criminals passing through St. Paul with whom her husband had associated. She gave the federal grand jury sitting in St. Paul plenty of ammunition to indict herself, Billie Frechette, Dr. May, and several other people for aiding and abetting fugitives from justice.[28]

IN THE COMING YEARS J. Edgar Hoover portrayed his agency's pursuit of Dillinger as scientific, methodical, and relentless. Others depicted the feds' efforts as incompetent. Both sides were right. A balanced view sees great thoroughness and amazingly amateurish mistakes. The Bureau was only coming into its own in these years, and Hoover and his men were learning their craft on the job. Agents did not routinely carry guns before 1934 because their cases involved fraud more than force, white-collar crime more than violent felonies. Moreover the number of federal agents was quite small in the winter of 1934, a serious liability in the labor-intensive task of surveillance, which the Bureau bungled repeatedly.[29]

Eddie Green's shooting was a sure sign that the heat was on, but by the time agents arrived at the address Green gave them, Dillinger and Frechette were back on the road, heading down to Iowa and east across Illinois. They were going to Mooresville, and they clearly assumed that they would be dodging cops all the way. When Billie had visited Johnnie's family there two weeks before, she came in the dead of night and slipped away within hours.[30]

Dillinger had not been home for several months, and we can only guess why he decided to go now. He always read his own press, and the news stories kept repeating how he couldn't hold out forever.

Literally thousands of law enforcement officials backed by millions of dollars pursued him, while senators, governors, and cabinet members called for his head. It must have been intoxicating and sobering at the same time. He had so successfully eluded the law, and become so famous doing it, that of course a man like Dillinger was tempted to press his luck. On the other hand, life had grown much more precarious in the past few weeks. In the month since the Crown Point breakout the gang's robberies became bloodier, and officials spoke frequently of taking people "dead or alive." That Dillinger had been shot twice in the past month must have taken a psychic toll. The slow-healing wound above his knee caused him to limp noticeably, and the heightened awareness of his own mortality contributed to his decision to return to Mooresville now. Dillinger knew that this might be the last time he would see his loved ones, and a moment of stability, of family warmth, was worth the risk. Mooresville, the town that bored him deeply as a young man and where his life took a bad turn, now became a haven in a heartless world, a place to rebuild dim memories of family togetherness.[31]

Dillinger Senior left us the most detailed account of Billie and Johnnie's visit. The old man told the Indianapolis reporter John Cejnar how he often lay awake at night, worried about his boy. Then, on Thursday, April 5, he heard a car outside. He came down the stairs and peered through the kitchen window and saw two dark figures approaching.

> I switched on the electric light in the room, and opened the door. "Hello, Dad!" came the tumultuous greeting from one of the figures. The next moment Johnnie, the most hunted person in America, was on me, hugging me and repeating over and over: "Hello, Dad! Gee, I am glad to see you!" I wanted to yell with joy. I wanted to scold him for running the risk of coming home. What I did say finally was: "Johnnie! My boy!" We stood for a moment, arms around each other. What a picture we must have made—he a debonair, good-looking young fellow, neatly dressed and I in my night shirt and bedroom slippers.

They parked the car in the barn to get it out of sight and brought in a suitcase and a machine gun. Johnnie went upstairs to wake his young sisters, Frances and Doris, then everyone stayed up for hours, talking long into the night.[32]

Johnnie's brother Hubert came by the next morning, and after more warm greetings, the two retired to the barn to do some work on the car. That night they went for a ride, east toward Indianapolis, where Hubert became nervous when they spotted a police car, but Johnnie, confident in his car's power and with a submachine gun at hand, assured his brother, "Don't pay any attention to them; we can run off and leave them anytime." They drove on into Ohio, all the way to the town of Leipsic to drop off some money for Harry Pierpont's family. They then turned around and drove back.[33]

At 3 a.m. on the way home Hubert fell asleep at the wheel near the town of Noblesville, Indiana. He sideswiped another car, then careened off the road before finally rolling to a stop. Amazingly no one was hurt. Dillinger removed the license plates from his car and grabbed his gear, and the two brothers started walking, hiding in ditches when oncoming traffic approached. They walked about three miles, Johnny limping all the way from his gunshot wound. As dawn broke they decided it was safest for him to hide in a haystack by the road. Hubert tied a handkerchief to a nearby fence post so he could find his brother when he returned, hitched a ride into Indianapolis, then on to Mooresville, retrieved his own car, then drove back to pick up Johnnie. They made it home by eight o'clock Saturday morning. Later Hubert drove Billie to Indianapolis, where she bought a new Ford V-8 sedan, counting out $722 in cash.[34]

Not long after Hubert and Johnny returned Emmett Hancock, husband of Johnny's sister Audrey, came by. He stood outside talking to the elder Dillinger when Johnnie stuck his head out the kitchen window and yelled, "What the Hell! Come on in here, you can talk to Dad any time!" Emmett bounded into the house, greeted his brother-in-law, and just as quickly rushed back to his car, returned to Maywood, and brought Audrey out to Mooresville. "Audrey rushed to his side," Old John reported of the brother-sister reunion, "broke down and cried. Johnnie kissed her, and big tears came into his eyes, too. He had an awfully loving nature that way." When Audrey realized that Johnnie had been shot, she helped him pour peroxide on the wound and bandaged it. Then they talked for a while, and they all agreed to have a big Sunday dinner after church the next day. Audrey and Emmett went home to fry chicken and bake coconut cream pie, Johnnie's favorite.[35]

Here Old John interrupted his family idyll. After Audrey and Emmett went back to Maywood, father and son stepped outside to the barnyard: "Suddenly we heard the roar of an approaching airplane. Johnnie ducked into the barn. The plane swooped down low over our house, almost skimming the top of the chimney. . . . Two men were in the cockpit of the plane. One of them had a pair of spy glasses and was leaning over looking at our place. The plane circled our home a couple of times and then disappeared." The intrusion of state surveillance broke the spell. Thinking back on that moment, Dillinger Senior said that those who sent airborne spies would stop at nothing to kill his Johnnie.[36]

The next day, while everyone else was at church, father and son took a walk in the woods. The old man later mused on this moment, asking himself why Johnnie had come back to Mooresville. "I believe it was a strong premonition of death that drove him out of hiding to make the risky trip home for a final reunion with his family. He felt that when he said goodbye to us it would be goodbye forever." Dillinger Senior was almost seventy years old, and since his son's crime spree started, he had been living, as he put it, like a parent whose child had inoperable cancer. There could be only one end to this story, so on this lovely spring morning, with new grass growing and trees and flowers budding out, father and son spoke about a final resting place. Johnnie told his dad that he wanted to be laid to rest beside his mother in Indianapolis. "We gripped each other's hands standing there in the wood, and stood for a moment silent and reverent. To me it will be always one of the most sacred moments of my life." Johnnie reassured his father that he was not as bad a man as the newspapers made him out to be. But he added, "There is no road back, Dad. I couldn't go back if I wanted to." To surrender meant that every man's hand would be turned against him, and officials would railroad him into the electric chair. "I've set my course and I'll have to follow it to the end," Johnnie concluded. "I will never go back to prison alive."[37]

The family reconvened after church, and thirteen members of the Dillinger clan sat down to dinner. "What a feast they set out," Old John recalled. "There were fried chicken, mashed potatoes that were almost like whipped cream, luscious gravy, peas, lettuce, celery, hot biscuits, honey, jellies, and to top it all off the best coconut cream pies that Audrey ever made." Sitting at the table were Emmett and

Audrey, their four children, Hubert and his wife, Dillinger Senior, his two young daughters, Doris and Frances, and of course Billie and Johnnie. Emmett asked the blessing: "Father, we thank thee for the privilege of meeting together again in this house. . . . God guard and direct us and at last save us without the loss of one. We ask it for Christ's sake. Amen!" In Old John's telling, joyousness and fear warred with each other at the table, but finally the warmth of kin could not hold: "Here we were gathered around a family meal while hostile eyes even then were watching our home. The world's most hunted person sat in our midst. I noticed with a start that there were thirteen of us around the table. Wasn't there a saying that thirteen at a table meant that one was soon to die?" He spoke his worst fears: "At any moment the doors might be flung open and men with blazing guns invade our midst. Our feast might be turned into tragedy in the twinkling of an eye."[38]

The Dillingers did their best to "shake off the feeling of dread" and make the occasion what John Senior called a "joyous family event that will stand forth in our memories all of our lives." Johnnie, his father recalled, especially refused to give in to fear: "He was for the hour, at least, once more the happy-go-lucky, carefree boy whom we remembered from other days." He cracked jokes and the whole table laughed, but, his father observed, "I said we laughed, yet there wasn't a one of us who was not ready to cry the next moment." Even Johnnie's stories were double-edged: "I was sitting beside Charles Makley . . . in a car in New Mexico one day, listening to the radio. . . . Suddenly the announcer broke into the program with a flash. He said, 'John Dillinger just held up a bank in Indiana.' Makley roared with laughter. 'What do you think of that?' he asked. 'You certainly can step. You must have pulled that holdup while I was napping a while ago!'"[39]

After their big meal, the family went outside to take pictures, including the famous one of Dillinger smiling, his machine gun in one hand and his wooden pistol in the other. But even here the family worried about who might be watching, and they knew they must ask a friend to process the film, that to have it developed by a commercial lab could land them all in jail and jeopardize Johnnie's freedom.[40]

Their worries were well founded. The car Johnnie and Hubert had abandoned near Noblesville was traced to a Carl Hellman (Dillinger's alias) of St. Paul, and when the feds suspected that their man was back in Indiana two agents were dispatched to nose around Mooresville.

With his uncanny sense of danger Dillinger apprehended that the old homestead on this beautiful spring Sunday offered him no more shelter. The family said their goodbyes, and Johnnie promised to return in a few weeks. Then he lay down on the backseat of the new Ford, clutching his machine gun, and Billie covered him with a blanket. She took the wheel with Audrey's daughters sitting beside her. They headed toward Maywood, dropped the children off, then drove out of Indiana and away from the Dillinger family forever.[41]

Shortly after Johnnie and Billie left, the police raided the family's homes—Audrey's, Hubert's, and John Senior's. They came with weapons drawn, and Hubert later claimed that he counted fourteen squad cars in front of his house. The FBI considered arresting Dillinger Senior for harboring a fugitive, but Assistant U.S. Attorney General Joseph Keenan, who headed the legal case against Dillinger for the Justice Department, argued that the outlaw already was becoming a Robin Hood figure to many Americans and that arresting the father would only deepen public sympathy for the son.[42]

Dillinger Senior's telling of the Mooresville reunion was filled with sentimental touches: the walk in the woods to discuss Johnnie's funeral, the big country supper, the family's sheltering warmth against a cold world. But it was not just Old John who saw it that way. Journalists suspected that Mooresville, and maybe even people beyond Mooresville, operated as part of a big family, a family that harbored the fugitive. There was something new here: the notion that many people—citizens, common folk—so identified with their homeboy that they protected him, even at their own risk. Of course gangsters paid money to corrupt cops and politicians for protection, and whether for honor, pay, or self-interest thieves cosseted one another. But now the suspicion arose that others with nothing to gain were protecting Dillinger, that individuals with information of his whereabouts were holding back in solidarity with him. "Dillinger Is Regarded as Hero in Old Home Town," declared the headline in the Coshocton (Ohio) *Tribune* after his visit home was discovered; "Dillinger Given Warm Welcome in Home Town," the Chicago *Tribune* banner read, and the story added, "So great is the sympathy of Mooresville for its own Robin Hood that a petition is being circulated requesting Governor Paul V. McNutt to grant Dillinger 'amnesty' if he surrenders."[43]

Indiana State Safety Director Al Feeney exploded when he received news of the Mooresville reunion and the amnesty petition.

He assumed that citizens knew of Dillinger's visit and deliberately failed to notify officials. "The trouble is," he told reporters, "they are all for Dillinger down there," and he added that it was unusual "for a community to withhold such information for days and then to let it reach the newspapers in a way that disparages the police." Feeney accused the entire town of being "anti-social," by which he seems to have meant that Mooresville was so intent on protecting one of its own that it disregarded everyone else's welfare.[44]

Mooresville folk responded with anger of their own. "The town is humiliated by these charges that have been spread over the nation," declared W. A. Lyon, head of the town board of trustees. "If I weren't a church man I could cuss right now." Lyon added, "Mooresville is a God-loving, law-abiding American town." He focused on John Dillinger Sr. as the emblem of Mooresville's goodness. Old John was not only a fine Christian but a "hard-working, un-assuming, retiring, honest and God-fearing tiller of the soil." As Lyon put it, the old gentleman "does unto all as he would have them do unto him." The Indiana journalist John Cejnar argued that local folk agreed with the Dillinger family that the courts had dealt Johnnie, indeed his whole family a deep injustice, one that was emblematic of the hard life of those with little money or influence. Cejnar added that Mooresville residents appreciated the irony of their hometown boy becoming a master bank robber; their own bank had recently closed its doors in the financial crisis, vaporizing ninety thousand dollars' worth of life savings.[45]

The trip to Mooresville enhanced Dillinger's reputation for boldness, for defying those who would run him down, for laughing at his enemies. And there was more to laugh about. On the very day that Billie and Johnnie drove to Indiana for their reunion, federal agents were pursuing leads in New York City. On April 4 the Detroit Office informed the New York Bureau that Evelyn Frechette was aboard a Chicago United Airlines flight bound for Newark Airport. Francis X. Fay, special agent in charge in New York, reported to J. Edgar Hoover that the G-men had no difficulty picking out the suspect after the plane landed. Upon questioning, however, "she identified herself as Mrs. Betty Karp Marx, wife of Chico Marx, nationally known member of the four Marx brothers." The seven agents at the airport satisfied themselves that the woman they intercepted was who she claimed to be, not Billie Frechette. Special Agent Fay reassured Hoover that

Mrs. Marx accepted his office's apologies and "appeared to treat the matter as a lark and a new experience to write home about."[46]

The Bureau's fortunes rose a week later. From Mooresville Billie and Johnnie drove back to Chicago. As often was the case with women of the demimonde, Billie did the searching for a hideout. She arranged to meet Lawrence Strong, an underworld figure and former boyfriend of Opal Long at the Austin-State Tavern on the night of April 9. According to the FBI report Billie entered the bar and approached Strong, who had been drinking heavily. It is unclear whether Strong himself tipped off the FBI (it seems unlikely from the Bureau's memos), but someone called the feds, and within minutes several agents raided the tavern, arresting Billie and Strong. They held her incommunicado, and Billie later claimed that they not only handcuffed and interrogated her under bright lights over the course of days, but deprived her of food and sleep. She apparently betrayed no significant information about the gang.[47]

The FBI delayed releasing news of Frechette's arrest. The problem was that having captured her they once again let Dillinger slip away. To enter the State Street bar the feds must have walked right past his car, but they never thought to ask themselves how Frechette got to the tavern. Agents later claimed that they simply failed to notice Dillinger parked at the curb, and when he realized what was happening and that a rescue attempt was hopeless he drove away. Frechette spoke to the press a few days after her arrest, and her version was even more embarrassing to the Bureau:

> John Dillinger and I sat in the tavern quite a long time eating and drinking. . . . Suddenly these agents came bursting in—from the front and the rear and all sides, it seemed. They had all kinds of shotguns and rifles. There were more agents than I knew existed. John saw the agents come in. He got up and walked up to the front and sort of mingled with the people and the agents. Then he walked outside and sat in his automobile. I sat still and soon the agents came along and started to question me and then they took me away. John was sitting in his car when the agents brought me out but when he saw I was pinched, he drove away.

Melvin Purvis, who directed the raid, called Frechette's comments "ridiculous," but it was undeniable that once again Dillinger had been within reach and gotten away.[48]

Despite her capture and her treatment by the feds, Frechette was determined to put on a good face. According to the Associated Press she talked her captors into postponing her extradition for a day, allowing her to buy a new spring outfit in Chicago. "I want to go to St. Paul in style," she told reporters. The United Press reported that she taunted the federal agents and state police who escorted her to the airport, "Watch out for John. . . . He's the big bad wolf, you know. . . . You've got the date now, but he's liable to cut in on you."[49]

Louis Piquett, representing Dillinger's "dusky Menominee girl friend" in court, tried but failed to get her out on a writ of habeas corpus. Then he argued that her bail be set very low because all she had done was aid a man charged with violating the Dyer Act. Here Piquett went to extravagant lengths, claiming that Dillinger was a good boy, that a great wrong had been done him, that he even had a fine Sunday school record. How could the court set Billie's bond at eighty thousand dollars when the man she abetted committed a crime whose bail should be a mere fraction of that figure? Piquett got nowhere.[50]

Meanwhile Dillinger had disappeared again. Word spread that at any moment he would break Billie out of prison; other stories placed him far afield. Three days after her capture the Associated Press reported that he was on his way to Shreveport, Louisiana; local authorities closed the Dixie Highway on a tip from federal agents in the New Orleans Office, causing "wild excitement" among local folk. A few days later the Indianapolis *News* reported that a French clairvoyant, a "professeur des sciences occultes" visiting town from the University of Paris, claimed that she could "see" Dillinger hiding in San Francisco and predicted his imminent capture or death. These leads were as solid as any the feds were following.[51]

DILLINGER MUST HAVE BEEN on a roller-coaster of emotions during these days. The feds picked up Billie just twenty-four hours after the lovers left Mooresville, so he was still feeling the afterglow of the family reunion, as well as the sadness of its abrupt ending, and anger at his pursuers, who seemed to be getting closer all the time. On their ride back to Chicago, Billie and Johnnie had spoken once again of finding a place where they could settle down together and live quietly. Hours before Billie was picked up, Dillinger had contacted Arthur O'Leary, and in the course of their conversation (which included a promise of further payment) he asked about a plastic surgeon who Louis Piquett knew. If he could only change his visage, Dillinger reasoned, he could hide in plain sight, and he and Billie could live happily ever after. A few days later Piquett passed on new rumors of Billie's mistreatment by the feds, evoking murderous anger in Dillinger.[52]

But he was powerless to do anything about it, powerless too to help his brothers in arms in Ohio. Back in March juries had convicted Pierpont, Makley, and Clark for the murder of Sheriff Sarber. Former gang member Edward Shouse had testified against them, and despite the protestations on the witness stand of Pierpont's mother that her boy had been home on the night of the Lima breakout, and of Makley's family that he was in St. Mary's, the jury believed Shouse. Pierpont and Makley were sentenced to die in the electric chair and Clark to serve a life term. Dillinger knew that Attorney Jessie Levy was appealing their cases, but time was running out, and there was nothing he could do. Meanwhile other friends were on the run, his money was being siphoned away by payoffs and lawyers' fees, and his wounds, which still had not fully healed, were constant reminders of the precariousness of his life. Dillinger, however, had witnessed sudden transformations before; he'd even crafted a few miracles of his own. He was not the sort of man to let feelings of powerlessness overwhelm him for long. His impulse, first, last, and always, was to act. The FBI was holding Billie in their headquarters in the Bankers Building in downtown Chicago. The place was too well fortified for a rescue attempt, but once the feds indicted her they would have to transfer her to St. Paul, and her captors might then be vulnerable.[53]

In preparation for such an opportunity, just three days after agents grabbed Billie, Dillinger and Homer Van Meter restocked their supplies. They raided the police arsenal in Warsaw, a small town in northern Indiana. Dillinger was so famous now that even a relatively minor act like this got instant press attention. The New York *Times* story described Dillinger as "the bank robber whom no jail seems strong enough to hold" and counted the mayhem wrought by his gang: in murders, kidnappings, and stolen dollars. Small-town newspapers agreed. The Sheboygan (Wisconsin) *Press* called him "a ruthless desperado with no compunctions about killing" and noted "the boldness, the sheer bravado of his moves."[54]

But if Dillinger was a bloodthirsty cop hater, "the killer," as newspapers sometimes called him, he certainly went out of his way not to kill anyone in Warsaw. Dillinger and Van Meter, brandishing two machine guns, stopped fifty-four-year-old veteran police officer Judd Pittenger on the street. Pittenger grabbed for one of the guns; his captors hit him, told him not to be a fool, and said they did not want to kill him. The officer led the outlaws into the Warsaw "armory," where they seized four bulletproof vests and two.38-caliber pistols; there were no machine guns. On the way out Pittenger made a break for it, but Dillinger and Van Meter did not even bother with him; they fled the scene without firing a shot. Police and vigilantes set up five thousand roadblocks in northern Indiana, but to no avail. "John Dillinger, America's No. 1 vanishing outlaw, has vanished again," reported the Associated Press. Dillinger "has again disappeared, without leaving a forwarding address," the Chicago *Tribune* added.[55]

Melvin Purvis assumed correctly that Dillinger had Billie on his mind and so would remain close to Chicago after the Warsaw raid. It became clear, however, that the feds now had sufficient firepower that a rescue attempt was out of the question. O'Leary, no doubt skittish about the blood that might flow in any direct confrontation with the G-men, argued that Billie's best chance was a good defense in court by Louis Piquett, which of course required money. Dillinger, assured O'Leary that he was good for the cash. O'Leary, as it turned out, was right that a battle with the feds would prove ugly, but when it came the showdown did not take place in Chicago and was not over trying to rescue Billie.[56]

Dillinger never stayed put for long, and once Billie was transferred to St. Paul he was on the move again. His life since his parole from Pendleton was one continuous road trip, an outlaw version of America's romance with the automobile. For all of the gang, men and women, the open road brought flight from danger, but it also connoted freedom, opportunity, camaraderie, love; more than just dodging authorities, it meant avoiding the deadening round of workaday life. But now Johnnie drove just to think. He agreed to take a road trip with John Hamilton and his girlfriend, Pat Cherrington, to Sault St. Marie, far north in Michigan's Upper Peninsula, to visit Hamilton's sister. They drove all day in two cars, 450 miles, Dillinger by himself. It was an emotional reunion for Hamilton, who, wounded like Dillinger and knowing that the cops' pursuit of the gang was getting hotter, longed for his family. Anna Steve cooked dinner for her brother and his friends, and Hamilton spent time with his nephews.

Mrs. Steve also found some scissors and gave both Johnnie and her brother haircuts. But Dillinger could not sit still. Fearful of a police raid, the three fugitives left just a few hours after arriving.[57]

Dillinger's sixth sense for danger was dead-on again; someone reported suspicious persons at the Steve home, and the day after the visit authorities showed up, searched the place, and arrested Hamilton's sister. The feds made an example of her, sending her to prison for three months for harboring the fugitives. By the time officers nabbed her, Dillinger, Hamilton, and Cherrington were back in Chicago, but almost immediately they went on the road again. The gang that pulled off the Mason City and Sioux Falls jobs agreed that both St. Paul and Chicago were now too risky. Despite the tension between Dillinger and Baby Face Nelson—Nelson and his wife thought that Dillinger brought unnecessary attention to the group, and Dillinger believed that Nelson was out of control in his violence—they needed to figure out their next move. So they took off in four separate cars for an obscure little resort in northern Wisconsin, a place where few tourists would go this early in spring, a place where they could plan their next moves.[58]

A trusted underworld operator, Louis Cernocky, who ran a roadhouse in the Chicago suburb of Fox River Grove, where the gang gathered after Sault St. Marie, suggested the lodge known as Little Bohemia, near Mercer, Wisconsin, deep in hunting and fishing country. Emil Wanatka, who knew Cernocky when he was a fellow Chicago barkeep, had named his establishment in honor of his home country. The lodge was reached by a narrow road, a long driveway really, overhung with trees, leading from the state highway. It had a bar, a restaurant, a small dance floor, and rooms for visitors upstairs. Wanatka approximated a legitimate small businessman, though he had had his share of questionable dealings in the past. The original Little Bohemia in Chicago was a bootleg joint, a speakeasy, and before running that Wanatka had faced charges of murder and auto theft, both of which he beat.[59]

The gang arrived over the course of the afternoon on Friday, April 20: Dillinger along with Red Hamilton and Pat Cherrington; Homer Van Meter and his girlfriend, Marie Conforti; Tommy Carroll with Jean Crompton; Baby Face Nelson with his wife, Helen Gillis; and Pat Riley, a hanger-on and gofer. A party of ten staying for a few days in the off-season seemed like good fortune, but before long the Wanatkas, noting that Cernocky had sent these men and that they wore shoulder holsters, figured out the identity of their guests. Dillinger reassured Wanatka that all the gang wanted was to rest up, then leave quietly. The Wanatkas were not exactly prisoners in their own home, but they certainly felt trapped. The tension kept building, and as people came and went from the lodge—children heading to a nearby birthday party, relatives coming by to socialize, guests passing through for a beer or a meal—the felons grew increasingly suspicious of their hosts, watching them ever more closely. Not so closely, however, that they noticed when Emil's wife, Nan Wanatka, snuck a message into a pack of cigarettes and passed it to her brother-in-law, Henry Voss, who read it and drove to Rhinelander (where the phone lines were secure) to call the feds. He reached Melvin Purvis in Chicago in the early afternoon on Sunday. Once he felt sure of Voss's story Purvis called Hoover, who ordered men up to Wisconsin.[60]

Purvis knew that time was of the essence, having learned from Voss that Dillinger had promised Wanatka a Monday morning departure; the feds had less than twenty-four hours to act. Purvis rounded up agents by phone, and within a few hours he had roughly two dozen armed men—several driving up from Madison, five aboard a charter flight from St. Paul, a dozen more flying out of Chicago—converging on the town of Rhinelander, fifty miles from Little Bohemia. Once on the ground, with daylight waning, Special Agent Hugh Clegg from the St. Paul Office commandeered cars from local auto dealerships. It was dark and cold when they set out into the woods. But before they did, word reached them that the gang was making plans to leave that very night. Five cars sped toward Little Bohemia along a muddy, rutted road. Two of them slipped off into ditches, but rather than waste time pulling them out the agents simply grabbed their guns and mounted the running boards of the remaining vehicles, struggling to hang on, their hands freezing in the early spring night. They arrived around 9 p.m.[61]

Henry Voss had drawn a crude map of Little Bohemia for the agents. It seemed to indicate that the lodge backed directly onto Star Lake, so that rear exit was impossible. The agents drove up the spur road leading from the highway to the lodge, stopping well within the cover provided by the woods. Everything looked good for a surprise assault, so good that Purvis and Clegg imagined that, with luck, no shots need be fired. Nonetheless the Bureau was still not good at large confrontations against armed criminals. So far in the "war on crime" sieges had repeatedly failed, and this was the largest one the feds ever attempted. Moreover the situation at Little Bohemia was not as favorable as it initially appeared. For starters, the feds lacked an unambiguous chain of command: Purvis gave orders and Clegg gave orders, though who was in charge remained unclear. Second, agents were operating with limited information on strange terrain. Third, news of the gang's presence in northern Wisconsin had come in so unexpectedly that there had been no time to devise a plan of action. Given Hoover's aversion to working with local law enforcement agencies the feds had not sought information, equipment, or assistance from police in the area; Wisconsin law enforcement had no idea the FBI was operating in their territory and therefore had not set up roadblocks around the lodge.[62]

As soon as the agents got out of their cars dogs began barking, eliminating, the G-men feared, the advantage of surprise. Purvis saw men on the lodge's porch, three of whom now headed toward a parked car. They got in, turned the vehicle around in the lot (agents could hear the radio playing), and drove onto the long driveway that led to the road. Agents assumed that their prey was coming to them, that they would be heroes, like the Tucson police, taking the gang by surprise and without bloodshed. Or maybe they were sitting ducks and the Dillinger gang was bearing down on them, headlights making them targets for the heavy firepower of known killers. The feds identified themselves and shouted for the car to stop. When the vehicle kept coming, Purvis and Clegg ordered their men to open fire, and a fusillade of machine-gun and small arms bullets shattered windows and flattened tires. The car rolled to a stop.[63]

Now pistol shots came at the feds, fired not from the car but from the lodge. Inspector William Rorer and two other men wove through the woods toward the left side of the building. Rorer saw two men at a second-floor window and shouted to them. Machine-gun bullets whizzed by; the agents ducked behind trees. After another few seconds one of the feds returned fire with a shotgun, but now no one was visible at the window. Rorer later said he was certain that the two men had gone back inside when the feds shot at them. Just at this moment another car turned up the driveway toward Little Bohemia, coming from behind the federal men. The agents demanded that the driver stop and identify himself. Instead he threw his vehicle into reverse and sped back to the highway. Gunfire hit at least one tire, and the feds later said they could hear the vehicle speeding away on its rims.[64]

In a matter of a few moments the FBI had fired hundreds of rounds at unidentified cars and men. But whom had they shot? One man staggered out of the car that had come at them from the lodge and fell wounded to the pavement. Asked to identify himself, he groaned the name "John." Once the agents managed to shine some lights on him, they saw he was elderly, certainly not the famous fugitive they sought. Another man had leaped from the car and ran into the woods, only to emerge later with a gunshot wound in his arm and facial lacerations. A third remained inside the car, and Inspector Rorer carefully crawled toward him. The G-man turned off the radio and the engine, felt the man for a pulse, detected none, reached for the dead man's wallet, and found his identification. His name was Eugene Boisneau, a thirty-five-year-old worker for the New Deal's Civilian Conservation Corps. As it turned out, he and the others—another CCC worker and a local gas station attendant—had come to Little Bohemia for a Sunday night drink. The feds had killed one civilian and shot two more, but they were still sure that Dillinger and his gang were pinned down inside Little Bohemia. In fact, having heard the gunshots, three men emerged from the Lodge in the next few minutes, hands up, including Emil Wanatka, who told Purvis that the gang was upstairs. Even with dead and wounded civilians, this still could come out all right if the FBI captured Dillinger. Rather than storm the lodge, Purvis decided to wait for a teargas gun, on its way by car from St. Paul.[65]

In this brief interim one of the agents, Carter Baum, became increasingly distraught over Boisneau's death. Baum had wielded the machine gun that strafed Boisneau's car and was horrified that he had killed an innocent man. To get him away from the scene, Purvis sent him out with Agent Jay Newman to find a phone at a nearby lodge and call the Rhinelander airport, where, Purvis guessed, the men bringing in teargas equipment might be waiting for instructions. When Newman made his call the switchboard operator informed him that a mysterious car had been spotted at a nearby home. Newman decided to investigate. On the way he and Baum picked up a local peace officer, Carl Christianson. They found the car and pulled up to it. There were several people inside, and Newman asked them to identify themselves. One stepped out, a small man, who pulled a gun and fired point blank at Newman, Baum, and Christianson before they could even reach for their weapons. Newman received a superficial head wound and revived after a few minutes. Christian received more serious injuries. Baum died quickly from several bullets to the neck. The shooter stole their car and headed up Highway 51. It was Baby Face Nelson; he had been in the middle of kidnapping some local residents and hijacking their car when the agents drove up.[66]

Word of what had happened got back to Purvis. It dawned on him now that the entire gang was not holed up in Little Bohemia, and it became all the more important to capture whoever was left. In the very early hours of the morning, with the teargas equipment finally on the scene, the feds decided to attack the lodge. But the teargas gun failed to work, so Agent John McLaughlin, declaring that he was not married and so could most afford to give up his life, volunteered to charge the building and toss in a canister. Teargas flooded Little Bohemia with poisoned air, but only three people emerged from the building: Helen Gillis, wife of Baby Face Nelson; Jean Crompton, who had left her husband six months before and hooked up with Tommy Carroll; and Marie Conforti, Homer Van Meter's lover. They were all arrested, taken to Madison, Wisconsin, then held incommunicado for a month as federal agents questioned them.[67]

In fact, Dillinger and his men were long gone. When the shooting started—when Inspector Rorer came up firing at the left side of the lodge—Dillinger was the one who returned fire with his machine gun. In those few seconds when the agents took cover, Hamilton, Van Meter, and finally Dillinger had all leaped from the second-story window into a deep snow bank behind the building. Tommy Carroll and Baby Face Nelson were already on the ground, and they ran around the right side of the lodge to join them.[68]

Once out of the lodge, the gang scrabbled down some stairs leading to the lakeshore, ran along the strand a short way, reentered the woods, then started looking for lights. They did not stay together. Tommy Carroll procured a car quickly and got out of harm's way, though later he bogged down on a logging road and was forced to hitchhike the rest of the way to St. Paul. Pat Riley had not even been in Little Bohemia during the assault; he and Pat Cherrington had gone out looking for ammunition. It was their car whose tires the FBI agents shot out earlier in the night; they drove out of danger. Things were more complicated for the others. Within minutes after leaping from the building, Dillinger, Hamilton, and Van Meter stumbled across another lodge; some elderly people there directed them to the nearby cabin of a local carpenter, and on pretext of a medical emergency the fugitives took his car and got away smoothly. Of course, the fact that no roadblocks had been set up helped them immeasurably.[69]

Hours later, with Van Meter at the wheel, the three approached St. Paul from the south, assuming that only the northern entrances to town might be blocked. They were wrong; a local sheriff and his deputies recognized the car's license number from an FBI bulletin and gave chase. The two vehicles hurtled toward St. Paul, guns blazing. Dillinger broke out the back window and blasted away with his machine gun, while the cops returned fire. As they neared the city, Van Meter managed a sharp right turn onto a secluded road and lost his pursuers, but not before Red Hamilton received a mortal gunshot wound in his lower back. They abandoned their bullet-riddled car, flagged down another, and took it at gunpoint from its owner. Dillinger helped Hamilton, in agony and bleeding heavily, into their new ride and headed back to Chicago.[70]

Meanwhile the car that Baby Face Nelson had commandeered broke down on him. He walked twenty miles through the woods and ended up at the home of Ollie and Maggie Catfish near Lac Du Flambeau. Difficult as it is to imagine the sharply dressed little thug and the elderly Chippewa couple together, Nelson, claiming to be a game warden, stayed with them for several days. Finally, growing worried or tired, he forced Ollie at gunpoint on a trek to find a car. Nelson stole a Plymouth and made the old man show him the way to State Highway 70. Nelson let Catfish out along the road, then drove down the length of Wisconsin and finally back toward Chicago. He went straight to Louis Cernocky's tavern in Fox River Grove, which, remarkably, still was not under surveillance, though several snitches had told the FBI that Cernocky's place was a safe house for the Dillinger gang.[71]

The Little Bohemia fiasco only reinforced Dillinger's fame. For days the media was saturated with the story. "Dillinger Reported Surrounded" was the block-letter headline across the St. Louis *Globe-Democrat*; "End of Bloody Trail in Sight," the Meriden (Connecticut) *Record* agreed. As that hope grew faint, other newspapers hyped the bloody deeds of the outlaws. The AP reported that the Dillinger gang, not the feds, had left two dead and four wounded before fleeing Little Bohemia, as well as the patently false details that the gang took Little

Bohemia by force, then mounted a machine gun on the roof in anticipation of a gun battle. The Chicago *Tribune*, like the other papers,
led with the casualties suffered by law enforcement officials and the
imminence of the gang's capture. Even the *Tribune*, however, could
not help but report the confusion on the ground. At 2:30 a.m., shortly
before the paper went to press, Hoover declared Dillinger to be trapped
in the lodge, but simultaneously came reports of the wounded civilians, then of the federal dead, and the *Tribune* ended up asking out-
right whether Dillinger had indeed been caught.[72]

The coverage by the Chicago *Daily News* gives a clear sense of
how reporters struggled to conceptualize the rapidly changing story.
On the Monday after the shoot-out, the paper's lead story carried the
headline "2 Die, 4 Shot, as Killer Escapes Wisconsin Trap." The very
next day, however, the *Daily News* gave mixed messages, juxtapos-
ing a story on the one hundred new agents sent in by the FBI with
a column highlighting unnamed authorities' incompetence, titled
"Those Guarded Bridges Not So Well Guarded in Hunt for Dillinger."
Describing the manhunt for Dillinger around St. Paul, the *Daily News*
staff writer Robert J. Casey questioned police claims that Dillinger
would be in custody within a few hours, and as for the FBI, Casey
added that in the future agents should be less distracted "by such
decoys as CCC workers."[73]

Struggling to get the story right also meant trying to understand its meaning. For as long as they could newspapers cleaved to
the heroic cops and brutal robbers theme, emphasizing the larger-
than-life drama. One Associated Press story declared that "the toll
of lives forfeited along the trail of John Dillinger" now stood at thirteen, including six peace officers. The United Press depicted "grim
federal agents and hundreds of local officers" stalking the Dillinger
gang through dark forests and cold northern towns. The AP described
Dillinger as "crafty as a fox and ruthless as a wolf." Reports portrayed
the criminals as so cunning and fearless that they would soon assault,
guns blazing, jails in Columbus, Ohio, St. Paul, and Madison to free
their comrades and lovers.[74]

Other stories, sometimes on the very same pages, repeated the feds'
position that the "Dillinger luck" had run out, that the "cop-killer,
bank robber, highwayman and jail fugitive" would soon make his last
stand. The New York *Times*, America's "newspaper of record," kept up
the melodrama for days after Little Bohemia, declaring that "fear of

[Dillinger's] depredations" brought panic throughout the region. But all was not lost; the *Times* added that Department of Justice agents "engaged in one of the greatest desperado hunts the country has ever known," that the FBI would make Dillinger eat his words that no jail in the country was strong enough to hold him. In the immediate aftermath of Little Bohemia most newspapers simply accepted the FBI line. They would get their man.[75]

But as the days passed "the Battle of Little Bohemia," as some reporters now called it, played poorly for the feds. Initially Attorney General Homer Cummings put the best spin he could on events for the Department of Justice and its Division of Investigation. He described how Boisneau and the others had not responded to agents' orders to stop their car: "They were commanded to stop and were informed that the men ordering them to stop were government officers. They did not stop, and agents of the division shot at the tires of their automobile. Immediately upon this being done machine gun firing started from the house and in the exchange of fire between the houses and our agents, the three men were shot." The notion that agents first aimed at the car's tires then accidentally shot the men in a crossfire did not mesh with the facts on the ground, and reporters let their readers know it. The feds came in for more criticism when Hoover coldheartedly justified the deaths of the civilians killed by his agents, claiming that the dead men were drunk and had refused to obey orders to halt. Nor was it good publicity when the government offered the Wanatka family a pittance for the damages done to their property, when the Rhinelander Ford dealership from which Purvis commandeered vehicles for the raid had to sue to recover the costs of wrecked cars, nor when one FBI agent decided to assault a photographer during the arraignment of the captured molls in Madison.[76]

Three days after first reporting the tragedy of brave federal officers shot by bloodthirsty felons, the Chicago *Tribune* led with the headline "Charge U.S. Men with Bungling Dillinger Hunt." The "criminal stupidity" of the feds, declared the *Tribune*, now overshadowed the manhunt itself as a news item. The lead story by midweek in American newspapers was the petition circulating in northern Wisconsin questioning the FBI's competence and calling for Melvin Purvis's resignation. Citizens singled out the Bureau's wanton disregard for human life and its insulting failure to seek aid from those who best knew the terrain.[77]

As in Crown Point, the absurdities of the story began to sink in. The United Press laid out the contradictions in the coverage of John Dillinger:

> He is mild mannered and never swears, but is evil-tempered and curses all the time. . . . He is a maniac but quite sane, and a moron but intelligent.
>
> Dillinger has robbed 5, 16, 32, 78 banks in 4, 6, 7, 8 states and killed 2, 3, 11, and 17 men.
>
> If you want to verify this, ask Dillinger. You will find him in Wisconsin, Montana, Arizona, Minnesota, Ohio, Texas, or Idaho.

As Dillinger sightings poured in by the thousands another article declared, "To date, there are still 12 states in which Dillinger has not been seen in the last 40 hours." Arthur Brisbane, famed columnist for the Hearst newspapers, declared the fact that the Dillinger gang blasted its way out of a trap with law enforcement officials in hot pursuit was not news: "If police officers should meet Dillinger, and not have their revolvers and bullet-proof vests taken from them, that would be news."[78]

Perhaps the most pointed comments came from the pen of Will Rogers, humorist, actor, syndicated columnist, and one of the most famous Americans of the 1930s. The day after the news of Little Bohemia broke he wrote, "Well, they had Dillinger surrounded and was all ready to shoot him when he come out, but another bunch of folks come out ahead, so they just shot them instead." Rogers added, "Dillinger is going to accidentally get with some innocent bystanders sometime; then he will get shot." A few days later Rogers noted the success of the feds at picking up Dillinger's women; the problem was that Dillinger always managed "to keep at least two women ahead of 'em."[79]

DILLINGER'S STORY, the New York *Times* noted, had "taken on the qualities of myth and legend," but his life could not have been more ordinary before his friends killed Sheriff Sarber:

> The story of his early life is far from being either glamorous or exotic. When it is stripped to the bone, one finds in it resentment, idleness, stupidity, cowardice, hysteria and bravado, nothing that is heroic or

very unusual. Indeed, the outstanding characteristic in this man's life, up to the moment when the shooting begins, is its extreme ordinariness. Behind the figure of the bandit who has defied the police officers of half a dozen states, and run through traps laid by Federal authorities, is a person who, so far as early evidence goes, might have been stamped out in gross lots.

The *Times* disparaged the sheer dullness of a commonplace family in a commonplace state. The story had the "uncertain flicker of an old film," and it took little imagination to picture young Dillinger, the "grimy little boy," who grew to be an average man in an average town. Probably he drank and smoked, maybe he was a sharp dresser, but nothing distinguished him from his fellow citizens. Only a dull-witted felony that led him into those schools of crime, Pendleton and Michigan City, broke the pattern of unspeakable ordinariness.[80]

The rank elitism of the *Times* article, its Menckenesque contempt for Middle America notwithstanding, gets at something important. The very ordinariness of Dillinger's life before the summer of 1933 was precisely why the man took on such legendary proportions just a year later. Becoming a master criminal might not have been the approved way of breaking through the banality of daily life, but John Dillinger had accomplished something quite extraordinary. He had "become somebody." He was famous. He had imposed himself on the nation's consciousness. After years of pent-up frustration at the breakdown of the American dream, here was a man stealing from banks rather than the other way around, going in with guns blazing, declaring, according to the newspapers, that he would not be taken alive. Parents, of course, did not want their children to identify with him. But the sense of rage at the system that had failed them, at institutions that now oppressed them, at the sheer dullness of life lived with diminished hopes made Dillinger's saga all the more compelling, even inspiring, to Americans. And the very ordinariness of his early life only enhanced their fascination with him.[81]

The more that bankers and congressmen, attorneys general and journalists condemned him, the more John Dillinger's celebrity status seemed to grow. Between newspaper photos and newsreels in the theaters, his face had become one of the best known in America, as had his persona. Or more precisely, his personas, for in addition to the bloodthirsty gang leader and the magician-bandit he was also the man who performed small gallantries for women and children. A United Press story noted that he added a "Robin Hood touch" to his escape from northern Wisconsin. As Dillinger and his companions held a family at gunpoint, demanding an automobile, E. J. Mitchell, an elderly man, protested that his wife was ill. "With a grand gesture, the desperado grabbed a blanket, wrapped it around the woman and said: 'Here you are, mother.'" Mrs. Mitchell described this bit of chivalry herself in a Pathe newsreel, and she added that Dillinger had assured her that no harm would come to her. Homer Cummings was outraged that Dillinger had been depicted favorably on film. Worse, theater audiences cheered when the outlaw's picture came onscreen. The Justice Department investigated, initiating a sharp exchange of letters between the attorney general's office and the president of Pathe News.[82]

But Dillinger's fame just kept growing. In the weeks after the shoot-out, Emil Wanatka reported that business was booming at Little Bohemia. "I guess I'll have to build an addition and get more help," he told reporters, as scores of traveling salesmen and tourists now made their pilgrimage to the lodge to stare at the bullet holes in the walls and relive the shoot-out.[83]

Countless Americans identified with Dillinger. Even as it condemned the "silly sentimentality" that made a hero of him, the Edwardsville (Illinois) *Intelligencer* acknowledged that he had "caught the imagination of a good part of his fellow countrymen." The Lima *News* agreed; there was a "sneaking admiration for the outlaw," which caused many to hope secretly that he would "[elude] the clutches of the law." Dillinger's exploits, declared an editorial in the Sheboygan *Press*, "read like fiction from the wildest criminal stories." He differed from the "Chicagoese gangsters" of the Capone era, who shunned glamour for efficiency and who killed each other in turf wars. The Edwardsville editorialist concluded, "Dillinger is more like a throwback to the bad men of the old west. He has traded shots with his victims in the old-time style and risked his neck plenty in his forays. As a result, he has been built up into an impossible character; a sort of combination of Jesse James, Billy the Kid, and Robin Hood." Dillinger's was a success story forged with a strange amalgam of larceny, technology, and the Old West of memory: male, white, stoic, with a violent but fair code of honor. And there was humor too. Should he ever pass that way, a big billboard for a roadhouse on the highway near Loretto, Pennsylvania, greeted the outlaw. "Hello Dillinger," it read. "You'll Like Lee Hofmann's Food." That was part of his persona too—one could imagine him stopping in, breaking bread with the locals, regaling them with stories of his exploits, charming them one and all.[84]

FIVE

"Dillinger Land"

Little Bohemia was no joking matter for Melvin Purvis and J. Edgar Hoover, both of whom were in jeopardy of losing their jobs. Attorney General Cummings had sharp words for Hoover. As the Chicago *Tribune* put it, "Because of the criticism which is gathering around him, Hoover's dismissal is regarded here as inevitable unless he succeeds in putting an abrupt close to Dillinger's career." Senator Thomas Schall of Minnesota called for more detectives and fewer politicians in the Bureau of Investigation, and Indiana Senator Arthur Robinson publicly denounced the agency's bungling. In the coming days the criticism intensified, especially as it became apparent that just two roadblocks across key bridges would have trapped the entire Dillinger gang. The feds blew it, and by the end of April everyone knew it. Perhaps, as one editorialist put it, Dillinger was "in a hell of his own making, a grim, unrelenting hell of inevitability with death at the end." But here in early spring such talk seemed hollow. John Dillinger was on the loose and living large.[1]

The crescendo of anger at law enforcement was only beginning. Senator Royal Copeland, chairman of the Anti-Racketeering Committee, called the lack of cooperation between federal, state, and local authorities a "pathetic failure." Congressman Jennings Randolph of West Virginia declared on the floor of the House that Dillinger's rampage highlighted the problem of crime, of the one hundred thousand assaults, twelve thousand murders, three thousand kidnappings, and fifty thousand robberies that cost fifteen billion dollars every year. The common enemy imperiling the nation, Randolph told his fellow congressmen, "hunts in packs, using high-powered automobiles . . . and machine guns for persuasion." Worse, they subvert the law by bribing or intimidating police, attorneys, judges, and even prison officials into doing their bidding. When wild animals become too destructive, he concluded, the state declares open season; it was time to declare open season on criminals.[2]

The Roosevelt administration seized the moment. "Aroused by the latest escapade of the bandit John Dillinger, President Roosevelt has requested early enactment by Congress of a sheaf of bills greatly enlarging the police powers of the federal government," the New York *Times* reported the day after the Little Bohemia shoot-out. Attorney General Cummings went on the offensive, turning the bungling at Little Bohemia into an opportunity. He placed the blame for the north woods debacle squarely on Capitol Hill, and he challenged Congress to authorize pending legislation for armored cars, airplanes, and more federal agents. Citing outdated equipment, the attorney general told the press with considerable disingenuousness, "If we had an armored car up there in Wisconsin our men could have driven right up to the house where Dillinger was. . . . The terrible tragedy then would not have happened."[3]

Dillinger had become quite useful to the Justice Department. Federal attorneys extended the government's reach with creative new charges against him. Before Little Bohemia their case against Dillinger was based on his violating the Dyer Act when he transported Sheriff Holley's car across state lines. Now a grand jury sitting in Madison charged all of the gang members with harboring each other. More, Dillinger became the poster boy for the stalled anti-crime package. Roosevelt's proposed legislation would allow the government to offer enormous rewards for the capture, dead or alive, of federal offenders, Dillinger prime among them. And the new laws authorized hiring two hundred additional men for the Division of Investigation, increasing the force by half. Whereas agents previously carried guns on an ad hoc basis, now all would be armed and trained in the use of the most sophisticated weaponry.[4]

Before the Little Bohemia debacle Congress had proceeded with caution, and the package of twelve laws languished in the House

Judiciary Committee in early spring. State and local authorities protected their prerogatives, and many Americans were deeply suspicious of the federal government's lengthening reach under the New Deal. But after the fiasco the House Judiciary Committee sped the bills to the floor for passage. "Public opinion demands action," declared Judiciary Chairman Hatton W. Summers. The Senate had already approved its own anticrime package, which made it a federal offense to flee a state to avoid prosecution; to transport stolen bonds, checks, securities, or other monetary instruments across state lines; to shoot a federal officer; to rob banks operating under the Federal Reserve System; to transport kidnap victims across state lines; or to extort money by telephone or telegraph. The Roosevelt administration also pressed for much stricter regulation of machine guns and other weapons, though not without considerable opposition from arms manufacturers and sportsmen's groups. Congressman Summers noted that he personally would prefer local solutions to the crime wave, but American citizens sought swift and sure federal action. "A wrath like that which kindled the frontier when the vigilantes cleaned out the gunmen is sweeping America," Summers declared. His committee bowed to this alleged popular uprising against the countervailing demands of states' rights. The congressman concluded, "These laws will smash the criminal gangs and make another Dillinger impossible."[5]

And it was not just Dillinger. Other famous criminals of the 1930s—Bonnie and Clyde, Pretty Boy Floyd, Machine Gun Kelly, the Barker gang, Baby Face Nelson—not only were frightening in their own right, but they threatened, in journalists' fevered imaginations, to join forces. To give just one example, a May 3 United Press article declared that Clyde Barrow, along with "his cigar smoking sweetheart," Bonnie Parker, were rushing north to Chicago, fresh from their depredations in Oklahoma, Texas, and Missouri, their route "marked by wanton gun play," to join up with Dillinger. For this reporter the fearful scenarios were endless: such noted gang leaders as Doc Barker and Alvin Karpis ran with Dillinger in Wisconsin and Minnesota, and both had been members of the Barrow gang "when it cut a swath of lawlessness" through the Great Southwest. The threat of an interlocking directorate of crime hell-bent on bloody mayhem, motivated a "grimly tense 'shoot to kill' army of 7,000 police and federal agents" to find Dillinger before the outlaws consummated their unholy alliance. But according to the United Press writer, it was the feds who would get the job done. Melvin Purvis had just recalled one hundred of his "ace detectives" to Chicago, and the article ended with the special agent's reassuring voice: "We think we're on the verge of running this crew to earth."[6]

Dillinger's escape from Little Bohemia recharged the debate on crime, its causes and cures, and newspapers amplified the discussion. "Editorial writers have nearly reached an exploding point," declared the *Literary Digest*, "as they dug into dictionaries for sarcastic epithets to hurl at authorities who let the outlaw slip through trap after trap." Inept police, incompetent prosecutors, corrupt prison officials, and lenient parole boards came in for the usual condemnation; so did sympathetic local folk who harbored criminals, wide-eyed editors who sensationalized crime, naïve "molls" who enabled their exploits, even arms merchants like the one in Texas recently arrested for retooling stolen guns into repeating weapons, then selling them to criminals, including members of the Dillinger gang. The Van Nuys (Calif.) *News* argued that Dillinger was just a pool hall loafer until prison, that college of crime, taught him his trade. A few editorials advocated federal laws requiring serial numbers on all guns, permits for those who carried them, and character references for anyone applying for a permit. Some went so far as to suggest banning weapons for all but the police. England, where constables carried no guns, was the model, and confiscating all contraband arms the goal.[7]

Equally prominent were calls to get tough, to expand police powers in the face of crime's spread, and to get Dillinger. Editors evoked "the helplessness of the country," declared that "killers are defying society," and argued that men like Dillinger were "stimulating the gun-courage of the jungle, arousing the blood-lust." The answer was tougher sentencing, more trained lawmen on the streets, and, above all, centralized policing. It was time, they argued, for the federal government to lose its remaining scruples about state and local autonomy.[8]

On June 24, 1934, two months after Little Bohemia, the Department of Justice officially made John Dillinger the mascot for its anticrime drive. The attorney general, bolstered by new legislation authorizing the payment of large bounties, issued the following proclamation:

> I, Homer S. Cummings . . . , by virtue of the authority vested in me by
> the Act of Congress approved June 6, 1934, and by virtue of all other

authority vested in me, do hereby proclaim and offer the following rewards:

1. For the capture of John Dillinger, $10,000.
2. For information leading to the arrest of John Dillinger, $5,000.
3. For the capture of Lester M. Gillis, alias "Baby Face" Nelson, $5,000.
4. For information leading to the arrest of Lester M. Gillis, alias "Baby Face" Nelson, $2,500.

Newspapers began calling Dillinger "Public Enemy Number One" because the law Cummings referred to was dubbed informally the "Public Enemy Bill." Although the attorney general's proclamation avoided the phrase "dead or alive," Cummings made it clear that he favored saving the cost of a trial for John Dillinger.[9]

The law authorizing large bounties was only the beginning; Congress quickly passed the full New Deal on Crime. "There will be no relenting," declared Roosevelt on signing the legislation, and he chided citizens who tolerated known criminals, who winked at public officials corrupted by gangsters, or who romanticized crime. As Congress and the Roosevelt administration crafted these measures, Dillinger's depredations were never far from their minds. "The name of John Dillinger, Middle Western desperado," the New York *Times* declared, "rang through the House chamber time and again today during debate on the crime bills." Endorsing the new legislation, the editors of the Washington *Times* titled their article "Lawmaker Dillinger."[10]

Ironically Dillinger was all but invisible during the two months between Little Bohemia and the attorney general's edict. The one bank robbery he did commit, assisted by Homer Van Meter, in Fostoria, Ohio, was not attributed to him with certainty until weeks later. But his absence from the public stage only made his reputation grow. On the very same day that the Chicago *Tribune* carried the attorney general's statement, the newspaper also ran an enormous article comparing Dillinger with Jesse James, the "most notorious of all in American crime annals."[11]

As POLICE HUNTED HIM, stories appeared that Dillinger and his men were living in dungeons, mines, or caves; some reports had him holed up in the country; some put him back in Chicago. One story claimed he had stowed away on the ocean liner *Duchess of York*; when the ship landed near Glasgow, Scottish authorities boarded and searched her. Another report had him convalescing from life-threatening wounds at a ranch near Branson, Missouri; sixty state and federal agents found nothing when they raided the place. Officials worried that Dillinger would flee the country, so police added extra security at airports.[12]

Daily the newspapers printed stories large and small: Dillinger had been seen, Dillinger had not been seen, the trail was hot, the trail was cold, Dillinger died, Dillinger lived. The speculation grew pretty wild: Dillinger's gang disarmed a squadron of suburban police, Dillinger machine-gunned carloads of officers, Dillinger planned to kidnap the governor of Ohio and exchange him for Makley, Pierpont, and Clark. *Time* magazine, which earlier had given Dillinger only passing notice, devoted four full pages to Little Bohemia and its aftermath, declaring that the story "held the Midwest enthralled" with its "unmatched heights of dare-devil ruthlessness." *Time* included three pages of photographs, of Dillinger, his father, his accomplices, the Wisconsin lodge, the dogs that barked, the gang's weaponry, the molls whom police arrested, Billie Frechette, and a map labeled "Dillinger Land" that traced his path through the Great Lakes states since he had broken out of Crown Point.[13]

Newspapers and newsreels continued to focus on the fortitude of the men who tracked the outlaws, such as Sergeant Frank Reynolds, the earnest new straight-shooting leader of Chicago's "Dillinger Squad" (which was redeployed to capture the Hoosier bandit after he broke out of Crown Point), and Joseph B. Keenan, the single-minded assistant attorney general who headed the federal government's legal efforts. Nonetheless many writers could not resist the increasingly absurd quality of the Dillinger story. As Robert Forsythe said in the radical journal *New Masses*, even those crying for vengeance sometimes found it hard to keep a straight face. The Keystone Kops' inability to guard a single prisoner, the farce at Little Bohemia, the family reunion in Mooresville—where, Forsythe claimed, Dillinger openly walked around town, had his car lubed, got a haircut, and exchanged pleasantries with townsfolk—all were surreal. Beneath the absurdity, Forsythe argued, the story was deeply serious: Dillinger's ruthlessness and his pursuers' incompetence were part and parcel of the larger

John Wilson Dillinger and Mary Ellen "Mollie" Dillinger. They married in 1887 and moved to Indianapolis, where their children Audrey and Johnnie were born. (Note: unless otherwise identified, photos are Courtesy John Dillinger Museum.)

J. W. Dillinger's grocery store in the Brightwood section of Indianapolis.

Audrey and Johnnie.

John Dillinger,
about age ten, on a
visit to the country.

The Dillinger farm house in Mooresville, where the family moved when Johnnie was in his teens.

John Dillinger (far left) enlisted in the Navy in 1923 but soon went AWOL.

Johnnie was quite a good local baseball player (standing, second from right). The man seated first from left is umpire Ed Singleton, Dillinger's first partner in crime.

Old John Dillinger
at the plow.

Dillinger and Mary Longnacker at the Century of Progress World's Fair in Chicago, July, 1933.

Evelyn "Billie" Frechette, the "Indian Beauty," as newspapers called her. She left Wisconsin for Chicago, where she met Dillinger in October, 1933. By all accounts, they were very much in love.

A Chicago policeman points out bullet holes on Dillinger's abandoned Essex Terraplane after a high-speed chase on Irving Park Road in November 15, 1933.

WANTED

Bank Robbery - Escape - Murder

$5000.00 REWARD

JOHN DILLINGER
DEAD OR ALIVE

May be Accompanied By One or More of The Following Men

HARRY PIERPONT   JOHN HAMILTON
HOMER VAN METER   CHARLES MARKLEY

Dillinger is 5'11", 170 lbs., 31 Years Old   Notify Your Local Police or FBI

The most wanted man in America. Courtesy Chicago History Museum.

The Dillinger gang in court after their capture in Tucson, Arizona.

Dillinger on his way back to Indiana to stand trial for murder, January 30, 1934.

Sheriff Lillian Holley, Prosecutor Robert Estill, and their prisoner, Crown Point, Indiana.

The escape from the Lake County jail, March 3, 1934.

John Dillinger, back home in Mooresville, Indiana, for Sunday dinner, April 8, 1934. Bass Photo Company Collection, Indiana Historical Society.

Little Bohemia Lodge, near Rhinelander, Wisconsin, scene of a bloody shootout with the FBI, April 22–23, 1934.

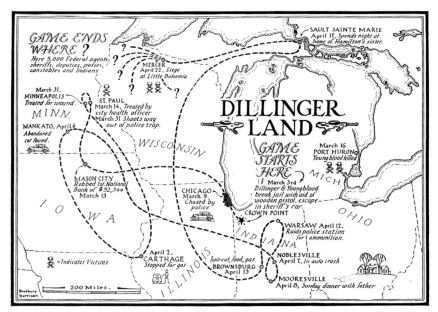

Time magazine gave several pages to the Dillinger story in its May 7, 1934, issue, including this map of a game the editors called "Dillinger Land." Note that the game ended in mid-sentence; the outcome was anybody's guess.

The cover of *True Detective Mysteries*, June 1934. Of course Makley, Clark, and Pierpont had been in custody since January, but Dillinger remained at large.

FBI Director J. Edgar Hoover.

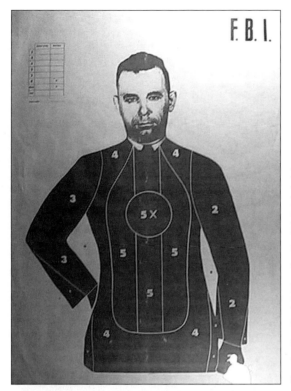

Left: Bringing down John Dillinger, Public Enemy Number One, became an obsession of the FBI. His likeness was used for target practice. Below: Melvin Purvis took advantage of his reputation as a heroic G-man in unexpected commercial opportunities.

Sergeant Martin
Zarkovich.

Anna Sage,
the "Woman in Red."

Artist's sketch of the Biograph shooting, July 22, 1934. Courtesy Chicago History Museum.

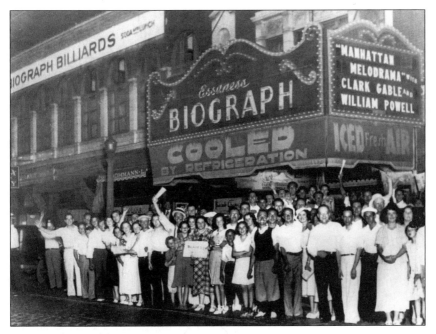

Crowds on Lincoln Avenue, Chicago, shortly after Dillinger's death.

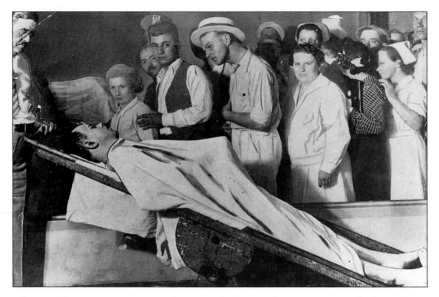

Thousands came to view Dillinger's body in the morgue, including these two Chicago show girls. Top: Courtesy John Dillinger Museum; bottom: Courtesy *New York Daily News*.

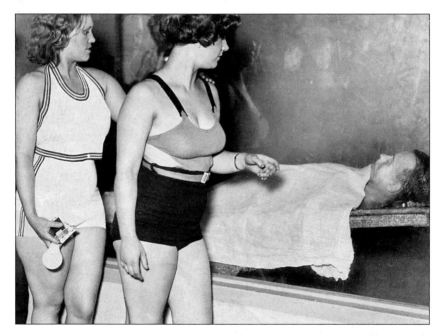

moral corruption of capitalism, a corruption made obvious to all by the economic collapse.[14]

Ideology aside, writers found it difficult to resist the story's sheer zaniness. The *Literary Digest* argued that Dillinger must have magical powers, *Time* magazine said he leaped through the Midwest like a demented Indian's ghost, the *New Yorker* described in mock fear the danger of meeting Dillinger on Fifty-second Street. Clearly the story had penetrated the culture pretty deeply when Kansas peace officers took target practice at Dillinger's image; when high school kids in Barberton, Ohio, put on a play about him and children in Sheboygan, Wisconsin, impersonated the Dillinger gang in the May Day parade; when a farmer in Henderson, North Carolina, named his mule for the outlaw; when a traveling carnival displayed "the car that John Dillinger used"; and when a theater company offered Dillinger Senior the chance to go on stage and talk about his son.[15]

Ordinary citizens took the story seriously enough to send letters to their public officials. Many offered advice on how to capture the outlaw. Writing from his home in Poughkeepsie, New York, James Crouch suggested to President Roosevelt that federal troops comb the Indiana countryside to find Dillinger, much as the Marines did recently in Nicaragua in search of the rebel leader Sandino. F. E. Frisbie of Milanville, Pennsylvania, declared that God had revealed a plan to him that would bring Dillinger in within a month, and for just five thousand dollars he would put it into effect (details were not included). A. E. Zeiske from Dallas suggested that law enforcement agencies needed properly armed "Autogiros" (helicopters) that his company just happened to sell. Eva Dumbeck of Houston offered her version of what was a very popular idea: because Dillinger was close to his family, kidnap one of them to lure the fugitive in. E. H. McColloch agreed: "Slap the old rooster [John Senior] in jail. . . . Let it be known far and wide that the authorities are putting the old boy through a third degree." When Dillinger breaks in to save his father, "that's where a life-size ambush would come in—anything from machine guns up to rapid-fire one-pounders; and the Lord have mercy on their souls." "Cherchez le femme!" declared an anonymous writer in a similar vein; let Billie Frechette "escape" and lead the feds to Dillinger. O. W. Johnson of Geneva, Ohio, assured the attorney general that a reward of one hundred thousand dollars for anyone who brought in Dillinger's body would get the job done, and Johnson added that the offer could be a standing one as each new thug rose to the position of "public enemy number one." Glenn Russelo of Leamington, Ontario, described Dillinger's hideout to the Justice Department in detail: a "dirty squatty shack" full of foreigners, about eight miles south of St. Paul, just waiting to be taken. Russelo knew this for a fact; he had dreamed of it, vividly and repeatedly.[16]

Other letters were more sympathetic. One man wrote to the attorney general's office that Dillinger was just smarter than his pursuers, and because he killed only when forced to they should simply let him be, thereby saving themselves further humiliation and bloodshed. Another correspondent, who identified himself as a Greek immigrant, described the approach to criminals in his homeland: "We do not destroy the brave; we make them useful for our fatherland." Dillinger, he argued, successfully evaded whole armies of sheriffs. Such a man would make an unrivaled general or an outstanding police officer; all that was needed was Dillinger's word of honor that he would "return to the straight road, and would remain worthy to be called an American." Another man suggested that the government invite Dillinger, with his inside knowledge, to head an anticrime organization. Edgar Clark of New York City wrote to the president that Dillinger should be treated with the spirit of Christian forgiveness, and he implored Roosevelt to recognize the outlaw as a "rugged individualist" who simply never had the advantages of wealth or influence. Josephine Aunt of Chesterton, Indiana, asked Roosevelt how a man like Dillinger knew which banks had lots of money. She intimated that the real blame should fall on those bankers who, because they were insured, did not mind being robbed and might even have encouraged it.[17]

Class divisions came out often in the letters. Many who wrote to Washington vented their anger at hard times, at the gap between rich and poor, and sympathy for Dillinger became one way to express such feelings. A citizen from Colorado explained to Attorney General Cummings why so many Americans applauded the outlaw: "There are millions of good people that are starving in this country that are living like rats." When a man like Dillinger had the guts to take matters into his own hands, it was all right with them. If folks had jobs and could feed themselves, he added, if government protected citizens from the banks that preyed on them, then they would feel like they were part of the country and wouldn't make heroes of men like

Dillinger. But if hard times continued, he warned, only bullets would keep people in line.[18]

Mrs. W. B. Grant of Butler, Tennessee, agreed. Addressing the first lady, Eleanor Roosevelt, Grant declared that John Dillinger was a great man, that he deserved a fair trial, that he was made an outlaw by an unjust legal system. She claimed to have met Dillinger and his gang in passing and found them to be good men: "If he holds up a bank what of it? Hasn't most of the bankers them selves been crooked, that is how they became wealthy, by cheating the honest man." Grant believed the rich had separated themselves from the poor and that their selfishness forced good people like Dillinger into bank robbery and other crimes. The law, she declared, was "filthy" for it deprived men of a fair chance in life. She added that great men like Jesus and John the Baptist were persecuted in previous eras. "I believe that John Dillinger is a man of such type, and I believe he should be given a fair trial in this, the Age of the 'New Deal.'"[19]

The theme of rich men robbing the poor was repeated again and again. Joseph Edwards wrote Roosevelt that Dillinger robbed banks from the outside, but that thousands of his fellow Chicagoans were starving because of the bankers who robbed them from the inside. Franklin Davis, a real estate man from Houston, suggested that the way out of the Depression was to develop land into farms for poor families. He added that it was wrong to castigate the John Dillingers and Clyde Barrows of the world, men of intelligence and aspiration who found every door of opportunity shut in their faces. In fact, Davis suggested that Dillinger could lead a settlement of convicts onto their own land, where the opportunity to farm and build homes would reform them into citizens.[20]

W. Guyer Fisher of Redlands, California, wrote that America's poor were more concerned with businessmen who "fleeced the rank and file out of . . . their hard earned cash" than all of the John Dillingers in the world. Fisher deplored the "wholesale thieves that use a sharp pencil" to rob a bank or steal a public utility. Businessmen, not gangsters, turned solid citizens into paupers. Other writers echoed this sentiment. One man asked the president point blank how Americans could remain loyal "when the government only prosecutes the poor and leaves the rich alone." He wished Roosevelt luck in finding Dillinger and asked when the feds would go after "the real racketeers," J. P. Morgan and Andrew Mellon. "A Citizen and a Tax Payer" agreed and urged the Justice Department to forget the "small rollers" like Dillinger and go after the "big ones," the "legalized robbers" who pull their jobs "Under Cover of the 'Law.'"[21]

Class divisions manifested themselves in another way as well. All of the newspaper stories about Mooresville and all of the images on newsreels of Old John Dillinger spoke to a Middle American sensibility born of class. "Dillinger Family Seeks Peace at Farm While Storm Whirls about Desperado," reported the Indianapolis *Star*, and below that headline were photographs of the modest Dillinger home, including one of the old man with his daughter Frances doing the dishes in their simple kitchen. By the spring of 1934 the image of the Dillinger household was firmly fixed in people's minds: Johnnie's sisters attending church, the simple meals prepared by their father, the girls pitching in with the household chores, the old man at his plow. Even back in April, when the people of Mooresville petitioned for a pardon for their native son, they contrasted Johnnie's acts with the criminality of banks "which have robbed our citizens without any effort being made to punish the perpetrators." Such language was always implicit when Dillinger Senior spoke of justice for his son. As late as June, Old John suggested that Johnnie might turn himself in if the courts promised him a "square deal," the assumption being that fairness was to be bargained for, not assumed.[22]

Ironically, several Indiana officials agreed with the Dillinger family and with Mooresville's citizens who argued that the criminal justice system had created John Dillinger. At the Central States Parole Conference, meeting on the grounds of the Century of Progress World's Fair in Chicago, Indiana attorney general Phillip Lutz and Wayne Coy, secretary to Governor Paul McNutt, both declared that John Dillinger became a public menace because of the inhumane treatment he received after he pled guilty in 1924. "There does not seem to be any escape from the fact that the state of Indiana made John Dillinger the public enemy No. 1 he is today," Coy told the delegates.[23]

JOHN DILLINGER EMBRACED the criminal stardom bestowed by the media and spent hours poring over the latest newspaper coverage of his activities. One can only imagine the giddy rush he must have felt. After a reasonably normal youth, then a feckless young adulthood, came nine years of incarceration—of iron bars, bullying guards, petty infractions, solitary confinement, mind-deadening labor, jailhouse politics, and, above all, boredom. Prison denied him his manhood, his will to independence, his sense of self. Now, in a few short months, he was famous. The sociologist Jack Katz refers to "the seductions of crime," by which he means the allure of life on the edge. According to Katz, armed stickups are not just instrumental activities, designed to garner cash. Men are attracted to this sort of crime for the sheer rush it provides.[24]

There is an old joke, sometimes attributed to Dillinger but more accurately to his contemporary Willie Sutton, in which the thief responds to the question "Why do you rob banks?" with "Because that's where the money is." Bank heists *are* about money, but they are also about glamour, excitement, danger, and camaraderie—about the sheer sexiness of risk taking. In his autobiography Sutton himself gave a fuller reason for why he robbed banks: "Because I enjoyed it. I loved it. I was more alive when I was inside a bank, robbing it, than at any other time in my life." He added, "During the planning of a robbery, you are in a constant state of excitement. From the time you disarm the guard to the time you enter the vault, all of your juices are flowing." And on top of the high-stakes thrills and the risk-filled life, Dillinger got to see it all magnified on the screen and in the press, and then to watch millions of awed spectators watching him.[25]

The problem was that the knife-edged dance with death sometimes ended in, well, death. Notoriety made life dangerous for the Dillinger gang. Red Hamilton's luck ran out immediately after Little Bohemia. He was seriously wounded in the East Chicago robbery, and now one of the bullets that pierced the backseat of their Ford as he and Dillinger and Van Meter fled toward St. Paul drove into his intestines. Dillinger and Van Meter eluded the police, exchanged their bullet-riddled car for a fresh one, lifted Hamilton into the new vehicle, and headed toward Chicago. They bandaged their friend as best they could, but he was bleeding heavily and writhing in pain. By the time Dillinger and Van Meter hooked up with underworld figures in Cicero and got Hamilton to a safe house in the town of Aurora, he was in his death throes. They dug a grave in a quarry near town, laid Hamilton down, and poured cans of lye over his face and hands to efface his identity. "Red, old pal," Dillinger allegedly said to his dead friend, "I hate to do this, but I know you'd do the same for me."[26]

It was not only Hamilton. The entire Dillinger gang from the Michigan City breakout was gone. Back in March, after Crown Point, there had been much talk of Dillinger rescuing Pierpont, Makley, and Clark. One news story even had him preparing his pals by slipping them religious pamphlets with key passages underlined: "Have no fear"; "Believe also in me"; "I will come again and receive you unto myself; that where I am there shall ye be also." In response to the threat of a breakout, the State of Ohio flooded the streets surrounding Lima's courthouse with national guardsmen, the county provided a twenty-four-hour guard of deputies, and authorities built a wooden fence around the jail with strategically placed machine-gun nests. When a rumor spread that Dillinger intended to kidnap Ohio governor White, national guardsmen patrolled the governor's mansion in Columbus. With such security there was no chance that Dillinger might ride to the rescue, and through the month of March the trials of the three ground on. Dillinger supplied money to attorney Jessie Levy, but despite her best efforts assembling the case, challenging procedures, and appealing decisions, the three were found guilty. Now Pierpont and Makley waited to die in Ohio's electric chair and Clark began serving a life sentence.[27]

Nor was there any possibility of rescuing Billie from St. Paul; the best Dillinger could do was to keep smuggling money for her defense. According to one story, Dillinger surprised Louis Piquett in the Twin Cities: "As [Piquett] left the courthouse he heard his name called softly by a voice in a waiting automobile. He turned, and there was Dillinger sitting at the wheel of the car and grinning broadly." Dillinger nonchalantly told Piquett that he wanted to see how the trial was coming along. Piquett responded that it was going to be tough for Billie to win this one, but Dillinger assured him that he and the other attorneys would get paid either way. Dillinger left as cool as he came, saying, "Well, so long, counsel. See you in Chicago." Late in May the court found Billie guilty and sentenced her to two years in federal prison and a thousand-dollar fine. Dr. Clayton May, who had treated Dillinger's wounds after the St. Paul shoot-out, received a similar sentence.[28]

During the month following Little Bohemia, outlaw life turned pretty grubby. For one thing, Dillinger needed money to pay off those who helped him hide, for attorney's fees, for his family, and for friends in need, such as Red Hamilton's old girlfriend, Pat Cherrington.

Robberies all over the country were being attributed to Dillinger, though he pulled only one during the month. On May 2 he and Van Meter robbed the First National Bank of Fostoria, Ohio, just south of Toledo, of seventeen thousand dollars. They wounded five people, including a policeman, and badly frightened some hostages but got away cleanly. Although they now had money to throw around it did not buy them much pleasure or peace-of-mind. For a few weeks they lived in an abandoned shack on the outskirts of East Chicago, then in a red panel truck with a mattress in the back. They drove the back roads of Indiana by day and pulled over to secluded spots at night. They probably paid East Chicago officials handsomely for the privilege of living so poorly. Arthur O'Leary, Piquett's assistant, visited them a few times, bringing cold medicine when Dillinger was sick, passing notes from Billie, promising Dillinger that his replies would make it to his beloved's hands.[29]

On May 24, right after Billie's conviction and the day following the ambush and killing of Bonnie and Clyde on a secluded road near Shreveport, Louisiana, two East Chicago policemen were murdered on the Gary highway. Plainclothes detectives Martin O'Brien and Lloyd Mulvihill drove a clearly marked police car into the country. Witnesses later reported seeing four suspicious men in a sedan near their vehicle. The Chicago *Tribune* easily made the leap: "While there was no direct evidence that the Dillinger gang was responsible for the killings . . . circumstantial evidence, and the manner in which the victims were machine-gunned without warning, and without a chance to draw their weapons, smacked of the methods of America's most notorious outlaw." The Indianapolis *News* made the connection even tighter, noting that Mulvihill would have been a star witness against Dillinger for the slaying of Officer William O'Malley, leaving the clear impression that the murders were premeditated. Other newspaper headlines leaped to the same conclusion: "Dillinger Suspected"; "Dillinger Sought"; "Slain in Dillinger Style."[30]

The larger story involved corruption that split the East Chicago Police Department wide open. Arthur O'Leary later claimed that Dillinger confessed to him that the two cops had pulled over his red panel truck and Homer Van Meter, rather than risk arrest, simply opened fire from the back of the cab. Dillinger expressed remorse for the killings but implied that the two officers were not there by accident. In fact O'Leary claimed that Dillinger told him that O'Brien and Mulvihill knew too much about the Crown Point breakout and about how other East Chicago policemen were taking bribes to hide the fugitives, so the two were "put on the spot" on that swampy midnight road. One version of the story that circulated months later made a fellow officer, Martin Zarkovich, the trigger man. Dillinger told O'Leary that Zarkovich knew exactly who was lurking out on the road and coldly had sent the officers to their deaths. Zarkovich, it turns out, had spent a lot of time at Crown Point while Dillinger was an inmate there—exactly why remains unclear—and he would show up again at the end of the Dillinger saga on a steamy July night in Chicago.[31]

Indiana back roads clearly were no longer safe for the fugitives, so Dillinger and Van Meter decided to risk the city once again. They drove to Wauconda, north of Chicago, where they hooked up with Baby Face Nelson and Tommy Carroll. Nelson had maintained contacts with Louis Cernocky, and with a fence named Jimmy Murray, who ran a place called the Rain-Bo Inn. Murray briefly rented a room to Dillinger and Van Meter, but before the end of May they found their way to Jimmy Probasco's seedy North Side house. Probasco was a friend of Piquett's and, like most of the attorney's circle, was not a model of probity. He had been a teamster and a boxer, then made his living fencing stolen goods, selling bootleg liquor, and other small-time scams. His underworld reputation was based not on the scale of his activities but on his luck at avoiding the law; no charge against him had ever stuck. Probasco apparently drank excessively, though this did not stop him from bargaining hard with Dillinger and Van Meter; they paid sixty dollars a night to share a room.[32]

Dillinger continued to toy with the idea of changing his face. Newspapers and the pulp press had speculated in recent years that the art of plastic surgery, developed in part to deal with the carnage of World War I, might allow criminals to alter their appearance. Dillinger pestered O'Leary and Piquett about it, and finally they made the arrangements. Piquett introduced him to Wilhelm Loeser, a middle-aged German émigré trained in American universities, who had been in and out of trouble with the law for drug abuse. Loeser then violated his parole when he traveled to Mexico to obtain a divorce from his wife, after which he practiced under the name "Dr. Ralph Robeind." Loeser agreed to perform plastic surgery on Dillinger, assisted by Dr. Harold Cassidy, a much younger man with legal difficulties of his own; he had been caught perjuring himself during a robbery trial and also performing abortions. Loeser and Cassidy needed the money, and the price for reconfiguring Dillinger's face was five thousand dollars.[33]

O'Leary brought the doctors to Dillinger the night after he moved into Probasco's house. Loeser asked Dillinger what he had eaten that day; toast and grapefruit in the morning, the outlaw replied. In fact, Dillinger had just finished a heavy meal but did not want to delay the surgery. His eagerness was balanced by Van Meter's caution, who refused an operation until he saw how Dillinger's came out. Dillinger lay down on a cot. Cassidy dripped ether into a towel and placed it over his face. When the patient failed to lose consciousness, Cassidy dumped the whole can of ether onto the towel. Within moments Dillinger stopped breathing and turned blue. Cassidy began screaming and Loeser came in from scrubbing up and began to pound his patient's chest. Finally Dillinger began breathing again. The doctors proceeded with the surgery.[34]

The operation was a bloody mess; several times Dillinger came out of anesthesia vomiting. Loeser cut away three moles, tightened the skin on Dillinger's face, built up his nose, and filled in his chin dimple. Dillinger awakened an hour after the doctor finished and said he felt all right. Two days later Loeser removed the bandages. The surgery did not fully transform Dillinger's visage; even with the puffiness and scarring, one of America's most recognizable faces was still familiar. Nonetheless Dillinger said he was pleased with the results, and the job was good enough that Van Meter anted up five thousand dollars too. Unlike Dillinger the morose Van Meter was not happy with Loeser's work and grumbled for days about retribution. If the pain from surgery was not enough, Loeser also effaced the two men's fingerprints, first by cutting away the epidermis, then treating their raw fingertips with alternate applications of hydrochloric acid and a strong alkali solution, then finally scraping away any remaining ridges. Neither man could use his hands for days afterward.[35]

These attempts at permanent disguise came as the noose continued to tighten around the Dillinger gang. Even before Loeser had removed all of his patients' bandages, sisters Opal Long and Pat Cherrington, Harry Copeland's and Charles Makley's girlfriends, were picked up by the police when they tried to retrieve some stolen jewelry from a safe-deposit box. On June 7 word arrived that Tommy Carroll was dead. Described in the newspapers as the "ace machine gunner" and the "hard-boiled Dillinger Gang's . . . most feared killer," Carroll had several outstanding warrants for his arrest, including one for murdering FBI Agent W. Carter Baum. When a mechanic in Waterloo, Iowa, working on Carroll's car noticed a machine gun on the backseat, he called the police, who realized they were dealing with a fugitive. The cops surrounded Carroll when he came to pick up his car. He died in the hospital, but not, newspapers said, before federal officer O. H. Dewey had asked him for Dillinger's whereabouts. Carroll allegedly replied that he hid his boss, and the papers speculated that meant he had buried Dillinger's body in a secret place.[36]

Carroll had seven hundred dollars in his pocket, and before he died asked the police to give it to his companion, Jean Crompton. "Be sure the little girl gets it," he told them. "She doesn't know what its all about." Twenty-two-year-old Crompton, who claimed to have just married Carroll, was not so innocent; she was also known as Jean Delaney from Aberdeen, South Dakota, one of the three women arrested when the feds stormed Little Bohemia. One report claimed that Crompton's composure was ruffled only when Carroll's real wife called from St. Paul. The feds grilled Crompton but she gave them nothing; they hauled her back to the grand jury in Madison for violating her probation, and she was sentenced to a year in the federal women's prison in West Virginia.[37]

Carroll's death was yet another reminder of the dangers of life on the lam, so with their scars still obvious Dillinger and Van Meter stayed close to home—at first. Dillinger read newspapers and magazines; Van Meter listened to the police radio; both played cards with Arthur O'Leary and Jimmy Probasco. Perhaps because time weighed heavily on their hands, or maybe because they felt fate closing in, Dillinger and Van Meter began to speak of people they needed to "take care of": the cops in Waterloo who shot Tommy Carroll; Agent Harold Reinecke, who had mistreated Billie just after her arrest; Art McGinnis, who fingered Dillinger months before; Melvin Purvis, their chief pursuer in the FBI. O'Leary and Louis Piquett later claimed that they dissuaded Dillinger from going on a rampage against his enemies. They told this story as they faced jail time for harboring the fugitive, hence they had good reason to make themselves appear to have been moderating influences. It is certainly possible that Dillinger thought about revenge, but it seems somewhat out of character. Bank robbers expect to shoot and be shot, but there is no real evidence that he developed any taste for blood in his year of freedom. Unlike Baby Face Nelson, who always felt challenged and was ready to fire away, Dillinger enjoyed his image as a cool customer who preferred dancing through danger to blasting his way out of it. If O'Leary and Piquett talked Dillinger out of going after his enemies, it probably took little effort.[38]

As far as the public was concerned, however, Dillinger had disappeared. The Little Bohemia affair happened at the end of April, and there had been little hard news about him for two months. There were the usual fugitive sightings: an unemployed cabbie told reporters that he bummed a cigarette from the outlaw in Northfield, Minnesota; a woman from Baraboo, Wisconsin, had the feds swarming all over her town in pursuit of, as it turned out, a traveling salesman Dillinger-look-alike from Chicago; and a retired private detective from Canton, Ohio, claimed that he saw Dillinger at the local diner, and he asked the attorney general's office for permission to make a citizen's arrest if the outlaw appeared again. But with no confirmed bank robberies, shoot-outs, or jailbreaks, the speculation that he had died fleeing Wisconsin seemed a real possibility. Even one of the gang's hangers-on, Pat Riley, told the feds he thought Dillinger was dead.[39]

Then, toward the end of June, a small notice appeared in the Maywood, Indiana, newspaper, one that got reprinted all over the country: "Birthday greetings to my darling brother, John Dillinger, on his 31st birthday. Wherever he may be, I hope he reads this message." Sister Audrey also told a reporter that the family had heard from John and that he was well. She added that she did not know where he was hiding, but she was sure he wouldn't surrender. A couple of days later Dillinger Senior confirmed that his son was still alive. He showed members of the press a letter from Chicago that he had received just three weeks before: "Dad, I got here all right and find I still have some friends who will not sell me out. Would liked to have stayed longer at home. . . . I enjoyed seeing you and the girls so much. I have been over lots of country, but home always looks good to me. Tell that little Frances . . . to keep smiling. This sure keeps a fellow moving. I will be leaving soon and you will not need [to] worry any more. Tell the girls hello. Hope everybody is well—Johnnie." It is such a poignant yet elusive little note: Johnnie's longings for home and family, his road-weariness, his suggestion that someone had tried to betray him, the hint that he was about to go somewhere far away where he would be safe. Neither Audrey nor John Senior gave any further details to the feds or to reporters; if they knew anything more about Johnnie, they weren't saying.[40]

As his incisions healed and the summer approached, Dillinger stepped out more and more. Instead of seeking revenge he took his new face, adorned with glasses, a mustache, and his hair dyed black, and embarked on some serious fun. Van Meter advised keeping a low profile, especially as that profile still showed fresh scars. Besides, the attorney general's newly issued offer of up to ten thousand dollars for America's "Public Enemy Number One"—roughly five times what an average family earned during an entire year in the middle of the Depression—was an enormous incentive. Dillinger made light of the danger, joking that he was worth twice the money offered for Baby Face Nelson and that Van Meter did not even rate a federal reward. He recklessly began to hang out at Wrigley Field by day, where the Cubs were well into a promising season, and by night at cabarets and houses of prostitution. He loved to dance, and he showed up at black-and-tans, jazz clubs considered disreputable because of their racially mixed clientele and their lascivious music.[41]

On June 21 he spent his thirty-first birthday with a new girlfriend, Polly Hamilton. She was born Rita Keele, and her husband, a Gary, Indiana, policeman, had divorced her just a few months earlier amid accusations of infidelity. Polly worked in an uptown sandwich shop, moonlighted in less respectable ways, and bore a striking resemblance to Billie Frechette. They went to the French Casino Night Club, and during the coming month Johnnie and Polly, sometimes accompanied by Van Meter and his girlfriend, Marie Conforti, were seen together in restaurants, bars, and movies. They even took in the wonders of the coming age of prosperity and technology at Chicago's Century of Progress World's Fair, where Johnnie had taken Mary Longnaker almost exactly a year before.[42]

There was also work to do. Dillinger, Van Meter, Baby Face Nelson, and one or two others cased some banks and got together several times at an abandoned schoolhouse in the northwest suburbs to discuss their next job. Testimony taken by the FBI months later indicated that Nelson, who expressed the opinion that Marie Conforti was a security risk and that Dillinger was living too openly, almost ended up in a shooting match with Van Meter. Despite the tension the gang made some decisions. For a while they talked seriously about the banks in Louis Piquett's old hometown, Plattesville, Wisconsin, but he let it be known that if they were serious they could look elsewhere for legal counsel. They settled on the Merchant's National Bank in South Bend, Indiana. This was to be the Dillinger gang's last bank job, and it was their most bloody and chaotic.[43]

"Dillinger Raiders Kill One, Injure Four in Bank Foray," screamed the headline in the Reno *Evening Gazette*. "Dillinger Head of Fatal Bank Raid," the Chicago *Tribune* echoed. Reports were contradictory. Some eyewitnesses positively identified Dillinger, others denied that he was there. Even the number of participants was uncertain, and some stories had the Oklahoma outlaw Pretty Boy Floyd, who had never been associated with the Dillinger gang before, joining in. We know that Dillinger, Van Meter, Nelson, and one, probably two others drove a brown Hudson sedan with Ohio plates into town a little before noon on Saturday, June 30. The street was filled with cars and passersby as Van Meter and Nelson took up positions outside the bank. Dillinger led the others in, announced that a holdup was in progress, and began clearing cash from the tellers' cages. Some of the two dozen customers held their hands aloft, some dropped to the ground, others hid themselves in back rooms. One of the robbers pumped a burst of machine-gun bullets into the ceiling. The noise alerted a traffic cop, Howard Wagner, who left his post and came toward the bank. Van Meter drew a bead and fired; Wagner fell backward, mortally wounded. Citizens out on the street screamed, panicked, and ran for cover. A local jeweler, Harry Berg, got a shot off at Nelson, hitting him squarely in the chest, right in the middle of his bulletproof vest. Berg managed to scamper back into his store before Nelson recovered and raked the street with machine-gun fire, badly wounding two bystanders.[44]

Van Meter took half a dozen hostages, and as three cops approached him, he fired through this cordon, scattering the police behind parked cars. Just then Dillinger and another unidentified robber came out of the bank, carrying nearly thirty thousand dollars and surrounded by their own cluster of hostages. As the bandits edged toward their car, the police began firing, wounding two of the hostages. Nelson returned with a long fusillade of his own, but the cops kept firing, and Van Meter took a bullet in the head. Dillinger came out from behind his hostages, grabbed his friend under the armpits, and dragged him into the car. They all sped away, the police riddling the vehicle with buckshot and rifle fire as it went. Van Meter was bleeding profusely, but what looked at first like a mortal wound turned out not to be life-threatening. Four farm boys reported several hours later seeing the men abandon their Hudson near Goodland, Indiana, and get into another waiting car.[45]

The gang made it back to the schoolhouse, three or four hours away, and that night slipped back into the city, taking refuge in Jimmie Probasco's house. The next day, when it was clear that Van Meter would be all right, the mood relaxed, and Dillinger regaled O'Leary, Piquett, and Probasco with stories of the robbery. The bandits even talked about going back to South Bend to get the "little jew"—Berg, the jeweler—who fired on them. But their cockiness hid the fact that they were lucky to be alive; a good hundred rounds were fired during the siege. The police had been surprisingly willing to shoot despite the hostages, and their presence on the roads radiating out of Chicago was larger than ever.[46]

Nonetheless, with the intoxicant of a successful heist, money in his pocket, and Chicago beckoning, Dillinger was more ready than ever for some fun. Out on the west edge of town, away from Lake Michigan and far from the city's nightlife, Jimmy Probasco's house grew increasingly claustrophobic. Dillinger had been at Probasco's for a month, longer than anywhere since prison, and now he sought new quarters. His friend Anna Sage, a Romanian immigrant formerly known as Ana Kumpanis, then Ana Chiolek when she married Mike Chiolek in 1917, then finally the Anglicized Anna Sage with a brief marriage to one Alexander Sage, was a prostitute turned brothel keeper who offered Dillinger a room in her North Side apartment house. He moved into 2420 Halstead Street on July 4. Sage even gave him a locked closet where he kept his machine guns, bulletproof vests, and other tools of his trade.[47]

Dillinger's main incentive for moving was no doubt Polly Hamilton, the twenty-six-year-old uptown waitress and part-time hustler also living at Sage's place. Later denials to the contrary, Anna had introduced the two. For the next three weeks Polly and Johnnie were constantly in each other's company. Dillinger, Hamilton later claimed, told her that his name was Jimmy Livingston and that he was a clerk at the Board of Trade; she said she met him at a nightclub, then brought him around to meet Sage, and that she never knew his real identity. In the spirit of plausible deniability Anna Sage told the FBI a similar story, claiming that she first met Dillinger just days before his death. In fact she was part of a network of underworld contacts going back to East Chicago; some writers have even speculated that Dillinger knew her before being sent to prison in 1924.[48]

Homer Van Meter was right: his partner was getting sloppy, and not only because he appeared in public too much. "I've got no use for that whole East Chicago bunch," Van Meter allegedly told Dillinger; "You're going to get yourself killed." Sage should have made Dillinger uneasy, for he must have known that her crowd, the same corrupt pack that probably helped him out of Crown Point, including prominent Lake County underworld figures like Hymie Cohen and Jimmie Regan, would just as quickly sell him out. They had a lot to fear from Dillinger if, once in custody, he decided to bargain for clemency. Even Sage had plenty of baggage. She had worked her way up from a single mother who supported herself as a waitress and part-time prostitute in East Chicago to a brothel owner in some of the toughest towns along the industrialized lakefront in northeast Indiana, and now on the North Side of Chicago.[49]

Payoffs were routine in Sage's line of work, and police and politicians in East Chicago and Gary had always managed to fix her legal troubles before. But in 1933 Indiana's new McNutt administration was less willing than its predecessors to pardon the likes of Anna Sage. When she was arrested yet again for practicing her trade, the charges against her stuck, and worse, officials turned her case over to the federal government. On July 12, 1934, a week after Dillinger moved in, Sage received final notice from the U.S. Immigration Service that her appeals to remain in the country had been turned down and a warrant issued for her deportation. Helping the feds bring down Public Enemy Number One, she reasoned, might well save her from being shipped back to Romania.[50]

If nothing else, Sage's friendship with East Chicago detective Martin Zarkovich should have been a big red flag for Dillinger. For the flamboyant Zarkovich, Sage's erstwhile lover and protector, whose amorous attentions were raised by her first husband in their divorce proceedings, the reward money offered by the feds was reason enough to betray Dillinger. Zarkovich had been brought up on corruption charges three times during the 1920s; money spoke eloquently to one for whom brokering daily transactions between politicians, prosecutors, and the underworld was a way of life. But if, as many researchers have suggested, the detective was also involved in arranging Dillinger's breakout from Crown Point (he showed up at the prison several times, then became deeply involved in the escape investigation—some have even speculated that Zarkovich arranged the whole wooden gun episode), or in securing Dillinger places to hide after Little Bohemia, or in sending officers Mulvihill and O'Brien to their deaths in late May because they knew too much about him, then Zarkovich had all the more reason to see Dillinger dead.[51]

While Dillinger was growing less cautious, his enemies were sharpening their blades. The humiliation of Little Bohemia caused J. Edgar Hoover to find scapegoats and make changes. Hoover's pet, Melvin Purvis, had not done well, and the director's hand-picked squad of clean young men, lawyers and accountants retooled as dedicated crime fighters, blundered over and over. Hoover began to assemble a new group, not of vaunted scientific criminologists and efficient managers, but of tough lawmen, many of them Texans, who above all could shoot. Herman Hollis, Charles Winstead, and J. C. "Doc" White all came from within the Bureau. Hoover also recruited new men, including Dallas's chief of detectives, Bob Jones, as well as Buck Buchanan from Waco and two officers from Oklahoma City, Jerry Campbell and Clarence Hurt. They trained together for a month in Washington, where it was made clear that bringing Dillinger down was their top priority.[52]

Meanwhile Purvis's run of bad luck laced with incompetence continued. Again and again promising stakeouts failed to produce results, snitches proved useless, surveillance went nowhere. After several embarrassing clashes with the press Purvis got a new chance in late May when a federal court released from custody Helen Gillis, Marie Conforti, and Jean Delaney, all captured at Little Bohemia. Agents watched them, hoping they would lead the feds to their men. But somehow all three slipped beneath the Bureau's eyes and disappeared. This was the last straw. Though he did not officially demote Purvis, Hoover placed him on a side rail. By the end of June, Samuel Cowley, an efficient, hard-working office cop with real street experience, was leading the Dillinger investigation with a beefed-up squad of twenty-two men. Purvis and Cowley worked side by side in the Bankers' Building in Chicago, and though many newspapers continued to refer to Cowley as Purvis's special assistant, in fact Cowley now had over-sight over the entire operation and reported directly to Hoover.[53]

What may have allowed Dillinger to suspend disbelief about the danger around him was a plan he and Van Meter concocted. It would be their ticket out of trouble if only they could hang on a few weeks more. In his retelling of the Dillinger story, G. Russell Girardin quoted the words Dillinger allegedly spoke to Arthur O'Leary: "Van and I are going to pull off the biggest job of our lives. It will be one of the biggest jobs in the world. Just me and Van—we're not cutting anybody else in on this. I'll tell you what it is—we're going to take a mail train. . . . We'll have enough to last us the rest of our lives, and right after it's over, we're lamming it out of the country." There had long been rumors that Dillinger planned to escape to Mexico or some-where in Latin America. He had mentioned the idea in a letter to Mary Longnaker the previous summer, and it might have been the mail train robbery that he had in mind when he wrote his father in early June that he would be leaving soon and that the old man wouldn't have to worry about him any more. Dillinger and Van Meter took long drives out of Chicago and spent hours along the railroad tracks, timing trains, learning their routes, looking for vulnerable places to strike and get away. They also worked at procuring "soup," nitroglyc-erin. Apparently they were after a particular train and believed that when they blew the doors off the armored car they would find them-selves richer than ever, rich enough to leave the country and never come back. For the last American outlaw, heir to Jesse James, a great train robbery and escape to Mexico would be the perfect end to a spectacular career. And if all of this weren't enough, Dillinger and Van Meter talked about trying to write a screenplay and sell the rights for a movie about their exploits. With such big schemes, Dillinger needed to believe that his luck would hold for just a few more weeks.[54]

Perhaps Dillinger had read so many sensationalized newspaper accounts about himself and seen so many newsreels depicting his narrow escapes that he felt invulnerable. Or possibly all the false Dillinger sightings convinced him the cops would never capture him. Maybe he believed that the plastic surgery rendered him invisible. Certainly he was sick of lying low. In any event, rather than become paralyzed by fears that the law was closing in, Dillinger chose to act as though he was untouchable. He and Polly were all over Chicago in July, dining out, going to shows, gambling, taking in movies, haunting amusement parks. They were a good-looking couple, both stylish dressers and filled with easy self-confidence. Polly told the Chicago *Herald and Examiner* three months after his death, "There was the night at a near North Side nightclub. [Johnnie] was always interested in the entertainers, for he loved a good floor show, and he and I were chatting with one of them when a police squad car, one of those big ones, drew up in front, full of detectives. . . . He hurried right up to the front to see it, just as interested as could be. Afraid? Why, not at all. The police could have caught him right there if they'd known. . . . That must have been why it took so long to catch him; he was always right under their noses, where they weren't looking for him."[55]

Steve Chiolek, Anna Sage's son, sometimes double-dated with Johnnie and Polly, and he remembered a man who always picked up the tab, was invariably good-natured, and above all loved going to the movies. "He didn't act tough and he didn't talk rough," Chiolek said. Dillinger was "an all around fellow." He drank moderately, was not ostentatious with his money, but generally talked and laughed a lot and seemed entirely unconcerned about being recognized.[56]

HIDING IN PLAIN SIGHT worked until Saturday, July 21, a day most notable for its record-setting heat. Late that afternoon Melvin Purvis received a call in his office on the nineteenth floor of the Bankers Building. Captain Timothy O'Neil of the East Chicago Police wanted to meet right away. Like his friend Sergeant Zarkovich, O'Neil was not a model of probity; his name came up often when issues of questionable police work arose, including the deaths of officers O'Brien and Mulvihill. Purvis and O'Neil got together on the sweltering street below FBI headquarters. O'Neil brought Zarkovich with him, and after a brief convocation in the lengthening evening shadows all three men drove to the Great Northern Hotel, Samuel Cowley's quarters. Zarkovich laid it out: Anna Sage had informed him that she and her friend Polly Hamilton planned to accompany John Dillinger to a movie the following night. Sage, Zarkovich said, would provide exact details as the time approached, and he made it plain that he, O'Neil, and Sage expected the federal reward money for their trouble.[57]

The feds wanted to talk to Sage to check out her story. Zarkovich had anticipated this, and the four men drove in two cars to the corner where Halsted, Lincoln, and Fullerton converged, steps from Sage's home and the Biograph movie theater. She approached them on foot as night fell. She got into Purvis's car and asked to see his identification. Then she told him that she wanted help with her immigration problem. He replied that the issue was not within his jurisdiction but that he would do his best. Sage, wishing to avoid all suspicion of harboring a fugitive, never revealed that Dillinger lived in her building, and she denied that she had ever known him before Polly started bringing "Jimmy Lawrence" around. He visited regularly, and she figured out from newspaper photographs that he was really John Dillinger. She told Purvis that she had contacted Zarkovich and that the two of them finally met last Thursday. Zarkovich persuaded her to do her duty and come forward to the FBI. Above all, she repeated what Zarkovich told Purvis a few hours earlier: Sage, Hamilton, and Dillinger were going to the movies tomorrow night.[58]

Purvis and Cowley had reason to be suspicious. Still, Dillinger's alleged ties to the Lake County underworld were well known, and it was apparent that these people had the means and motives to deliver Dillinger. For now it seemed wise not to ask too many questions. In a case that generated literally thousands of leads, this was the strongest since Henry Voss's call came in from Rhinelander reporting that the gang was holed up at Little Bohemia.[59]

After what must have been a sleepless night, Purvis and Cowley prepared for Sunday. Sage had said she, Hamilton, and Dillinger would go to either the Marbro theater downtown or the Biograph up on the North Side, probably the former. Agents knew something was up when the office called, telling them to show up for work on a Sunday afternoon. Purvis and Zarkovich briefed them on the situation. The G-men began familiarizing themselves with the theaters, learning the streets, the lobbies, the emergency exits. Covering two venues stretched their ranks thin, so the same old problem that had plagued the Dillinger investigation all year cropped up again: How much should the feds cooperate with other law enforcement agencies? The East Chicago Police Department was already in; several of their detectives accompanied the G-men. Should the Chicago cops also be let in on the stakeout? The FBI and the Chicago police had not worked particularly well together, especially because the former suspected that Dillinger had informants planted inside the latter. Besides, Hoover desperately needed for himself and his agency to get the credit for bringing down Dillinger. If a Chicago cop tipped off the outlaw, who then failed to show, the Bureau would once again look incompetent. No, this was the FBI's show, and no locals would screw it up. Agents spread out at both theaters and waited for Sage's call.[60]

Word finally came a little after 8:30 p.m. Sage called to say that they were going to the Biograph. She told the feds she would be wearing an orange skirt and a white hat. Just a few minutes later Purvis watched a man and two women walk up to the theater, where the movie *Manhattan Melodrama*, starring Clark Gable, William Powell, and Myrna Loy, was playing. Dillinger was unaccompanied by any of his henchmen, and he was coatless too, so he could not be hiding much weaponry. The three walked into the air-conditioned theater to enjoy the show. Meanwhile Cowley led his agents up to the North Side from the Marbro theater. Deciding that it would be safer to take Dillinger on the street after the show rather than hunt for him inside, Cowley and Purvis deployed the men in pairs along the sidewalk in front of the Biograph, across the street, in the alley a few doors to the south, and at the emergency exits along the back and sides of the building. Agents spent the next two hours pacing, chatting, and smoking, trying to break the tension. At one point some Chicago police officers pulled up, guns drawn, on reports of strange men, possibly robbers, lurking on Lincoln Avenue. The feds identified themselves (but not their mission) and the cops left. In a doorway just south of the Biograph, in the path the three moviegoers walked as they approached the theater, stood Charles Winstead and Clarence Hurt, two of Hoover's new recruits.[61]

Manhattan Melodrama was a surprise summer hit. Two boys, Jim Wade (William Powell) and Blackie Gallagher (Clark Gable), are orphaned when the boat carrying their families sinks in New York harbor. They grow up together. Jim, studious and ambitious, becomes district attorney. Blackie loves the good life; he owns a casino, is a major underworld figure. Eleanor (Myrna Loy) loves them both. The movie resonated with years of gangster films—law, justice, and righteousness neatly arrayed against moral compromise. But Jim Wade is a bit cold and officious; Blackie, though a murderer, has an easygoing manner, is filled with charm; he is the film's emotional hero. Blackie is tried and convicted, but his old friend, now governor of New York, comes to death row and offers to commute his sentence. Blackie refuses to let Jim compromise his principles, and *Manhattan*

Melodrama ends with the gangster walking boldly to the electric chair, a priest giving him the last rites, his friend looking on mournfully.[62]

At 10:20 p.m. patrons began emerging from the theater. Purvis stood by the ticket booth, waiting, looking right and left, the crowd enveloping him, an unlit cigar in his mouth. Suddenly, just a few feet away strode Dillinger, Polly Hamilton on his left arm, Anna Sage beside her. In a prearranged signal to his men on the street Purvis lit his cigar. Many of the agents could not see Purvis through the crowd, but Winstead and Hurt were ready. As the throng streaming south on Lincoln Avenue thinned a bit, Dillinger walked right past them. They fell in behind, joined by Agent Ed Hollis, who had been standing beside a parked FBI car. According to the reports given by federal agents, Dillinger turned, saw the three men in suits, and knew. He crouched, broke free of Hamilton and Sage, and strode forward toward the alley, his hand reaching into his pocket, pulling a gun. No words were spoken, though Purvis later claimed that he called out to Dillinger to halt. Their guns ready, Winstead, Hurt, and Hollis fired six shots at the fleeing man. Two bullets grazed Dillinger, another struck him on the left side. The fatal shot entered his neck, pulverized the vertebra at the top of his spinal cord, crashed into the lower part of his brain, and exited below his right eye. He pitched forward a couple more steps, fell face down on the pavement in front of the alley, muttered a few unintelligible words, and died.[63]

SIX

"You Can't Get Away with It"

OLD JOHN DILLINGER LEARNED THE NEWS WHEN A LOCAL journalist awakened him late on Sunday. He had not been feeling well and went to bed early that night. Barefoot and wearing overalls, hearing that his greatest fear had come to pass, the old man stammered, "Is it really true? . . . Are you sure there is no mistake?" Then he collapsed into a chair and wept. Soon Johnnie's sisters Doris and Frances awakened, and their dad comforted them the best he could. Audrey and her husband, Emmett, arrived, and she and Old John cried together for a while. When they regained their composure they began planning the funeral. Just as Johnnie requested, they would bring his body back to Indiana and bury him next to his mother in Indianapolis's Crown Hill Cemetery. Now more reporters began to show up, and father and daughter told them that Johnnie was a good son, a generous brother, kind-hearted and thoughtful, that only the raw deal he got, sending him to jail for nine years, had turned his hand against the law.[1]

The next day, Ed Harvey, Mooresville's undertaker, picked up Dillinger Senior and Johnnie's brother Hubert in his old hearse and drove them to Chicago. As they waited to claim the body at McCready's Funeral Home, where it was laid out for burial, Dillinger told reporters, "They shot him down in cold blood. . . . I don't approve of shootin' a fellow in cold blood," and he asked why, if the feds had so many guns trained on his son, did they need to kill him. But he added cryptically that maybe it was better that Johnnie was killed than captured. Finally, they let Old John see his son.

> With tears glistening in his aging eyes, the elder Dillinger gazed for a few moments at the bullet-torn face of his son.
> "My boy!"
> Those were the only words that escaped his lips as he struggled to hold back his emotion. Hubert . . . put his arm around the old man and led him away.[2]

Dillinger's death created a scene, first on Lincoln Avenue, then at Alexian Brothers Hospital, where he was pronounced dead, then at the coroner's office, and finally at the funeral home. Gestures of genuine compassion mingled with the truly grotesque. One Chicago cop grasped Old John's hand and offered sincere condolences; hundreds more gave him their warmest feelings. Others behaved with cold indifference. For reasons never fully explained, the Cook County coroner removed Dillinger's brain. Dillinger Senior told reporter John Cejnar:

> All of us were embittered concerning the treatment of Johnnie's body. It was mutilated during the postmortem and part of the brain was removed. . . . The embalming had been done at the morgue in the presence of all of the curious thousands who could fight their way in. It was said that this procedure was followed in order to present a lesson to all who looked on. I can't see why they had to do that to my boy's body. It seems to me they did enough when they shot him in his tracks. I can't see why, after he was dead, his body could not have been turned over to me as it was. His body was all I had left.

Then there was the paltry seven dollars returned by the coroner's office. Was it possible Dillinger died so broke? His father had hoped there would be more money than that: "I was in the plight of the average farmer. The funeral expenses worried me heavily. I didn't know how I would pay the bill."[3]

By the time they were ready for the five-hour drive back to Mooresville, the old man was sick with grief and from the heat. Chicago police did their best to clear a path through the crowds on Sheridan Road. Six men carrying the oilcloth-covered wicker basket shoved their way through the multitude and deposited Dillinger's body in the hearse. Then they all drove out of the city Johnnie loved, back to Mooresville, back to the farm. But they did not, Old John remembered, travel alone: "Men, women and children lined the streets of

Chicago, and throughout the entire trip through Indiana, automobiles filled the roads and crowds assembled to see John Dillinger's last ride." A violent thunderstorm outside Indianapolis, he added, seemed like a "mighty requiem for John Dillinger's last homecoming."[4]

They approached Mooresville at sunset, spotting the spires in the distance across the prairie. The crowds thickened again:

> People hung on fence rails and stared. Cars drew aside. We crossed the town limits. Home folks lined the streets. We rolled up to Ed Harvey's funeral home. A crowd had gathered there. The hearse stopped. The crowd became strangely silent. Men removed their hats. John Dillinger had come home for good. As I watched them carrying the casket from the hearse into the mortuary, tears trickled down my face onto my shirt front. I wiped them away carefully, for I remembered suddenly the shirt was my birthday present from Johnnie. It would be only three more days until I had another birthday, my 70th.[5]

Virtually the entire population of Mooresville came out for the viewing at the Harvey Funeral Parlor on Tuesday. Mary Kinder, Harry Pierpont's old girlfriend, drove down from Indianapolis, as did hundreds of others. Reporters wrote that Mary Longnaker was there in the crowd; some also spotted Red Hamilton, who had been dead for months. Late that evening Johnnie's body, dressed in a gray herringbone suit, white shirt, and polka-dot tie, was taken to Audrey's bungalow in Maywood for the next day's ceremonies. It was to be an outdoor religious service, quiet and respectful, with hymns and prayers, but as the Chicago *Tribune* put it, thousands of "curiosity seekers" turned the event into a spectacle: "Despite the religious atmosphere and the respect shown the dead by relatives and friends, the presence of morbid throngs of spectators charged the obsequies with an undercurrent of excitement. The drone of photographers' airplanes circling overhead and the commands of the heavy police guard deployed about the place repeatedly cut in on the service." Audrey's pastor, Reverend William Evans, led the gathered in prayer, and Reverend Charles Fillmore, loyal friend of Dillinger Senior, writer of famous religious songs such as "Tell Mother I'll Be There," and pastor to Johnnie when he was a boy back in Indianapolis, gave a brief sermon. At times the clergymen competed to be heard over the airplanes' roar.[6]

Audrey and Old John did their best not to let the publicity detract from the decent Christian burial Johnnie deserved. Indeed the whole town of Mooresville treated the event with dignity out of deference to the Dillinger family, especially the elder Dillinger. The Mooresville *Times* made it clear that although no one condoned Johnnie's life, his homecoming deserved seriousness and respect. Even in death, however, controversy swirled around John Dillinger. Some indignant plot owners in Indianapolis's grand old Crown Hill Cemetery assailed the burial ground's managers for allowing a desperado—the "motorized Jesse James of the thirties," as the Indianapolis *Star* referred to him—to be interred in the same ground as former president Benjamin Harrison, two vice presidents, Indiana Senator Albert J. Beveridge, and the Hoosier poet James Whitcomb Riley. Others upheld the right of Dillinger Senior to give his son a proper burial in a plot he had paid for. The cemetery's custodians not only ruled in his favor, but the heads of the State Public Safety Office, the Indianapolis State Police, and the Indiana attorney general all agreed, over considerable protest, to provide police protection.[7]

Wishing to avoid a spectacle at the gravesite, the family hedged on announcing the burial time. Only the inner circle knew to go immediately from Audrey's Maywood home to Indianapolis, where forty policemen at Crown Hill stood ready to keep the event orderly and dignified. A summer rainstorm began just as friends and family gathered at the graveside. "Finally," the Chicago *Tribune* reported, "the drenched mourners in their shirt sleeves and thin summer dresses stood about a hastily dug grave, over which had been stretched a canvas canopy." As the ministers led them in the final prayers, Audrey collapsed against her husband, Mary Kinder keened loudly, and Old John and his daughters Frances and Doris quietly wept. "Then they all turned away and three Negroes began indifferently to shovel dirt onto the casket. Mourners and the curious tore flowers from the wreaths as souvenirs and many of the policemen on duty did likewise." After they all left a police guard remained at graveside, to be maintained day and night indefinitely. According to the *Tribune*, "Fear of grave robbers, who may seek to place the body on exhibition, and morbid souvenir hunters caused the precautions to be taken." The security detail failed to catch whoever left a note on the grave two days later: "I am going to get her, John. So long, old boy—J. H."[8]

HIS DEATH DOMINATED THE NEWS for several days. "Dillinger Slain in Chicago," was Monday morning's headline in the New York *Times.*

All of America's big-city newspapers that day led with the story. "Dillinger Slain in Ambush," the San Francisco *Chronicle* declared across the top of page 1; "Dillinger Killed by Federal Officers," the Los Angeles *Times* echoed; "Kill Dillinger Here," the Chicago *Tribune* headline screamed with perverse local pride. The smaller towns did their part too. Citizens of Butte, Montana, sipped coffee over the banner "Federal Men Kill Dillinger" in Monday morning's *Standard*; residents of Lima, Ohio, awoke to "Dillinger Killed by U.S. Agents in Chicago Alley"; across the state, in Mansfield, the headline read, "Dillinger Dies in Trap after Woman 'Tips Off' U.S. Agents," and Nevadans preparing for the new work week opened the *State Journal* and read atop page 1, "U.S. Agents Kill Dillinger." For days Dillinger was the lead story as newspapers gave over entire front pages to the coverage, including eyewitness reports, chronologies of the banks robbed and people killed, and speculation on the whereabouts of remaining gang members.[9]

Coverage was not limited to the North American press. The front page of Bogota's *El Tiempo* told Colombians of the "Tragico final del famoso pistolero," how the "enemigo publico numero 1" emerged from the cinema "con dos amigas," and how "la muchacha del traje rojo" gave him up to the police. In São Paulo Brazilians read a detailed account of the killing of the "Famoso Bandido" on page 1 of *O Estado*. The headline for the *Times of India* asked, "Dillinger Betrayed by a Jealous Woman?" The report, based on a Reuters News Service account, noted how Dillinger had become such a legendary figure that officials attributed every holdup in America to him ("It is a wonder they don't charge me with crimes committed in Europe," Dillinger allegedly once quipped), how his hometown friends supported him and petitioned for clemency, how fifteen crack federal agents waited for him outside the theater while he watched a gangster movie, how he died with a picture of his lover, Evelyn Frechette, in his watchcase.[10]

The Peiping *Chronicle* portrayed a more ruthless Dillinger, a violent man from youth through his last day on earth: "When he emerged from the theatre, Dillinger scented danger, and savagely whipped out his automatic pistol from his pocket, and had half raised it when the agents of the Department of Justice opened fire." The London *Times* agreed, labeling him a remorseless killer, adding that no American outlaw, including Jesse James, was ever more hunted than Dillinger, who until the night before had always managed to shoot his way out of danger. The Manchester *Guardian* noted how life imitated art, or at least Hollywood's version of art: "The pursuit of him from State to State, his escapes from prison, his large-scale affrays with the police have made a tale as sensational as any the film could muster." From Reykjavik to Melbourne, people read of the life and death of the Hoosier outlaw.[11]

Dillinger's demise even became a footnote in the nascent propaganda war between the United States and Nazi Germany. The *Volkischer Beobachter* was critical of how American law enforcement had dealt with Dillinger and even more critical of how the press covered the story. Less than a month before the events on Lincoln Avenue American newspapers had roundly condemned as barbaric the courts-martial and executions in Germany of several enemies of the Reich. Under the title "Barbarism?" the editors of *Volkischer Beobachter* wondered why American newspapers, so concerned with German abrogation of civil liberties just a few weeks earlier, said nothing about due process in the Dillinger case. Where were America's vaunted liberties? "Right out in the street they shot him down like a mad dog; he was riddled like a sieve." The editors mocked Americans' admiration for the likes of Melvin Purvis: "A great fellow, eh? Calls out 'Hello, John' and simply shoots the surprised gangster down, without giving him a chance to say a word. . . . Does a country in which such things happen deserve the name of a constitutional state?" Which was the nation of barbarians, the editors asked, Germany, which executed traitors according to the rule of law, or the United States, where gangsters were gunned down in the streets? The American Embassy in Berlin considered the article so troubling that it translated a copy and sent it home to the State Department.[12]

The German editors were right: mainstream America offered little criticism of the federal men in those very first days after Dillinger's death. Attorney General Homer Cummings set the tone when he called Dillinger's slaying at the hands of Hoover's agents "gratifying as well as reassuring." Indiana Governor Paul McNutt reacted with one word, "Delighted," and state Public Safety Director Al Feeney said that all glory belonged to the federal men. Of course the Justice Department was in a position to spin the initial coverage. The Division of Investigation's Chicago Office fed information to the press, which cranked out a pretty uniform product, especially because so much of the Dillinger coverage came through news agencies such as the United

Press and the Associated Press. Five days after Dillinger's death the New York *Times* ran a long story that read like a collective résumé of the G-men, enumerating the law degrees, foreign languages, sporting feats, military experience, and academic achievements of Hoover's elite five hundred.[13]

Melvin Purvis, the goat of St. Paul and Little Bohemia, suddenly found himself a national hero. Newspapers ran stories about his life, and some of the coverage of this "greatest manhunt in contemporary criminal annals," as one Indianapolis newspaper put it, was presented in his voice. Purvis emphasized the importance of careful police work. Having received information of Dillinger's impending visit to the Biograph, he told the nation in a syndicated (and no doubt ghost-written) column, "I hurriedly made arrangements to surround the theater with picked men from among my investigators." He issued only pistols, no rifles or machine guns, in order to minimize the danger on the street. Then Purvis waited in his car. "It was shortly before 9 o'clock when I first noticed Dillinger. He was coatless, but wore a hat and gold spectacles. He had passed my car before I saw him, but I have studied every available photograph of him so carefully that I recognized the back of his head immediately." Dillinger bought tickets and entered the Biograph with his women. "Those two hours that he spent in the theater," Purvis recalled, "two hours and four minutes to be exact, were the longest I ever spent." By the time Dillinger reemerged, Purvis told reporters, his "men were covering the neighborhood . . . so thoroughly that a cat couldn't have gotten through." At the prearranged signal agents appeared as if out of thin air. "Dillinger gave one hunted look about him, and attempted to run up an alley, where several of my men were waiting. As he ran, he drew an automatic pistol from his pocket. . . . As his hand came up with the gun in it, several shots were fired by my men, before he could fire. He dropped, fatally wounded. I had hoped to take him alive, but I was afraid that he would resist to the last." The federal agents' hometown paper, the Washington *Post*, breathlessly praised their heroics: "The fragmentary report of Dillinger's capture . . . told of almost incredible daring by Agent Purvis, who seized a gun from the gangster's hand."[14]

The jury sitting in the Cook County coroner's office offered no dissent. It took but a few minutes to reach its decision of justifiable homicide. In his autopsy report, Dr. J. J. Kearns described Dillinger as "a medium developed white man, 32 years of age, 5 feet 7 inches tall, weighing 160 pounds, scalp hair brown (dyed black), mustache same, eyes brown." Four gunshot wounds pierced his body, the fatal one entering at the back of his neck, passing through the spine and out his right eye. Coroner Frank Walsh opened his inquest by questioning fingerprint expert Earle Richmond, who testified that though they had been disfigured, the fingerprints of the body with the toe tag marked "No. 116, July, John Dillinger, by District 37, 7–22–34" matched those of the Indiana State Prison inmate paroled the year before. Walsh also interviewed Samuel Cowley, whom the papers referred to as Melvin Purvis's assistant. Cowley testified that as federal agents approached him, Dillinger drew a gun but was shot and killed before he was able to aim and fire it. Then the clerk of the coroner's office gave his testimony that Dillinger had $7.70 in his pocket. And that was that. The jury went out and came right back with its verdict, adding, "The government agents are to be highly commended for their efficient participation in the occurrence, as shown by the fact that there was no further loss of life in the capture of a man of this type." They did not mention the two women bystanders wounded by stray bullets who were compensated months later by an act of Congress.[15]

For the next few days news coverage continued to heap praise on Dillinger's conquerors and reprised the previous year's themes. More prominent than ever, newspapers focused on the attraction of women to the outlaw. "No. 1 Public Enemy Slain as He Strolls out of Theater in Chicago, a Girl on Each Arm," the subhead of one paper read; "Women Figured Prominently in Dillinger's Life," another declared. As one paper put it, "Dillinger always had one or more women with him when the officers closed in. Usually they were left behind and when he turned up again it was with another 'moll.'" A United Press story managed to link death, dirt, violence, and women: "A stiffening corpse in the county morgue and a muddied pool of blood in the filth of an alley was all that was left today of John Dillinger, arch criminal of modern times. Dillinger died as he lived—in a hail of bullets and a welter of blood. He died with a smile on his lips and a woman on each arm."[16]

Along with attraction came betrayal. These "last of an ever changing stream of feminine favorites" abandoned him when the shooting started. Anna Sage's name remained unknown to newspapermen for a few more days, but the phrase "the woman in red" appeared within hours after Dillinger's death (despite the fact that Sage wore orange).

It resonated perfectly with themes of erotic pleasure and easy virtue, and it vivified a new motif, sexual treachery. Hard-bitten newsmen assumed that Dillinger's fast life of sex, money, and violence inevitably led to his being "put on the spot." And they fell back easily on the old stereotype of women's fickleness. Journalists also reported the day after Dillinger's death that federal agents guarded the mysterious woman in red in a downtown hotel suite, fearful of reprisals from the remnants of the Dillinger gang. Less prominent was the more logical explanation that the feds were interrogating Sage to gather facts, find Dillinger's accomplices, and close out the case.[17]

The end of the Dillinger story broke so suddenly that it left reporters groping for answers, and what they did not know they often made up. This was particularly true for the outlaw's supposed dalliances, a fertile field for the male journalistic imagination. The United Press had Dillinger traveling back to Rhinelander, Wisconsin, on July 7, a trip on which he made the error that led to his death: "He was not content with one woman. He took two, thereby sowing seeds of jealousy." A later UP story referred to "Dillinger's craze for wom[e]n," which led him to fall for one motivated by greed and jealousy, who "left him with a bullet torn body, blood streaming from his mouth, his face twitching in agony and fear, scurrying like a frightened rat up an alley . . . to pitch dead in the gutter as his pursuers closed in."[18]

Every paper told a different story. The Chicago *Tribune* declared that Dillinger had stolen another gangster's girl—again, the woman in red—and that the aggrieved hood ratted him out to stalwart Martin Zarkovich, who had sworn to bring down the killer of his lifelong friend Officer William O'Malley. The *Tribune* further speculated that Zarkovich had then persuaded the two-timing woman to betray Dillinger, as the outlaw was out of funds anyway and she stood to gain the reward money. The New York *Times* spun the story a bit differently: O'Malley and Zarkovich were partners, and after the former's death in East Chicago, Zarkovich took a furlough without pay from his job to hang out among hoodlums and hunt for his buddy's killer. An AP "inside story" had Zarkovich meeting Sage in a North Side bar; he "played up" to her and persuaded her to sell out the outlaw for a share of the reward. About the only thing such "news" stories got right was that there was indeed a tie between Sage and the sergeant. All of them made Zarkovich the hero, while missing his long-standing entanglement in webs of East Chicago corruption. Such accounts were patently absurd, but journalists insisted on rounding the story out, connecting the dots, finding meaning. Above all, the early reporting stuck to the well-worn elements of crime melodrama: noble cops loyal to each other, sociopathic criminals, weak and selfish women who betray men to satisfy their need for money, sex, and love.[19]

Not just women but Hollywood was said to have betrayed Dillinger. A United Press story headlined "Dillinger's Weakness for Movies Leads to Sudden Death" noted that it was much easier for the feds to ambush him in a theater than in one of his hideouts. An early news story even claimed that agents knew to look for him at the Biograph because an underworld informant told them he showed up there every time a new film appeared. Reporters repeatedly noted the irony that Dillinger's last moments were spent watching a gangster film that ended with Blackey Gallagher going to the electric chair. Dillinger's love of movies, especially gangster movies, was mentioned almost as often as his weakness for women. Both had caused his downfall—women because they "put him on the spot," movies because he couldn't resist their glamour, couldn't stay out of glittering film palaces.[20]

Of course these ideas reinforced each other. Portraying women as dangerous yet alluring sex objects, as femme fatales, was a standard Hollywood theme, so that Dillinger's weakness for them was readily available as an explanation for his fate. Women of easy virtue were merely part of the slick life of bars and cabarets, the whirl of fancy cars and clothes that had become Hollywood staples, part of the good life stunted by the Depression (and in film, by the Hays Commission). As the years passed after his death, Dillinger's own life story would be recycled in movies containing these same themes; just as Hollywood helped him imagine the life of crime, Dillinger himself would be taken up by Hollywood's fantasies of the underworld.[21]

The paradox of the Dillinger story is that coexisting with titillating tales of his fast life was copious moralizing on the poisoned fruits of crime. Readers had it both ways: the salacious story covered by the fig leaf of stern condemnation, a chance to glare at the scandal while denying that they liked it. The Chicago *Tribune* was probably most heavy-handed. It printed a cartoon right under its "Dillinger Dies" banner headline titled, "An Object Lesson for a Mourning Hero Worshiper." In it, a seated man wearing a coat and tie holds up a newspaper for his young son, who has a toy holster and gun strapped on his hip. "Dillinger Killed; Most Notorious Criminal Since Jesse James" is the headline. The caption reads, "See there, son! That's the way they all end—a short life and a quick death."[22]

In story after story the fact that Dillinger had only seven dollars on him was taken as evidence that he was broke, that he no longer had the wherewithal to pay his underworld contacts for protection, despite all of the money he had stolen. In case anyone missed the lesson, government officials and journalists repeatedly cautioned that crime did not pay. A Washington *Post* editorial castigated the sentimentalists who hailed Dillinger as the greatest criminal of his era. The fact that he killed people, stole money, lived like a hunted animal, and was finally betrayed by his friends, then "shot down like a rabid dog in a Chicago alley," said it all. The *Post* wondered about the "morbid second-hand pride" some took from his defiance of the law. Desperation, not courage, the editors concluded, marked Dillinger's short, ignominious life. As if to underscore the point, the *Post* ran a story in the same issue titled "Dillinger's Death Pleases Agent's Widow," which discussed the family of Federal Agent Carter Baum, left bereft after Little Bohemia, and their satisfaction that finally justice had been served.[23]

Dillinger's end offered an object lesson to "all who place themselves beyond the pale of society," declared the Montana *Standard:* "There is no rest, no peace, no comfort or pleasure for them even in the remotest hiding place." The New York *Times* editorialized, "The glamour of outlawry fades when its supposed loyalties and comradeships are shown to be fiction, and its men and women are ready to sell each other for cash." The Mansfield (Ohio) *News-Journal* argued that Dillinger's story revealed the fragility of social progress. But more than just outlaws declaring war on law and justice, the argument invoked the "stages of civilization," with Dillinger representing a throwback to more primitive ways. Humankind's rise from its "original state of savagery to the present imperfect stage of civilization" had been a "slow process of mental development coupled with spiritual influence." The veneer of civilization was fragile at best, and "at worst the uncontrolled impulses of the jungle become dominant and the restraint required to live in accord with civilization's standards is put aside." What needed to be done now, the *News-Journal* concluded, was to study what made Dillinger a fiendish killer and "to provide influences for the children of today that will make them disciples of civilization instead of permitting them to revert to elemental savagery."[24]

After a few days of intensive coverage and editorializing, the story seemed tired and ready to be put to bed. The "woman in red" had been identified as Anna Sage, the keys in Dillinger's pockets matched her door locks, his guns and ammunition were found dumped in Lake Michigan. The dangers not only of crime but of the fast life in the city had been hammered home. Like newspaper editors the feds were now in a mop-up operation. J. Edgar Hoover told reporters that soon the rest of Dillinger's friends would fall too, that "any one who ever gave any of the Dillinger mob any aid, comfort or assistance will be vigorously prosecuted." An AP story quoted Hoover saying of Dillinger, "He was just a yellow rat that the country may consider itself fortunate to be rid of. There are other rats still to be gotten, however, and we are not taking any time off to celebrate about Dillinger." Hoover announced Baby Face Nelson as the new Public Enemy Number One, and he added that John Hamilton (the feds still had not found his body) and Homer Van Meter were also in his agency's sights. Crack federal "man hunters" were closing in on the remnants of the Dillinger gang, on the hundreds of thousands of dollars they had stolen, and on those dupes who aided and abetted them.[25]

THE DILLINGER STORY QUIETED DOWN, but it did not go away, partly because the facts refused to stay still. Anomalies, large and small, kept cropping up. The controversy over Dillinger's brain was one. At the end of July undertaker Ray McCready announced that it was already gone when the Cook County Morgue delivered the body to his Chicago funeral home. Coroner Frank Walsh denied the report and said that only a few ounces of brain, heart, and kidney had been removed for chemical analysis. Dr. Jerome Kearns, who performed the autopsy, concurred. Dillinger Senior, not knowing what to think, spoke about having the body disinterred and about a possible lawsuit. But a day later he retracted his statement and said that maybe Johnnie's brain could be useful to scientific understanding of the origins of crime. No sooner had he backed off taking legal action than Kearns admitted that the brain had in fact been removed, sent out for analysis, then destroyed after scientists determined there was nothing unusual or pathological about it.[26]

Another significant organ came up. Among the first images released after Dillinger's death was one of him in the morgue. A sheet covers his body, and the slab on which he lies is tilted upward. Between his knees and his neck, the sheet rises at least a foot, tent-like, from around where his loins would be. The photograph was never explained; perhaps Dillinger's arm stiffened in rigor mortis with his hand hovering several inches above his groin, or maybe some other object on the table was covered by the sheet. Whatever the reason, the photo makes it look as if Dillinger died with an enormous erection. The autopsy report (which, incidentally, also disappeared months after the outlaw's death, and did not reemerge for decades) mentioned nothing unusual about his physique. The photograph appeared in some early-edition newspapers, though not all, apparently because editors realized how viewers might read the image. Whenever the photo reappeared in the next few days the tent was airbrushed flat. Decades later the "missing" appendage became part of an urban legend.[27]

There were other unanswered questions. Did Dillinger reach for his gun as the feds closed in? Some eyewitness accounts made the shooting sound more like an execution than a gunfight. Two days after his death Mrs. Esther Gusinow told reporters that from her window, just a few feet from the action, it looked as if Dillinger had been shot at point-blank range: "The man and the women with him passed the two agents and started across the alley. Suddenly one of the agents pulled out a gun and fired. The man fell and the women disappeared." Edgar l'Allemand, an auto mechanic working across Lincoln Avenue, said he witnessed the whole thing too: "Suddenly I saw a tall man fire two shots in quick succession. He seemed to be standing almost beside the man who was shot. The wounded man fell to the alley without uttering a sound." Chicago police later confirmed the presence of powder burns on Dillinger's body, indicating that the shots were fired at very close range.[28]

There were other contradictions. How much money was Dillinger carrying? Seven dollars and seventy cents, most papers declared, but rumors spread that thousands of dollars in his pocket mysteriously disappeared. Audrey Hancock claimed that her brother always wore a well-stuffed money belt and a valuable ruby ring, and police suspected that somewhere Dillinger may have stashed tens of thousands more. None of it ever turned up. Even the lovely story of Dillinger carrying Billie's picture, his "pretty Indian sweetheart," in his watchcase proved elusive. Samuel Cowley told reporters that the blurry image was Billie's, but Melvin Purvis said no, the photo in the watchcase was not of Frechette, but of Mary Longnaker. The New York *Times* championed this interpretation, declaring that Mary had harbored Dillinger after his escape from Lima, and that of his many sweethearts she was "the one woman in his life." Other newspapers, however, reported that the photo was actually Polly Hamilton, Dillinger's last girlfriend. Incidentally, Polly too had also gone missing since the shooting. Initial news stories said she had returned to her mother in Fargo, North Dakota; others reported that she never made it home, and they speculated about foul play, maybe even suicide.[29]

Other facts in the case did not square. What were those East Chicago cops doing at the Biograph anyway? In early reports Melvin Purvis implied that they just happened to drop by the feds' offices at a propitious moment and came along for the ride. But then Captain O'Neil accused Purvis of being a publicity hound and told the press that the East Chicago boys were not getting the credit they deserved. Like Purvis, O'Neil did not want to make Anna Sage a hero of the story, and he denied she had anything to do with Dillinger's demise. It was all good police work by Sergeant Zarkovich, whose contacts led him to the Biograph. In O'Neil's telling, the East Chicago cops brought about the good results with the purest of motives. The Chicago *Tribune*, however, had already begun to see the case a bit more cynically; federal agents were not permitted to receive reward money, but the East Chicago cops could, so a deal was struck: "The feds got the credit, the East Chicagoans the money."[30]

A few days after Dillinger's death Sage's connections with Zarkovich began to emerge in the newspapers, as did her troubles with immigration authorities. Her professions of innocence did not survive close scrutiny. Soon everyone knew that she ran brothels in East Chicago, that Dillinger had stayed in her Halsted Street apartment building in the days leading up to his death, and that she and Zarkovich had been lovers. In fact just a week after the killing the *Tribune* ran a long story tracing an interlocking directorate of sleaze, including recent photos of Zarkovich and Sage together (the "Sheik," as the sharp-dressing Zarkovich was known, had denied seeing Sage since 1928), and interviews with Zarkovich's ex-wife and Polly Hamilton's ex-husband about sex, politics, and the police departments of northwest Indiana. Lake County once again came off as a sinkhole of corruption, and Chief Matt Leach of the state police vowed to investigate.[31]

If all of this was not enough, there was the death of Jimmy Probasco. The feds brought him up to their headquarters on the nineteenth floor of the Bankers Building for questioning late Wednesday night, on a tip that he had harbored Dillinger. Sam Cowley testified at a coroner's inquest the following morning that, left alone for a few minutes, Probasco brought a chair to the conference room window and leaped to his death. The coroner's jury accepted the suicide story at face value, but Hoover, eager to deflect any possible criticism, released Probasco's rap sheet to the press. At his funeral a few days later Probasco's sister denied that her brother had killed himself; she said that the feds roughed him up when they arrested him, implying that they either murdered him or caused him to take his own life. Years later Doris Lockerman, Melvin Purvis's secretary, speculated that Probasco might have been driven to suicide, assuming that agents in Chicago subjected him to the usual routine of keeping suspects awake and starved for hours as they badgered them with questions.[32]

A week after Dillinger died, the Chicago *Tribune*'s piecemeal gripes against the feds became a full-fledged critique. Although Dillinger's demise was a public benefaction, the government's lack of accountability was disturbing and, an editorial implied, part of a larger problem of growing federal arrogance. The *Tribune* accused the feds of treating a local police matter like "princely politics in medieval Italy" and Melvin Purvis of retiring to his ducal castle and refusing to answer questions. These "new ideas of autocratic government" all flowed out of the New Deal's arrogation of power and the denigration of local autonomy. The *Tribune* wanted an explanation of why federal agents were joined by officers from another city, indeed from another state, while the Chicago police were deliberately kept away. The feds had bungled Little Bohemia, and without the East Chicago cops they would have bungled the Biograph too. A casual observer might assume that the FBI's reticence was designed to cover incompetence, enhance federal prestige, and "justify invasion of the states by United States policemen." Hoover, Purvis, and the rest owed Americans a full accounting of the case; without it, "Dillinger dies as he lived, in a cloud of mystery and to the great hazard of other people."[33]

Hoover, ever vigilant of his agency's reputation, was incensed. In an act of damage control he sent the *Tribune* editorial to the attorney general's office with a memo declaring the newspaper to be openly hostile, accusing the editors of meddling in government business, and intimating that they had underworld ties and needed to be watched. With characteristic petulance, the Director refused to meet with *Tribune* reporters or respond to their written questions, and he urged the attorney general's office to do the same. Hoover's anger went back to that paper's harsh coverage of Little Bohemia. Now the *Tribune* was asking difficult questions about the FBI's relationship to Martin Zarkovich and Anna Sage. Matt Leach, no doubt resentful that the feds had kept the Indiana State Police out of the action, leaked the story to the *Tribune* that Zarkovich and Sage conspired to set up Dillinger, take whatever was left of the money he stole, and claim the government bounty. Hoover warned Attorney General Cummings's office not to comment on Leach's allegations on the grounds that corruption in northeast Indiana was a local, not a federal matter.[34]

Most notable was Hoover's self-righteous tone. Both the Chicago Police Department and the Indiana State Police had been involved in the Dillinger hunt from the beginning; of course they wanted to share the credit for bringing him down. Hoover was utterly indifferent to them. His goal, pure and simple, was to keep the glory and deflect bad publicity from the Division of Investigation, He was equally uninterested in pursuing charges that Zarkovich and Sage had visited Dillinger several times in the Crown Point jail, that they and others in East Chicago helped bribe local officials to aid his escape, and that they took money to keep him hidden. Quite the contrary, quashing information about those two was necessary to building the legend of the FBI. Yet for all of Hoover's efforts to showcase Dillinger's death as the fruits of clean, modern police work, it was in fact a dirty old story: the fugitive knew too much, he was worth more dead than alive, paid informers brought him down.[35]

HOOVER SUCCEEDED IN PROTECTING the Bureau's image to the extent that many Americans accepted the story of good triumphing over evil, a predator run to earth, justice served. For many, however, it was not so simple. The sheer size of the crowds following Dillinger's death reveal the story's power. By midnight on July 22 hundreds, perhaps thousands were out on Lincoln Avenue, posing for newsreel cameras and holding up newspaper headlines. Scores of them dipped their handkerchiefs or even the hems of their dresses in Dillinger's blood. As Monday dawned the Cook County Morgue drew "gaping thousands" of "morbid curiosity-seekers," as one United Press report put it. "For several hours they swarmed," the Chicago *Tribune* reported of those hoping for a glimpse of the body, "pushing and shoving, down the steps leading from the first floor to the basement."[36]

An Associated Press reporter described the scene at the morgue: a gray basement room smelling of formaldehyde; a bare light bulb suspended over the corpse on the operating table; policemen moving the crowd along a narrow aisle. One blond woman brandishing scissors tried to sneak up to the body to steal a lock of hair; an attendant forcibly pushed her out. A young nurse from nearby Cook County Hospital gazed wide-eyed at the dead man, commenting on how neatly trimmed his moustache was; police noted that she had visited three times the day before. A United Press story described a mother and her young daughter who had come to view the body. When a cop suggested that the morgue was no place for a kid, the woman shot back, "Who says so . . . ? It'll be good for her. Teach her what happens to boys and girls that don't be good."[37]

Newspapermen painted the morgue scene as an all-night party: Camera crews set up lights and filmed the gunman's corpse, as show girls, bartenders, nurses and interns from nearby hospitals, night-hawk cabbies, and drunken revelers all lined up to view the dead man. Deputy Coroner Jack Schewell gave the whole scene a morbid benediction when he remarked of gangland Chicago, "They all show up here; sooner or later we get them all." When the morgue released the body on Tuesday for burial preparations, another five thousand people crowded outside McCready's Funeral Home in uptown. "Throngs Fight for Glimpse of Dead Dillinger," the *Tribune* reported.[38]

Were the people there to celebrate Dillinger's death? Were they the "sentimentalists" newspapers accused of trying to make a hero of the dead outlaw? Many were attracted by the excitement and glamour, the celebrity moment, the break from ordinary life. Others were fascinated by the story's grotesqueness. Looking at Dillinger lying in the morgue or even at pictures of his body gave people the opportunity to gaze at that from which they normally averted their eyes, the freak-show pleasure of staring at the forbidden. Dillinger's death, like his life, was absorbed into the culture of spectacles. Newsreel footage from the Biograph theater and the photographs of onlookers at the morgue had a carnivalesque quality to them. The merger of crime, journalism, and showbiz grew doubly apparent when, to help defray the costs of the funeral, Dillinger Senior, Hubert, Audrey and her husband Emmet took to the stage. An Indianapolis vaudeville house announced immediately after Dillinger's funeral that his family would do six shows per day, answering questions about their outlaw kinsman, especially his visit to Mooresville the previous April. The shows sold well and audiences gave the family respectful applause; the troupe even had some success on the road.[39]

The Dillinger family tour was but one instance of small-scale entrepreneurs capitalizing on the dead outlaw's charisma. Right after the shooting street peddlers offered the public bits of paper stained with the outlaw's blood for a quarter, and handkerchiefs for half a dollar, with plenty of takers. One man offered one thousand dollars for Dillinger's shirt, another one hundred dollars each for Lincoln Avenue's blood-stained bricks, in the hope of displaying them at fairs and carnivals. Over the next few weeks Mary Kinder and Evelyn Frechette sold tell-all stories to the press. What horror was next, Indianapolis politician Carlton McCulloch wrote to his friend Meredith Nicholson, American minister to Paraguay? John Dillinger five-cent cigars? John Dillinger talcum powder to soothe a chafed world?[40]

Other self-appointed arbiters of taste saw nothing but cultural degradation in the events of late July. "Never before in history," the *Literary Digest* declared with alarm, "have so many millions of both sexes and all ages contemplated the mutilated corpse of a criminal." In addition to the thousands who degraded themselves at the morgue, the *Digest* noted, newspaper photos of the body circulated everywhere. Editors argued that Dillinger's bloody carcass gave stark and conclusive evidence that crime did not pay, but the *Digest* was having none of it. On the day the photo of Dillinger in the morgue appeared, a twenty-year-old man in Los Angeles shot and killed a policeman, allegedly shouting, "I'm the new Dillinger!" "So much," the *Digest* declared, "for the deterrent effect of gruesome pictures on impressionable youth," adding that though it was no surprise that the tabloids ran graphic photos to increase circulation, the publishers of family newspapers ought to know better. Had the *Literary Digest* article appeared a few days later, its editors might have noted the story of three Maryland robbers, the self-styled "black Dillingers," all sentenced to hang for killing the white owner of a barbecue stand.[41]

Those on the political left were equally appalled, not so much by Dillinger as by the circus surrounding his demise. *New Masses* noted that strikers in recent months had often taunted police, "Why don't you get Dillinger": Why don't you do your job, arrest criminals, and leave working folks struggling against their bosses alone? The feds did get their man, *New Masses* observed, "and a lovely spectacle they have made of it": the media frenzy, the "revolting exhibition" of the corpse, the hawking of souvenirs, Dillinger Senior trying to maintain his dignity through it all. "By every measure of current capitalist entertainment," the editors scoffed, "the exit of Dillinger was a glorious success." The communist *Daily Worker* editorialized in similar mocking tones that it took only fifteen armed men to shoot down Dillinger in cold blood, and they managed to wound only two bystanders in the process. Banks were safe again, the article continued, and the Marines could return to Haiti, Nicaragua, and Cuba "to help teach 'self-government' to the colonial possessions of the American Empire." Dillinger's father, the *Daily Worker* concluded, was emblematic of American parents, struggling unsuccessfully against an unjust system to keep their children from turning to crime. His son, however, was less a Jesse James than an amateurish version of the old Robber Barons, "men who really knew how to rob a community." Dillinger was just a small-timer, born too late: "Gould, Vanderbilt, Fisk, Rockefeller and the rest had the country in the bag, and their descendants still have the racket sewed up." Theirs was "a record for plunder that Dillinger could never approach."[42]

Underneath many of these accounts of Dillinger's death lay contradictory feelings. Even as they condemned the outlaw, newspapers often expressed a sense of awe at his wild year. One Associated Press reporter referred to him as the "arch criminal of the age" and "the most dangerous desperado of the decade." He also called Dillinger "swashbuckling" and described how he came out of obscurity "to astound the world with his deeds of depredation." Another journalist declared that Dillinger and his men vanished and reappeared "like so many headless horsemen." "His name," the story continued, "was bruited in the Senate chamber and mouthed on the stage. He was the subject of endless editorials, an object lesson to law enforcement officials, a factor in politics. Humorists found in him a fruitful source of gags, and some civic authorities the cause of chagrin." No other felon in American history, the Chicago *Tribune* concluded, "ever so captured the imagination of the public." The paper added that Dillinger's insouciance and good humor were as much a part of this "super-criminal's" legend as his courage under fire.[43]

Even as the Washington *Post* wrote glowingly of the brave federal men it carried such subheads as "Dillinger Blazed His way to Throne of Underworld with Machine Guns," "Bandit's Success in Bank Robberies and Jail Breaks Amazing," and "Outlaw Shot Way out of Many Traps Set by U.S. Agents." Over and over editorial writers condemned the dead man's acts only to return to his popularity. Dillinger had hero worshippers all across the country, the Sheboygan (Wisc.) *Press* noted, and women everywhere were ready to be his companion.[44]

The guilty pleasure of a criminal being so attractive was a big part of the Dillinger story's appeal. An article by Joseph K. Shepard in the Indianapolis *Star* captured some of this paradox by noting the dead outlaw's odd combination of fatalism and flippancy. It was his sense of humor, Shepard believed, that got him into trouble. Dillinger did not take the world seriously enough, but always played the wise guy, toyed with life itself. Shepard wrote that he gained insight into Dillinger when he met him in the Tucson jail, then talked about him for two days with Pierpont, Makley, and Clark as they rode the train back to Ohio to stand trial. Dillinger's whole philosophy since prison centered on living life to the fullest: "Might as well go early in the morning," he used to say, "stay all day, bring your lunch and enjoy the fireworks at night." He joked, "The world's a very dangerous place; few get out of it alive."[45]

Dillinger's "wise cracks," his assumption that life was fleeting and nihilistic, did not amuse Shepard, but he had to admit that the outlaw lived and died by his code. If something as serious as prison was absurd—"'A jail is just a nut with a worm in it. The worm can always get out'"—then everything was absurd: "It was meat and good red wine to him to walk right by a Federal agent and flash his twisted smile when the whole United States was in arms against him. It was the bread of life to him to walk in disguise into night clubs and amusement places, flaunting his presence, in the hottest spots in the country. He couldn't leave the cities and the night life alone. . . . Every 'coup' of Dillinger's was just one more joke on the world." It was this jocularity—living life on the edge, thumbing his nose at the law, laughing all the way—that carried him out of Crown Point singing "The Last Roundup" in March, that brought him to Mooresville for a family dinner in April, that took him in the end with not one but two women to the Biograph. And he did it all knowing "that every time he stepped into the street the lightning might strike." Shepard clearly was torn, admiring Dillinger's swagger and style yet deeply disturbed by his refusal to take life seriously, his insistence on running through his wild year as if deeds had no consequences. An outlaw bloody of tooth and claw was bad enough. For him to morph into a charismatic man, full of life, one who invited us to join him in mocking grim-faced authority, in laughing at the self-important likes of J. Edgar Hoover and Homer Cummings, that was truly unsettling.[46]

Robert J. Casey underscored these same themes in his three-part column, "Dillinger, the Country Boy Killer," published in the Chicago *Daily News* during the week after the outlaw's death. Following a childhood of small-town boredom, Dillinger "settled down to a life which promised to be just as deadly dull as his boyhood had been." Something in the young man rebelled; he got drunk, mugged Frank Morgan, and spent his twenties behind bars. Folks in Mooresville would never let him forget he was an ex-con, so Dillinger embraced his fate. "I said to myself, 'Johnny, you're a criminal now. . . . by the free gift of a judge and jury and the best thing you can do is to study for the job ahead in your new profession.'" So he sprung his friends from prison and then carried out a string of spectacular bank robberies. "He had a magnetic personality and a ready smile," Casey wrote, and after Crown Point he had the stage he craved. Dillinger bantered easily with reporters, charmed everyone he met, and soon the public leaned back and laughed along with him. "With no foundation at all, he was generally looked upon as a Robin Hood—a sort of benevolent robber who seemed to wear a hero's laurels because he stood alone (except for a gang of talented murderers) against the police." He made the law look ridiculous, and the story's tone of comic relief blunted the horror of the death of innocents. Dillinger's nonchalance as agents of justice pursued him only added to his legend. So too did the stories of women who flocked to him like moths to a flame. "He lilted lightly from love to love and left a trail of deserted boudoirs while trusting their disgruntled owners to keep faith with him." Most kept faith, even did prison time for him, but inevitably one betrayed this enthralling rogue.[47]

The Dillinger of legend beguiled writers and journalists, despite their ambivalence. He was the shape-shifter, the con artist, the bandit Houdini of a thousand escapes. This was the charismatic Dillinger, fearless, clever, beating the system, the one who played it for laughs, who drove the best cars, wore the snappiest clothes, dated the sexiest women. If the straight and narrow was the shortest path to American manhood, then Dillinger showed them all an alternative route, winding, exhilarating, fun. Even J. Edgar Hoover was fascinated by him. Hoover repeated for reporters Dillinger trickster stories. Assuming, no doubt, that it made the outlaw appear unmanly, he recounted that Dillinger had once dressed up as a nun to case a bank; another time he posed as a salesman of ventilation systems to get inside a vault. Hoover described how once Dillinger claimed to be a writer of detective stories looking for authentic detail and quizzed policemen about their arsenals. Another time he asked officers what they would do if this Dillinger fellow showed up. In both cases the police displayed the weaponry at their disposal, guns Dillinger stole a few days later. Hoover claimed that Dillinger had even passed himself off as a banker to plead for cooperation in crime prevention; the ploy got him invited to the financiers' banquet.[48]

HOOVER WON THE PUBLICITY WAR, at least in the short term, and bringing down Dillinger became the FBI's founding myth. Within months after his death, agents had rounded up or killed the remaining public enemies from the Dillinger days: Homer Van Meter, Baby Face Nelson, Pretty Boy Floyd, and the rest. The Agency was well on its way to becoming a truly national police force, and the power of its director grew proportionally. Hoover understood the need for good public relations, for image control, and he became ever more skilful at it.[49]

Children were enrolled as "Junior G-Men" and told to be on the lookout for new Dillingers. In the anteroom to his office Hoover set up a miniature Dillinger museum, complete with the outlaw's death mask, the pistol he allegedly carried into the Biograph, his pocket change, and other memorabilia. (Years later legend had it that the director also kept Dillinger's private parts, preserved in a jar of formaldehyde.) Hoover maintained good relations with many journalists, including the era's most famous celebrity reporter, Walter Winchell. Another famous commentator on the news of the day, Lowell Thomas, narrated a thirty-minute promotional film for the Bureau. In *You Can't Get Away with It* (1936) agents showed their mettle with Thompson machine guns, firing away at targets plastered with Dillinger's picture. The film emphasized systematic police work and featured images of Bureau scientists poring over fingerprints in a high-tech crime lab. The director himself appeared on camera and told viewers how his men had brought down Dillinger and protected the public from blood-thirsty criminals. Hoover's lesson was obvious: Wrongdoers, with their meager intelligence and limited abilities, were no match for the Bureau. As Thomas intoned at the end of the film, "You can't get away with it."[50]

The emphasis on technological sophistication and bureaucratic efficiency proved to be effective publicity. Yet even while he promulgated that image Hoover also encouraged his men to apply different methods—threats, coercion, violence—and to use the tools that worked: bribes, bounties, payoffs. Far more than scientific policing, these were what brought down the Dillinger gang and made the Bureau's reputation.[51]

Perhaps Hoover's most effective weapon in the crime wars was publicity itself. He was masterful at stamping the FBI image across American popular culture. James Cagney, who made a career out of playing criminals in the movies throughout the early 1930s, starred in *G-Men* in 1935, a film that signaled the shift in popular culture away from telling crime stories from the felons' perspective toward telling them from the cops' point of view. Made with Hoover's blessing, *G-Men* roughly followed the outlines of the Dillinger story, with the slightly effete, very bloodthirsty Danny Leggett brought down by the charming but tough working-class kid, Buck Davis, played by Cagney.[52]

But much as Hoover tried to make his agency the hero of the story, finally it was Dillinger himself who remained center stage. Americans might be impressed by how the FBI got its man, but Dillinger, not Hoover or Purvis or Cowley or the whole cadre of efficient young G-men, fascinated them most. "Dillinger died with millions of admirers because he was a brave man, and a figure of romance, appealing to the imagination, and a hunted man, and the underdog in the fight," declared an editorial in the Clarendon (Va.) *Chronicle*.[53]

A fearless rogue, Dillinger resembled the old tricksters of oral tradition, pushing cultural limits, violating customs, breaking the rules.

His story also evoked the picaresque heroes of fiction. The *picaro* was a man of low birth who made his way up the social ladder with laughter, cunning, physical bravado, and sexual prowess. Most of all Dillinger embodied the American road trip, that liminal journey filled with freedom and adventure, even sex and violence, set apart from the crushing ordinariness of daily life. The Dillinger story was all about the freedom of the open road, where, in fantasy anyway, men and women fled the conventions of law, custom, and respectability. Few Americans endorsed bank robberies, yet during the Depression they could not help but admire a man who pulled them off with such élan. Most citizens, if asked directly, hated crime and considered gangsters social predators. But there was something undeniably refreshing about someone whose deeds mocked the moralists and the guardians of propriety—not to mention that he stole from those whom many people assumed had been robbing them all along. Americans had watched it all on the silver screen for years, but now the film heroes and antiheros had a real analogue in John Dillinger. Life and art did not just imitate each other, they became each other.[54]

The Dillinger of legend was a "social bandit," a concept described by the English historian Eric Hobsbawm. Hobsbawm points out that there is a long tradition in peasant societies of men on the fringes opting out of respectable life, often to attack the wealthy and powerful. Some, like Robin Hood, became legendary social benefactors. Other social bandits were less generous yet still were seen as heroic because they would not bend to an unjust order. The story of an impoverished son of the countryside might begin with some slight at the hands an aristocrat, or sometimes a nobleman insults the hero's family. Blood is shed and the hero flees, but he returns to continue the battle against injustice. Social bandits not only avenged wrongs done to them by the rich and powerful, they also fought in the name of something larger: their family, their village, their region, their people. They came to see their personal troubles as part of the larger plight of their class or group, and listeners to the heroes' stories made that same leap.[55]

Dillinger of legend fit the social bandit mold, but only imperfectly. Occasional kindnesses and gallantries were attributed to him, and his defenders said that he killed only when forced to. His ties to the countryside and the fact that the gang mostly robbed small-town banks in the heartland also connected him to the rural bandit tradition. Despite the economic crisis, however, few thought of Dillinger as a social benefactor. The emotional power of his story stemmed less from any connection to "his people," or from his social largesse than from his assault on banks, those symbols of a system seen by many in 1934 not just as a failure, but as predatory. He might not embody a new social order, but he assaulted institutions of the corrupt old one. Dillinger's rebellion against injustice was not communal, it was personal, or more precisely, it extended no further than the band he led. His goal was to even the score, to get his own back, to take what society had denied him, but he was no harbinger of a new day.[56]

Nonetheless his violent assault on the citadels of wealth carried deep emotional resonance. Dillinger and his men could not be more American in their desire to seize the good life for themselves. The 1920s marked a watershed when nationally marketed consumer goods became available to masses of Americans. Supermarkets and department stores opened their cornucopias to all, movies revealed a world of glamour, radio provided a free and endless cycle of entertainment, automobiles offered proof on every street that life was getting better, more modern, more affluent. Along with it all came a loosening of mores, of social restraints, a letting down of inhibitions against drinking, sex, indebtedness. The burgeoning consumer society of the post–World War I years became the very definition of the American way, and citizenship came to mean the right to seek a life of material comfort and pleasure, to have things, to enjoy life.[57]

Dillinger and his ilk were not going to be deprived of the good things in life just because of the economic cataclysm. We sometimes have to remind ourselves that photos of Depression-era celebrity criminals, fashionably dressed, standing beside expensive cars, were taken in the 1930s, not the 1920s. The John Dillingers of the world grabbed these trophies of status, taking a sort of 1930s revenge on the 1920s. Many of their countrymen cheered them on. Both government and business had failed middling people, and the resulting anger took several forms as the decade unfolded. Some citizens directed it inward and experienced economic failure as personal shame. Others were drawn to the raw populist politics of a Huey Long or the ugly anti-Semitic binging of a Father Coughlin; right-wing authoritarianism found a significant minority of adherents. Still other Americans sought radical solutions to social problems through the Communist Party, or looked to liberal alternatives within the Popular Front. Councils of the unemployed, marches to demand social justice, general strikes, food riots, confrontations with the police, militant new labor unions were all as much a part of the Great Depression landscape as the dustbowl and the New Deal.[58]

But some of the rage in those hard times also got channeled into the stories of men like Dillinger, who with smiles on their faces and guns in their hands took what they wanted. The carnage of the Dillinger days mesmerized people losing faith, people who felt victimized. Dillinger might be nihilistic, violent, destructive, but at least he was not passive. On the contrary, he answered the inertia, the paralysis of the era with elemental male action. He was no Robin Hood, but he was no victim either.[59]

In memory, the face of the Great Depression comes down to us from the great photographers Walker Evans and Dorothea Lange, who worked for the federal government's Farm Security Administration, producing images like those of Floyd Burroughs and Florence Owens Tompkins, rural folk, bereft in the economic crisis. These were American faces, careworn and tired, with hopeless eyes. Such documentary photographs persuade by their literalness; they are black-and-white images of spare composition using candid subjects, producing artless art. They capture in haunted glances the harsh reality of the era. But an equally authentic representation of the 1930s was a photograph of another heartland American. With a Thompson machine gun in one hand, a wooden pistol in the other, a smile on his face, and a sharp suit on his back, John Dillinger was the very picture of a man who would get his due, have a good time doing it, and damn the consequences. Dillinger was a man crafting his own image, his own life, his own way. His was a deeply American story of obscurity and fame, poverty and wealth, self-creation and self-immolation. It was not, however, a story of martyrdom.[60]

SEVEN

Dillinger's Ghost

ONE MORE RUMOR AROSE SOON AFTER HIS DEATH: IT WASN'T John Dillinger lying on that slab in the morgue. It was a look-alike who had stood in for him at the Biograph and who, unaware that he'd been set up, took the FBI's bullets. Dillinger had faked his own death. He was alive.

It's a common theme in the legends of heroes. From King Arthur to John F. Kennedy, charismatic figures cheat death, and careful research reveals the hidden truth. Here, for example, Dillinger's autopsy reported that the corpse had brown eyes; Dillinger's eyes were gray. A generation after the shooting at the Biograph theater, old-timers in Morgan County, Indiana, believed that whoever was in that casket at Harvey's Funeral Home back in '34, it wasn't Johnnie Dillinger.[1]

Many have speculated how Dillinger staged his own end, who acted as his surrogate, who was in on the con, and how the scheme got pulled off. Jay Robert Nash advanced the idea furthest in *The Dillinger Dossier*, a well-researched work, though not finally a convincing one. Nash argues that there really was a Jimmy Lawrence (the name of the man Polly Hamilton said she was dating) and that it was he who died on July 22. Nash argues that getting Dillinger was the linchpin of salvaging the FBI's reputation, that enormous rewards had already been paid to his killers, and that his "death" helped Indiana state agencies cover up their incompetence. In other words, lots of influential people would be better off if the public continued to believe that Dillinger was dead, so officials suppressed evidence that he was still alive. Nash implies that the deaths of Jimmy Probasco and of Anna Sage after she was deported to Romania, were part of the cover-up. He also offers the transcript of an interview he conducted with a bank robber named Blackie Audette, who claimed that he and Dillinger drove west from Chicago just after July 22 and hid out on an Indian reservation in Oregon. Finally Nash reprints a letter allegedly written by Dillinger and a photograph of him sent to Emil Wanatka Jr., from Hollywood, California, dated July 1963. Squint hard enough and the handwriting could be Dillinger's; stare at the picture, and the head and ears of the sixty-year-old man staring back do have the same shape as those in photos of the thirty-year-old criminal.[2]

The notion that Dillinger did not die in July 1934 gained currency. In a long article in the Indianapolis *Star* written fifty years after the outlaw's death, L. Spenser Riggs described the scene in Mooresville on the day they buried Dillinger. Riggs's father, an Indianapolis barber, joined others in conversation as they stood outside Harvey's funeral home in Mooresville, having just viewed the body: "If that's John Dillinger in there, then I never cut his hair!" Ivan Riggs said, and his boss agreed: "That man has never been in my shop. . . . He's too short . . . and he's too fat." A local woman declared, "If that's Johnnie in there . . . then I never made love to him, and that would be a lie." "'Who do they think they're kidding?' yelled a well-dressed drunk who nearly fell into the casket. 'That ain't Johnnie in that box! Some sort o' trick!' Plainclothes police hustled him into a car and drove off." That Dillinger did not die in July 1934 became the basis for a 1980 short story by John Sayles, "Dillinger in Hollywood," and a 1995 film starring Martin Sheen and F. Murray Abraham, *Dillinger and Capone*.[3]

Of course he really did die on July 22 in Chicago, but like so much else in the Dillinger legend it is best to treat the notion that he survived the shoot-out at the Biograph allegorically. During his wild year Dillinger walked away from one hair-raising encounter after another, broke out of "escape-proof" jails, got shot repeatedly, yet always turned up a few weeks later to pull another bank job. His intrepidness, indeed his seeming unstoppability, made him part of American lore. It seemed almost too much to believe that he was dead. And metaphorically, of course, he did not die on that sweltering Chicago night in the middle of the Depression. Over the next seventy-five years, journalists, novelists, crime writers, historians, poets, artists, public relations men, filmmakers, storytellers, songwriters, chamber of commerce types, and local history buffs, all have kept his memory alive.[4]

FIRST, THE BALLADS. The old Anglo-American ballad tradition never fully died out, especially in rural America, and broadsides—printed songs originally sold long ago by hawkers on the streets of London—remained popular. Broadsides told of spectacular events, dark murders, and bold bad men. It is impossible to know how many songs were written and sung about John Dillinger, but the Library of Congress has collected a dozen or so, all created in the months immediately following his death. Some of these were printed with cover art, musical scores, and lyric sheets. More of them seemed to be homemade, never formally published, intended for local musicians and family ensembles.[5]

The lyrics were sung to well-known tunes, often printed with visual aids for chording guitars and ukuleles (popular in that era as a home instrument and on the stage). "John Dillinger" by Rieley "Singing Mountaineer" Lausch and Cliff "The Hill Billy" Grey begins with an author's note: "This song was written expressly for the prevention of crime and not to glorify the public enemy—CRIME DOES NOT PAY." The story is a morality play from the very first stanza:

> Oh come all you people
> A story I will tell
> A story of a bad man
> You all know very well
> His name is John Dillinger
> Public enemy number one
> Now lies a sleeping
> In a graveyard on a hill.

Similarly "Killer John Dillinger" sings of a murderer whom all decent people feared. A recording by the Frank Luther Trio (distributed under the title "Outlaw John Dillinger") is done in waltz time, with guitar and fiddle backing a single voice:

> That's the end of the foolish outlaw,
> Take warning all young men,
> Just stay on the Path that's narrow,
> And stay away from sin.

A bad man wreaks havoc, good men restore order, the straight and narrow is straightened and narrowed.[6]

Broadside conventions such as the formulaic "come all ye" openings make the songs feel old, and phrases like "lies a-sleeping" lend them a countrified air, as do writers' nicknames such as "The Hill Billy." Historically broadsides were vehicles for spreading the news, so the Dillinger ballads, much like their predecessors, had simple titles: "John Dillinger," "The Death of John Dillinger," "The Life and Death of John Dillinger." Broadsides were perfectly designed for telling the Dillinger story in the centuries-old outlaw tradition of American folk song. They were nostalgic throwbacks in an age of mass media, placing Dillinger in the lineage of Jesse James and Billy the Kid.[7]

Most of the songs condemned Dillinger's deeds while admiring his courage. "The Life and Fate of John Dillinger" warned of seeking riches only to find disgrace, but still called him "a gangster bold and true" and "our bravest gangster," whom the authorities captured only after a woman betrayed him. "John Dillinger" by Forrest Herbert admonished with stock pieties—"Children, look on the outlaw's grave / and know that crime does not pay"—yet still depicted Dillinger quite sympathetically. Many people feared the "little gunman," but more loved him dearly. Though he stole from banks, his conscience was clear because he refused to harm widows and orphans and he always fought fair. Only trickery allowed the federal men to get him:

> Right into a trap she led him,
>> Set by men with coward's fear;
> Men who shot and killed the gunman,
>> From behind, John Dillinger.

Americans from "every town and hamlet," the song concluded, came to Mooresville to pay their respects to the dead outlaw.[8]

The contrast between the virtues of the country and the corruptions of the city lay at the heart of these songs. "The Life and Death of John Dillinger" begins with two joyful parents in their Indiana home fussing over their "curly-headed boy." But as Johnnie grew to manhood he left this circle of love, and in Chicago, "the home of noted gangsters, where many a man is slain," he met his fate:

> And then began the manhunt, the greatest ever known,
> With plots and plans to trap him, both brains and skill were shown;

His draw was fast as lightning, rewards stood on his head,
"Go bring in this great criminal, whether he be alive or dead."

The bad man must be stopped, justice served, the innocent protected. Yet the law relied on cold-blooded calculation and deception, whereas Dillinger was an old school outlaw of the Wild West. The feds surrounded him and shot him down, "he had not a chance to draw." His death was necessary yet tragic. Dwight Butcher's "John Dillinger" invokes similar sentimental conventions of rural home and family. The song opens with a farmer's wife in Indiana, "famous for its waving corn," giving birth to a baby. As he grows up the boy wanders from the family hearth to the city and takes up drinking corn liquor and "bumming around" with loose women; soon he is robbing banks and taking his "share of evil fun." Good mothers versus evil women, corn in the fields versus corn whiskey, rural happiness versus urban vice; the song ends with the image of Ma and Pa back in Indiana, "grieving their poor old hearts away." Dillinger was emblematic not only of the individual's fall from grace, but of the nation's fall from rural virtue.[9]

Another song, "The Death of John Dillinger," seems, in its opening stanza, unequivocal in its condemnation of Dillinger:

For against God's mighty will
Many people he did kill
As he robbed the banks and terrorized the land.

As in the other songs, however, the descriptions of Dillinger's daring acts, especially his many escapes with "the dicks from Uncle Sam" in hot pursuit, form the ballad's emotional core. Thus the song ends not in a triumph of law and order, but in death by betrayal:

Like all other desp'rate men
This is the way he met his end
A WOMAN, and lies, and deceit.
And so ends this tail of woe,
Justice Agents dealt their blow
As he left the show and walked out on the street.

As if to underscore the point, the cover art for "The Death of John Dillinger" features a sketch of Lincoln Avenue, the Biograph theater on the left, two women in the center peeking out from a recessed doorway, and in the lower right-hand corner three G-men close behind Dillinger, one of them shooting him in the back as he lies face down in the alley. Bill Cox's recording of "Gangster's Yodel" describes how Johnnie swore revenge after the "dirty deal" that put him behind bars, how he escaped prison with a wooden gun, and how the police killed him after the woman in red betrayed him. His many friends thought it "a dirty shame the way they shot Johnny down."[10]

Dillinger is no sugary Robin Hood in these songs; he is not romanticized as a noble outlaw or public benefactor. His end is both predictable and necessary. But he is braver than the men who bring him down and represents something that many people feared was passing from America: manly valor, physical courage, and honor. The farm boy's end is tragic because he is not a bad man, just one who succumbs to the evil blandishments of the city: money, women, glamour, fame. H. Robinson Vaughan and Dorothy Hardy's "John Dillinger" make his death sound like an execution:

> In Chicago he was found, at the show he was shot down
> By Purvis and his men all there in line.
> They hunted day and night hoping just to get in sight
> Of the country's great outlaw of his time.[11]

Even more than the unmanly feds it was Anna Sage who bore the stigma of the betrayer. The red dress was the outward sign of a fallen woman, one who took money for love, who sold out for cold cash the man who trusted her. There is a powerful misogyny here, a fear that women might abandon their true roles as nurturers. Again, implicit is the notion that greed eroded all other values, and the city, with its riches and blandishments, was the breeding ground of avarice. Once he fell into its clutches, Chicago, America's most corrupt city, with its loose women, its flashy shows, its rich banks, killed the country boy.[12]

THROUGH THE MID-1930S the Dillinger saga remained newsworthy, especially as the last members of the gang met their ends. Just a month after Dillinger's demise, St. Paul policemen surrounded Homer Van Meter on a busy street and shot him down after a brief gun battle. Then in September Harry Pierpont and Charles Makley, largely forgotten as Attorney Jessie Levy ground out their death sentence appeals, grabbed headlines once again when, armed with fake pistols, they attempted to break out of the Ohio State Prison. Both were shot, Makley fatally. Newspapers reported that Pierpont begged his captors to finish him off, but instead the State of Ohio patched him up, then executed him in October.[13]

Meanwhile the Justice Department charged Louis Piquett, his assistant, Arthur O'Leary, the two plastic surgeons, Wilhelm Loeser and Harold Cassidy, as well as three others with harboring Dillinger. The legal maneuverings garnered front-page coverage, and J. Edgar Hoover himself took a hand in the case. FBI agents and Justice Department attorneys told reporters that the gang had planned some of their bank jobs in Piquett's rooms and that Dillinger's attorney was the "mastermind" of many of their operations. The case dragged on for months. Despite the feds' best efforts, on January 14, after just four hours of deliberation, the grand jury found Piquett not guilty of harboring Dillinger. The jurors agreed with Piquett's claim that the attorney-client relationship was a privileged one. The Chicago *Tribune* declared the verdict to be one of the biggest surprises in a federal case in years, and the paper described how Piquett, his wife, and friends danced down the hallways of the federal courthouse, shrieking with laughter as camera flashbulbs popped. But the celebration was short-lived. Piquett stood trial next on the charges of harboring Van Meter, who had never been his client, and this time the grand jury convicted him. He was sentenced to two years in prison and fined ten thousand dollars; two months later the Chicago Bar Association took away his license.[14]

Baby Face Nelson remained at large through much of this. The Justice Department had named him the new "Public Enemy Number One." Late in November the feds confronted Nelson, his wife, and another gangster, John Paul Chase, north of Chicago in the town of Barrington, Illinois. Two agents engaged in a running but inconclusive battle with the Nelson vehicle; a few minutes down the road two others pinned down Nelson and Chase, and Nelson opened up with machine-gun blasts that "avenged the slayings of his partners in crime," as the New York *Times* put it, for Baby Face had killed Samuel Cowley, who headed the team that brought down Dillinger, and Herman Hollis, one of the three shooters. Early reports claimed that Nelson escaped unscathed. In fact Hollis and Cowley shot him multiple times in the chest, abdomen, and legs. Chase and Mrs. Nelson drove him a few miles further, to Niles Center, Illinois, where he got out of the car and walked a short way, stripped off his clothes, fell into a ditch, and died. The following summer the FBI found John Hamilton's body and thereby crossed the last important member of the Dillinger gang off their list.[15]

By the end of the year the Dillinger story was a fading echo in the press. The reward money was given to Martin Zarkovich and Timothy O'Neil; James Probasco's sister received the payout on his life insurance policy; the by-standers hospitalized due to gunshot wounds they sustained at Little Bohemia and in front of the Biograph theater were compensated by an act of Congress. There continued to be arguments over who really took down Dillinger, FBI agents or East Chicago cops, and which officer fired the fatal shot. Other controversies still got some coverage: Had the authorities been too quick to fire their guns, too eager to pursue the end of criminals rather than the ends of justice? Was there truth to the reports that Dillinger and his father had been negotiating for a peaceful surrender to Indiana authorities just before the shooting on Lincoln Avenue? One of the most surprising announcements was the resignation of Melvin Purvis from the FBI almost exactly a year after Dillinger's death. Purvis denied there was tension between himself and J. Edgar Hoover. He said he left for "purely personal" reasons, but added, "Frankly, I'm glad to get out of here." Anna Sage also made it back into the papers. Ruled an undesirable alien for her criminal past running brothels in Gary, Indiana, federal agents late in April 1936 arrested her in Chicago, placed her on a train to New York City then on a boat across the Atlantic, on her way back to Romania.[16]

With the first anniversary of Dillinger's death in July 1935, the story began its passage from news to memory. Reporters marked the event with long retrospectives about Dillinger's life and fate. The Chicago *Tribune*, for example, gave two full pages to retelling the saga, and the article speculated how Dillinger got the gun that sprung him from Crown Point, who protected him, who betrayed him, and why. Was it true that Dillinger was on the verge of surrender when he was shot? Or that he was about to flee to Mexico? And probing a little below the surface the article asked once again why the FBI seemed uninterested in either posing or answering such disturbing questions.[17]

The Dillinger family continued their "Crime Does Not Pay" tour for a couple of years. Billie Frechette also went on the road when she got out of prison, giving lectures about her time with the gang. She even wrote a booklet about her experiences, emphasizing her regrets over them. Of course this was one way for a poor woman to make some money. The whole "crime does not pay" theme was always double-edged; the stories of life on the lam titillated audiences, not the moral lesson "don't you do it." But there is no reason to assume that Billie and the others were insincere. They had paid dearly for lives of crime—deaths of loved ones, jail time, guilt over the blood of innocents. Take the phrase "crime does not pay" literally, not morally, and it was true; the FBI, the police, and the courts exacted a high price from those who crossed the line. In Billie's case, years after she served her prison time, the Justice Department even attached her allotment—a small stipend given to Native Americans who can prove their lineage—to pay off the $1,000 fine she still owed the federal government.[18]

The feds also commemorated the anniversary. Hoover's office helped in the making of a radio drama. The National Broadcasting Corporation premiered a new series, *G-Men*, in prime time on Saturday, July 20. The very first episode told the story of "John Dillinger's reign of terror and its dramatic finish with the killing of the outlaw," written by the radio actor, director, and producer Phillips Lord. Newspapers reported that Hoover personally approved the script, that he insisted on vetting it. This doubtless explains the absence of any mention of Little Bohemia or of Melvin Purvis, though all the other G-men were named. Moreover, sensitive to charges that the Bureau was careless of civilians, the inaugural episode of *G-Men* described how a federal agent walked Lincoln Avenue dressed as a beggar just before the others gunned Dillinger down, the idea being that because people shunned mendicants, it gave agents both a clear path to their man and a way of preventing needless bloodshed. Bringing down Dillinger was the rock on which Hoover built his agency's reputation for toughness, efficiency, and morality, and he was more than willing to sacrifice accuracy for good publicity. With this auspicious beginning, *G-Men* reassured Americans week after week that a strong national police force protected them from evil.[19]

The feds marked their triumph over Dillinger in one more way. In the waiting room outside Hoover's office several display cases featured memorabilia of the FBI's war on crime. "The most compelling decorative object," the *New Yorker* reported in a 1937 profile of

Hoover, "is a startling white plaster facsimile of John Dillinger's death mask. It stares, empty-eyed, from under the glass of a display case. There are other exhibit cases in the anteroom, but this one, like a prize scalp, is significantly located closest to the Director's office. Grouped about the mask are souvenirs of the memorable night when the spectacular outlaw was cornered and shot down after he had emerged from a motion-picture theatre in Chicago." Hoover must have bristled at the phrase "spectacular outlaw"; he hated how people romanticized this "rat," this "foul murderer," this "cheap, boastful, selfish, tight-fisted plug-ugly," as he called Dillinger in his book, *Persons in Hiding*.[20]

Nonetheless the display case revealed just how much cop and robber, hunter and hunted, hero and antihero had needed each other, shaped each other's myth. Dillinger was not the most dangerous, violent, or sociopathic criminal of his day. His gang set no records for banks robbed, money stolen, or civilians murdered. Dillinger himself stood accused of killing only one man, Officer William O'Malley, when he allegedly returned O'Malley's fire. But Dillinger was the era's most charismatic criminal. What upset Hoover most was that the public *liked* him, all the more as he eluded his pursuers across the Depression-era landscape, more still as he fled the burdens of law, morality, and poverty. Dillinger proved that the old American fascination with movement, with flight, with lighting out for the territories was still alive, still glorious, even if the journey lasted only long enough to flame out and die. To die, his friends would add, not like a rat, but like a man.[21]

ADMIRING DILLINGER ALWAYS was a guilty pleasure. Toward the end of 1935 an attendant at Crown Hill Cemetery noted that visitors from out of town invariably found their way to his grave. They would ask where the Hoosier poet James Whitcomb Riley was buried, then look for Dillinger's tombstone. The next few decades were like that. Dillinger clearly had not slipped from public memory, but he made fewer and fewer appearances in print. Through the remainder of the Depression, World War II, and into the 1950s his name and story faded from public view.[22]

No books about him were published until twenty-five years after his death. Then a handful of novels appeared in the late 1950s and early 1960s, cheap paperbacks with characters named Dillinger,

Pierpont, and Frechette and lots of midwestern bank robberies, jail-breaks, and killings. But these books merely used the Dillinger narrative as a very rough outline for their own sex-and-murder plots. They cleaved to the FBI version of the story, portraying the gang as a bunch of bloodthirsty predators and Dillinger himself a megalomaniac, a sex fiend, and a brute. Even as their plots revealed that the wages of sin are death and that crime does not pay, they in fact paid handsomely by titillating readers and selling copies. You *can* tell these books by their covers: "The sordid story of Dillinger's love affairs is almost unbelievable," one jacket blurb declared. "No jail could hold him; no bullet could kill him." Whole events and characters were made up in these novels: a jewel heist at a New Year's Eve party in one, a "professor" who aids the gang by supplying weapons and planning bank jobs in another. The name Dillinger still resonated enough with sex and violence that publishers wanted it on their books' covers. Nonetheless the details of his story were sufficiently distant that authors felt free to make up whatever they pleased.[23]

Still, these novels marked the beginning of a Dillinger revival in popular culture. Newspapers covered the twenty-fifth anniversary of his death in 1959, though they did not give it prominence. One AP article opened by noting how distant it all seemed now: "Today the name Dillinger is nothing but a faint, bitter taste of memory for his family and the veteran policemen and reporters who were caught up in his sensational, bullet-pocked career." The article briefly reprised the highlights of his rampage and concluded that for the first few years after his death the path to his grave was well-worn. "All that is over now. Scarcely a dozen persons have inquired the way to the grave this twenty-fifth summer."[24]

The first substantial nonfiction works appeared in the early 1960s. In 1962 McGraw Hill issued Robert Cromie and Joseph Pinkston's painstakingly researched *Dillinger: A Short and Violent Life*. Cromie and Pinkston's work remains one of the best books available on the Dillinger gang. Theirs was the first book based on primary sources, and they did a remarkable job of piecing together the story. A year later Random House published John Toland's *The Dillinger Days*. Though it was also well researched—his papers at the Library of Congress reveal that he immersed himself in 1930s newspapers and conducted extensive interviews—Toland was a popular historian, and *The Dillinger Days* contains fictional dialogue and sensationalized events. Toland succeeded, however, in placing Dillinger at the center of a larger crime saga.[25]

Both works were part of the repackaging for a new generation of the "golden age of crime," the era stretching from Capone through Dillinger. Bootlegging, machine-gun wars, sexy gun molls, and high-speed chases in antique cars, all were part of a renewed interest in both celebrity gangsters and heroic G-men. Television was also part of this larger cultural revival of crime history. *The Untouchables* (1959–1963), a popular television series starring Robert Stack, dramatized several crime stories from the 1920s and 1930s. Beginning with the history of Treasury Department agent Elliot Ness, whose men had pursued and brought down Al Capone, *The Untouchables* based its stories loosely on the most famous felons. Crime quickly became a popular television genre, with the narratives invariably told from law enforcement's perspective. For example, week after week throughout the 1950s Los Angeles cops in the popular series *Dragnet* brought criminals to justice and kept the city safe. Such crime stories were integral to the culture of cold war America; dedicated government agents rooted out dangerous but unseen enemies, deviants and malcontents who threatened the social order.[26]

Dillinger had never disappeared from film as completely as the Hays Commission wanted, and movies, more than any other popular culture genre, helped revive his memory. Even in the 1930s elements of his story made it into theaters in various disguises and under assumed names. As we have seen, James Cagney made the shift from gangster to federal agent in the 1935 film *G-Men*, in which his humble yet heroic character, Buck Davis, pursued ruthless criminals through scenes that evoked Little Bohemia, Crown Point, and the Biograph. Just a year later a new star rose in American movies, one who looked remarkably like John Dillinger. Humphrey Bogart played Duke Mantee in the 1936 film *Petrified Forest*. Like *G-Men* the movie does not so much tell the Dillinger story as allude to it. The action takes place in a barbecue joint on a dusty road outside Flagstaff, Arizona, where the bleak landscape suggests the emptiness of desert lives. The gang terrifies citizens across the Southwest, though they were less bloodthirsty thugs than frightened men on the run. Mantee himself was not a monster but an amoral and laconic man, consumed with his own impending doom.[27]

Five years later, in 1941, Bogart starred in *High Sierra*, in which he played Roy "Mad Dog" Earle, a stickup artist recently sprung from prison in Indiana. Earle was no mad dog at all; he longed for life back on the farm and for the love of a woman, but he was pulled into a California jewel heist. At one point a crusty old character called Doc reminds Earle that Johnnie Dillinger himself said guys like them were just rushing toward death. Earle is a tough man but a good one, older but wiser, handsome and generous, well-spoken, with a soft spot for dogs and ill-treated women. He lives by his code: pride in his craft, loyalty to his friends, generosity toward those who depend on him. When the big heist goes bad, he ends up in a shoot-out high in the mountains from which he never returns.[28]

Such films whispered Dillinger's name with guarded sympathy. Not so when Hollywood broke the Hays Commission ban and released Monogram Studios' 1945 film *Dillinger*, a B movie that did surprisingly well at the box office. There was nothing at all sympathetic in actor Lawrence Tierny's portrayal of Dillinger. Craven, needy, scheming, ruthless, Tierny gives us a moral monster. In fact Chicago censors kept the film out of that city for years due to its violence. In seventy low-budget minutes *Dillinger* managed to retain some elements of the real story: smuggling guns for the big breakout, a shoot-out in the north woods, betrayal by a woman dressed in red. Director Max Nosseck danced around Hollywood's Motion Picture Production Code, getting away with depicting Dillinger by demonizing him and in the process stretching the code's limits of acceptable violence. The movie's most shocking scene involves a waiter who humiliates young Dillinger, insisting that he pay cash in advance for his drinks. Years later, unrecognized, Dillinger returns, buys him a drink, then another, then breaks a beer stein on a table and attacks him. We never see the assault itself, merely Dillinger's hand with the jagged glass coming at the man, then an empty place at the table where the waiter had been sitting and the tablecloth being pulled down toward the floor, clutched, no doubt, in his dying hand.[29]

A few years later Hollywood began to make movies more sympathetic to drifters and outlaws. James Dean, Marlon Brando, and Paul Newman embodied new men onscreen, rebels and renegades, defiant antiheroes, sometimes laconic or sullen, sometimes picaresque. It was only a matter of time before 1930s gangsters were reworked into the new mold. In 1967 Warner Brothers brought out *Bonnie and Clyde*, directed by Robert Penn and starring the little-known actors Warren Beatty and Faye Dunaway as the southwestern couple whose saga of holdups and murders overlapped with Dillinger's. Bonnie Parker and Clyde Barrow were never nearly as famous as Dillinger during the 1930s; indeed it is probably fair to say that the film made them better known in the late 1960s than in 1934. But with its main characters played by two striking actors who went on to become major stars, the relatively open sex and graphic violence, the depiction of life on the lam as an antidote to impoverished small-town ways, the clear sympathy for the outlaws and disdain for the police (especially in the depiction of the couple's death), *Bonnie and Clyde* became an iconic film of the 1960s. Amid that era's larger questioning of law and authority—over and over again during the decade, local police, the FBI, and the military were seen as forces of repression against the freedom struggle of African Americans, in the growing movement against the Vietnam War, in the loosening of moral strictures by the counterculture—the movie represented Hollywood's return to portraying crime as romance.[30]

Bonnie and Clyde set the tone for several new outlaw films in the late 1960s and early 1970s, all of them inflected with an antiestablishment sensibility. Like *Bonnie and Clyde*, director John Milius's 1973 feature *Dillinger* was a surprise hit. The narrative is highly fictionalized, yet many of the film's details are accurate. More important, *Dillinger* takes pains to convince us that we're getting the real story. The set design, the use of incidents like Little Bohemia and Crown Point, the graphic violence, all lend verisimilitude. From its very beginning the movie blurs the border between documentary and fiction. As the popular 1930s song "We're in the Money" plays, the opening credits roll across iconic scenes of hobo camps, breadlines, and the dust bowl. The film closes with a sequence of photos and texts enhancing its historicity. For example, next to a picture of the Woman in Red, played by Cloris Leachman, appear the words, "Anna Sage was deported to Romania in 1935 and never returned to the United States."[31]

Such details, however, ultimately served the purpose of myth more than history. *Dillinger* is pitched as a struggle between the outlaw and Melvin Purvis, played here by Ben Johnson, a big, rough looking, late-middle-aged man. Purvis announces that his goal is to smoke a cigar over the dead body of every public enemy, and given that his voice narrates the story we begin with the expectation that the film is about the triumph of law and order. But before it is over Purvis is the cold-blooded killer, Dillinger and his gang the more sympathetic, human, and finally tragic figures. Actor Warren Oates's John Dillinger has a mean streak, and sometimes he seems a bit hapless, but he is also courageous, honest, the moral center of the film.[32]

The first scene gives us a robbery in which Dillinger tells a bank filled with terrified people, "Nobody get nervous. You ain't got nothing to fear. You're being robbed by the John Dillinger gang, and that's the best there is. These few dollars you lose here today, they gonna buy you stories to tell your children, your great-grandchildren. This could be one of the big moments in your life. Don't make it your last."[33]

Throughout the film it is the outlaws, not the G-men, who forge emotional bonds with others. Billie Frechette, Mary Kinder, and the other molls are loved and loving. Harry Pierpont predicts more than once that a woman eventually will get Dillinger killed, but Johnnie and Billie (played by Michelle Phillips) are deeply alive to each other. Above all director Milius always keeps the Great Depression in view. The crisis that impoverished so many Americans is omnipresent, not just for background color, but as part of how people look, how they live in history and respond to the tragedy. In the 1945 *Dillinger* the Depression was barely noted at all, making it easier to render the outlaw a sociopath; in the 1973 film the historical context is key to understanding the story.[34]

Purvis does J. Edgar Hoover's bidding, yet the deaths of Dillinger's men are depicted less as the fruits of justice than executions. Pretty Boy Floyd, played by Steve Kanaly, joins the gang toward the end (there had long been rumors that he was with them for their last robberies), and the film portrays him as thoughtful, respectful, fully capable of the deeds of generosity which Depression-era bard Woody Guthrie sang. Separated from the gang and on the lam, sharing dinner with an elderly farmer and his wife as the feds gather outside, Floyd is offered a Bible by the woman. "I've sinned," he says to her gently, earnestly. "I've been a sinner. But I enjoyed it. And I've killed men. But the sons of bitches deserved it. No matter now. I figure it's too late for no Bible. But thanks just the same, ma'am." With that he goes out the back and tries to outrun his pursuers. They line up as a firing squad and shred his body at Purvis's command. The same brutality brings the end of Homer Van Meter. Played by Harry Dean Stanton, Van Meter is a violent man, not romanticized in the film. When he is wounded by vigilantes in a small town and asks for mercy, a dozen of them stand around his prone body, some wearing American Legion caps, and fire round after round into him.[35]

Scenes like these are far uglier than the gunfights depicted during bank robberies. Just before he goes to his death at the Biograph—just before Purvis himself guns Dillinger down—the outlaw returns to Indiana, where he parks his car a hundred yards from his father's home and looks longingly at the old farmstead as the venerable western theme "Red River Valley" plays. When his sister and father call to him, he drives away, back to Chicago and his fate. The movie leaves the viewer not with a sense of satisfaction that justice has been done, but with a feeling of emptiness. *Dillinger* in the end is a romantic film, the dead outlaw its tragic hero.[36]

SOMETIME AROUND THE LATE 1960S a new story about Dillinger began to circulate widely. Or more precisely, it was an old rumor slightly retooled. Joseph Snurr from Hagerstown, Pennsylvania, wrote to the Smithsonian Institution to ask whether John Dillinger's penis really was thirty-six inches long during an erection, as he had heard for years. And was it true that it resided in the Smithsonian Institution, preserved in alcohol for the benefit of researchers? Snurr was not alone in contacting the Smithsonian about "this nationally famous story," as another correspondent put it. The editors of the *Book of Lists*, urged on by letters from their readers, inquired of the Smithsonian whether the object in question might not be added to the "Preserved Human Parts" section in the new edition of their reference book.[37]

From roughly the beginning of the 1970s through the early 1990s the Smithsonian received a steady flow of inquiries on the subject. In the spirit of pure research, a student from San Antonio wrote that she was completing an undergraduate paper and needed to know if the Smithsonian held "any of Mr. Dillinger's personal belongings, especially anything unusual." A writer from Westwood, New Jersey, asked if the museum's exhibits centered "on a particular part of [Dillinger's] anatomy." A man from Durham, North Carolina, wrote that he had learned of the Smithsonian story from *Playboy* magazine but added that he wondered if the story was true, given the "filthy reputation" of that publication. One woman admitted that she was embarrassed to write but determined to settle a household dispute.[38]

Most asked about the legendary object as circumspectly as they could, but not everyone. One writer requested a photo of "the famous rod." Others simply inquired where it was displayed so they might come and get a look. Several correspondents asked about its dimensions. One can imagine the conversation that led to a brief and straightforward query—Do you have it and if so, where?—signed with elegant simplicity by "The Regular Customers of this Bar."[39]

Of course the letters' very existence betrays doubt about the object's reality, or at least its presence in the Smithsonian. A medical researcher from the University of Alabama, Birmingham, wrote that Dillinger's member was the subject of recurrent debate at local parties. A woman from Boston wanted to settle among friends the truth or falsehood of this "extraordinary vital organ." The president of a financial services firm in Palm Beach, Florida, was sure he had seen Dillinger's penis, but he didn't remember if it was at the Smithsonian or FBI headquarters, so he asked for clarification.[40]

In fact the Smithsonian was only the most prominent venue where legend placed Dillinger's manhood. In "A Quiz You Can't Refuse," a short test for gangster buffs published in *Playboy* in 1991, the question was asked, "Which place keeps insisting it does not have Dillinger's prodigious pecker pickled in formaldehyde?" The possible answers were (a) the National Museum of Health and Medicine in Washington, D.C.; (b) the Smithsonian Institution; (c) the Mutter Museum in Philadelphia; and (d) the Cook County, Illinois, Coroner's Office. The correct answer was all of the above, though the Smithsonian was the most frequently mentioned venue. One additional site might have been added: some claimed that the object in question lay for years in a jar of formaldehyde on J. Edgar Hoover's desk.[41]

The Smithsonian took pains to deny that it ever had anything to do with Dillinger's penis. A boilerplate memo from the Division of Medical Sciences stated in 1971 that the museum did not possess any part of his anatomy, adding, "We have never had an exhibit on Dillinger, nor do we have anatomical specimens in our medical collection." Twenty years later Museum Specialist Judy Chelnick composed a new memo for general circulation, noting that "this particular rumor has been running rampant for years" and denying that the Smithsonian or any other organization she knew of had any part of

Dillinger's body. In 1991 the museum's Public Inquiry Mail Service sent out more than one hundred copies of the denial. But the calls and letters kept coming. Chelnick said that she enjoys urging callers to be explicit: "Now, what exactly about John Dillinger interests you?"[42]

The notion of Dillinger's unusual endowment had been whispered around since that morgue photo in 1934. The crime scholar William Helmer notes that an eight-page pornographic pamphlet, a popular genre in the 1930s, featured Dillinger. In Indiana, stories about the outlaw's "prodigious pecker" circulated for years. One Hoosier believed that the "Lady in Red" betrayed Dillinger because they were lovers, and she just couldn't take it any more. Another claimed that although Dillinger's penis was twenty-three inches long flaccid, he was not a great lover because whenever he got an erection he passed out from lack of blood in his brain. One man from Washington, D.C., recalled hearing in junior high school during the 1950s that Dillinger's organ was so big and powerful that he had to strap it down to his leg for fear of it ripping through his pants.[43]

Stories of Dillinger's legendary manhood were usually told with a wink and a nod, not with a sense of leering at violent pornography. But in a few tellings the tale grows dark as it merges fantasies of sex and violence into rape. One letter to the Smithsonian, for example, asked if it was true that Dillinger's organ had killed several women during intercourse. Even without such overtly violent imagery, the Dillinger story was always about male prerogatives. What gave the whole Dillinger mythology its giddy quality was the vicarious breaking of rules and social conventions, but more, the letting go of tight self-control. While the dominant tone of the Smithsonian story was not violent misogyny or sexual aggression, it sometimes expressed such brutish fantasies. The Dillinger legend's ever-present themes of sex and violence invited listeners to envision abandoning self-restraint, which took a sadistic turn in some men's imaginations.[44]

Above all, the Smithsonian story is best thought of metaphorically. Dillinger had to be well endowed because he was so poised, so nervy, so fearless and so free. It makes sense that the Smithsonian legend, no doubt circulated mostly among men by word-of-mouth, seems to have arisen in the '60s and continued through the century. Dillinger's phallus is a fitting symbol for that era, when male fantasies of sexual adventure, of breaking through social constraints, of personal indulgence found heightened expression in popular culture.

As Barbara Ehrenreich observes, these years witnessed a range of male responses to domestic life, but a dominant theme was flight from commitment, more precisely flight from the burdens of marriage and family. Although no one made the connection at the time, Dillinger in some ways fit the bill as the cool, attractive outsider Norman Mailer had in mind when he coined the phrase "the white negro" to describe the disaffection of many American men from mainstream culture. Looked at this way, the letters to the Smithsonian constitute a palpable record of Dillinger's mythic capacities, preserved in the nation's official repository of memory.[45]

If the Smithsonian legend was a product of male desires of the '60s, '70s, and beyond, the sexualization of Dillinger was nonetheless there from the beginning. He was, after all, betrayed by "the woman in red," an image redolent with erotic pleasure, easy virtue, and sexual treachery. Sex was always central to the story, but so too was death, and the two were linked.[46] As reporters wrote back in 1934, he lived as he died, with a smile on his face and a woman on each arm, and in an instant, with a burst of gunfire and a spray of blood.

Even as the Smithsonian legend underscored fantasies of male sexual liberation for a new era, it undercut them too, as surely as the story of Anna Sage's betrayal. What could better symbolize the uneasiness, the ambivalence with Dillinger's alleged sexual potency—and with men's new erotic freedom—than death and castration, the outlaw's manhood safely pickled in formaldehyde and stashed away in the federal bureaucracy? How better to reaffirm the official version of the story—"The FBI always gets their man" and "You can't get away with it"—than imagining Dillinger's giant penis in a jar on J. Edgar Hoover's desk? In that light the Smithsonian story was at once about glorying in wild male sexuality and fears of its consequences. The price of uncurbed virility was death then castration at the hands of those who enforced the rules.[47]

BY THE TIME THE FIFTIETH ANNIVERSARY of Dillinger's death came along in 1984, his fame clearly was on the rise again. Most of those alive in 1934 were dead now, so Dillinger was barely part of living memory, and the sense of menace at the very bottom of the Great Depression engendered by ruthless gangsters firing Thompson machine guns from high-powered automobiles had largely faded. In July 1984 the

Associated Press began its story, "He stepped out into the sultry summer night feeling invincible, America's most notorious desperado with a woman on either arm. Shielded from the glow of streetlamps, a G-man lit a cigar and taking their cue, two more stepped from the shadows of the Biograph Theater." Though a factual account, it felt nonetheless like detective fiction, or like a movie in which the criminal must die.[48]

The Chicago *Sun-Times* anniversary article acknowledged that, to the police, Dillinger was nothing but a cop killer, a desperado, deserving death. But for the common man during the Great Depression, he was "Dillinger, the ladies man, phoning to taunt lawmen obsessed with his capture. Dillinger, the friend of the little guy, telling a bank customer during a robbery: 'I don't want your money. Just the bank's.' Dillinger, the country boy, seizing control of his own destiny." The *Sun-Times* noted that ten thousand people went to Mooresville for his wake and that his gravestone had been replaced four times because souvenir hunters kept chipping away at it. Similarly the Chicago *Herald* emphasized local color and Dillinger's personality, describing him as a folk hero of the Great Depression, a farm kid who robbed banks when banks were looked on as thieves, a modern-day Jesse James. The *Herald* told how Dillinger once wrote a letter to Henry Ford, praising his motorcars for their ability to outdistance other vehicles (the letter proved a forgery). The story concluded by calling the outlaw "a legendary womanizer who resembled Humphrey Bogart, gave his money away like Robin Hood, and thumbed his nose at authorities while managing to stay one step ahead of them."[49]

By the late twentieth century Dillinger had become a conduit of local Midwest color and nostalgia. "Town Can't Forget the Daring Dillinger," a 1991 *USA Today* feature declared, describing how folks in Fostoria, Ohio, still talked about his raid on their bank. "Loot in hand, Dillinger and Van Meter . . . came out of the bank firing wildly." The author underscored the story's filmic quality by noting at the end that the actor Mark Harmon would soon portray the outlaw in a new made-for-TV movie.[50]

The Dillinger of memory embodied a search for identity in what was perceived as a modern, homogenizing world. In 1987 the student newspaper at DePauw University in Greencastle, Indiana, ran an article discussing their town's moments of notoriety. "Nothing has come close to the day John Dillinger and three other men stole nearly $75,000, the largest haul of Dillinger's 15 month crime spree."

The article went on to quote from the Greencastle *Daily Banner* published just days after the robbery: "The story was soon on the press wires all over the country, because of the huge amount lost and it was not long before radio reports were made from stations even in New York City. Greencastle was heavily featured in glaring eight-column headlines. . . . It will be a long time before such a break comes for this city again." But Greencastle's "break" was renewable; retelling the Dillinger story as local history became a way of embracing the past. And it was not just Greencastle. In 1998 the public library in Bluffton, Ohio, put up a display of books and newspaper pieces on the outlaw and the local paper reprinted Dillinger articles from the 1930s. Story after story appeared in Indianapolis newspapers, and they got larger and better illustrated as the years passed. The Chicago *Tribune* travel section ran a story called "The Dillinger Trail" in 1994 that took up three full pages and laid out the sights for tourists—Little Bohemia, the Biograph theater, Crown Hill Cemetery—like stations of the cross.[51]

With time mellowing memories of the gangster era, and with crime stories now routinely on display in the media, the unthinkable half a century earlier now seemed reasonable. The Convention and Visitors Bureau of Lake County, Indiana, searched for a community willing "to sponsor a Dillinger attraction that might grow into something as big as Valparaiso's Popcorn Festival or Holland, Michigan's Tulip celebration." The executive director of the bureau predicted that "a Dillinger festival would spark the interest of the Midwest, as well as sparking an economic boon for Lake County." The Crown Point Chamber of Commerce appointed a committee to study the possibility of a Dillinger celebration. Some objected to making a notorious criminal the town's poster boy, but the city of East Chicago was already considering an annual reenactment of its Dillinger robbery, and a member of the Crown Point Chamber's executive board declared that it would be a shame for his town to be left behind: "We glorify events in our history all the time, good and bad. . . . People come to our town every day asking where it happened. If they want to ask the question, we should be providing the answer." Northwest Indiana had suffered an economic cataclysm during the deindustrialization of the 1980s and 1990s. Factories folded and unemployment rates soared. Perhaps tourism was the answer, and maybe the first Public Enemy Number One, the man whom the Hays Commission banned from

American theaters and J. Edgar Hoover called a rat, could help bolster civic pride and boost commerce.[52]

Lake County got its attraction when the Visitors Bureau opened the Dillinger Museum in 1999. Hammond, however, not Crown Point or East Chicago, was the winning town. In 1975 the Dillinger chronicler Joe Pinkston had used his extensive memorabilia collection as the basis for the John Dillinger Historical Wax Museum in Nashville, Indiana. On display with typewritten labels were Dillinger's baseball spikes, his original headstone, yellowing newspaper clippings, a copy of his death mask, the infamous wooden gun, his 1933 Essex Terraplane-V8, and the blood-stained pants he wore on his last night on earth. The museum had something of a carnival sideshow atmosphere. Pinkston commissioned several wax figures depicting gory moments in Dillinger's life, as well as effigies of Pretty Boy Floyd, Baby Face Nelson, Bonnie and Clyde, Ma Barker, and others.[53]

When Pinkston died in 1996 his family sold everything to the Lake County Convention and Visitors Bureau for four hundred thousand dollars. For another one million dollars the Bureau hired the ICON Exhibits Company, which specializes in creating trade shows, to design a "hands-on historical adventure." The new museum is located in the Lake County Visitors Center, at the Illinois-Indiana border on the interstate highway to Chicago. It has not been without controversy. Just before the museum opened, the Lake County sheriff—Lillian Holley's successor almost three generations later—denounced the whole idea as a monument to a criminal and a cop killer. Other Lake County officials reassured him that the place would be as much about crime fighting and crime's victims as criminals. The sheriff relented. Then Dillinger's grandnephew sued the museum, arguing that the anticrime tilt slandered his uncle. He claimed that under Indiana law he had the right to protect the Dillinger family name and that the museum defamed it by calling Dillinger a murderer, when in fact he had never been charged with or convicted of homicide. The courts took the suit seriously, and the museum closed for a few years. The parties finally reached an out-of-court settlement in 2008, and the Dillinger Museum reopened that year.[54]

Tucson too got on the Dillinger heritage bandwagon. Beginning in the 1990s the Hotel Congress began sponsoring special events to commemorate the gang's apprehension, and by the next decade the whole town was involved. "The capture of outlaw John Dillinger at the historic Hotel Congress in downtown Tucson is one true tale that is celebrated every year," Rio Productions, the company responsible for inventing the tradition, declared in a 2005 press release. Set to coincide with the anniversary of the gang's moment in that western town, "Dillinger Days" featured a reenactment of their capture by Action Unlimited Entertainment, a mock fire in the Hotel Congress, a street festival, an antique car and truck show, a display of the Dillinger gang's arsenal, and a walking tour of important sights. The following year Action Unlimited included a bank robbery and car chase during the festival (neither of which actually happened in Tucson in 1934). The Tucson Downtown Alliance filled in with an antiques market, craft fair, puppet show, rope-trick demonstration, bluegrass band and swing band, as well as more displays of antique cars, guns, and clothes, while the Congress's restaurant offered such special dishes as "killer apple pie," and "hit man's omelet." Unfortunately the 2006 festivities were marred when a sixteen-year-old boy stole a car, drove down-town, then plowed through a police barricade. He hit an off-duty cop, scattered terrified citizens, and came to a stop only when another offi-cer unloaded his gun at the stolen vehicle. Fortunately no one was seriously injured. The boy was taken into custody for grand theft auto and aggravated assault, crimes certainly in keeping with the spirit of the day.[55]

One thing that clearly had changed as the twentieth century gave way to the twenty-first was the balance between Dillinger as pub-lic menace and Dillinger as attractive rogue. "Felonious and Urbane, Dillinger Still Charms," a New York *Times* headline declared on the seventieth anniversary of his death in 2004, arguing that "the debo-nair bank robber" had, in the 1930s, "reached a level of fame equaled only by Charles Lindbergh and Franklin Roosevelt." During the Depression openly admiring Dillinger was controversial. By the late twentieth century, as Dillinger's name became associated with street festivals, vintage cars, and even punk bands (the Dillinger Escape Plan) and hip-hop artists (Daz Dillinger), the rawness of his story became less and less accessible. Like so much else in American culture, the more that people sought authentic experience, the more they found media creations. The more that marketplace efficiency and bureau-cratic obligations filled their days, the more they craved "real life." And the more that boredom drove them to look for authenticity, the more the marketplace sold them pale simulacra.[56]

There was a related change. During the 1930s authorities tagged Dillinger a public enemy in part because of his image as a social avenger. J. Edgar Hoover considered Dillinger dangerous not only because he stole money and shot people, but because citizens found in his story a conduit for their own rage. From the beginning many interpreted Dillinger's life through the prism of class. His rampage against banks crystallized the anger they felt against the economic system that had betrayed them. With time the Depression, poverty, and social injustice became less central to the telling of his story, but class never disappeared entirely; it was quite present in Milius's 1973 film, for example, which came out in an era when exposing social inequality was very much on the national agenda. But in the last years of the twentieth century Dillinger's role as a social avenger grew lighter, the emphasis on nostalgia, on antique cars and old guns and vintage clothes heavier. Rebellion became more than ever a matter of style. The old outlaw had been domesticated.[57]

THE AMOUNT OF MATERIAL on Dillinger keeps growing, and books about his life appear with increasing frequency. Jay Robert Nash assembled his case that Dillinger did not die that night at the Biograph in his 1982 book, *The Dillinger Dossier*. In 1990 William Helmer discovered Russell Girardin's manuscript and edited it as *Dillinger: The Untold Story*. Five years later Paul Maccabee brought out *John Dillinger Slept Here*, a study of crime in St. Paul, with special focus on the Hoosier bandit. Academics have also stepped in. In her excellent 1998 book, *War on Crime: Bandits, G-Men and the Politics of Mass Culture*, the historian Claire Bond Potter argues that the federal government's initiatives against the underworld were part of a larger effort at New Deal state building, and bringing down Dillinger became central to making the FBI indispensable to that goal. The literary critic William Beverly includes a long chapter on Dillinger and the meanings of being a fugitive in his thoughtful 2003 book, *On the Lam: Narratives of Flight in J. Edgar Hoover's America*.[58]

New books continue to appear. Perhaps the most original one is journalist Ellen Poulsen's 2002 work, *Don't Call Us Molls: Women of the John Dillinger Gang*, noteworthy because Poulsen helps us understand the feelings and motivations of the working-class women who ran with the gang. Dary Matera brought out a new biography, *John Dillinger: The Life and Death of America's First Celebrity Criminal*, in 2005, and it is far richer in detail than anything that preceded it.

Brian Burrough's *Public Enemies*, also published in 2005, uses Toland's structure of jump-cutting from one big crime story to another, with Dillinger at the center, but with far more detail and much greater fidelity to primary sources, including the FBI's enormous Dillinger dossier. Two more books appeared that same year. Jeffrey S. King's *The Rise and Fall of the Dillinger Gang* focuses on Pierpont, Makley, Nelson, and the rest, while Melvin Purvis's son Alston (with Alex Tresniowski) published *The Vendetta: FBI Hero Melvin Purvis' War Against Crime, and J. Edgar Hoover's War Against Him*, a vindication of Agent Purvis and a critique of the FBI.[59]

Painters, poets, and novelists also have turned to Dillinger. A few years after the outlaw's death the publishing mogul Henry Luce commissioned Reginald Marsh to paint the bandit as part of a series on recent history. Luce reproduced the work on a full page of *Life* magazine in March 1940. Marsh was famous for his street scenes, including the late-night revels of gamblers, prostitutes, and underworld characters. He called his painting *The Death of Dillinger*. The perspective is from the sidewalk, looking back up Lincoln Avenue toward the Biograph theater. In the foreground Anna Sage—by far the brightest object in the painting in her red dress—and Polly Hamilton casually walk out of the frame. Behind them several G-men stand shoulder-to-shoulder, shooting Dillinger in the back. He is halfway between standing and falling, reaching for his gun, just on the verge of crumbling to the ground, caught between the one who betrayed him and those who used her information to destroy him.[60]

Years later the poet Todd Moore wrote an epic cycle on the Hoosier outlaw, an early example of what has come to be known as "outlaw poetry." The first poem, "The Name Is Dillinger" (1980), evokes Walt Whitman and Carl Sandburg:

> I sing my name Dillinger
> I have heard it in the wind off Lake Michigan
> I have heard it crossing the Mississippi
> I have heard it driving across Jesse James' Missouri at night.

Moore's protagonist tells us boldly,

> I can take a bank or a girl w/a look
> they will make movies about me
> they will tell stories about me

they will yell at the top
of their lungs about me.

For Moore, Dillinger's identification with America, and America's
identification with him, are all about masculine power, expressed in
images of factories and blue-collar work:

dillinger of the machines
freight engines automobile plants
foundries coal mines barges
I drive past them and feel that
power lift into my body
energy of all that floats through me

Above all Dillinger has the nerve of an outlaw. "I'm still dillinger
goddamit," he shouts,

the dillinger of the shot out headlights
the dillinger of shotguns at close range
fast take dillinger
hideout dillinger
distant dillinger
10 wanted Dillinger

Dillinger's manic energy, his fearlessness, wild ambition, and love of
life embody America, and it is America itself that is betrayed when
he is gunned down.[61]

Fiction writers too have turned to the Hoosier outlaw as part of
their fascination with the demimonde. Jack Kelly's 1992 novel *Mad
Dog* embraces Dillinger as an existential hero, a man true to his code
of honorable action. The backdrops for Kelly's story are the small prairie towns and plains crossroads where circus and medicine-show per-
formers scratched out a living night by night in hard times. *Mad Dog*
tells the Dillinger story from the point of view of an unnamed narrator who happened to look like the Indiana bandit and used that resemblance to go on the road, reenacting scenes from the life of the outlaw
in a traveling carnival. Playing Dillinger, embodying him, then thinking back on the '30s, he came to understand what his life meant: "We
were all desperate then, as the young are always desperate—in good
times too, but especially in bad. We were all desperate and we were
all scared and we needed somebody to display our desperation. . . ."

Dillinger was the one who had the courage to act when courage was so hard to come by, and his life gave voice to bottled-up yearnings and desires. "People loved John Dillinger," the actor blurts out to his audience in the end, his life now deeply entangled with the outlaw's: "They love him to this day. Because he dared. . . . He didn't lie down and take it. He didn't hang his head over hard times. He didn't bemoan his fate. He carried his courage into the world and he took what he wanted. And they shot him down. . . . He was a man who had the nerve to do what thousands would have done, but were afraid to."[62]

James Carlos Blake's 2004 novel *Handsome Harry* echoes some of the same themes. Blake begins with the old rumor that Harry Pierpont was the brains behind the Dillinger gang. Pierpont tells his story as a flashback on the eve of his execution in Ohio. We learn of his early troubles with the law, his time in the Indiana State Prison, and the gang's wild four months on the lam before being captured in Tucson. What is most striking about the book is Blake's ability to imagine the daily lives and feelings of the gang. Pierpont, Dillinger, Mary Kinder, and the rest do not come across as particularly antisocial or misanthropic, though the author certainly does not tidy up their crime scenes, or the blood they spill. Nor does he depict them as singularly accomplished or unusual, except in their loyalty to each other and their devotion to rejecting the restraints imposed by the straight life—conventional marriage, a regular job, bureaucratic rules, deference to authority, the limits of a paycheck. Theirs is the courage of not giving in to life's crushing dailiness, right up to Pierpont's final moment of life before the current surges in the electric chair.[63]

"The Name Is Dillinger," *Mad Dog*, and *Handsome Harry* all capture the defiance that lies at the heart of the Dillinger story. Being the last outlaw meant lighting out for the territories, both literally and metaphorically, heading into the borderlands between legal jurisdictions, the new highways through rural America, Chicago's anonymous urban neighborhoods. Hoover provided the counterpoint, law versus outlaw, social order versus personal freedom, the manliness of the rule giver versus the manliness of the bandit. Hoover was the ultimate Washington bureaucrat, not just in the 1930s but throughout his life. His career and his power were based on gathering information—fingerprints, field reports, dossiers, wiretaps—and systematizing it to unmask hidden truths, and then to coerce, pressure, and blackmail others. Of course most Americans did not reject

Hoover's rule of law and order, of conventional morality late in the twentieth century and into the twenty-first. Quite the contrary. Still, the world of rational, calculating ways and regimented bureaucratic power often felt so spiritually empty, so aesthetically bankrupt. Kelly's narrator in *Mad Dog* warns his half-comprehending listeners in the end not to go home and tell their children that crime does not pay: "What does pay? Does selling off your life by the tablespoon pay? Does spending all your time counting what you've got to lose pay?" In fantasy, anyway, decades after his death, Dillinger still channeled Americans longings for the outlaw's free skies, for a wild ride on the open road.[64]

SEVENTY-FIVE YEARS AFTER HIS DEATH, the Hoosier outlaw is with us still. Even as this book goes to press Hollywood is making a new blockbuster movie about John Dillinger, starring Johnny Depp, one of America's most popular actors, directed by the respected film-maker Michael Mann and filled with a stellar cast. Moreover, as I write these words in the fall of 2008 America's financial system tee-ters on the brink of collapse, and the most serious economic down-turn since the Great Depression is upon us. Newspapers are filled daily with stories of bank failures, home foreclosures, and rising unemployment; comparisons to the 1930s, whether they prove accu-rate or not, are everywhere. A recent column by a film critic noted the coincidence of these two facts, the soon-to-be-released Dillinger film and the economic crisis. "I always wanted to be a Depression era rural bandit and folk hero," he fantasizes, "sticking up greedy banks with my hot, cheap-looking, even more psychotic moll at my side. And what a way to go—dying in a hail of gunfire while screaming, 'You'll never take me, coppers.'" Art and life are imitating each other once again, and John Dillinger, I suspect, armed and dangerous, is smiling at us from somewhere beyond the grave.[65]

Acknowledgments

I've wasted an otherwise promising career writing about the likes of boxers and brawlers, labor organizers, and bank robbers. All the words I've written over the years while working history's city desk are connected by the generous help I received along the way.

Four good friends read the entire manuscript and suggested important changes. Timothy Spears at Middlebury College, Lynn Dumenil at Occidental College in Los Angeles, Timothy Gilfoyle of Loyola University, Chicago, and Arthur Casciato of Rutgers University all proffered commas and active verbs, encouragement and ideas. They made me look smarter than I am. Good friends will do that for you.

My first writing about John Dillinger appeared in a book of articles by several students of Lawrence Levine, *The Cultural Turn in U.S. History*, published by the University of Chicago Press and edited by Michael O'Malley, Jay Cook, and Lawrence Glickman. The book showcases how much Larry influenced all of us. He passed away before it appeared, but I think he would have liked it. I really miss Larry; we all do.

John Aubrey, librarian extraordinaire at the Newberry Library, first suggested Dillinger as a topic when I approached him and said, "I'm getting interested in crime in the '30s; what have you got?" The Newberry has long given me a fine place to work in my real hometown, Chicago. A year's leave of absence in my original hometown, generously provided by a Los Angeles Times fellowship at the

Huntington Library in 2005–2006, allowed me to write the first draft of this book. Over the years, the Huntington's Roy Ritchie has provided a wonderful environment for scholars, as has the Newberry's James Grossman.

Other archives were generous with their time and resources: the Library of Congress, the National Archives, the Federal Bureau of Investigation, the Indiana Historical Society, the Indiana State Library, the Indiana State Archives, the Chicago History Museum, the Popular Culture Archives at Bowling Green State University, the Wisconsin State Historical Society, and the John Dillinger Museum in Hammond, Indiana, as well as the film archives at the University of South Carolina and at UCLA. I also got important research assistance from Carson Cunningham, Christopher Lamberti, Alexa Rosenbloom, and Consigliere Ken Glaspey.

I received help with images from John Russick, Peter Alter, and Rob Medina, all of the Chicago History Museum; from Christopher Lamberti, Dustin Edward Arnold, and John Kappelman; and especially from Erika Sheeringa of the John Dillinger Museum, housed in the Lake County Welcome Center in Hammond, Indiana. My friend Stephen Wade found and recorded several old Dillinger ballads for me, and Lisa Maria Olavaria kindly shared her research.

Don Lamm and Christy Fletcher at Fletcher Agency helped bring this project to a good home, and at Oxford University Press, Timothy Bent, Dayne Poshusta, and Joellyn Ausanka all made it a better book. Judith Hoover gave the manuscript a thorough copy editing, and John Bealle supplied a fine index.

At Brown University, where I work, Mary Beth Bryson, Julissa Bautista, Cherrie Guerzon, Karen Mota, Jean Wood, and Rosanne Neri have been unfailingly helpful, and more, nice to me. I have been lucky to have supportive colleagues at Brown; let me mention Robert Self, Seth Rockman, Naoko Shibusawa, Michael Vorenberg, Karl Jacoby, Howard Chudacoff, Maud Mandel, and Ken Sacks in History, and Robert Lee, Susan Smulyan, Patrick Malone, Ralph Rodriguez, Richard Meckel, Beverly Haviland, Steven Lubar, Sandy Zipp, Matt Garcia, Robert Emlen, Rhacel Parreñas, and Mari Jo and Paul Buhle, all in the American Civilization Department.

And then there are friends who supplied ideas or gave support or laughed at my jokes or made me laugh at theirs. In no particular order they include Arthur Casciato, John Powell and Genai Stoneburner,

Ashley Dodge, Harvey Kaye, Paul Mapp, Chris Elzey, Ben Johnson and Michelle Nickerson, Jack Kirby, John Donoghue, Thomas Jundt, Danny Greene, Tony Cardoza and Cathy Mardikes, Michael Khodarkovsky, Robert Warde, Steven Smith, John Schulian, Tom Silfen, Larry Malley, James Farr, Gary Ogimachi, Fred Hobson, Bruce Levine and Ruth Hoffman, Kate Rousmaniere, Susanne Kaufman and Bill Sites, Margaret Vines, Mike and Christine Gorn, Roberta Wollons, Frank and Marie Travisano, William Stout, Arnold Barnes, Amanda Marquez, Damian Fischer, Vicki Perez, and Mr. Sack. And let's not forget Dr. Blair, Curtis Davison, Piper Pfister, Yoda, and Landau.

Finally, in all the years I've known him, Terry Bouton did nothing.

Notes

Chapter One

1. James Finan, "Our Foot-Loose Correspondents," *New Yorker*, May 19, 1934, p. 67.

2. Ibid., pp. 67–68.

3. Ibid., p. 69.

4. Ibid., pp. 70–71.

5. On the deep history of the rural ideal in America, see Henry Nash Smith, *Virgin Land: The American West as Symbol and Myth* (Cambridge, Mass.: Harvard University Press, 1970), and Leo Marx, *The Machine in the Garden: Technology and the Pastoral Ideal in America* (New York: Oxford University Press, 2000). On Chicago, see William Thomas Stead, *If Christ Came to Chicago* (Chicago: Laird and Lee, 1894), and Herbert Asbury, *Gem of the Prairie: An Informal History of the Chicago Underworld* (New York: Knopf, 1940).

6. Lynn Dumenil, *The Modern Temper: American Culture and Society in the 1920s* (New York: Hill and Wang, 1995), p 11. On agriculture during the Great Depression, see Theodore Saloutos, *The American Farmer and the New Deal* (Ames: Iowa State University Press, 1982), and Donald Worster, *Dust Bowl* (New York: Oxford University Press, 1979).

7. Newspapers ran stories under such titles as "Dillinger: The Country-Boy Killer" by Robert J. Casey, Chicago *Daily News*, July 25, p. 5, July 26, p. 5, July 27, p. 9.

8. The Indiana Division of the Indiana State Library (hereafter ISL) in Indianapolis has an excellent genealogy of the Dillinger family, including the marriage certificate for Matthias and Mary Dillinger and United States manuscript census information for the Dillingers in Shelby County in 1870 and Marion County in 1880; Dillinger Genealogy File.

9. *Indianapolis City Directory* (Indianapolis: R. L. Polk), 1892, p. 300, 1897, p. 314, 1900, p. 352, 1903, p. 376, 1907, p. 417, 1913, p. 504; Dillinger Genealogy File,

ISL; Dillinger marriage documentation from www.Ancestry.com. On populism, try Lawrence Goodwin, *Democratic Promise: The Populist Moment in America* (New York: Oxford University Press, 1976); and Michael Kazin, *A Godly Hero: The Life of William Jennings Bryan* (New York: Knopf, 2006).

10. Dillinger's original birth record can be found in the collection of documents labeled "John Dillinger" in the Mooresville Public Library (hereafter MPL). See "Obituaries: Audrey Hancock," Mooresville *Times*, April 8, 1987, p. 2a, Dillinger Genealogy File, ISL. The Manuscripts Division of the State Library also houses an untitled, unpublished manuscript of John Dillinger Sr. telling the life of his son to the reporter John Cejnar. Cejnar published pieces of it as articles, but here I cite the full original. Mrs. John Cejnar Collection, LL29, box 1, folder 7, p. 1 (hereafter Dillinger Sr. ms), ISL.

11. Dillinger Sr. ms, p. 2, ISL. For an abbreviated version of these years in Indianapolis, see G. Russell Girardin with William J. Helmer, *Dillinger: The Untold Story* (Bloomington: Indiana University Press, 1994), pp. 10–12.

12. Dillinger Sr. ms, file 6, pp. 4–5, ISL; Robert Cromie and Joseph Pinkston, *Dillinger: A Short and Violent Life* (1962; Evanston, Ill.: Chicago Historical Bookworks, 1990), pp. 6–9; Girardin, *Dillinger*, p. 11; Dillinger Sr. ms, file 6, p. 12, ISL.

13. John Toland is most given to such psychological explanations in *The Dillinger Days* (New York: Random House, 1963), pp. 5–9. Toland's papers at the Library of Congress include a "handwriting analysis" of Dillinger's script. Such analyses were popular in the 1950s and 1960s, and they supposedly revealed deep traits of character. "He was obsessed by a love of and desire for power. To him money meant his kind of power. With that basic urge women were to be used and cast aside when they no longer added to his sense of power. . . . He was greatly over-sexed. . . . He was driven by a desire to have everything he wanted in his own way. He carried a life-long resentment toward society and toward religion." "Analysis of Writing of John Dillinger," September 3, 1961, John Toland Papers, box 57, Dillinger Miscellany, Library of Congress. Dary Matera, John Dillinger's most recent biographer, repeats many of Toland's suspect stories and adds a few more in *John Dillinger: The Life and Death of America's First Celebrity Criminal* (New York: Carroll and Graf, 2004), pp. 9–15. Brian Burrough also relies on Toland for his book *Public Enemies* (New York: Penguin Press, 2004), pp. 134–36. The evidence on young Dillinger is not only fragmentary and contradictory, but much of it was filtered through memories of who he became: neighbors and acquaintances were interviewed decades after his crime spree, when he was already legendary. Audrey Dillinger gave a long interview to Bette Walls, titled "Has John Dillinger's Real Story Been Told?" Martinsville (Ind.) *Daily Reporter*, October 12, 1971, p. 6. She complained that none of the writers who interviewed her over the years ever accepted her story: that John was a good boy, not a troubled kid, that he was contrite for the crime that landed him in prison, but that nine years of incarceration changed him.

14. Toland, *The Dillinger Days*, pp. 5–8. Toland's notes from interviews with those who knew young Dillinger are found in box 57 of his collected papers in the Library of Congress (hereafter, LC). Matera too builds a case for a pathological young Dillinger, but it is not convincing. For example, he quotes an interview with the lad's Sunday school teacher, Elsa Ellsbury: "Johnnie was mischievous like the rest of them, but he was such a healthy, normal specimen of a boy that you couldn't help liking him." From this Matera says that Ellsbury was one of the first to recognize the outlaw's "bipolar charm." Matera, *John Dillinger*, p. 14.

15. See Walls, "Dillinger's Real Story," p. 6; Dillinger Sr. ms, chapter 1, ISL; Tony Stewart, *Dillinger, the Hidden Truth* (n.p.: Xlibris, 2002), pp. 89–103.

16. Dillinger's prison records document his work history; Indiana State Archives, Indiana Commission on Public Records, Department of Corrections, Indiana State Prison and Indiana State Reformatory, Dillinger Gang Papers and Packets, DV 13, boxes 1–4 (hereafter Dillinger Gang Papers and Packets, ISA); see especially Jas. P. Burcham to A. F. Miles, October 6, 1924. Also see Dillinger Sr. ms, pp. 6, 9, 28.

17. Walls, "Dillinger's Real Story," p. 6; Cromie and Pinkston, *Dillinger*, pp. 8–10; Girardin, *Dillinger*, pp. 12–14; Matera, *John Dillinger*, pp. 15–20. Dillinger Senior describes this ill-fated courtship in Dillinger Sr. ms, pp. 6–7, ISL. In his autobiographical statement to officials at the Indiana Reformatory Dillinger described himself as having left home at age sixteen; in other words, he considered himself independent from his family after they moved to Mooresville.

18. W. R. Shoemaker, Chief, Bureau of Navigation, Navy Department, to Warden A. F. Miles, Pendleton Reformatory, December 1, 1924, Dillinger Gang Papers and Packets, box 4, file 1, ISA. The Navy gave this information to the Bureau of Investigation, and it was circulated in a memo from Washington; see report by R. P. Burruss, Washington, D.C., March, 17, 1934, pp. 1–3, Dillinger File, 62–29777.145, FBI. Dillinger's father failed to mention his son's enlistment and discharge at all in Dillinger Sr. ms, ISL. One story had it that Dillinger did not go home after leaving the Navy until spring, that he spent the winter in Indianapolis.

19. Stewart, *Dillinger*, pp. 81–104; Walls, "Dillinger's Real Story," p. 6; Dillinger Genealogy; records reproduced from www.Ancestry.com, Indiana Marriages, 1845–1920, in Dillinger Sr. ms, ISL, p. 9.

20. Walls, "Dillinger's Real Story," p. 6; Cromie and Pinkston, *Dillinger*, pp. 8–12.

21. Information on Dillinger's kin is scattered throughout Dillinger Genealogy File, ISL.

22. Taken from a typescript oral history interview with Ralph Morgan Townsend, from the *Hendricks County History Bulletin*, May 1991, pp. 8–9, Dillinger file, MPL. Dillinger's confession is found in Dillinger Gang Papers and Packets, box 4, file 1, ISA; "An Attempted Holdup," Mooresville *Times*, September 12, 1924, reprinted in Martinsville (Ind.) *Daily Reporter*, September 23, 1971, clipping in Dillinger file, MPL. Also see Girardin, *Dillinger*, p 16; Walls, "Dillinger's Real Story," p. 6.

23. Dillinger Sr. ms, file 7, pp. 9–17, file 8, p. 1 ISL; John Cejnar interview with John Dillinger and Audrey Hancock, Mrs. John Cejnar Collection; Dillinger Sr. ms, pp. 21–26, ISL.

24. Cromie and Pinkston, *Dillinger*, pp. 12–14, give a detailed account of the crime and arrest. In addition to the stiff jail term, Judge Williams fined Dillinger one hundred dollars for each of the two counts and disenfranchised him for twelve years. Mooresville *Times*, September 19, 1924, p. 1, October 17, 1924, p. 1, both in Dillinger file, MPL; Dillinger Sr. ms, file 7, pp. 9–17, file 8, p. 1 ISL; Cejnar interview with Dillinger Sr. and Hancock, pp. 21–26, ISL. The version that Cejnar wrote emphasizes liquor as the source of Singleton's evil influence over Johnnie more than the interview with Old John and Audrey does. Also in the interview, Dillinger Senior claims that the court was prepared to set Johnnie free for lack of evidence until he, a self-described ignorant farmer, intervened and told his son to plead guilty.

25. Dillinger Gang Papers and Packets, box 4, file 1, ISA, including "Biographical Statement."

26. Ibid.; H. L. to the Indiana Reformatory, December 31, 1924, Dillinger Gang Papers and Packets, box 4, file 1, ISA; John Dillinger to Mary Hancock, March 2, 1930, in Cromie and Pinkston, *Dillinger*, p. 21. Most of the few surviving Dillinger's letters were in the possession of Joe Pinkston, who collected them for years, then displayed them in the Dillinger Museum he founded in Nashville, Indiana. They ended up in the archives of the latest incarnation of the Dillinger Museum, the Indiana Visitors Center in Hammond. In spring 2008 the Visitors Center settled a lawsuit out of court brought by Jeffrey Scalf, Dillinger's great-nephew, who claimed that the museum defamed his ancestor. The lawsuit made the letters unavailable to me, and they were still unavailable as I finished this book. Fortunately Cromie and Pinkston and Toland reprinted most of the Dillinger correspondence that survives; copies of several of the letters are also on display once again at the Dillinger Museum, and a few are transcribed in the Toland Papers, LC.

27. Superintendent A. F. Miles, printed form letter; Jas P. Burcham to A. F. Miles, October 6, 1924, Dillinger Gang Papers and Packets, box 4, file 1, ISA.

28. E. F. Hadley to A. F. Miles, September 22, 1924; T. H. Greeson to A. F. Miles, October 31, 1924, both in Dillinger Gang Papers and Packets, box 4, file 1, ISA.

29. Matera, *John Dillinger*, pp. 26–37. The Pendleton Dillinger file contains several Officers Reports for Violation of Rules; the one quoted above is #105, dated October 17, 1928; Assistant Superintendent H. S. (?) to Superintendent A. F. Miles, November 22, 1928, Dillinger Gang Papers and Packets, box 4, file 1, ISA. The State Reformatory file also contains summaries of prisoner infractions, in this case, for #14395, John Dillinger, Dillinger prison file, ISA.

30. Mrs. John W. Dillinger to Superintendent A. F. Miles, no date; Mrs. Audrey Hancock to Superintendent A. F Miles, July 21, 1927; A. F. Miles to Mrs. John W. Dillinger, June 17, 1926, all in Dillinger Gang Papers and Packets, box 4, file 1, ISA; John Dillinger Sr. quoted in Jack Cejnar interview, Dillinger Sr. ms, folder 8, p. 2, ISL.

31. Stewart, *Dillinger*, pp. 102–3; Cromie and Pinkston, *Dillinger*, pp. 16–17; Toland, *The Dillinger Days*, pp. 21–22; Matera, *John Dillinger*, p. 29. Matera argues (p. 21) that before the attack on Frank Morgan, Beryl was increasingly upset at Dillinger's frequent absences from home.

32. Cromie and Pinkston, *Dillinger*, pp. 17–18; Matera, *John Dillinger*, pp. 31–32.

33. Dillinger Sr. ms, folder 6, p. 34, ISL; Mary Hancock to John Dillinger, March 2, 1930, quoted in Cromie and Pinkston *Dillinger*, pp. 19–20; Cromie and Pinkston, *Dillinger*, pp. 17–18; Matera, *John Dillinger*, pp. 31–32.

34. Cromie and Pinkston, *Dillinger*, pp. 18–19.

35. Ibid. Also see Susan Bell, "Transcript of Taped Interview with Nellie Daly," Manuscript Division, p. 7, ISL.

36. Mary is quoted in Cromie and Pinkston, *Dillinger*, p. 16.

37. John Dillinger to Beryl Hovious Dillinger, August 18, 1928, in Cromie and Pinkston, *Dillinger*, p. 17.

38. John Dillinger to Elizabeth Dillinger, May 11, 1929, quoted in Cromie and Pinkston, *Dillinger*, pp. 17–18.

39. John Dillinger to Mary Hancock, December 25, 1929, Dillinger Gang Papers and Packets, box 4, file 1, ISA.

40. Ibid.; letter from the Office of the General Superintendent of Pendleton to Frank A. Muncey Company, in Cromie and Pinkston, *Dillinger*, p. 19; John Dillinger to Mary Hancock, March 2, 1930, in Cromie and Pinkston, *Dillinger*, pp. 19–20.

41. John Dillinger to Hubert Dillinger, January 17, 1932, in Cromie and Pinkston, *Dillinger*, pp. 20–21, also reprinted in Martinsville (Ind.) *Daily Reporter*, September 23, 1971, in Dillinger File, MPL. A long article in the Martinsville *Daily Reporter*, informed by Joe Pinkston's research, speculates that prison changed Dillinger, that he went in a callow and naïve youth, but divorce, hard labor, constant trouble with the guards, association with serious felons, and so forth set him on his path toward crime; Bette Walls, "What Happened to Dillinger in Prison?" September 21, 1971, n.p., Dillinger File, MPL.

42. The prison statistics come from "The Report of the Indiana Committee on the Observance and Enforcement of Law," January 5, 1931, p. 14, as cited in Paul Musgrave, "'A Primitive Method of Enforcing the Law': Vigilantism as a Response to Bank Crimes in Indiana, 1925–1933, *Indiana Magazine of History*, 102(3) Sept. 2006, online at www.historycooperative.org/journals/imh/102.3/musgrave.html, pp. 7–8.

43. J. E. Comer to Governor Paul McNutt, February 24, 1933, and J. W. Williams to Indiana Parole Commission and Clemency Board, March 14, 1933, in Dillinger Gang Papers and Packets, box 4, file 1, ISA; John Dillinger to Mary Dillinger, March 5, 1933, in Cromie and Pinkston, *Dillinger*, pp. 21–22. The petition of clemency was addressed to His Excellency Paul V. McNutt, Governor of Indiana, and dated February 23, 1933. Alfred F. Dowd, a parole officer at Pendleton, argued that Dillinger's case for parole was a very strong one: the prosecuting attorney, sentencing judge, Dillinger's victim, and dozens of townsmen all supported his release, and no one objected. Jerry Handfield, "Transcript of Taped Interview with Alfred F. Dowd," Oral History Project, 1979, Indiana Division, transcript pp. 68–72, ISL.

44. State of Indiana, Executive Department, Governor Paul McNutt, Executive Order #7723," May 20, 1934, in Dillinger Gang Papers and Packets, box 4, file 1, ISA.

45. Dillinger Sr. ms, box 1, file 6, pp. 35–38, ISL.

46. Dillinger Sr. ms, Paul Cejnar interview with Audrey Hancock, box 1, file 6, pp. 31–32, 39, ISL.

47. The story that Frank Morgan called for help with the distress signal of the Ku Klux Klan when Dillinger and Singleton attacked him in 1924 captures some of these cultural tensions. The second Klan, founded in Indiana in the early 1920s, carried the same racist assumptions as the Reconstruction-era Klan, but its overall aims were different. New Klansmen styled themselves the protectors of an older America, one that was racially and ethnically pure. The new Klan longed for an America cleansed of its cosmopolitan ways, an America of rural virtue and chaste morals, of teetotaling, hard-working, God-fearing men and women. Whether he intended to or not, Dillinger Senior of Mooresville also came to symbolize that America. Over the course of his crime spree, with his fancy clothes, big cars, and wild behavior, his son seemed to embody the other America: of urban pleasures, easy morals, and modern hedonism. On the Klan in Indiana, see Leonard Moore, *Citizen Klansmen: The Ku Klux Klan in Indiana, 1921–1928* (Chapel Hill: University of North Carolina Press, 1991).

48. The debate over the transformation from a culture of "character" to a culture of "personality" is long and contentious. For some of the seminal thinking on the issue, see David Riesman, Nathan Glazer, and Reuel Denney, *The Lonely Crowd: A Study of the Changing American Character* (New Haven, Conn.: Yale University Press, 1965); William H. Whyte, *The Organization Man* (New York: Doubleday Anchor, 1957); Christopher Lasch, *The Culture of Narcissism: American Life in an Age of Diminishing Expectations* (New York: Norton, 1991); and Warren Susman's

collected essays, *Culture as History: The Transformation of American Society in the Twentieth Century* (New York: Pantheon, 1984), especially chapters 7, 8, 9, and 14.

49. Lizabeth Cohen, *Making a New Deal: Industrial Workers in Chicago, 1919–1939* (New York: Cambridge University Press, 1990), pp. 246–49.

50. David Kennedy, *Freedom from Fear: The American People in Depression and War, 1929–1945* (New York: Oxford University Press, 1999), pp. 130–37

51. Ibid., pp. 190–96.

52. Ibid., pp. 162–63; Robert McElvane, *The Great Depression: America, 1929–1941* (New York: Times Books, 1984), pp. 224–29.

53. William Helmer with Rick Mattix, *Public Enemies: America's Criminal Past, 1919–1940* (New York: Barnes and Noble, 1998) is a remarkable work of research on crime, based on newspapers, police records, FBI files, and more. See chapters 4–6.

54. Ibid., chapter 4.

55. Ibid.

Chapter Two

1. "The Farmer Turns Gangster," *Commonweal*, May 19, 1933, pp. 65–67.

2. Ibid.

3. My thinking about culture and the Great Depression has been powerfully shaped by Lawrence W. Levine's essays in *The Unpredictable Past: Explorations of American Cultural History* (New York: Oxford University Press, 1993), especially chapters 11–14.

4. Dillinger Sr. ms, file 7, pp. 26–27, Indiana State Library (hereafter ISL). Roughly a year later Pastor Reinier declared that the press had misrepresented her, that she never defended John Dillinger or excused his behavior. She explained, however, that no man was beyond redemption and that all deserved justice and mercy: "Dillinger Stand Told by Mooresville Pastor," Dillinger file, n.d., Mooresville Public Library (hereafter MPL). Dillinger also visited his ex-wife, Beryl, shortly after he was released from prison: Tony Stewart, *Dillinger, the Hidden Truth* (n.p.: Xlibris, 2002), pp. 95–96.

5. "3 Escape with $10,000 Loot," Mansfield (Ohio) *News Journal*, June 21, 1933, p. 1; "New Carlisle (O.) Institution Is Again Held Up," Zanesville (Ohio) *Times Recorder*, June 22, 1933, p. 1; "Attempt to Rob Thread Mills," Monticello (Ind.) *Herald*, June 29, 1933, p. 1; Dillinger Sr. ms, file 7, pp. 29–31, ISL. The FBI later turned up some inconclusive evidence for the Gravel Switch robbery; see Field report by N. B. Klein, Cincinnati Office, April 10, 1934, p. 16, Dillinger File, 62–29777–447, FBI. Hubert Dillinger was interviewed by Jack Cejnar; see Dillinger Sr. ms, box 1, file 6, pp. 39–40, ISL; also see Cejnar's notes, box 1, file 3, p. 1, ISL.

6. From Statement of William Allen Shaw, REG. #23546" copied July 29, 1933, Dillinger Gang Papers and Packets, Indiana State Archives (hereafter ISA).

7. Shaw's stories grew more elaborate with time; his initial confession following his arrest mentions both Dillinger and Harry Copeland but does not implicate them specifically. He describes their activity in Muncie: "Claycombe knew Harry Copeland and invited him to go with us the following night. Dillinger, Claycombe, Copeland, and I drove to the restaurant in the stolen DeSoto. Copeland got the money and was to divide it the following morning. Dillinger had driven down with us the night before from Indianapolis. He and Copeland were planning on a bank

job, and were going to use the proceeds of the restaurant robbery . . . in the bank job." From Statement of William Allen Shaw, REG. #23546" copied July 29, 1933, Dillinger Gang Papers and Packets, Indiana State Archives (hereafter ISA). Brian Burrough discusses Shaw's importance to chroniclers of the Dillinger story such as Toland and Pinkston in *Public Enemies* (New York: Penguin Press, 2004), p. 64. Dillinger's most recent chroniclers, Burrough and Dary Matera—*John Dillinger, The Life and Death of America's First Celebrity Criminal* (New York: Carroll and Graff Publishers, 2004)—did excellent research for their books, yet both, especially Matera, are sometimes overly trusting of their sources.

8. Dillinger Sr. ms, file 7, pp. 29–31, ISL; "Bandits Loot Daleville Bank," Muncie *Evening Press*, July 17, 1933, p. 1.

9. Dillinger Gang Papers and Packets, box 4, file 1, ISA.

10. Dillinger Sr. ms, file 7, pp. 27–28, ISL.

11. On the emotional attractions of crime, see Jack Katz, *Seductions of Crime* (New York: Basic Books, 1990).

12. "No Trace of Montpelier Yeggs Found," Fort Wayne *News Sentinel*, August 5, 1933, p. 1; "Clews to Bank Robbers' Trail Are Indefinite," Fort Wayne *Journal Gazette*, August 5, 1933, p. 1.

13. "Bluffton Bank Held Up by Daylight Bandits," Lima (Ohio) *News*, August 14, 1933, p. 1; "Clues Sought in Bank Holdup," Lima (Ohio) *News*, August 15, 1933, p. 1; "Five Bandits Rob Bank Here; Escape with Loot of $2,000," Bluffton (Ohio) *News*, August 17, 1933, n.p., all in box 57, file labeled "Bluffton, Ohio," John Toland Papers, Manuscript Division, Library of Congress (hereafter LC).

14. "City Bank Robbed," Indianapolis *Star*, September 7, 1933, p. 1. In all of these early holdups two men entered the bank. In the case of Indianapolis, however, the newspaper claimed that a total of eight men were involved in the robbery, that five large armed men waited in a second car, which followed the first car out of town. This must be erroneous.

15. The individual prisoner files are available in Dillinger Gang Papers and Packets, ISA. Robert Cromie and Joseph Pinkston, *Dillinger: A Short and Violent Life* (1962; Evanston, Ill.: Chicago Historical Bookworks, 1990), chapters 3 and 4, give the richest account of Dillinger's early underworld affiliations.

16. See Paul Musgrave's excellent "'A Primitive Method of Enforcing the Law': Vigilantism as a Response to Bank Crimes in Indiana, 1925–1933," *Indiana Magazine of History*, 102(3), Sept, 2006, on line at www.historycooperative.org/journalimh/102.3/musgrave.html, pp. 7–11.

17. Field report from Cincinnati office filed by N. B. Klein, April 10, 1934, pp. 7–9, Dillinger file, 62–29777–447, Division of Investigation (the name was changed to the Federal Bureau of Investigation in 1935, hereafter FBI). John Toland reports the rumor about James Jenkins in *The Dillinger Days* (New York: Random House, 1963), pp. 28–29.

18. John Dillinger to Mary Longnaker, July 25, 1933, box 57, file "Dayton, Ohio," Toland Papers, LC; second letter quoted in Toland, *The Dillinger Days*, p. 77.

19. Ibid.

20. Toland, *The Dillinger Days*, pp. 74–77; Cromie and Pinkston, *Dillinger*, pp. 38–40; Report of N. B. Klein, pp. 7–10, Dillinger file, 62–29777–447, FBI.

21. Cromie and Pinkston, *Dillinger*, pp. 40–46. Leach was a Serbian immigrant who came to America in 1907 at age thirteen (his given name was Matija Licanin). He followed his father into the steel mills in Gary, then joined the Army, served

in Mexico and on the Western Front during World War I, returned to Gary as a policeman, and in the American Legion met Paul McNutt, who became national chairman of that organization and in 1932 the Democratic governor of Indiana. McNutt appointed Leach to his post in the state police just months before the Dillinger story broke. Dillinger file, 62–29777–447, FBI, p. 7; Burrough, *Public Enemy,* pp. 94–95.

22. "Police Arrest 3 in Bank Holdups," Indianapolis *Star,* September 22, 1933, p. 1; "4 Name Man as City Bank Robber," Indianapolis *Star,* September 23, 1933, p. 1; "Suspect in Numerous Bank Robberies Nabbed," Zanesville (Ohio) *Signal,* September 22, 1933, p. 1.

23. "Alleged Bandit Remains Silent in County Jail," Lima (Ohio) *News,* September 29, 1933, p. 2. Dillinger was also identified as having committed robberies that he had nothing to do with, such as a heist of twenty-four thousand dollars in Farrell, Pennsylvania: "Robber Suspect Again Identified," Newark (Ohio) *Advocate,* September 28, 1933, p. 1; Cromie and Pinkston, *Dillinger,* pp. 50–57, 67–69.

24. John Dillinger to John W. Dillinger, September 29, 1933, in box 57, Toland Papers.

25. John Dillinger to Mary Hancock, October 4, 1933, quoted in Cromie and Pinkston, *Dillinger,* pp. 68–69.

26. Sarber's killing is best told by Cromie and Pinkston, *Dillinger,* pp. 73–77; Matera, *John Dillinger,* pp. 104–7.

27. Matera, *John Dillinger,* pp. 31–35.

28. See Van Meter's prison admission summary, July 31, 1926, in Dillinger Gang Papers and Packets, ISA.

29. Homer Van Meter petition for parole, March 30, 1933; Rev. Robert Hall to Thomas Arbuckle, April 6, 1933; Homer Van Meter to James McRae (his cousin in Brooklyn), n.d., all in Dillinger Gang Papers and Packets, ISA; Burrough, *Public Enemies,* p. 138.

30. Much of Pierpont's record is contained in box 4, file 2, Dillinger Gang Papers and Packets, ISA; Burrough, *Public Enemies,* p. 138.

31. Files containing documents on the gang members are scattered throughout the Dillinger Gang Papers and Packets, ISA, but information on the gang is nicely summarized in the collection's finding aid. Also see Letter from C. F. Williams to Superintendent Miles, July, 1925, box 4, file 2, Dillinger Gang Papers and Packets, ISA; Cromie and Pinkston, *Dillinger,* pp. 59–60; "10 Shoot Way from State Prison," Indianapolis *Star,* September 27, 1933, pp. 1, 3.

32. The FBI credited Walter Dietrich, who was eventually picked up and shipped back to Michigan City, with revealing how the guns were brought in: Report from T. F. Millian, Chicago Office, March 10, 1933, Dillinger file, 62–29777–172, FBI; Cromie and Pinkston, *Dillinger,* pp. 58–59. Newspapers came to view the Michigan City breakout as part of a larger pattern of riots and escapes in recent years. See the Associated Press story, "Series of Prison Riots and Escapes in Last Five Years," Chicago *Tribune,* February 18, 1935, p. 12. For a very good fictional rendering of the breakout, see James Carlos Blake, *Handsome Harry* (New York: William Morrow, 2004), pp. 87–108.

33. Alfred F. Dowd, a guard at Pendleton, tells the story of the breakout well in Jerry Handfield, "Transcript of Taped Interview with Alfred F. Dowd," Oral History Project, 1979, pp. 62–63, Indiana Division, ISL; Cromie and Pinkston, *Dillinger,* pp. 59–63.

34. On Sheriff Neel's convoluted story, see "Felon's Hostage Is Safe in Gary," Indianapolis *Star*, September 30, 1933, p. 1, and "Captured Sheriff Set Free; His Own Story of How Felons Kidnaped Him," Chicago *Tribune*, September 30, 1933, pp. 1–2. Matera, *John Dillinger*, pp. 82–93, is especially strong on the breakout. Also see Cromie and Pinkston, *Dillinger*, pp. 58–67.

35. These stories in the Indianapolis *Star* appeared under the banner "10 Shoot Way from State Prison," September 27, 1933, pp. 1, 3. The day after the breakout the Indianapolis *News* began calling for an investigation, claiming that more than half of the prison employees were recently appointed by the new governor, Paul McNutt, as part of a corrupt spoils system: "Prison Trustees to Study Escape," September 27, 1933, p. 1. "All Trace of 10 Convicts and Kidnaped Sheriff Lost," Gary *Post-Tribune*, September 28, 1933, p. 1. For AP and UP stories, see, for example, Stevens Point (Wisc.) *Daily Journal*, September 27, 1933; Helena (Mont.) *Daily Independent*, September 27, 1933; and the Zanesville (Ohio) *Times Recorder*, September 27, 1933, all front-page stories.

36. "10 Felons Flee Indiana Prison," Chicago *Tribune*, September 27, 1933, pp. 1, 2; "Guardsmen Join Dragnet; Prison Inquiry Starts," Indianapolis *Star*, September 28, 1933, p. 1; "Fugitives Foil Police Here, Escape," Indianapolis *Star*, September 30, 1933, p. 1; "False Radio Report on Hunt Charged," Indianapolis *Star*, September 29, 1933, p. 1; "Faking Radio News," Indianapolis *Star*, September 30, 1933, p. 8.

37. "Lima Gets Bandit Suspect," Lima (Ohio) *News*, September 28, 1933, p. 1; Cromie and Pinkston, *Dillinger*, pp. 68–74.

38. The story is well told in a memo dated October 20, 1933, to J. Edgar Hoover from William Larson, special agent in charge of the Detroit office of the Division of Investigation. Larson had gone to Lima to report back to Washington, and he wrote a very detailed nine-page memo that included information from Fred Pierpont, Harry's brother, who aided and abetted the gang. After the Lima breakout the Bureau of Investigation was asked repeatedly to enter the case. Hoover publicly refused to intervene, but his agency got involved covertly, using fingerprint analysis, sending out bulletins describing suspects, and, most important, keeping tabs on events and circulating detailed memos from regional offices in Cincinnati, Detroit, and Chicago. Not until March 1934, however, did the FBI become officially involved. See William Larson memo, pp. 1–9, Dillinger file, 62–29777–12, FBI. Before the Lima breakout, newspapers had linked the need for tighter security around Dillinger with the Michigan City breakout; see, for example, "Accused Bank Robber under Heavy Guard," Lima (Ohio) *News*, September 27, 1933, p. 9. For good local coverage of the Lima shooting and subsequent manhunt, see "Sheriff Is Slain in Jail Delivery" and "Sheriff Slayer Is Hunted Here," both Bluffton (Ohio) *News*, October 14, 1933, p. 1. Cromie and Pinkston, *Dillinger*, pp. 73–78; Burrough, *Public Enemies*, pp. 140–44; and Matera, *John Dillinger*, pp. 103–4, tell the story well. Matera suggests that Sarber reached for his gun before Pierpont shot him.

39. "Kill Ohio Sheriff, Free His Prisoner," New York *Times*, October 13, 1933, p. 10; "Kill Sheriff, Take Robber from Ohio Jail," Chicago *Tribune*, October 13, 1933, p. 1.

40. Ibid.; "Sheriff Slain, Gang Leader Freed by Pals," Gary *Post-Tribune*, October 13, 1933, pp. 1, 7.

41. "Fugitive's Father Blames Judge," Mooresville *Times*, October 19, 1933, p. 1.

42. John Martin Smith, "Auburn-Dillinger Arsenal," Auburn-DeKalb (Ill.) *Vanguard*, July 1969, pp. 41–43; "3 Raid Auburn Police Station and Take Guns,"

Lima (Ohio) *Sunday News,* October 15, 1933, p. 1; "State Police Probe Auburn Jail Escapade," Fort Wayne *Journal Gazette,* October 16, 1933, pp. 1, 2; "Bold Gunmen Hold Up Police, Take Weapons," Peru (Ind.) *Republican,* October 27, 1933, p. 1; Cromie and Pinkston, *Dillinger,* pp. 78–81. The Thompson Machine gun, technically a "sub" machine gun because it uses pistol, not rifle, ammunition, was invented toward the end of World War I, though it saw little use in that conflict, and was then marketed (rather unsuccessfully) as a police weapon to stop criminals' getaway cars. Its first real success came when Al Capone's men adopted the "Chicago typewriter," as it became known, for their own purposes, especially drive-by shootings. Its most spectacular use came with the St. Valentine's Day Massacre on February 14, 1929. By then radio, newspapers, movies, and newsreels had adopted the Thompson machine gun as the symbol of gangland crime. William J. Helmer is the authority on the history of this weapon; see *The Gun That Made the Twenties Roar* (New York: Macmillan, 1970).

43. For AP coverage, see "Four Bandits Force Cashier to Open Vault," Mansfield (Ohio) *Journal-News,* October 24, 1933, p. 2, and "Bank Robbers Get $70,000 at Greencastle, Ind.," Zanesville (Ohio) *Times-Recorder,* October 24, 1933, p. 1. Detailed local coverage can be found in the Greencastle *Daily Banner,* October 24, 1933, p. 1. The Greencastle Public Library keeps a file of materials on the robbery, including copies of the Putnam County grand jury's indictments of Dillinger, Pierpont, Makley, and Copeland. Matera, *John Dillinger,* pp. 40–41, gives a good description of the technology of successful robberies.

44. "Eight Men Hold Up Indiana Bank and Flee with $70,000," Chicago *Tribune,* October 24, 1933, p. 2.

45. Ibid.; Cromie and Pinkston, *Dillinger,* pp. 83–87; Matera, *John Dillinger,* pp. 112–18. For coverage of the gang's alleged involvement in the South Bend holdup, see "Armed Gang Gets $11,000 in South Bend; May Be Same Robbers Who Got $75,000 in Greencastle Monday" and "Dillinger's Hand in Crime Wave," Gary *Post-Tribune,* October 24, 1933, p. 1. The *Post-Tribune's* headline on the South Bend robbery, incidentally, is a fine study in exaggeration, for although the robbers did steal more than three thousand dollars in cash and negotiable bonds, they also stole more than seven thousand dollars in defaulted mortgage bonds, worth pennies on the dollar.

46. Such reporting was widespread; see, for example, "Hunt Gang of Outlaws in Indiana," Elyria (Ohio) *Chronicle-Telegram,* October 25, 1933, p. 4; "Indiana Governor Acts to Protect State from Bandits," Reno *Evening Gazette,* October 26, 1933, p. 1; "Militia Ready to Hunt Gang of Outlaws," Mansfield (Ohio) *News,* October 26, 1933, p. 1; "Indiana National Guardsmen Are Detailed to Bandit Hunt," Zanesville (Ohio) *Times-Recorder,* October 27, 1933, p. 1; "Indiana Calls on Troops to Curb Bandits," Chicago *Tribune,* October 27, 1933, p. 1.

47. Ibid. Decades after these events Matt Leach claimed that he deliberately tried to stir dissension among gang members by calling them the "Dillinger gang," knowing that Pierpont was the real brains of the organization. It was a very self-serving story, though Brian Burrough repeats it in *Public Enemies,* citing the Indianapolis *News,* June 15, 1955. Given Dillinger's ability to keep going long after Pierpont, Makley, and Russell Clark were in custody, and given other reports of how the gang operated, such as Mary Kinder's in "Four Months with the Dillinger Gang," Chicago *Herald and Examiner,* July 30, 1934, Leach's boasts seem dubious. The story of the Bonus Expeditionary Army is well told in Paul Dickson and Thomas B. Allen, *The Bonus Army: An American Epic* (New York: Walker, 2004). On fear of social unrest during the '30s, see Robert S. McElvaine, *The Great Depression: America, 1929–1941*

(New York: Times Books, 1984), pp. 224–49, and David M. Kennedy, *Freedom from Fear: The American People in Depression and War, 1929–1945* (New York: Oxford University Press, 1999), pp. 218–48. Hope and fear are inextricable in Studs Terkel's oral history of the era, *Hard Times: An Oral History of the Great Depression* (New York: Pantheon, 1970).

48. Cromie and Pinkston, *Dillinger*, pp. 87–88.

49. "Voice of the Reader," quoted in Cromie and Pinkston, *Dillinger*, p. 88.

50. Ellen Poulsen does a remarkable job of recreating the relationships and domestic life of the gang in *Don't Call Us Molls: Women of the John Dillinger Gang* (Little Neck, N.Y.: Clinton Cook Publishing, 2002), especially pp. 69–91. Also see Cromie and Pinkston, *Dillinger*, p. 82; Matera, *John Dillinger*, pp. 119–121; Burrough, *Public Enemies*, pp. 154–157.

51. Poulsen, *Don't Call Us Molls*, pp. 69–91; Kinder, "Four Months with the Dillinger Gang."

52. Poulsen, *Don't Call Us Molls*, pp. 69–91; Kinder, "Four Months with the Dillinger Gang"; and Evelyn Frechette, "What I Knew About John Dillinger," a five-part series appearing in the Chicago *Herald and Examiner*, August 27–31, 1934. On their movements, see Melvin Purvis memo to J. Edgar Hoover, March 31, 1934, p. 2, Dillinger file, 62–29777–226, FBI; H. H. Clegg to J. Edgar Hoover, April 13, 1934, pp. 5, 8, Dillinger file, 62–29777–5XX (file number illegible), FBI. As Ellen Poulsen points out, the gang spent lots of time going to dentist offices, not surprising for working-class people who suddenly had come into enough money for such a luxury.

53. The earliest and in many ways still the best research done by writers of the Dillinger story remains Cromie and Pinkston's *Dillinger: A Short and Violent Life;* the authors carefully followed Huntington's paper trail, pp. 92–98.

54. "Fight 16 Police; Elude Trap," Chicago *Tribune*, November 16, 1933, p. 1; "Raid Apartment to Seize Outlaw Who Fled Trap," Chicago *Tribune*, November 17, 1933, p. 1; "Indiana Bandit Evades Police," Detroit *Times*, November 17, 1933, n.p., all in Dillinger file, 62–29777–32, FBI. Also see Cromie and Pinkston, *Dillinger*, pp. 92–98; Burrough, *Public Enemies*, pp. 158–61. Matera, *John Dillinger*, p. 3, credits an unpublished Pinkston manuscript, along with the work of the Chicago journalist Tom Smusen, as the basis for much of his own work.

55. Dillinger Sr. ms, file 7, p. 34, ISL; "Fight 16 Police," Chicago *Tribune*, November 16, 1933, p. 1. For an example of the Associated Press coverage, see "Desperado Shoots Way from Trap Set by Chicago Police," Sheboygan (Wisc.) *Press*, November 16, 1933, p. 18; "Sixteen Officers Stage Running Fight with Man Wanted for Murder," Lima (Ohio) *News*, November 16, 1933, pp. 1–2.

56. Huntington was in the car following Dillinger, and Cromie and Pinkston quote him at length in *Dillinger*, pp. 101–2. He reported that no return fire came from Dillinger's car. Also see Chicago Police Patrolman Howard Harder to Chief of Detectives, November 15, 1933, Box 57, Dillinger Miscellany file, Toland Papers, LC. "Detective Describes Thrilling Gun Fight with John Dillinger," Lima (Ohio) *News*, November 17, 1933, p. 1, also reported that a local detective, Bernard Roney, was in on the attempt to capture Dillinger; he gave a detailed account and concluded that Dillinger was just lucky, that "the same thing couldn't happen again in a thousand years."

57. Cromie and Pinkston, *Dillinger*, pp. 105–12, do a fine job of piecing together the story from eyewitness accounts. Helmer, in his notes to Girardin, claims that Red Hamilton was also there for the Racine heist; see Russell Girardin with William J.

Helmer, *Dillinger: The Untold Story* (Bloomington: Indiana University Press, 1994), p. 273. "Bandits Rob Bank at Racine," Sheboygan *Press*, November 20, 1933, p. 1; Burrough, *Public Enemies*, p. 162–64; Matera, *John Dillinger*, pp. 134–38.

58. Cromie and Pinkston, *Dillinger*, pp. 112–17; Burrough, *Public Enemies*, pp. 164–66; Matera, *John Dillinger*, pp. 139–44.

59. Copeland was quoted in "Copeland, Accused Murderer, Blames Liquor for Arrest," Lima (Ohio) *News*, November 21, 1933, p. 1. Also see "First Member of Jail Raid Gang Is Taken in Chicago" and "Sheriff Prepares to Protect Prison against Gangsters," Lima (Ohio) *News*, November 20, 1933, p. 1; "Copeland Back in Penitentiary," Lima (Ohio) *News*, November 24, 1933, p. 1; "Seize Indiana Outlaw, Pal of Dillinger," Chicago *Tribune*, November 20, 1933, p. 1.

60. On Shanley, see "Escaped Convict Slays Police Hero," Chicago *Tribune*, December 15, 1933, pp. 1, 12; Burrough, *Public Enemies*, p. 178; Cromie and Pinkston, *Dillinger*, pp. 126–29. Wire service stories of the Dillinger gang were now penetrating into the smallest towns. On Hamilton's killing of Shanley, see "Officer Slain by Fugitive," Salomanca (N.Y.) *Republican-Press*, December 15, 1933, p. 1; "Policeman Slain by Desperado in Chicago Garage," Van Wert (Ohio) *Daily Bulletin*, December 15, 1933, p. 1.

61. For examples of newspaper claims that smaller crime rings were consolidating into larger organized units, see "Great Crime Ring Is New Challenge to Chicago Police," Bismarck (N.D.) *Tribune*, December 16, 1933, p. 7; "Robberies Laid upon New Gang," Charleston (W.Va.) *Daily Mail*, December 17, 1933, p. 14; "Organize Hunt All Over U.S. for 4 Outlaws," Chicago *Tribune*, December 17, 1933, p. 7; "Forty Marksmen Picked to Hunt Outlaw Gangs," Chicago *Tribune*, December 20, 1933, p. 17; Melvin Purvis to J. Edgar Hoover, December 19, 1933, Dillinger file, 62–29777–44, FBI. For the next six months John Dillinger was sighted all over America, pumping gas, eating breakfast, and robbing local shops. See, for example, "Dillinger Battles Police in Chicago," New York *Times*, January 1, 1934, p. 1; "Two Dillinger Men Believed Shot in Battle," Chicago *Tribune*, January 1, 1934, p. 5.

62. "Another Pal of Dillinger Goes to Jail," Lima (Ohio) *News*, December 24, 1933, p. 1; "Dillinger's Gang Called 'Kill-Crazy,'" New York *Times*, December 26, 1933, p. 28. Shouse allegedly made advances toward Billie Frechette; see Cromie and Pinkston, *Dillinger*, pp. 133, 155; Matera, *John Dillinger*, pp. 133, 149–50.

63. "Jail Raider Trapped in Illinois City," Lima (Ohio) *News*, December 20, 1933, p. 1; "Officer Slain in Gun Battle; Convict Seized," Chicago *Tribune*, December 21, 1933, pp. 1, 4; "Nab Convict as 'Outside Man' of Dillinger Gang," Chicago *Tribune*, December 24, 1933, p. 4; "Dillinger Plans Fight to the Death," Lima (Ohio) *News*, December 26, 1933, p. 1; "Slay Three Gunmen in Trap," Chicago *Tribune*, December 22, 1933, p. 1. The Chicago *Tribune* coverage included an editorial, "A Mighty Good Killing," praising the Chicago police on the deaths of the three Rogers Park men, Katzewitz, Tittlebaum, and Ginsberg.

64. Field report from R. L. Shivers, Jacksonville Office, April 9, 1934, p. 2, Dillinger file, 62–29777–424, FBI; H. H. Clegg to J. Edgar Hoover, April 15, 1934, p. 9, Dillinger file, 62–29777–5XX (file number illegible), FBI. Apparently they bought at least two of the cars in Jacksonville; see Memo from R. A. Alt, Jacksonville Office, to the Chicago Office, April 2, 1934, pp. 2–3, Dillinger file, 62–29777–293, FBI.

65. Mary Kinder later reported that Frechette and Dillinger had been fighting and that he blackened her eye; Ellen Poulsen, *Don't Call Us Molls*, p. 94, writes that her interviews with Frechette's family contradict any domestic troubles.

66. "Dillinger Gang Named as Chief Public Enemies," Chicago *Tribune,* December 29, 1933, p. 1; "This Describes Desperados of Dillinger Gang," Chicago *Tribune,* December 30, 1933, p. 3. This last story described the "gang of fugitive convict desperadoes" who "have sworn to die in battle rather than be captured alive."

Chapter Three

1. Field report from R. L. Shivers, Jacksonville Office, April 9, 1934, pp. 2–3, Dillinger file, 62–29777–424, FBI.

2. Billie later claimed that they met at a prearranged time on a bridge in St. Louis, but the best evidence is that they met in Chicago. Ellen Poulsen, *Don't Call Us Molls: Women of the John Dillinger Gang* (Little Neck, N.Y.: Clinton Cook Publishing, 2002), pp. 98–101; Dary Matera, *John Dillinger: The Life and Death of America's First Celebrity Criminal* (New York: Carroll and Graf, 2004), pp. 169–71; Robert Cromie and Joseph Pinkston, *Dillinger: A Short and Violent Life* (1962; Evanston, Ill.: Chicago Historical Bookworks, 1990), pp. 133–36; Brian Burrough, *Public Enemies* (New York: Penguin Press, 2004), pp. 186–89.

3. Steck quoted in "Outlaws Rob Bank, Kill a Policeman," New York *Times,* January 16, 1934, p. 4. Steck's words were reprinted with slight variations elsewhere, including in the Chicago *Tribune* as part of the day's lead story, "Dillinger Robs Bank, Kills Policeman," January 16, 1934, p. 1.

4. For United Press coverage, see "Notorious Bandits Escape," Hammond (Ind.) *Times,* January 16, 1934, p. 1. For an Associated Press story, see "Dillinger Gang Slays Policeman," Mansfield (Ohio) *News-Journal,* January 16, 1934, p. 1; "Spread Dillinger Hunt to Four States," Gary (Ind.) *Post-Tribune,* January 16, 1934, p. 1; "Outlaws Rob Bank, Kill a Policeman," New York *Times,* January 16, 1934, p. 4. Wilgus is quoted in "Wilgus Tells of O'Malley Death in Bank Robbery," Arizona *Star,* January 29, 1934, n.p., in Dillinger clipping file, Arizona Historical Society (hereafter AHS). Also see "Thrilling Robbery Story Recounted," Tucson *Citizen,* January 29, 1934, n.p., in Dillinger clipping file, AHS; Cromie and Pinkston, *Dillinger,* pp. 133–35.

5. Brian Burough, *Public Enemies: America's Greatest Crime Wave and the Birth of the FBI, 1933–1934* (New York: Penguin Press, 2004), pp. 187–88; Russell Girardin with William J. Helmer, *Dillinger: The Untold Story* (Bloomington: Indiana University Press, 1994), pp. 47–55.

6. "Bullet Riddled Car Used by Dillinger in Holdup Found," Chicago *Tribune,* January 17, 1934, p. 3; Field report, St. Louis, April 7, 1934, pp. 4–7, Dillinger file, 62–29777–353, FBI; Matera, *John Dillinger,* pp. 168–169.

7. Of course Dillinger never wrote his own column, but the Tucson police did let him speak to reporters, and one of them cobbled his words into a "statement" that made the rounds in several newspapers; see "Rotten Deal says Leader of Gun Gang," Gary (Ind.) *Post-Tribune,* January 26, 1934, p. 1.

8. Field report, Cincinnati Office, January 6, 1934, pp. 3–6, Dillinger File, 62–29777–49, FBI.

9. J. Edgar Hoover to Homer Cummings, January 31, 1934, p. 3, Dillinger File, 62–29777–70, FBI; Field report, Cincinnati Office, February, 26, 1934, pp. 3–4, Dillinger File, 62–29777–81, FBI. Charles Makley insisted in an interview that Tucson was a good hideout, but that this time "the boys got the breaks," especially when the firemen recognized the photos in *True Detective* magazine: "Makley Sorry

for Family, Less Concerned over Self," Arizona *Star,* January 27, 1934, n.p., Dillinger file, 62–29777–72, FBI.

10. The fullest telling of the arrests is found in the account given by Tucson Chief of Police C. A. Wollard to J. F. Weadock, "Clark! Makley! Pierpont! Dillinger! Captured," in *True Detective Mysteries,* June 1934, pp. 6–13, 80–84. Also see "Salesmen Identify Leaders of Gang," Tucson *Citizen,* January 26, 1934, in Dillinger clipping file, n.p., AHS; "Who Gave Tip for Dillinger Arrests Explained by Chief," Arizona *Star,* February 3, 1934, Dillinger clipping file, n.p., AHS. Also see the United Press story allegedly written by Police Chief Wollard reprinted in the Mansfield (Ohio) *News-Journal,* "Tucson Police Chief Tells How Men Trapped Noted Gang," January 26, 1934, p. 1.

11. Wollard, "Clark! Makley!" 13, 80–84; Cromie and Pinkston, *Dillinger,* pp. 135–41.

12. Wollard, "Clark! Makley!" 13, 80–84; Cromie and Pinkston, *Dillinger,* pp. 135–41.

13. Wollard, "Clark! Makley!" 13, 80–84; Cromie and Pinkston, *Dillinger,* pp. 135–41. Newspaper reports vary in details; see "Dillinger Caught with Three Aides" and "Dillinger Caught on Fireman's Tip," New York *Times,* January 26, 1934, p. 1; "Dillinger Gang Is Held under $100,000 Bonds as Fugitives from Justice," Tucson *Citizen,* January 26, 1934, p. 1. Also see C. L. Sonnichsen, "Hard Times in Tucson," *Journal of Arizona History* 22, no. 1 (Spring 1981): 54–58. See Matera's version of events, *John Dillinger,* pp. 170–75, and Burrough, *Public Enemies,* pp. 199–205.

14. "Crack Shots Guard Jail in Tucson," Hammond *Times* (from the International News Service), January 27, 1934, p. 1; "Bandits Fare Poorly," New York *Times,* January 27, 1934, p. 1; "Tamed Dillinger and Gang," Chicago *Daily News,* January 27, 1934, p. 1; "As Dillinger Was Arraigned in Tucson," Chicago *Daily News,* January 29, 1934, p. 1. Of course the Arizona *Star* agreed that "Tucson can be proud of its Police Force": January 27, 1934, editorial in Dillinger clipping file, n.p., AHS.

15. "Catch Dillinger and 3 Aides," Chicago *Tribune,* January 26, 1934, p. 1; "50 Guard Dillinger and Gang," Mansfield (Ohio) *News-Journal,* January 26, 1934, p. 1; "Dillinger and Three Aides Guarded in Tucson Jail," Chicago *Daily News,* January 26, 1934, p. 1.

16. "$400,000 Bail Set for Dillinger Gang," New York *Times,* January 27, 1934, p. 3; "Speed Extradition of Dillinger Gang," New York *Times,* January 29, 1934, p. 1; "'I'll Kill You Yet, You Dirty Rat': Pierpont," Arizona *Star,* January 29, 1934, n.p., in Dillinger clipping file, AHS; "Dillinger Gang Is Held under $100,000 Bonds as Fugitives from Justice," Tucson *Citizen,* January 26, 1934, p. 1; Oral history interview with Emma Walk Finney, November 2, 1989, transcript pp. 24–25, AHS Archives.

17. "Dillinger Gang Is Held under $100,000 Bonds as Fugitives from Justice," Tucson *Citizen,* January 26, 1934, p. 1; Oral history interview with Roy Drachman, April 3, 1980, transcript pp. 1, 13–14, AHS Archives; Cromie and Pinkston, *Dillinger,* p. 141.

18. "Leader of Bank 'Mob' Tells How He Was Captured," Tucson *Citizen,* January 26, 1934, n.p., in Dillinger clipping file, AHS.

19. "Desperado Tells Arizona He Will Fight Extradition," Mansfield (Ohio) *News-Journal,* January 26, 1934, p. 1; "Arizona Rules Indiana Gets Dillinger," Chicago *Tribune,* January 28, 1934, p. 3; Joseph U. Dugan, "Dillinger, Archenemy of Society, Another of Crime's Muddleheads," Chicago *Tribune,* April 22, 1934, pp. G1, G3; "Still Hopes He Will Shoot Way Out," Elyria (Ohio) *Chronicle-Telegram,* January 31, 1934,

section 2, p. 1; "Tucson's Police Show They Can Beat 'Em to Draw," Chicago *Tribune*, January 27, 1934, p. 2; "Pierpont Wisecracker," Hammond (Ind.) *Times*, January 29, 1934, p. 5; Fred Finney, "Smartest Cops We Have Seen, Says Pierpont," Arizona *Daily Star*, January 28, p. 1.

20. "Makley Sorry for Family, Less Concerned over Self," Arizona *Daily Star*, January 27, 1934, n.p., in Dillinger File, 62–29777–72, FBI.

21."Dillinger Gang Facing Death as States Act," Chicago *Tribune*, January 27, 1934, p. 1.

22. "Wires to Dillinger Spur $150,000 Hunt," New York *Times*, January 28, 1934, p. 28; also see the AP story in, for example, the Reno *Evening News*, "Dillinger Linked in Kidnapping," January 28, 1934, p. 1; "Indiana Indicts Dillinger for Murder; Arizona Sets Huge Bond for Outlaws," Chicago *Daily News*, January 26, 1934, p. 1. Some of the accounts connecting the gang to the St. Paul kidnapping implied that there was a larger scheme afoot to free the prisoners: "Indiana Police Take Plane in Race for Gang" and "Dillinger Gangsters May Be Divided in Two States," Arizona *Daily Star*, January 27, 1934, p. 1.

23. The Chicago *Tribune*, among other papers, was outraged by Wisconsin's efforts to extradite the Dillinger gang; justice demanded that they be tried for their most heinous offenses and that they be put to death. The *Tribune* editorial was reprinted in, for example, the Oshkosh *Northwestern* as "Dillinger's Gangsters," February 1, 1934, p. 6. Also see "Outlaws Struggle to Return to Wisconsin as Dispute Rages," Tucson *Citizen*, January 29, 1934, n.p., in Dillinger clipping file, AHS; "Snarling Gangsters Fail to Make $100,000 Surety and Remain in Pima Jail," Arizona *Star*, January 27, 1934, pp. 1, 7; "The Value of Civil Service," Arizona *Star*, January 30, 1934, n.p., in Dillinger clipping file, AHS. Kinder was wanted for harboring the fugitives from the Michigan City prison breakout, but the other women were released for lack of evidence.

24. "Plane Rushes Dillinger East," Arizona *Star*, January 30, 1934, p. 1; "Tucson Sighs as Gangsters Leave Arizona," Arizona *Star*, January 31, 1934, p. 1; "Three Dillinger Bandits and Woman Confederate Are Sent East by Train," Tucson *Citizen*, January 30, 1934, p. 1, all in Dillinger clipping file, AHS; "Dillinger in Plane on Way to Indiana," New York *Times*, January 30, 1934, p. 4; "Dillinger Is Back in Indiana Jail," New York *Times*, January 31, 1934, p. 9; "Speed Dillinger to Lake County," Gary (Ind.) *Post-Tribune*, January 30, 1934, p. 1; Cromie and Pinkston, *Dillinger*, pp. 146–50; Burrough, *Public Enemies*, pp. 206–9; Matera, *John Dillinger*, pp. 176–185.

25. "Outlaw Wants 'Best Lawyer,'" Mansfield (Ohio) *News-Journal*, January 27, 1934, p. 4; "The Law Catches Up," Sheboygan (Wisc.) *Press*, January 26, 1934, p. 10; "Power of Criminals Being Broken," Edwardsville (Ill.) *Intelligencer*, February 5, 1934, p. 2, reprinted in slightly modified form in Clearfield (Pa.) *Intelligencer*, February 5, 1934, p. 4, and in the Helena (Mont.) *Independent*, February 6, 1934, p. 4.

26. "Fighting It Out," Arizona *Star*, January 29, 1934, n.p., in Dillinger clipping file, AHS.

27. Ibid.

28. Ibid.

29. Ibid.

30. "Speed Dillinger East by Air," Chicago *Tribune*, January 30, 1934, p. 1; "Meek Dillinger Is Jailed," Chicago *Tribune*, January 31, 1934, p. 1; "Dillinger Is Delivered to Hoosier Jail," Arizona *Star*, January 30, 1934, p. 1; "Dillinger and His Gangsters,"

Chicago *Tribune*, January 31, 1934, p. 14. The *Tribune*'s rival paper preferred its signature hard-boiled style in headlining the rendition of Clark, Pierpont, and Makley to Michigan City: "Dillinger's Three 'Stooges' Tucked Safely Away in Their Old 'Alma Mater,'" Chicago *Daily News*, February 1, 1934, p. 1.

31. For especially detailed coverage of Dillinger's return to Indiana, see Hammond (Ind.) *Times*, January 30–February 2, 1934, under the page-one banners "Dillinger Due Here Tonight," "Dillinger to Be Arraigned at Crown Point Friday," and "Dillinger Re-Indicted Today." For Dillinger bantering with reporters, see "Dillinger in Indiana Jail; Tells of His Crime Career," Chicago *Daily News*, January 31, 1934, p. 1. On the *How to Be a Detective* story, see typed manuscript written by Indiana journalist John Cejnar, called "Crown Point," dated January 31, 1934, Dillinger Sr. ms, file 1, ISL.

32. John Dillinger to Doris Dillinger, February 20, 1934, transcribed in box 57, Dillinger Miscellany, John Toland Papers, Library of Congress; also reproduced in G. Russell Girardin with William J. Helmer, *Dillinger: The Untold Story* (Bloomington: Indiana University Press, 1994), p. 77. Helmer, who edited Girardin, attributes the letter to the John Dillinger Museum; Pinkston collected most of the extant Dillinger correspondence.

33. "22 Who Saw Killing Identify Dillinger," New York *Times*, February 1, 1934, p. 2; "One Happy Family," New York *Times*, February 2, 1934, p. 16.

34. "Holdup Victims Name Dillinger as Police Killer," Chicago *Tribune*, February 1, 1934, p. 3; "Dillinger in Lake County Jail," Gary *Post-Tribune*, January 31, 1934, p. 1; "Fear Dillinger Jail Delivery; Bolster Guard," Chicago *Tribune*, February 5, 1934, p. 1; "Dillinger Outlaw Gets 20-Year Term," New York *Times*, February 18, 1934, p. 16; Accused Outlaw Still Defiant," Reno *Evening Gazette*, February 23, 1934, p. 7; "Organize Police 'Racket' Detail as Strike Looms," Chicago *Tribune*, February 25, 1934, p. 9; "Woman Sheriff Takes Task of Dillinger Guard Calmly," Tucson *Citizen*, January 31, 1934, n.p., in Dillinger file, AHS; "Start Dillinger Gang Back to Ohio," Mansfield (Ohio) *News Journal*, February 10, 1934, p. 1. The United Press carried a story under Lillian Holley's byline assuring the public that Dillinger was going nowhere: "Woman Sheriff Has Charge of John Dillinger," Sheboygan *Press*, January 31, 1934, p. 2.

35. "Jail Will Keep John Dillinger in Crown Point," Chicago *Tribune*, February 13, 1934, p. 6.

36. "John Dillinger Escapes," Gary *Post-Tribune*, March 3, 1934, p. 1; "Dillinger Flees from Jail," Chicago *Daily News*, March 3, 1934, p. 1; "Notorious Gangster Escapes from County Jail," Hammond (Ind.) *Times*, March 3, 1934, p. 1.

37. "3 States Hunting Dillinger," Chicago *Tribune*, March 4, 1934, p. 1; "Dillinger Coolest Criminal Alive, Declares His Hostage," Arizona *Star*, March 4, 1934, p. 1; "Dillinger's Record Is Unprecedented," Sheboygan *Press*, March 3, 1934, p. 6; "Dillinger Escapes Jail Using a Wooden Pistol," New York *Times*, March 4, 1934, p. 1. From the El Paso *Herald-Post* to the Syracuse *Herald*, from the Billings *Gazette* to the Hagerstown *Daily Mail*, John Dillinger's escape was the leading news. Early reports that police in northern Indiana trapped him proved false, though an International News Service story in, for example, the March 3 Hammond (La.) *Times* was prophetic: "No Federal Warrants for Dillinger," the headline read, but the story indicated that the Justice Department finally might be ready to pursue him. Also see Burrough, *Public Enemies*, pp. 234–40; Matera, *John Dillinger*, pp. 186–203; Cromie and Pinkston, *Dillinger*, pp. 145–69. The most detailed account comes from Girardin, *Dillinger*, pp. 65–108, especially as it is supplemented by editor William Helmer's wonderful commentary on pp. 291–94.

38. "Locks Up Deputies and Flees in Sherif's [sic] Car," Chicago *Tribune*, March 4, 1934, p. 1; telegram, Melvin Purvis to J. Edgar Hoover, March 3, 1934, Dillinger file, 62–29777–89, FBI; "John Dillinger Escapes," Gary *Post-Tribune*, March 3, 1934, p. 1; "Dillinger Escapes Jail, Using a Wooden Pistol; He Locks Guards in Cell," New York *Times*, March 4, 1934, p. 1; "Toy Pistol Fashioned from Old Washboard," Hammond (Ind.) *Times*, March 5, 1934, p. 1; "Dillinger May Be Hiding in Chicago Area," Chicago *Tribune*, March 3, 1934, p. 1.

39. For United Press stories, which were reprinted all over the country, see, for example, "Dillinger Raid on Ohio Jail Is Feared," *Nevada State Journal*, March 4, 1934, p. 1; "Dillinger Vanishes 'Into Air,'" *Nevada State Journal*, March 5, 1934, p. 1; "Think Bandit Has Rejoined Gang Members," Stevens Point (Wisc.) *Daily Journal*, March 5, 1934, p. 1. For the Associated Press, see "John Dillinger Escapes Prison," Clearfield (Pa.) *Progress*, March 3, 1934, p. 1; "Dillinger Breaks Out of Bastile [sic]," Helena (Mont.) *Independent*, March 4, 1934, p. 1. After the Crown Point escape the Division of Investigation intensified its intelligence gathering on Dillinger. For example, four days after the breakout the Division began to monitor the mail of Welton Sparks, Billie Frechette's former husband, in Leavenworth prison, assuming that she or Dillinger himself might tip their whereabouts. See Special Agent M. C. Spear to Special Agent in Charge Melvin Purvis, March 8, 1934, Dillinger File, 62–29777–118NR5, FBI. For another example of the Division's intelligence work, see the twenty-one-page report written by T. F. Mullen, March 9, 1934, Dillinger file, 62–29777–115, FBI.

40. "Police Locate Dillinger Car," Sheboygan (Wisc.) *Press*, March 6, 1934, p. 6; "Dillinger's Pals Await Delivery from Lima Jail," Chicago *Tribune*, March 5, 1934, p. 2.

41. See the three page-one New York *Times* articles on March 4, 1934: "Dillinger Escapes Jail Using a Wooden Pistol," "Captive Recounts Dillinger Flight," and "Dillinger 'Rose' in 6-Month Spur."

42. Saager's syndicated story appeared under his own byline; see, for example, "Dillinger Coolest Criminal Alive, Declares His Hostage," Arizona *Star*, March 4, 1934, p. 1; "Dillinger Cherishes Toy Pistol," Hammond (La.) *Times*, March 5, 1934, p. 1.

43. "Locks Up Deputies and Flees In Sherif's [sic] Car," Chicago *Tribune*, March 3, 1934, p. 1; "Steps in Dillinger's Notorious Career," Chicago *Tribune*, March 4, 1934, p. 2.

44. "Dash of Dillinger Frightens Bronx," New York *Times*, March 8, 1934, p. 13; "Hunt for Dillinger Spurred in Chicago," New York *Times*, March 9, 1934, p. 40; "Dillinger Shoots Way out of Chase," New York *Times*, March 10, 1934, p. 1; "Dillinger Hunt Extended to State," Frederick (Md.) *News*, March 14, 1934, p. 1; "Dillinger Seen on South Side; Push Manhunt," Chicago *Tribune*, March 9, 1934, p. 1; "New Dillinger Hunt On; Shots Halt Police Car," Chicago *Tribune*, March 10, 1934, p. 1.

45. "Dillinger Tips Reach State Police at Rate of 1 Every 5 Mins.," Gary *Post-Tribune*, March 5, 1934, p. 1; United Press story in Sheboygan *Press*, "Dillinger Opens Fire to Halt Trailing Car," March 10, 1934, p. 1. One prankster even wrote a letter signed John Dillinger to Harry Flannery, whose radio program out of Fort Wayne, Indiana, covered the Crown Point escape. In the letter Dillinger denied there was any collusion in his escape; rather, the guards were simply filled with the product that sponsored Flannery's show, Kamm's beer. "John Dillinger" to Harry Flannery, March 8, 1934, box 1, 80AF, Harry Flannery Papers, Wisconsin State Historical Society. Also see the broadcast transcripts in box 19.

46. All from the Gary *Post-Tribune*: "Dillinger a Robin Hood to Boys in Backroom; They're Glad He's Loose," March 10, 1934, p. 1; "Boom in Crown Point as Thousands Visit Scene of Jail Break," March 5, 1934, p. 1; "Dillinger Escape Cheers Mary Kinder," March 4, 1934, p. 1; "This Man Dillinger—What Is He? Killer and Humorist," March 10, 1935, p. 1.

47. "Fiction and Realism," Sheboygan (Wisc.) *Press*, March 13, 1934, p. 26; "The Defeat of Justice," Arizona *Citizen*, March 6, 1934, n.p., in Dillinger clipping file, AHS; "Capital Punishment," Sheboygan (Wisc.) *Press*, March 19, 1934, p. 16.

48. "The Dillinger Escape," *Nevada State Journal*, March 5, 1934, p. 4; "Breaking Out of Jail," Monessen (Pa.) *Daily Independent*, March 7, 1934, p. 2; "The Public Is Sore," Wellsboro (Pa.) *Gazette*, March 8, 1934, p. 4; "Dillinger's Obligation," Mansfield (Ohio) *News-Journal*, March 14, 1934, p. 4.

49. Reporter John Cejnar reproduced this interview with Hancock, who allegedly repeated the breakout story as Johnnie told it to his family: John Cejnar interview with Emmett Hancock, in Dillinger Sr. ms, file 6, pp. 19–20, file 7, pp. 54–64, ISL. The problem with a story like this is knowing whose voice we are hearing, Dillinger's, Hancock's, Cejnar's, or some blend of all three.

50. See articles in Chicago *Defender*: "Dillinger Jibes Jailer about Youngblood as He Quits Prison," "World, Meet Mr. Dillinger," and "So Dillinger Escaped," March 10, 1934, pp. 3, 4.

51. Dillinger Sr. ms. file 7, pp. 54–64, ISL. Sheriff Holley apparently agreed with Will Rogers; see "Sherif [sic] Holley Says Her Men Were 'Yellow,'" Chicago *Tribune*, March 6, 1934, p. 2. It is a third-hand account, but when Emmett Hancock was interviewed by Jack Cejnar he reported Dillinger's telling of the Crown Point breakout as follows: "As they were being led into the bullpen he managed to get right behind a guard named Cahoon, and he shoved the gun into his back while in the corridor and told him to 'stick 'em up.' Then he asked who was in the next room and if the guard in the next room was armed. Cahoon said 'No.' John said: 'All right, call him in' and tell him to come through the door with his hands in the air. Cahoon objected, and said 'I am not going through with this.' John told him: 'I just got eight shots in this automatic and I have just to touch the trigger and you are done. Would you rather be a live coward or a dead hero? Well, we are beginning to understand each other. Call him in.'" When Blunk hesitated Dillinger said to him, "'You are a married man, aren't you, and got children?' Blunk said 'yes.' John continued: 'It is a beautiful world outside, the sun is shining, and spring is here. You would hate to leave this beautiful world, wouldn't you? Would you rather be a live coward or a dead hero?'" Emmett Hancock interview, Dillinger Sr. ms., file 6, p. 19, ISL.

52. On early questions about how he escaped, see, for example, "Seek Dillinger Gang Hideout; Quick Getaway Indicates Help from His Aids," Chicago *Tribune*, March 5, 1934, p. 1; "Dillinger Hunted in Chicago," Chicago *Tribune*, March 6, 1934, p. 1. For the United Press report, see "Two Guards of John Dillinger Are Arrested," Sheboygan *Press*, March 6, 1934, p. 1. Between March 5 and March 15 the Hammond (Indiana) *Times* gave particularly detailed coverage to the political fallout of Dillinger's escape. For early FBI reports on Crown Point, see the memo by T. F. Mullen, March 9, 1934, Dillinger file, 62–29777–115, FBI, and Ernest Blunk's long statement to the feds, March 10, 1934, Dillinger file, 62–29777–134, FBI. A year after Crown Point, Department of Justice agents claimed (probably erroneously) that Dillinger had escaped with a real pistol, not a wooden one.

53. Girardin, *Dillinger*, pp. 67–81, tells the story from Louis Piquett's point of view. We know so much about Piquett because Chicago advertising man G. Russell

Girardin cooperated with him on a series of newspaper articles and then a book manuscript. Decades later William J. Helmer edited and published the manuscript, and though it certainly cannot be taken at face value, it is a remarkable document.

54. Ibid.; J. Edgar Hoover to Homer Cummings, June 25, 1934, Record Group (RG) 60, 95–57–8, section 4, box 14022, National Archives and Records Administration (hereafter NARA), Department of Justice (hereafter DOJ). For good local coverage, see "Dillinger to Present Alibi as His Defense," Brazil (Ind.) *Daily Times,* February 20, 1934, n.p., in Dillinger file, Mooresville Public Library. One gets a good sense of Piquett from an exchange of letters he had with a woman named Eulalia Callender days after the breakout. Callender wrote to Piquett that she believed Dillinger was a good man whose escape was providential. One can imagine Piquett and O'Leary shaking with laughter as the attorney composed his response: that Dillinger intended to "travel in the path of righteousness," that he was "a great student of the Bible," and that "it was his intention to give the balance of his life in this world to God." Piquett closed by thanking Callender for her prayers of deliverance: Louis Piquett to Eulalia Callender, RG 60, 95–57–8, section 3, box 14022, NARA, DOJ.

55. Girardin, *Dillinger,* pp. 104–5.

56. "Confidential Report Concerning the Crown Point Jail Break by J. Edward Barce, Special Investigator for Governor Paul V. McNutt of Indiana, Philip Lutz, Jr., Attorney General," Hubert Hawkins Collection, S1854, Manuscript Division, ISL. The Indianapolis newspapers covered Barce's investigation; see, for example, "State Ready to Reveal Dillinger Pay-Off," Indianapolis *Times,* April 18, 1934, p. 1.

57. William Helmer, who edited the Girardin *Dillinger* manuscript, offers a sharp critique of the Barce memo on pp. 98–99. For coverage of the detentions, see "Indiana Seizes 8 in Dillinger Escape Inquiry," Chicago *Tribune,* October 31, 1934, p. 1; "Seizure of 8 in Calumet," Indianapolis *Star,* October 31, 1934, p. 1; "Demands M'Nutt Bare Hideout of Dillinger 'Quiz,'" Chicago *Tribune,* November 1, 1934, p. 6; "Indiana Frees 8; Dillinger Quiz 'Failure,'" Chicago *Tribune,* November 2, 1934, p. 1. Bogue turned up in a new scam at the end of 1935; see "Trap Diamond Robber Gang," Chicago *Tribune,* December 12, 1935 p. 1; "Gem Plot Exposed as Hoax," Chicago *Tribune,* December 13, 1935, p. 1.

58. Girardin, *Dillinger,* pp. 98–99.

59. O'Leary told the story at the end of 1934, though he gave eleven thousand dollars as the amount delivered to unspecified persons; Girardin, *Dillinger,* pp. 81–88. The Associated Press story can be found in, for example, the Reno *Gazette,* "Dillinger Escape Not Paid For in Full Says Report," December 19, 1934, p. 1.

60. The Crown Point story remains very shadowy, but the best work on what we know and don't know can be found in Matera, *John Dillinger,* pp. 197–203, 381–82, and Girardin, *Dillinger,* pp. 65–108.

61. "Crime-Ridden America Blushes for Its Jails," *Literary Digest,* March 17, 1934, p. 39.

62. "Beck Contends Roosevelt Has Set Up Dictatorship," Chicago *Tribune,* March 11, 1934, p. 3; "Robinson Blames Indiana's Prison Woes upon Politics," Chicago *Tribune,* March 6, 1934, p. 2; "Dillinger Escape Perils Rule of Democrats in Crown Point," Chicago *Tribune,* March 6, 1934, p. 2; "John Dillinger Parole Under Fire of Jurors," Chicago *Tribune,* March 15, 1934, p. 3; manuscript news story by Jack Cejnar, Dillinger Sr. ms, folder 1, n.d., n.p., ISL. McNutt summarized his position nicely in a letter to Courtland Smith, who headed the Pathe News Company: the governor has no power to remove local officials from office, the ongoing investigation of Crown Point already bore results, it was Judge Murray's decision alone

whether Dillinger stayed in Crown Point or was transferred to Michigan City. As it turned out the fallout from Crown Point was limited; Prosecutor Robert Estill lost his bid for renomination in May, and Sheriff Lillian Holley stepped down and was replaced by her nephew, Carroll Holley. Dillinger's death in July apparently obviated him as a campaign issue in November. See Paul V. McNutt to Courtland Smith, n.d., RG 60, Central Files, Classified Subjects, Correspondence, 95–57–8, section 1, part 1, box 14021, NARA, DOJ.

63. "Cummings Rebukes Dillinger Jailers," New York *Times,* March 9, 1934, p. 40. For the United Press story, see "Estill Rebuked by U.S. Official," Hammond (Ind.) *Times,* March 8, 1934, p. 9.

64. "Anti-Toy Pistol Law Asked to Curb Dillingers," Chicago *Tribune,* April 4, 1934, p. 19.

65. "Open Jail Doors," New York *Times,* March 5, 1934, p. 14; "Yes! Dillinger Bade Us Goodbye!" Lake County (Ind.) *Star,* March 9, 1934, p. 1. The AP story describing Dillinger's "movie escape" can be found in "U.S. Hunting for Dillinger," Gettysburg (Penna.) *Times,* March 7, 1934, p. 1.

66. On Hollywood, see "Dillinger's Exploits Will Be Made into Movie," Chicago *Tribune,* March 9, 1934, p. 4; "Hardly a Crime Wave," New York *Times,* March 10, 1934, p. 12; "Ban on Dillinger Escape as Film Thriller Theme," New York *Times,* March 21, 1934, p. 25. For AP coverage of the Hays Commission, see "Hollywood Forbids Dillinger Picture" and "Ban on Dillinger Film Is Praised," Arizona *Star,* March 21 and 22, 1934, in Dillinger clipping file, AHS; "Timely Editorial—Will Hays Says No," Mansfield (Ohio) *News-Journal,* March 23, 1934, p. 4, originally printed in the Ohio *State Journal.* For letters from citizens condemning the movie industry for valorizing Dillinger and other criminals, see Mrs. Rachel Harris to Homer Cummings, March 14, 1934; Fern Marr Deneen to Franklin Roosevelt, March 4, 1934; Harry D. Townsend to J Edgar Hoover, March 12, 1934; Lucretia Dryman to Franklin Roosevelt, March 20, 1934; B. Purcell to Department of Justice, March 11, 1934, all in RG 60, 95–57–8, section 1, part 1, box 14021, NARA, DOJ. Months later *Commonweal* magazine still wasn't satisfied; the lead story on June 29 called for cooperation among Catholic, Protestant, and Jewish organizations to draw up a nationwide "white list" and "black list" of films, lest lack of unity evoke "the jeering laughter of the pagan crowd, and the more discreet, but even more delighted, snickers of the motion-picture ghouls." "Let Us Center Our Fire," 20, no. 9 (1934): 225–26.

67. "Not a Rob'n Hood," Gary *Post-Tribune,* n.p., n.d., clipping in RG 60, 95–57–8, section 1, part 1, box 14021, NARA, DOJ.

Chapter Four

1. J. Edgar Hoover to Melvin Purvis, March 6, 1934, Dillinger file, 62–29777–93NR1, FBI.

2. Dary Matera, *John Dillinger: The Life and Death of America's First Celebrity Criminal* (New York: Carroll and Graf, 2004), pp. 217–22; Brian Burrough, *Public Enemies: America's Greatest Crime Wave and the Birth of the FBI, 1933–1934* (New York: Penguin Press, 2004), pp. 244–47; G. Russell Girardin with William J. Helmer, *Dillinger: The Untold Story* (Bloomington: Indiana University Press, 1994), pp. 113–16. The FBI in the Dillinger case was mostly diligent, repeatedly unlucky, usually undermanned, occasionally incompetent, and often outsmarted. For an example

of surveillance of the gang's "molls" in which the feds were unlucky, including the reading of private telegrams and staking out suspect residences, see the memo of William Larson, special agent in charge of the Detroit Office, to the St. Paul Office, April 3, 1934, Dillinger file, 62–29777–301, FBI.

3. "Thugs Get $46,000, Kidnap 5 in Bank," New York *Times*, March 7, 1934, p. 2; "Bandits Raid Bank, Take Police Guns," Gary *Post-Tribune* March 6, 1934, p. 1; "Machine Gunmen Rob Sioux Falls Bank of $46,000," Chicago *Tribune*, March 7, 1934, p. 8; Burrough, *Public Enemies*, pp. 244–47; Matera, *John Dillinger*, pp. 217–22.

4. See, for example, the Associated Press story in the Reno *Evening Gazette*, "Five Persons Are Seized as Hostages in Daring Foray on Vaults," March 6, 1934, p. 1, and Coshocton (Ohio) *Tribune*, "Middle West Bankers Are All Set for Dillinger Raid," March 7, 1934, p. 1. According to the Chicago *Tribune* the bank president initially identified Dillinger from photographs, then said he wasn't sure, then declared it was indeed Dillinger: "Machine Gunmen Rob Sioux Falls Bank of $46,000," Chicago *Tribune*, March 7, 1934, p. 8. The wanted poster can be found in Dillinger file, 62–29777–114, FBI.

5. As the headline for typical coverage declared, "Outlaw Seen as Chieftain of New Gang"; an AP story in the Mansfield (Ohio) *News-Journal*, March 14, 1934, p. 1.

6. Ibid.; "Police Say John Dillinger Plans South American Trip," Arizona *Star*, March 13, 1934, n.p., in Dillinger file, Arizona Historical Society (hereafter AHS); Girardin, *Dillinger*, pp. 116–19; Burrough, *Public Enemies*, pp. 250–57; Matera, *John Dillinger*, pp. 226–32.

7. Girardin, *Dillinger*, pp. 88–94.

8. Ibid.; Matera, *John Dillinger*, pp. 197–203; Burrough, *Public Enemies*, pp. 244–60.

9. Alvin Karpis with Bill Trent, *The Alvin Karpis Story* (New York: Coward, McCann and Geoghegan, 1971), p. 100; Field report by V. F. Peterson, May 6, 1934, p. 4, Dillinger file, 62–29777–1222, FBI. Mortensen claimed until he died that he had not known that his patient was the famous outlaw; Hoover, wishing to make an example of all of the Bureau's enemies, made sure that the doctor served prison time. Maccabee, *John Dillinger Slept Here*, pp. 216–18, is especially strong on Hoover's ugly determination to bring down Mortensen. The AP story on Mortensen's suspension can be found in "Health Officer Suspended for Aiding Dillinger," Sheboygan (Wisc.) *Press*, April 26, 1934, p. 1. Also see J. Edgar Hoover to Homer Cummings, April 26, 1934, RG 60, Central Files, Classified Subjects, Correspondence, 95–57–8, section 2, part 2, box 14022, National Archives and Records Administration (hereafter NARA), Department of Justice (hereafter DOJ); "Health Official Aided Dillinger," New York *Times*, April 27, 1934, p. 1.

10. For Youngblood's death, see Memorandum to the Special Agent in Charge, from J. L. Murphy, Detroit Office, March 17, 1934, pp. 1–6, Dillinger file, 62–29777–169, FBI; "Aide, Shot, Reveals Dillinger's Trail," New York *Times*, March 17, 1934, p. 1; "Dillinger's Aid Kills Sherif [sic], Is Slain in Battle," Chicago *Tribune*, March 17, 1934, p. 1. AP coverage can be found in "Dillinger Aide Dies in Fight with Deputies," Arizona *Star*, March 17, 1934, in Dillinger File, n.p., AHS.

11. "Blunder in Killing of Dillinger Aid," Chicago *Defender*, March 31, 1934, p. 2; "Dillinger's Aid Is Slain in Michigan," Chicago *Defender*, March 24, 1934, p. 4.

12. See the United Press story, "Block Boundary in Watch for Dillinger," Elyria (Ohio) *Chronicle-Telegram*, March 17, 1934, p. 1; Girardin, *Dillinger*, pp. 119–20.

13. Piquett's story is best told in Girardin, *Dillinger*, pp. 120–24.

14. Dillinger Sr. ms., file 7, p. 55, Indiana State Library (hereafter ISL); Girardin, *Dillinger*, pp. 120–24; John Dillinger to Audrey Hancock, reprinted in Maccabee, *John Dillinger Slept Here*, pp. 219–20.

15. H. H. Clegg memo to J. Edgar Hoover, March 31, 1934, Dillinger file 62–29777–381, FBI, pp. 1–2; Samuel Cowley memo to J. Edgar Hoover, March 31, 1934, Dillinger file 62–29777–382, pp. 1–2, FBI; Cowley to Hoover, April 3, 1934, Dillinger file 62–29777–278, p. 1, FBI; D. L. Nicholson, Report # 26–2434, Dillinger file 62–29777–299, pp. 3–9, FBI; Dillinger file, 62–29777–224, FBI; Burrough, *Public Enemies*, pp. 266–70; Maccabee, *John Dillinger Slept Here*, pp. 219–21.

16. In addition to the FBI sources above, see, for example, the newspaper coverage of the event in the UP story, "Dillinger Shoots Way Out of St. Paul Apartment," Oshkosh (Wisc.) *Northwestern*, March 31, 1934, p. 1; "Bold Bandit Once More Foils Dicks," Helena (Mont.) *Daily Independent*, April, 1, 1934, p. 1.

17. H. H. Clegg memo to J. Edgar Hoover, March 31, 1934, Dillinger file 62–29777–381, FBI, pp. 1–2; Samuel Cowley memo to J. Edgar Hoover, March 31, 1934, Dillinger file 62–29777–382, pp. 1–2, FBI; Cowley to Hoover, April 3, 1934, Dillinger file 62–29777–278, p. 1, FBI; D. L. Nicholson, Report # 26–2434, Dillinger file 62–29777–299, pp. 3–9, FBI; Dillinger file, 62–29777–224, FBI.

18. "St. Paul Police Find Dillinger Fingerprints," Chicago *Tribune*, April 2, 1934, p. 9; H. H. Clegg memo to J. Edgar Hoover, March 31, 1934, Dillinger file 62–29777–380, pp. 1–2, FBI. The clothes are listed in D. L. Nicholson report, April 9, 1934, Dillinger file 62–29777–466, pp. 1–11, FBI. The photo descriptions and inscriptions differ slightly in these two FBI reports. Also see Burrough, *Public Enemies*, pp. 270–72; Maccabee, *John Dillinger Slept Here*, pp. 221–24.

19. The best summary of Dr. May and Nurse Salt's activities is found in J. Edgar Hoover to Homer Cummings, April 21, 1934, RG 60, Central Files, Classified Subjects, Correspondence, 95–57–58, section 1, part 2, box 14021, pp. 1–3, NARA, DOJ.

20. "Doctor Is Seized in Dillinger Case," New York *Times*, April 19, 1934, p. 29; "Dr. May Describes Dillinger Meeting," St. Paul *Dispatch*, May 19, 1934, n.p., in RG 60, 95–57–8, section 1, part 2, box 14022, NARA, DOJ; "U.S. Jury Indicts Six for Aiding Flight of John Dillinger," Chicago *Tribune*, April 21, 1934, p. 6; "The Doctor's Dilemma," Sheboygan (Wisc.) *Press*, April 20, 1934, p. 12; Maccabee, *John Dillinger Slept Here*, pp. 224–25; Girardin, *Dillinger*, pp. 135–36.

21. The story was reprinted, for example, as "Dillinger First Went to Prison a Callow Youth, Came Out a Hardened Criminal, Study Discloses," Mansfield (Ohio) *News-Journal*, March 27, 1934, p. 4.

22. "Dillinger Shoots Way Out of Trap," New York *Times*, April 1, 1934, p. 1; "A Fast Moving Life," Newark (Ohio) *Advocate*, April 3, 1934, p. 4; "Dillinger's Laugh," Nevada *State Journal*, April 9, 1934, p. 4; Melvin Purvis to J. Edgar Hoover, March 31, 1934, Dillinger file, 62–29777–226 p. 4, FBI; "Beauty Surgery for Busy Thugs," *Literary Digest*, April 7, 1934, p. 11.

23. Summary of phone conversation between J. Edgar Hoover and Melvin Purvis, April 1, 1934, in Dillinger file, 62–29777–269, pp. 1–2, FBI; summary of phone conversation between Hoover and William Rorer, April 1, 1934, Dillinger file, 62–29777–264, pp. 1–2, FBI; "Dillinger Hunted in Gang Hideouts," New York *Times*, April 2, 1934, p. 5; "Dillinger Hide-Out Yields New Clues," New York *Times*, April 3, 1934, p. 46. Hoover was quoted by the AP in, for example, "Declares War on Gang," Mansfield (Ohio) *Journal News*, April 4, 1934, p. 13. Agent William Rorer

of the St. Paul Office disagreed about cooperation with other agencies, arguing that the local police must be relied on because they were collecting as many leads as the feds. His feelings proved prescient by the end of the month; see H. H. Clegg memo to J. Edgar Hoover, April 2, 1934, Dillinger file 62–29777–371, pp. 1–2, FBI. On the FBI cultivating snitches, see memos and field reports detailing agents' contacts with underworld sources, Dillinger file, 62–29777–209, pp. 286, 308, 322, FBI; Burrough, *Public Enemies*, pp. 273–74; Maccabee, *John Dillinger Slept Here*, pp. 223–24. The AP placed the gang in California and Arizona at the end of March: "Dillingers in Arizona Again, Coast Reports," Arizona *Star*, March 28, 1934, in Dillinger clipping file, AHS. Ten days later San Francisco police checked out a sighting on the Sausalito-bound ferry: "San Francisco Is All Agog," Arizona *Star*, April 12, 1934, n.p., Dillinger clipping file, AHS.

24. Green's role in the case is described in FBI memos and affidavits under Dillinger file 62–29777–467.

25. For the wounded Green's interviews with federal agents, see D. L. Nicholson report, April 9, 1934, Dillinger file 62–29777–466, pp. 35–41, FBI; H. H. Klegg to J. Edgar Hoover, April 4, 1934, Dillinger file 62–29777–467, pp. 9–21, FBI; Samuel Cowley, "Memorandum," April 4, 1934, Dillinger file, 62–29777–294, p. 1, FBI. For newspaper coverage, see "Shoot Dillinger's Pal; Seize Woman," Chicago *Tribune*, April 4, 1934, p. 1; "U.S. Agents Shoot Aide of Dillinger," New York *Times*, April 4, 1934, p. 1. The *Times* story makes no mention of the feds asking Green to halt, just the agents firing at him. Samuel Cowley offered Hoover the following abbreviated description on April 3: "Two nigger women appeared at the apartment for Stevens' bags, which women were identified as former maids of Charley Harmon, a former bank robber, and Frank Nash. . . . Shortly afterwards a man appeared, opened the door of the apartment, and was immediately fired upon by the agents with the result that he is now in a dying condition in the hospital." FBI memo, Dillinger file, 62–29777–293, p. 1. But a week later Hoover's report to Attorney General Cummings stated, "A demand was made for him [Green] to halt whereupon he made a menacing gesture and was fired upon and shot." J. Edgar Hoover to Homer Cummings, April 11, 1934, RG 60, 14010, item 95–39–4, NARA, DOJ. The best secondary coverage is in Maccabee, *John Dillinger Slept Here*, pp. 232–35, and Burrough, *Public Enemies*, pp. 274–78, 290.

26. J. Edgar Hoover to Samuel Cowley, April 3, 1934, Dillinger file, 62–29777–325, pp. 1–4, FBI; Erik G. Peterson to J. Edgar Hoover, April 6, 1934, Dillinger file, 62–29777–341, pp. 1–2, FBI; Erik Peterson report, April 7, 1934, FBI Dillinger file, 62–29777–407, pp. 1–2, FBI; J. Edgar Hoover to Homer Cummings, April 20, 1934, RG 60, section 1, part 2, box 14021, NARA, DOJ.

27. For examples of newspaper coverage, see the UP story "Dillinger Pal Shot by Justice Agents," Sheboygan (Wisc.) *Press*, April 4, 1934, p. 1; and the AP stories, "Armories of Bandits Are Seized," Helena (Mont.) *Daily Independent*, April 5, 1934, p. 1, and "Federal Agents Concentrate on Dillinger Case," Lima (Ohio) *News*, April 6, 1934, p. 1.

28. Girardin, *Dillinger*, p. 137; Maccabee, *John Dillinger Slept Here*, pp. 235–36. For Bessie Green's testimony to the FBI, see H. H. Clegg to J. Edgar Hoover, April 13, 1934, pp. 1–15, Dillinger file, 62–29777–5XX (number illegible).

29. In fairness to the Bureau, the agent in charge of the Cincinnati Office asked for more men to cover Mooresville just days before Dillinger and Frechette showed up: Samuel. P. Cowley to J. Edgar Hoover, April 2, 1934, Dillinger file, 62–29777–297,

FBI. The feds also monitored the mail in and out of Mooresville: E. J. Connelley to the FBI Office in New Orleans, March 31, 1934, Dillinger file, 62–29777–320NR12, FBI.

30. John Dillinger Sr. ms, file 7, pp. 41–44, ISL.

31. Ibid.; Burrough, *Public Enemies*, pp. 281–86; Matera, *John Dillinger*, pp. 247–51; Robert Cromie and Joseph Pinkston, *Dillinger: A Short and Violent Life* (1962; Evanston, Ill.: Chicago Historical Bookworks, 1990), pp. 191–99.

32. John Dillinger Sr. ms, file 7, pp. 41–44, ISL. More information can be found in the long field report by agent E. J. Connelley, August 2, 1934, Dillinger file, 62–29777–3165, FBI.

33. Dillinger Sr. ms, file 7, pp. 44–48; and file 6, pp. 4–8, ISL, which is a transcription of John Cejnar's questions and his informants' answers.

34. Ibid. Cejnar often smoothed the prose of those he interviewed and guessed at facts he didn't actually know. The wrecked car quickly became the subject of newspaper speculation: "Hunt Dillinger after Auto Wreck," Zanesville (Ohio) *Signal*, April 7, 1934, p. 1. The FBI picked up the Dillinger trail from the new car Billie purchased in Indianapolis: E. J. Connelley to the Birmingham Office, Dillinger file, 62–29777–445nr3, April 9, 1934, FBI.

35. John Dillinger Sr. ms, file 7, pp. 48–50, ISL.

36. Ibid.

37. Ibid., pp. 50, 68–71.

38. Ibid., pp. 50–52.

39. Ibid.

40. Ibid., pp. 50–52, 71; Cejnar interview with Emmett Hancock, file 6, pp. 41–42.

41. Cejnar interview with Emmett Hancock, file 6, pp. 41–42.

42. Cejnar interview with Emmett Hancock, file 7, pp. 71–72, file 6, pp. 11, 42. Burrough, *Public Enemies*, pp. 284–86, describes how FBI agents spotted the Dillinger car, saw their man, but failed to recognize him. According to FBI reports after Dillinger's death, the getaway was more complex. Hubert Dillinger drove John's car into the center of Mooresville to draw the feds' attention, while Evelyn drove to the home of Audrey's friends, Mr. and Mrs. Macy Davis, in Mars Hill, Indiana. There Mary Kinder and Harry Pierpont's parents came to discuss their son's defense with John Dillinger. See E. A. Tamm memo to J. Edgar Hoover, August 7, 1934, pp. 2–3, RG 60, 95–57–8, box 14022, file 8, NARA, DOJ. The raids were discussed in "Dillinger Seen Here; Raiders Miss Him," Indianapolis *Star*, April 9, 1934, p. 1. According to the *Star* story, the raiding party consisted of eighteen men, a mixed group of federal agents, local police, even a St. Paul cop. They came bearing machine guns and wearing bulletproof vests. "'We're through taking chances,' one operative said decisively." The police also searched Mary Kinder's home in Indianapolis. Also see Joseph Keenan to Mr. Stanley, assistant to the attorney general, April 30, 1934, RG 60, 95–57–8, box 14021, section 2, file 1, NARA, DOJ.

43. Jack Cejnar, manuscript news story for the Central Press Syndicate, in Mrs. John Cejnar Collection, L29, Manuscript Division, box 1, file 3, pp. 1–4, ISL; "Dillinger Given Warm Welcome in Home Town," Chicago *Tribune*, April 20, 1934, p. 1; "Town Would Exonerate Dillinger," Mooresville *Times*, April 19, 1934, p. 1; "Dillinger's Camping Ground," New York *Times*, April 25, 1934, p. 20; "Dillinger Is Regarded as Hero in Old Home Town," Coshocton (Ohio) *Tribune*, April 22, 1934, p. 2.

44. "Dillinger Given Warm Welcome in Home Town," Chicago *Tribune*, April 20, 1934, p. 1; "Dillinger Is Regarded as Hero in Old Home Town," Coshocton (Ohio) *Tribune*, April 22, 1934, p. 2.

45. Cejnar, manuscript news story, in Mrs. John Cejnar collection, L29, Manuscript Division, box 1, file 3, pp. 1–4, ISL; "Town Board Decries Criticism of Feeney; Adopts Resolution," Mooresville *Times*, April 26, 1934, p. 1. To keep Mooresville's attitude in perspective, the fact was that most residents never knew Dillinger anyway, they had no idea he was in town until after he left, and the city's board of trustees passed a resolution rejecting Feeney's remarks but calling for Dillinger's capture. "Home Town Asks for Troops," Mansfield (Ohio) *News-Journal*, April 24, 1934, p. 1.

46. F. X. Fay to J. Edgar Hoover, April 5, 1934, pp. 1–2, Dillinger file, 62–29777–326, FBI.

47. Report of V. W. Peterson, May 6, 1934, pp. 5–6, Dillinger file, 62–29777–1222, FBI. According to Burrough in *Public Enemies*, p. 289, Melvin Purvis's personal secretary, Doris Rogers, confirmed Billie's charges that the feds treated her harshly. Austin is named Hubbard Street today, and the tavern stood at the corner of today's State and Hubbard. Girardin claims that Dillinger phoned Strong, an old friend, for Billie's appointment, but that Strong had turned informer, testimony to Dillinger's naïveté about people. The FBI reports, however, are less clear about Strong's status. Girardin, *Dillinger*, pp. 139–40, quotes conflicting testimony from the trial in St. Paul regarding the FBI's interrogation methods. Girardin also claims that Dillinger swore revenge against the agents who roughed up Billie.

48. "Dillinger's Girl Friend Held on Federal Charge," Chicago *Tribune*, April 13, 1934, p. 7; "Woman Friend Brags," Chicago *Tribune*, April 19, 1934, p. 3. The Chicago *Herald Examiner* of April 19 titled its story "Taunts Police on Dillinger's Escape Here" and referred to Frechette as the "dusky Menominee girl friend of Dillinger": n.p., Dillinger file, 62–29777–751, FBI.

49. In addition to the *Tribune* and the *Herald-Examiner*, above, also see "Dillinger Sits," Nevada *State Journal*, April 19, 1934, p. 1; "Evelyn Frechette Waives Extradition," Wisconsin Rapids *Daily Tribune*, April 19, 1934, p. 10; "Dillinger Does Not Keep Date," *Nevada State Journal*, April 23, 1934, p. 1; Girardin, *Dillinger*, pp. 139–40. J. Edgar Hoover, incidentally, wrote Attorney General Homer Cummings urging him to ask to have Frechette's bond increased; he feared that she might raise the sixty thousand dollar bail the court had set. He added, "There is no doubt that if she is released on bond, she will immediately rejoin Dillinger, and as we well know from our investigation of her, the Frechette woman . . . rendered material assistance to Dillinger in not only procuring firearms, but in aiding his rapid movement about the country." Memo dated April 16, 1934, RG 60, 95–57–8, box 14021, section 1, part 1, NARA, DOJ.

50. "Dillinger Just a Nice Boy Doing Right," St. Paul *Pioneer Press*, April 22, 1934, n.p., in Dillinger file, 62–29777–A, FBI.

51. "Dillinger Rumors Scare Shreveport," Tucson *Citizen*, April 13, 1934, in Dillinger clipping file, AHS; "Says Dillinger May Die Soon," Indianapolis *News*, April 14, 1934, p. 1.

52. Girardin, *Dillinger*, pp. 139, 141–42.

53. For the trials of Pierpont, Makley, and Clark, see, for example, "Pierpont Fights for His Life at Lima, O." Hammond (Ind.) *Times*, March 10, 1934, p. 1; "Dillinger Aide Doomed to Chair," New York *Times*, March 11, 1934, p. 1; "Makley Convicted in Dillinger Case," New York *Times*, March 18, 1934, p. 1; "Third Member of Dillinger Gang on Trial Monday," Zanesville (Ohio) *Times*, March 18, 1934, p. 5; "Harry Pierpont Guilty; to Get Electric Chair," Chicago *Tribune*, March 11, 1934, p. 3; "Makley Guilty; Dillinger Gang Aid Due to Die," Chicago *Tribune*, March 18, 1934, p. 10.

54. "Dillinger Raids a Police Station," New York *Times*, April 14, 1934, p. 1; "This Man Dillinger," Sheboygan (Wisc.) *Press*, April 17, 1934, p. 8; "Patrol Northern Indiana after Jail Raid by Dillinger," Chicago *Tribune*, April 14, 1934, p. 6.

55. J. Edgar Hoover to Homer Cummings, April 13, 1934, RG 60, 95–57–8, box 14021, section 1 part 1, NARA, DOJ; "Dillinger Loots Indiana Jail," Mansfield (Ohio) *News-Journal*, April 14, 1934, p. 1; "Dillinger, 'Here Today and Gone Tomorrow' Desperado, Again Shows Heels to Law," Wisconsin Rapids *Daily Tribune*, April 14, 1934, p. 1; "Officers 'Lose' Dillinger," Pittsburgh *Sun-Telegraph*, April 14, 1934, p. 1; "Dillinger Raids a Police Station," New York *Times*, April 14, 1934, p. 1; "This Man Dillinger," Sheboygan (Wisc.) *Press*, April 17, 1934, p. 8; "Patrol Northern Indiana after Jail Raid by Dillinger," Chicago *Tribune*, April 14, 1934, p. 6.

56. For UP coverage, see "Dillinger's Date with Girl Worries Officers," *Nevada State Journal*, April 22, 1934, p. 1; for AP, see "Raid Hideout of Dillinger in Michigan," Sheboygan (Wisc.) *Press*, April 21, 1934, p. 1. FBI Dillinger File, 62–29777–761, NARA, DOJ; "Dillinger Is Hunted in Michigan Woods," New York *Times*, April 22, 1934, p. 2; Burrough, *Public Enemies*, pp. 294–96.

57. The FBI traced the trip to Sault St. Marie; see memos by T. N. Stapleton, H. H. Reinecky, Hoover, and Cowley, April 26, 1934, Dillinger File, 62–29777–891–4, FBI; Burrough, *Public Enemies*, pp. 296–300; Matera, *John Dillinger*, pp. 256–57.

58. Reinecky and Stapleton memos, Dillinger file, 62–29777–891–4, FBI; Burrough, *Public Enemies*, pp. 299–301.

59. J. Edgar Hoover to Homer Cummings, June 27, 1934, RG 60, 95–57–8, section 4, box 14022, NARA, DOJ. Burrough, *Public Enemies*, pp. 300–304, sets the scene nicely. On Wanatka, see Matera, *John Dillinger*, p. 264.

60. For a good summary of the whole episode, see H. H. Clegg to Hoover, April 25, 1934, Dillinger file 62–29777–910, FBI, and field report from the Chicago office, April 28, 1934, Dillinger file 62–29777–934, FBI. Burrough, *Public Enemies*, pp. 304–16, and Matera, *John Dillinger*, pp. 262–75, tell the story well.

61. Clegg to Hoover, April 23, Dillinger file, 62–29777–910, FBI. Using a combination of local reporters and wire service stories, the Rhinelander (Wisc.) *Daily News* covered the story quite thoroughly; see especially April 23–25.

62. Many of the memos passing between Hoover and his men concerned the Bureau's image; for example, Cowley wrote Hoover about an editorial in the Milwaukee *Sentinel*, "The editorial is a good one from our standpoint, stating that the criticism is unjustifiable, that the best possible work was done under the circumstances; and criticized the other papers for their criticism of our Division without knowing the facts." April 26, 1934, Dillinger file, 62–29777–923, FBI; Burrough, *Public Enemies*, pp. 308–12.

63. Clegg to Hoover, April 23, Dillinger file, 62–29777–910, FBI.

64. Ibid. For a good example of how confused events on the ground looked, see S. P. Cowley's memo to Hoover asking the director to clarify queries coming in from the press: April 23, 1934, Dillinger file, 62–29777–840, FBI. The Justice Department put the best spin it could on these events; the Associated Press released a story quoting Attorney General Homer Cummings to the effect that federal agents acted admirably throughout the episode; see, for example, "Cummings Describes Escape of Dillinger," Philadelphia *Evening Bulletin*, April 23, 1934, n.p., in Dillinger file, 62–29777–A, FBI.

65. Hoover defended his agents and summarized his view of the shooting of the three CCC workers in a memo to Assistant Attorney General William Stanley,

April 25, 1934, Dillinger file, 62–29777–882, FBI; Burrough, *Public Enemies*, pp. 313–22; Matera, *John Dillinger*, pp. 279–80.

66. Clegg to Hoover, April 23, Dillinger file, 62–29777–910, FBI. For FBI reports on the death of Agent Baum, see Purvis to Hoover, April 25, 1934, Dillinger file, 62–29777–790; Purvis to the St. Paul Office, April 24, 1934, Dillinger file, 62–29777–903; and especially Cowley to Hoover, April 23, 1934, Dillinger file, 62–29777–852, all in FBI.

67. "Guard against Effort to Free Dillinger Girls," Chicago *Tribune*, April 30, 1934, p. 2. Ellen Poulsen describes the raid from the point of view of the women in *Don't Call Us Molls: Women of the John Dillinger Gang* (Little Neck, N.Y.: Clinton Cook Publishing, 2002), pp. 235–45.

68. A month after Little Bohemia the grand jury sitting in Madison, Wisconsin, returned indictments against the entire gang for harboring Tommy Carroll and John Dillinger; a copy of the indictments accompanied a memo from Joseph Keenan to Homer Cummings, May 21, 1934, RG 60, 95–57–8, box 14021, section 2, part 1, NARA, DOJ. The women were convicted on harboring charges, then released on probation; Crompton was rearrested in June when she was picked up with her lover: "Three Dillinger Women Placed on Probation," Chicago *Tribune*, May 26, 1934, p. 3. Also see Burrough, *Public Enemies*, pp. 321–22; Matera, *John Dillinger*, pp. 278–79.

69. Clegg to Hoover, April 23, Dillinger file, 62–29777–910; Cowley to Hoover, April 25, 1934, Dillinger file, 62–29777–932, both in FBI.

70. Descriptions of the "molls" were reported in Purvis to Hoover, April 24, 1934, and April 25, 1934, Dillinger file 62–29777–811, 818, and 838, FBI; "Tells of Driving Dillinger," New York *Times*, April 23, 1934, p. 3. On the gang's escape from Little Bohemia, see Burrough, *Public Enemies*, pp. 325–33; Matera, *John Dillinger*, pp. 276–83.

71. "Forced Indian to Shield Him Since Monday," Rhinelander (Wisc.) *Daily News*, April 27, 1934, p. 1; "Posse Closing in on Dillinger Aide," New York *Times*, April 28, 1934, p. 5. On the lack of roadblocks, see Cowley to Hoover, April 25, 1934, Dillinger file, 62–29777–862, FBI.

72. "Dillinger Reported Surrounded," St. Louis *Globe Democrat*, April 23, 1934, n.p., Dillinger file, 62–29777–A, section 9, FBI; "End of Dillinger's Bloody Trail in Sight, Officials Say," Meriden (Conn.) *Record*, April 25, 1934, n.p., Dillinger file, 62–29777–A FBI; "Four Others Hurt as Web Is Drawn on Famed Badman," Bismarck (N.D.) *Tribune*, April 23, 1934, p. 1; "Federal Agents Advance on Hideout," Zanesville (Ohio) *Signal*, April 23, 1934, p. 1; "Dillinger Trailed in Wisconsin Woods; 2 Slain, 4 Shot in Trap; Roosevelt pushes Crime War," Washington *Post*, April 24, 1934, n.p., Dillinger file, 62–29777–A-section 9, FBI; "Dillinger Escapes Posses after Two Running Fights; Two Killed, Five Wounded," New York *Times*, April 23, 1934, p. 1; "Hunt Dillinger; 2 Die, 4 Shot," Chicago *Tribune*, April 23, 1934, p. 1.

73. "Dillinger at St. Paul," p. 1; "Farmer Tells of Being Awakened and Forced to Drive Trio," p. 1; "Sheriff Tells Story of Dillinger Fight," p. 3; "Knew He Was Dillinger," p. 3; "Dillinger 'Host' Got Tip to U.S. in Cigarette Pack," p. 3, all in the Chicago *Daily News*, April 23, 1934. For April 24, see the two front-page stories in the *Daily News*: Robert J. Casey, "100 U.S. Agents Ordered after Dillinger" and "Those Guarded Bridges Not So Well Guarded." On page 3 the *Daily News* added the information that two of the three "molls" the feds picked up "were dressed in shabby lounging pajamas, the third in a sort of green riding habit"; they refused to

give their names and addresses, though they said they were from Chicago: "Girls Seized in Dillinger Fight Just Won't Talk," p. 3.

74. "OK Measures Aimed at Dillinger; 13 Slain Since John Escaped" Kingsport (Tenn.) *Times*, April 24, 1934, p. 1; "Stalk Dillinger Through a Snow Covered Forest," Chillicothe (Mo.) *Constitution-Tribune*, April 24, 1934, p. 1; "Dillinger Believed to have Fled From Woods," Brownsville (Texas) *Herald*, April 24, 1934, p. 1.

75. "Trail of Dillinger Gang Fades as Augmented Forces Press Hunt," New York *Times*, April 26, 1934, p. 1.

76. For wire service versions of the story, see "Attorney General Relates Story of Dillinger Battle," Sheboygan (Wisc.) *Press*, April 23, 1934, p. 19; "Department of Justice Makes Report on Dillinger Escape," Elyria (Ohio) *Chronicle Telegram*, April 23, 1934, p. 1. Matera, *John Dillinger*, pp. 279–80, is especially strong on the aftermath of Little Bohemia; also see Burrough, *Public Enemies*, pp. 324–25.

77. "Charge U.S. Men with Bungling Dillinger Hunt," Chicago *Tribune*, April 26, 1934, p. 1; "Lack of Police Cooperation in Dillinger Case Is Scored," Washington *Times*, April 24, 1934, n.p., Dillinger file, 62–29777–816, FBI; "Charge Stupidity in Attempts to Nab Elusive Outlaw," Reno *Evening Gazette*, April 25, 1934, p. 1; "Vilas County Is After Dillinger on Murder Charge," Oshkosh (Wisc.) *Northwestern*, April 25, 1934, p. 7.

78. "Apparently You Can't Believe All Dillinger Stories," Mansfield (Ohio) *News-Journal*, April 28, 1934, p. 1; "Loose Leaf from the Journal," *Nevada State Journal*, April 27, 1934, p. 3; "Suspension of Purvis Sought by Lake Group," Rhinelander (Wisc.) *Daily News*, April 25, 1934, p. 1; "It Was Bungled," Rhinelander (Wisc.) *Daily News*, April 26, 1934, p. 4; "Too Many Dillingers," Philadelphia *Evening Ledger*, May 24, 1934, n.p., Dillinger File, 62–29777–A, section 10, FBI; Arthur Brisbane quoted in the "The Dillinger Farce," Rhinelander (Wisc.) *Daily News*, April 26, 1934, p. 1. For some of the more absurd stories, see "Indians After Dillinger, Says London Paper," Chicago *Tribune*, April 26, 1934, p. 1; "Avers Dillinger Ought to Silence U.S. on Hitler," Chicago *Tribune*, April 25, 1934, p. 2.

79. "Will Rogers Says," Newark (Ohio) *Advocate*, April 24, 1934, p. 1; "Will Rogers Says," Frederick (Md.) *Post*, April 26, 1934, p. 4.

80. Mildred Adams, "The Evolution of a Criminal: The Case of John Dillinger," New York *Times*, April 29, 1934, p. 2. The *Times* saved a little of its contempt for the feds; see "Gibe at Raid on Dillinger," April 25, 1934, p. 3.

81. Adams, "Evolution of a Criminal," p. 2.

82. "Should Be Easy to Nab Dillinger, Just a 'Muddle-Head,' Officers Say," Rhinelander (Wisc.) *Daily News*, April 26, 1934, p. 1; "Psychologist Calls Dillinger Victim of Ego, Conquering Fear with Arrogance," Mansfield (Ohio) *News-Journal*, April 28, 1934, p. 2; "Robin Hood Touch Added by Dillinger," Sheboygan (Wisc.) *Press*, April 23, 1934, p. 19; Homer Cummings to Assistant Attorney General Joseph Keenan, April 30, 1934, Keenan to Courtland Smith, May 1, 1934, Arthur Breuer to Keenan, May 1, 1934, Smith to Cummings, May 5, 1934, Smith to Keenan, May 5, 1934, Smith to Assistant Attorney General William Stanley, June 6, 1934, Smith to Stanley, June 13, 1934, Smith to Cummings, June 13, 1934, all in RG 60, 95–57–8, box 14622, section 2, part 2, NARA, DOJ.

83. "Dillinger Visit Tonic for Business, Wanatka Tells Vilas Undersheriff," Rhinelander (Wisc.) *Daily News*, April 30, 1934, p. 1; Henry Winitt, "Dillinger," New York *Times*, April 29, 1934, p. E5.

84. "Dillinger, an Outlaw, Yet Hero to Some!" Edwardsville (Ill.) *Intelligencer*, April 24, 1934, p. 4; "Dillinger Not a Hero," Lima (Ohio) *News*, April 25, 1934, p. 4;

"This Man Dillinger," Sheboygan (Wisc.) *Press,* April 17, 1934, p. 8. The Lima editorialist clearly borrowed from the earlier Edwardsville work. Dillinger as western hero was a constant theme; see Harry Carr, "Dillinger's Weaving a Hang-Man's Rope," Los Angeles *Times,* Sunday Magazine, June 3, 1934; Charles Norman, "Dillinger Hits the Jesse James Trail," Tucson *Citizen,* May 15, 1934, both in Dillinger file, AHS. Photograph in "Invitation to Dillinger," Washington *News,* April 24, 1934, n.p., Dillinger file, 62–29777-A, section 10, FBI.

Chapter Five

1. "U.S. Agents Will Shoot Dillinger without Parley," Chicago *Tribune,* April 24, 1934, p. 2; "Vengeance Inevitable," Beloit (Wisc.) *News,* reprinted in Oshkosh (Wisc.) *Northwestern,* April 26, 1934, p. 6. Hoover responded to some of the newspaper accusations in an April 26 memo to the attorney general, RG 60, 95–57–8, box 14022 section 2, part 2, National Archives and Records Administration (hereafter NARA), Department of Justice (hereafter DOJ). Almost two months later Hoover was still answering criticism that the FBI "sent a group of young lawyers" rather than cooperate with real law enforcement agencies: Hoover to Cummings, June 20, 1934, RG 60, 95–57–8, box 14022, section 4, NARA, DOJ.

2. "Lack of Police Co-operation in Dillinger Case Is Scored," Washington *Star,* April 24, 1934, n.p., clipping in RG 60, 95–57–8, box 14022, section 2, part 2, NARA, DOJ; "Says Agencies Bungled Case," Newark (Ohio) *Advocate,* April 25, 1934, p. 12; Speech of Randolph Jennings, West Virginia, "Open Session on Criminals," in the House of Representatives, Wednesday April 25, 1934, *Congressional Record: Proceedings and Debates of the Second Session of the Seventy-Third Congress of the United States* (Washington, D.C.: U.S. Government Printing Office, 1934), vol. 78, part 7, pp. 7367–69.

3. "New Dillinger Killings Stir the President, and He Asks Quick Action on Crime Bills," New York *Times,* April 24, 1934, p. 1; "Trail of the Dillinger Gang Fades as Augmented Forces Press Hunt," New York *Times,* April 26, 1934, p. 1; "Anti-Gangster Action Is Plea of Roosevelt," Rhinelander (Wisc.) *Daily News,* April 24, 1934, p. 1; "Trail of Outlaw in Wisconsin Is Lost by Posses," Reno *Evening Gazette,* April 24, 1934, p. 1; "Says Armored Car Needed," Mansfield (Ohio) *News-Journal,* April 25, 1934, p. 11.

4. "Crime Bills Sped by Dillinger Hunt," New York *Times,* April 25, 1934, p. 3; "Dillinger and 9 Are Indicted by Wisconsin Jury," Chicago *Tribune,* May 20, 1934, p. 27; "Action Permit 25,000 Reward for Dillinger," Coshocton (Penna.) *Tribune,* April 27, 1934, p. 1; "Agents May Not Carry Firearms," Rhinelander (Wisc.) *Daily News,* April 25, 1934, p. 1. On the indictments, see Stanley Ryan, U.S. attorney, to Assistant Attorney General Joseph Keenan, May 19, 1934, Keenan to Homer Cummings, May 21, 1934, and the indictments themselves, all in RG 60, 95–57–8, box 14021, section 2, part 1, NARA, DOJ.

5. The story of the expansion of federal policing powers as part of the larger New Deal project of state building is the subject of Clair Bond Potter's thoroughly researched and admirably argued book, *War on Crime: Bandits, G-Men, and the Politics of Mass Culture* (New Brunswick, N.J.: Rutgers University Press, 1998); see especially chapter 6, subtitled "John Dillinger as Political Actor." "Crime Bills Sped by Dillinger Hunt," New York *Times,* April 25, 1934, p. 3; "Outcome in Dillinger Chase to Affect Anti-Crime Bills," Mansfield (Ohio) *News-Journal,* April 30, 1934,

p. 4. Citing the example of England, the Edwardsville (Ill.) *Intelligencer* declared, "We should greatly restrict the sale of firearms. There is no reason why anyone should carry them." But the paper was not "soft" on Dillinger; the editor castigated law enforcement officials for lacking courage, called for the outlaw's death, and added, "The unfortunate thing . . . is that officials did not 'crack down on him' with determination at the beginning of his career." "The Dillinger Case," Edwardsville (Ill.) *Intelligencer*, April 27, 1934, p. 4.

6. "Barrow and his Moll Speeding toward Chicago to join Dillinger, Say Police," Jefferson City (Missouri) *Post-Tribune*, May 3, 1934, p. 1.

7. "Dillinger Case Stirs Nation's Press to Sarcasm," *Literary Digest*, May 5, 1934, p. 9. See "Three Causes of Crime Waves" and "A Cure for Crime," Elyria (Ohio) *Chronicle-Telegram*, May 1, 1934, p. 20, and May 10, 1934, p. 16; "Steel Vests and Banjos," Bismarck (N.D.) *Tribune*, May 4, 1934, p. 4; "Disarm the Criminal," Sheboygan (Wisc.) *Press*, May 9, 1934, p. 20; "Pure Dumbness," Deming (N.M.) *Headlight*, May 18, 1934, p. 4; "Dillinger—American Made," Van Nuys (Calif.) *News*, May 21, 1934, p. 2. The arrested arms merchant was Hyman S. Lebman of San Antonio. According to William H. Helmer's outstanding research, Lebman and his wife hosted Baby Face Nelson, Homer Van Meter, and Marie Conforti for Thanksgiving dinner in November 1933. Despite his selling a variety of exotic weapons to known gangsters, neither Texas nor the federal government was able to put Lebman away for long: G. Russell Girardin with William J. Helmer, *Dillinger: The Untold Story* (Bloomington: Indiana University Press, 1994), 301–2.

8. See "Time to Do Something," Sheboygan (Wisc.) *Press*, May 18, 1934, p. 10; "Crime Has Upper Hand," Newark (Ohio) *Advocate*, May 14, 1934, p. 4; "Get the Killers," Oshkosh (Wisc.) *Northwestern*, May 31, 1934, p. 6.

9. "Rewards for Dillinger and Nelson," press release, June 24, 1934, RG 60, 95–57–8, box 14022, section 5, NARA, DOJ; "U.S. Sets Price of $10,000 upon Dillinger Head," Chicago *Tribune*, June 24, 1934, p. 13. The New York *Times* carried the story on page 1 on June 24, 1934, under the title "U.S. Offers $10,000 to Get Dillinger." Hearst columnist Arthur Brisbane lamented that so many people admired Dillinger that only a large reward might persuade them to turn state's evidence: "Arthur Brisbane," Newark (Ohio) *Advocate*, June 26, 1934, p. 4. The Federal Reward Bill, An Act to Authorize an Appropriation of Money to Facilitate the Apprehension of Certain Persons Charged with Crime, HR 9370, publication no. 295, chapter 408, was passed June 6, 1934. Also see, for example, "Public Enemy Bill Passes," *Nevada State Journal*, June 2, 1934, p. 1. The governors of Indiana, Illinois, Michigan, Minnesota, and Ohio each contributed an additional one thousand dollars, for a total bounty on Dillinger of fifteen thousand dollars.

10. "New Effort to Put Down Crime Is Inaugurated," Frederick (Md.) *Post*, May 19, 1934, p. 1; "Dillinger Hunt," Soda Springs (Idaho) *Sun*, May 17, 1934, p. 2; "Crime War Bills Passed by House," New York *Times*, May 6, 1934, p. 3; "Lawmaker Dillinger," Washington *Times*, n.d., p. 22, RG 60, 95–57–8, box 14021, section 2, part 1, NARA, DOJ.

11. John A. Menaugh, "Jesse James/John Dillinger," Chicago *Tribune*, June 24, 1934, p. G1. The Jesse James comparison had become quite common; see, for example, "Dillinger Hits the Jesse James Trail," Oshkosh (Wisc.) *Northwestern*, May 12, 1934, p. 7. Fingerprint evidence from Fostoria turned out to be inconclusive; it was only when the feds finally traced the getaway car to Dillinger a month later that the robbery was nailed down: "Fingerprints May Aid Cops," "Newark (Ohio) *Advocate*,

May 5, 1934, p. 1; "Consider Theory That Dillinger Gangsters Responsible for Bank Robbery in Which 5 Are Wounded," Wisconsin Rapids *Daily Tribune*, May 4, 1934, p. 1; "Insists Bank Raid Was Led by Dillinger," Coshocton (Ohio) *Tribune*, May 4, 1934, p. 1.

12. For examples, see "Gang Occupies Dungeon after Bohemia Escape," Helena (Mont.) *Daily Independent*, May 18, 1934, p. 1; "Find Hideout for Dillinger," Zanesville (Ohio) *Signal*, May 18, 1934, p. 1; "Report Dillinger Hiding at Farm on Wisconsin Border," Bismarck (N.D.) *Tribune*, May 5, 1934, p. 1; "Dillinger Is Not Found on Liner Bound for Europe," Oshkosh (Wisc.) *Northwestern*, May 5, 1934, p. 2; "Dillinger Hunted on Canadian Liner," New York *Times*, May 6, 1934, p. 2; "Dillinger at Sea?" *Nevada State Journal*, May 5, 1934, p. 1; "Airways Guarded to Keep Dillinger from New Getaway," Bismarck (N.D.) *Tribune*, May 4, 1934, p. 1.

13. "Police in Battle with Gangsters Who Escape in Automobile," Reno *Evening Gazette*, April 30, 1934, p. 1; "Dillinger Gang Disarms Police Squad," Monessen (Pa.) *Daily Independent*, April 30, 1934, p. 1; "Dillinger Hunted in Chicago Again," New York *Times*, May 3, 1934, p. 3; "Sight John Dillinger in Speeding Car," Sheboygan (Wisc.) *Press*, May 8, 1934, p. 1; "Receive Word Mob Seeks to Abduct White," Newark (Ohio) *Advocate*, May 10, 1934, p. 5; "Dillinger Death Theory Gaining Credence in Midwest," *Nevada State Journal*, May 23, 1934, p. 3; "Bad Man at Large," *Time*, May 7, 1934, pp. 18–21.

14. "Mild-Mannered Officer with Record for Sharp-Shooting Seeks Dillinger," Arizona *Star*, May 5, 1934, n.p., Dillinger clipping file, Arizona Historical Society (hereafter AHS); "Keenan Arrives to Aid Dillinger Hunt," Arizona *Star*, May 6, 1934, n.p., Dillinger clipping file, AHS; Robert Forsythe, "Dillinger's Dilemma," *New Masses*, May 15, 1934, pp. 13–14.

15. "Not Beelzebub, but Just a Dumb Crook," *Literary Digest*, June 30, 1934, p. 10; "Again, Dillinger," *Time*, April 23, 1934, pp. 17–18; "Dillinger's Ghost," *Time*, May 14, 1934, pp. 13–14; "The Talk of the Town," *New Yorker*, June 2, 1934, p. 11; "Kansas Police to Get Shots at Dillinger," Reno *Evening Gazette*, May 17, 1934, p. 10; "Dillinger Again!," Oshkosh (Wisc.) *Northwestern*, May 17, 1934, p. 12; "'Dillinger Gang' to Be Entered in Parade Next Week Saturday," Sheboygan (Wisc.) *Press*, May 12, 1934, p. 2; "John Dillinger Held! Not Bad Man . . . A Mule," Lima (Ohio) *News*, May 10, 1934, p. 18; "Invade Garage," Chicago *Tribune*, May 23, 1934, p. 5; "Americana," Elyria (Ohio) *Chronicle-Telegram*, June 28, 1934, p. 14; "Exploiting Crime," Newark (Ohio) *Advocate*, June 25, 1934, p. 4. This last article did not know who was most at fault: the theatrical company for glorifying crime, Dillinger Senior for cashing in on his son's "sins," or the public willing to pay for such nonsense.

16. The following sources are in RG 60, 95–57–8, box 14021, section 2, part 1, NARA, DOJ: James R. Crouch to Franklin Roosevelt, April 14, 1934; F. E. Frisbie to the Department of Justice, May 16, 1934; A. E. Zeiske to Homer Cummings, April 25, 1934; Eva Dumbeck to Franklin Roosevelt, May 18, 1934; E. H. McColloch to Joseph B. Keenan, April 24, 1934; "Psychologist" to Department of Justice, May 17, 1934; Russelo's story was communicated through a series of diplomatic contacts: O. W. Johnson to the attorney general, April 27, 1934; William Larson, FBI, to Marshall Vance, May 2, 1934; Marshall Vance to the secretary of state, May 3, 1934; secretary of state to attorney general, May 14, 1934.

17. Charles W. Ives to Joseph Keenan, April 24, 1934; "A Greek Subject" to Franklin Roosevelt, May 7, 1934; name illegible to Franklin Roosevelt, May 7, 1934; Edgar M. Clark to FDR, April 27, 1934; Josephine Aunt to Franklin Roosevelt,

registered at Department of Justice, May 9, 1934, all in RG 60, 95–57–8, box 14021, section 2, part 1, NARA, DOJ.

18. Albert Meglitock to Attorney General Homer Cummings, May 6, 1934, RG 60, 95–57–8, section 2, part 1, box 14021, NARA, DOJ.

19. W. B. Grant to Elinor [*sic*] Roosevelt, May 4, 1934, in RG 60, 95–57–8, section 2, part 1, box 14021, NARA, DOJ.

20. Joseph J. Edwards to Franklin Roosevelt, April 25, 1934; Franklin P. Davis to Department of Justice, April 29, 1934; Anonymous to Franklin Roosevelt, April 24, 1934; all in RG 60, 95–57–8, section 2, part 1, box 14021, NARA, DOJ.

21. W. Guyer Fisher to Homer Cummings, April 30, 1934; "A Citizen and Tax Payer" to Joseph B. Keenan, received May 1, 1934, all in RG 60, 95–57–8, section 2, part 1, box 14021, NARA, DOJ.

22. Such stories were extremely common. See the clippings in RG 60, 95–57–8, section 3, box 14022, NARA, DOJ, all from the Indianapolis *Star*: "Dillinger Attends Reunion as Officers Scour Indiana," April 18, 1934; "Dillinger Family Seeks Peace at Farm," May 18, 1934, "Mooresville Petition Asks Pardon for John Dillinger," April 19, 1934; "Dillinger's Father Seeks 'Justice' for Son," June 9, 1934, all without page numbers.

23. "Parole Experts Rush to Adopt New U.S. Law," Chicago *Tribune*, June 28, 1934, p. 9; "Indiana Blamed for Dillinger's Career of Crime," Chicago *Tribune*, June 29, 1934, p. 19.

24. A year after his death, Anna Sage, the "woman in red," discussed Dillinger's fascination with the media coverage: "Dillinger Avidly Read Accounts of Infamous Crimes," Bismarck (N.D.) *Tribune*, July 19, 1935, p. 1 (the story was widely reprinted); Jack Katz, *The Seductions of Crime* (New York: Basic Books, 1990).

25. "Engineered Escape of Gang from Jail Sept. 23 Last Year," Washington *Daily News*, April 23, 1934, p. 1; Willie Sutton, *Where the Money Was: The Memoirs of a Bank Robber* (New York: Viking Press, 1976), pp. 10–11.

26. Brian Burrough, *Public Enemies* (New York: Penguin Press, 2004), pp. 326–30; Dary Matera, *John Dillinger: The Life and Death of America's First Celebrity Criminal* (New York: Carroll and Graf, 2004), pp. 280–84. O'Leary told Girardin, *Dillinger*, pp. 152–56, a different story about Hamilton's burial: that Dillinger and Van Meter brought him all the way out to the south shore of Lake Michigan and buried him deep in the Indiana sand dunes. Though it was never conclusive, the feds were satisfied that the body exhumed two years later near Aurora was Red Hamilton.

27. "Underline Bible to Get Missives to Dillingerites," Chicago *Tribune*, April 21, 1934, p. 6. On the precautions taken at Lima, see especially the memo from Special Agent William Larson of the Detroit Office to J. Edgar Hoover, March 5, 1934, FBI Dillinger file, 62–29777–96, NARA, DOJ; Burrough, *Public Enemies*, pp. 249–50. A justice of the peace from Leipsic, Ohio, wrote to the Department of Justice that Levy had been overheard in a phone conversation, apparently with Dillinger, who wanted to come to Lima to liberate his friends: W. H. McClung to Department of Justice, March 11, 1934, FBI Dillinger file, 62–29777–165, NARA, DOJ.

28. One FBI informant told Agent F. E. Hurley back in April that Dillinger had considerable courage and craft, and although he was absolutely devoted to the members of his gang he knew that the jails were too well guarded now for a rescue attempt; all Dillinger could do was keep robbing banks and paying the lawyers: Field report of Special Agent Hurley, Cincinnati Office, April 3, 1934, FBI Dillinger File, 62–29777–308, NARA, DOJ; Girardin, *Dillinger*, pp. 160–62. The leading English medical journal, the *Lancet*, praised Dr. May for treating Dillinger: "For Dr. Clayton

May, however, there was only one question. Did Dillinger come to him for treatment, trusting in his professional honor? The answer is obvious, and Dr. May's colleagues in every country will applaud his action in not betraying a professional trust." "British Medics Praise Jailed Doctor Who Treated Dillinger," Chicago *Tribune*, June 2, 1934, p. 5, reprinted from the New York *Times*.

29. Girardin, *Dillinger*, pp. 158–60; Burrough, *Public Enemies*, pp. 338–47; Matera, *John Dillinger*, pp. 284–86. The Fostoria robbery was reported tentatively because the identity of the perpetrators was unclear until a month later, when the FBI confirmed that the license plates on the getaway car matched one driven by Dillinger in June. For newspaper reports, see "Four Wounded in Gun Fight at Ohio City," Stevens Point (Wisc.) *Daily Journal*, May 4, 1934, p. 1; "Trailed into Ohio," New York *Times*, May 6, 1934, p. 2; "Dillinger, Aid Linked in Robbery," Lima (Ohio) *News*, May 6, 1934, p. 1. The Lima paper reported that the bank was robbed by "Dillinger's master machinegunner, Homer Van Meter" and that Dillinger stood by in Toledo, waiting to help his friend if he needed it.

30. Girardin, *Dillinger*, pp. 162–63, tells the story of O'Brien and Mulvihill in some detail through O'Leary's eyes. For newspapers, see "2 Policemen Slain in Dillinger Hunt," Chicago *Tribune*, May 25, 1934, p. 1; "Five States Offer $5,000 Reward for John Dillinger," Chicago *Tribune*, May 26, 1934, p. 3; "Two East Chicago Detectives, One Star Murder Witness against Dillinger, Slain by Machine-Gun Fire," Indianapolis *News*, May 25, 1934, p. 1; "Two Officers Slain by Chicago Gunmen," Clearfield (Pa.) *Progress*, May 25, 1934, p. 1; "Two Chicago Policemen Killed, Dillinger Sought," Edwardsville (Ill.) *Intelligencer*, May 25, 1934, p. 1. For the deaths of Bonnie and Clyde, see Burrough, *Public Enemies*, pp. 347–61.

31. Girardin, *Dillinger*, pp. 162–63; Burrough, *Public Enemies*, pp. 362–64; Matera, *John Dillinger*, pp. 288–300.

32. With his ties to Piquett and O'Leary, Girardin was in the best position to tell this murky story; see *Dillinger*, pp. 167–68, 189. Also see Burrough, *Public Enemies*, pp. 363–67; Matera *John Dillinger*, pp. 289–91.

33. Girardin, *Dillinger*, pp. 167–71. On May's trial, see the AP stories "Doctor Believed He Was Followed by Dillinger Men," Bismarck (N.D.) *Tribune*, May 21, 1934, p. 1; "Deny Motions for Dismissal at St. Paul," Sheboygan (Wisc.) *Press*, May 19, 1934, p. 1. Billie Frechette, standing trial with Dr. May and Augusta Salt, was described in the Bismarck *Tribune* story: "Miss Frechette appeared in court Monday with a fetching white outfit trimmed in red which contrasted with her black hair and eyes."

34. Girardin, *Dillinger*, pp. 171–77. According to Girardin, the money was divided among O'Leary, Piquett, Cassidy, and Loeser. Also see Burrough, *Public Enemies*, pp. 365–67.

35. Girardin, *Dillinger*, pp. 171–77; Burrough, *Public Enemies*, pp. 365–67.

36. The story of Tommy Carroll and Jean Crompton is beautifully told by Ellen Poulsen, *Don't Call Us Molls: Women of the John Dillinger Gang* (Little Neck, N.Y.: Clinton Cook Publishing, 2002), pp. 307–17. Also see "Dillinger Pal Killed by Police," Edwardsville (Ill.) *Intelligencer*, June 8, 1934, p. 1; "Dillinger's Aide Is Slain in Iowa," New York *Times*, June 8, 1934, p. 3; "Dillinger Aid Shot to Death," Lima (Ohio) *News*, June 8, 1934, p. 1; "Machine Gunner Asserts That He Killed Dillinger," *Nevada State Journal*, June 8, 1934, p. 1; "Dying Gunman Hints Death of Dillinger," Coshocton (Ohio) *Tribune*, June 8, 1934, p. 1; "Dillinger Gang Gunman Slain by Iowa Police," Chicago *Tribune*, June 8, 1934, p. 2.

37. Poulsen, *Don't Call Us Molls*, pp. 307–17; "Dillinger Gang Gunman Slain by Iowa Police," Chicago *Tribune*, June 8, 1934, p 2. Apparently Carroll actually said

nothing about hiding Dillinger; in a memo to Homer Cummings, J. Edgar Hoover wrote that Carroll died at 7:00 p.m. without making any statement: June 8, 1934, RG 60, 95–57–8, box 14022, section 3, NARA, DOJ.

38. Girardin, *Dillinger*, pp. 183–88, 193–94. Girardin wants to have it both ways, claiming that Dillinger prepared a hit list and went out looking for his enemies, but that he was not really a violent man. Girardin's narrative is based largely on interviews he conducted with Louis Piquett, who claimed that he talked Dillinger out of going after his enemies. Amazingly, neither the FBI nor local police systematically tailed O'Leary or Piquett; both men took evasive measures when they approached Probasco's home, but because O'Leary visited Dillinger every other day and Piquett not much less frequently, they easily could have led lawmen to their prey. O'Leary and Piquett were prosecuted by the federal government after Dillinger's death; they could not deny they spent time with him, but they could make the case that they restrained him from committing worse depredations. In other words, they had reason to tell Girardin of their good deeds. Also see "Open Letters," Lima (Ohio) *News*, June 8, 1934, p. 6.

39. For examples of Dillinger being spotted in the Upper Great Lakes, see "Pick Up Dillinger's Trail in Northwest," Bismarck (N.D.) *Tribune*, June 13, 1934, p. 1; "Transient Says Dillinger Gave Him a Cigaret," Zanesville (Ohio) *Signal*, June 13, 1934, p. 1; "New Dillinger Clue Exploded," Elyria (Ohio) *Chronicle-Telegram*, June 13, 1934, p. 2; letters from H. E. Mickle (Canton, Ohio), Fred E. Frank (Bayonne, N.J.), Sam Stepanik (Edmonton, Alberta), "John Doe" (Calumet City, Ill.), Ellen Olmstead (Sioux Falls, S.D.), and F. T. Knichbaugh (York, Pa.), all in RG 60, 95–57–8, box 14022, file 4, NARA, DOJ. For an erroneous report of Dillinger's death, see, "Pat Reilly Tells of Story Related by Bandit's Slain Friend," New York *Times*, June 29, 1934, p. 42.

40. For Audrey Hancock's notice, see "Sister Greets Dillinger with a Birthday Ad," Chicago *Tribune*, June 23, 1934, p. 2; "Sister Conveys Birthday Greetings to Dillinger by Means of Newspaper Ad," Coshocton (Ohio) *Tribune*, June 23, 1934, p. 1. For Old John, see "Dillinger Is Alive, His Father Asserts," New York *Times*, June 29, 1934, p. 42; "Denies She Had Dillinger Letter," Frederick (Md.) *News*, June 23, 1934, p. 1; J. Edgar Hoover to Homer Cummings, June 30, 1934, RG 60, 95–57–8, box 14022, section 4, NARA, DOJ.

41. Girardin, *Dillinger*, pp. 188–90. Robert Volk, who was in the garage in Crown Point when Dillinger stole Sheriff Holley's car, claimed he saw Dillinger at Wrigley Field and said, "This is getting to be a habit, isn't it?" to which Dillinger replied, "Looks like it is." Dillinger slipped out quietly after the seventh inning stretch: "Pat Reilly Tells of Story Related by Bandit's Slain Friend," New York *Times*, June 29, 1934, p. 42.

42. Girardin, *Dillinger*, pp. 188–90. Van Meter hooked up with his old girlfriend, Marie Conforti, toward the end of the month, and they moved in together in Calumet City, Illinois; see "Third Girl Disappears," Chicago *Tribune*, June 23, 1934, p. 2. The Chicago *Defender* joked that the World's Fair organizers designated Tuesday, June 26, "John Dillinger Day," and that the Dillinger Squad would be on hand to fire a twenty-one-gun salute into Mr. Dillinger. The outlaw declined the honor, being busy writing his memoirs: "Mr. Dillinger's Day at the Fair," Chicago *Defender*, July 7, 1934, editorial page. For Dillinger's last weeks, see Burrough, *Public Enemies*, pp. 382–400; Matera, *John Dillinger*, pp. 294–306; Robert Cromie and Joseph Pinkston, *Dillinger: A Short and Violent Life* (1962; Evanston, Ill.: Chicago Historical Bookworks, 1990), pp. 240–48.

43. Girardin, *Dillinger*, p. 167–78, 299–303, is the best source on the surgery. Also see Matera, *John Dillinger*, pp. 307–18; Burrough, *Public Enemies*, pp. 384–87.

44. The most thorough newspaper coverage of the robbery can be found in "Dillinger Gang Kills Officer," South Bend (Ind.) *Tribune*, June 30, 1934, p. 1. The following day's *Tribune* carried several stories under the banner "Bank Slayers' Auto Found," July 1, 1934, pp. 1, 6–7. Also see "Dillinger Head of Fatal Bank Raid, Say Police," Chicago *Tribune*, July 1, 1934, p. 1; "Bank Robbed by Dillinger; Officer Slain," Coshocton (Ohio) *Tribune*, June 30, 1934, p. 1; "Dillinger Raiders Kill One, Injure Four in Bank Foray," Reno *Evening Gazette*, June 30, 1934, p. 1; "Another Clue in Dillinger Search Fades," Newark (Ohio) *Advocate*, July 2, 1934, p. 1.

45. "Dillinger Gang Kills Officer," South Bend (Ind.) *Tribune*, June 30, 1934, p. 1.

46. In Girardin's colorful but suspect telling of the story, Berg fired the shot that hit Van Meter, who was determined to return to South Bend for revenge: *Dillinger*, pp. 198–201. Newspapers also reported a hot lead on July 1, which grew cold by July 2. The day after the robbery, two men woke Dr. Leslie Laird of North Webster, Indiana, out of a sound sleep and demanded treatment of an arm wound as well as cocaine for pain. When the doctor refused the narcotic, they beat him. It was Dillinger, early reports declared, but subsequently Dr. Laird could not identify his assailants.

47. Girardin, *Dillinger*, pp. 304–5; Burrough, *Public Enemies*, pp. 388–91; Cromie and Pinkston, *Dillinger*, pp. 240–43. As proof that she didn't know that "Jimmy Lawrence" was John Dillinger, Anna Sage said in a widely reprinted story that her son spent lots of time with the outlaw; no mother would allow her son to be so much in harm's way, she argued: "Dillinger Avidly Read Accounts of Infamous Crimes," Bismarck (N.D.) *Tribune*, July 19, 1935, p. 1.

48. A week after Dillinger's death George Wright wrote a very insightful article piecing together Dillinger's end: "Indiana's Police Launch Quiz on Dillinger Death," Chicago *Tribune*, July 30, 1934, p. 3. Also see "Outlaw Trapped by Woman Hit by Jealousy, Claim," Oshkosh (Wisc.) *Northwestern*, July 24, 1934, p. 24; "Clear Up Dillinger Mystery," Chicago *Tribune*, July 25, 1934, p. 1; "Dillinger Cache Eludes the Police," New York *Times*, July 26, 1934, p. 40; "Hunt Dillinger Money, If Any; Girl in Flight," Chicago *Tribune*, July 26, 1934, p. 5; "Dillinger a Gay Boy on Parties, Says Companion," Chicago *Tribune*, July 26, 1934, p. 6.

49. Girardin, *Dillinger*, pp. 218–22. Sage tells her story in a sworn statement to Samuel Cowley, August 1, 1934, Dillinger file, 62–29777–3233, FBI.

50. Ibid.; Burrough, *Public Enemies*, pp. 388–91, 397–99; Matera, *John Dillinger*, pp. 334–45; Wright, "Indiana Police Launch Quiz," p. 3. Sage's statement to Samuel Cowley, August 1, 1934, Dillinger file, 62–29777–3233, FBI.

51. George Wright, "Indiana's Police Launch Quiz on Dillinger Death," Chicago *Tribune*, July 30, 1934, p. 3; Samuel Cowley to J. Edgar Hoover, August 2, 1934, Dillinger file, 62–29777–3233, FBI. Also see "Relentless Cop Spied on Bandit for Many Days," Newark (Ohio) *Advocate*, July 24, 1934, p. 2; Burrough, *Public Enemies*, pp. 390–91, 397–400.

52. Burrough, *Public Enemies*, pp. 367–71, convincingly makes the argument for Cowley's ascendancy.

53. Ibid. The AP story on the "Dillinger gang girls" can be found in Arizona *Citizen*, "Dillinger Women Elude U.S. Agents," June 23, 1934, n.p., in Dillinger clipping file, AHS. Alston Purvis and Alex Tresniowski, *The Vendetta: FBI Hero Melvin Purvis' War against Crime and J. Edgar Hoover's War against Him* (New York: Public Affairs, 2005), pp. 146–68.

54. Girardin, *Dillinger*, pp. 208, 303–4; Burrough, *Public Enemies*, pp. 393–94.

55. "Dillinger a Gay Boy on Parties, Says Companion," Chicago *Tribune*, July 26, 1934, p. 5; "Clear Up Dillinger Mystery," Chicago *Tribune*, July 25, 1934, p. 1; "Dillinger Cache Eludes the Police," New York *Times*, July 26, 1934, p. 40. Polly Hamilton is quoted at length in Cromie and Pinkston, *Dillinger*, pp. 340–42; she told her story to the Chicago *Herald-Examiner*, in October, 1934.

56. "Dillinger a Gay Boy on Parties, Says Companion," Chicago *Tribune*, July 26, 1934, p. 5; "Clear Up Dillinger Mystery," Chicago *Tribune*, July 25, 1934, p. 1.

57. Purvis, *The Vendetta*, pp. 157–58; Girardin, *Dillinger*, pp. 219–20; telegram to J. Edgar Hoover, July 22, 1934, Dillinger file, 62–29777–1–19X, FBI; Samuel Cowley memo to J. Edgar Hoover, July 24, 1934, Dillinger file 62–29777–1–14, FBI; Samuel Cowley to J. Edgar Hoover, August 2, 1934, Dillinger file, 62–29777–3233, FBI.

58. Anna Sage, sworn statement to Samuel Cowley, August 1, 1934, Dillinger file, 62–29777–3233, FBI; Girardin, *Dillinger*, pp. 219–20, 305.

59. Ibid.; Purvis and Tresniowski, *Vendetta*, pp. 158–59; Burrough, *Public Enemies*, pp. 397–99; Matera, *John Dillinger*, pp. 338–42; Anna Sage, sworn statement to Samuel Cowley, August 1, 1934, Dillinger file, 62–29777–3233, FBI.

60. See the testimony of several agents who were present at the Biograph on July 22, 1934: V. W. Peterson, C. O. Hurt, R. D. Brown, C. B. Winstead, and E. L. Richmond. Each submitted memoranda of their recollections to J. Edgar Hoover, all dated August 1, 1935, all in Dillinger file, 62–29777, FBI. Also see Purvis and Tresniowski, *Vendetta*, pp. 160–61; Burrough, *Public Enemies*, pp. 401–3; Girardin, *Dillinger*, p. 306; Matera, *John Dillinger*, pp. 342–45. J. Edgar Hoover submitted a summary of the Dillinger gang's history to the attorney general a year after Dillinger's death, on September 6, 1935, RG60, 95–57–8, Box 14022, Section 3, NARA, DOJ.

61. See the August 1, 1935, Peterson, Hurt, Brown, Winstead, and Richmond memos to Hoover. The FBI position is summarized in a memo on J. Edgar Hoover's letterhead dated October 3, 1935, Dillinger file, 62–29777–1–26, FBI; Samuel Cowley to J. Edgar Hoover, July 24, 1934, Dillinger file, 62–29777–2895, FBI; Burrough, *Public Enemies*, pp. 404–7; Matera, *John Dillinger*, pp. 346–54.

62. *Manhattan Melodrama*, DVD, directed by W. S. Van Dyke, 1934 (Burbank, Calif.: Warner Home Video, 2007).

63. August 1, 1935, Peterson, Hurt, Brown, Winstead, and Richmond memos to Hoover; J. Edgar Hoover to E. A. Tamm, July 23, 1934, Dillinger file, 62–29777–2958, FBI; Samuel Cowley to J. Edgar Hoover, July 24, 1934, Dillinger file, 62–29777–2895, FBI. The FBI's Dillinger file contains a copy of the coroner's report and minutes of the inquest: 62–29777–2941–2943, FBI. The FBI file on Dillinger's death contains literally hundreds of documents, but see J. Edgar Hoover to E. A. Tamm, July 23, 1934, Dillinger file, 62–29777–2958, FBI; J. Edgar Hoover to E.A. Tamm, July 24, 1934, Dillinger File, 62–29777–2964, FBI; J. Edgar Hoover to E. A. Tamm, July 27, 1934, Dillinger file, 62–29777–2966, FBI.

Chapter Six

1. John Dillinger Sr. ms, file 7, pp. 73–74, Indiana State Library (hereafter ISL); "Dillinger's Dad Here to Claim Body of Killer," Chicago *Tribune*, July 24, 1934, p. 2; "How the Hunted Bandit Chose His Own Grave," Sunday *Mirror*, magazine section, December 16, 1934, p. 13, in Dillinger Sr. ms, box 1, file 9, ISL.

2. "Homecoming in a Hearse for Outlaw," Oshkosh (Wisc.) *Northwestern*, July 24, 1934, p 1; "Dillinger Comes Home," Clearfield (Penna.) *Progress*, July 25, 1934, p. 1.

3. "John Wasn't Bad All Through Says Dillinger's Aged Father," Washington *Post*, July 24, 1934, p. 3; Dillinger Senior quoted in Dillinger Sr. ms, file 7, pp. 75–76, ISL.

4. "Dillinger's Dad Here to Claim Body of Killer," Chicago *Tribune*, July 24, 1934, p. 3; Dillinger Sr. ms, file 7, pp. 77–78, ISL.

5. "Dillinger's Body Taken Home by Aged Father He Disgraced," Zanesville (Ohio) *Times Recorder*, July 25, 1934, p. 1; "Dillinger's Dad Here to Claim Body of Killer," Chicago *Tribune*, July 24, 1934, p. 3; "Dad Takes Dillinger's Body Home; Police Raid Flat of 'Girl Friend,'" Chicago *Daily News*, July 24, 1934, p. 1; Dillinger Sr. ms, file 7, pp. 77–78, ISL.

6. "Dillinger Comes Home Last Time," Mooresville *Times*, July 26, 1934, p. 1; also see Virginia Gardner, "Crowds of Home Town Folks See Dillinger Body," Chicago *Tribune*, July 25, 1934, p. 2.

7. "Dillinger Comes Home Last Time," Mooresville *Times*, July 26, 1934, p. 1; "Objections to Burial of Dillinger's Body in Crown Hill Cemetery Overruled" and "Outlaw's Body to Be Buried beside Mother's in Indianapolis Cemetery," Coshocton (Ohio) *Tribune*, July 24, 1934, pp. 1, 8; Claude A. Mahoney, "Dillinger Comes Home to Mooresville," Indianapolis *Star*, July 25, 1934, p. 1.

8. Virginia Gardner, "Dillinger Given Church Burial as Downpour Soaks Curious," Chicago *Tribune*, July 26, 1934, p. 6; "Note Pledges Revenge for Death of Dillinger," Oshkosh (Wisc.) *Northwestern*, July 27, 1934, p. 3.

9. All of the headlines quoted above come from the July 23, 1934, editions of these newspapers; all were the day's lead story on page 1.

10. "Denunciado Por Una Mujer, John Dillinger Fue Muerto," Bogotá (Colombia) *El Tiempo*, July 24, 1934, p. 1; "Foi Morto, Nost Estados Unidos, O Famoso Bandido John Dillinger," São Paulo (Brazil) *O Estado*, July 24, 1934, p. 1; "Dillinger Betrayed by a Jealous Woman?" *Times of India*, July 24, 1934, p. 10.

11. "Dillinger, U.S. Public Enemy No. 1, Shot Dead in Chicago," Peiping *Chronicle*, July 24, 1934, p. 1; "The Career of Dillinger," *Times of London*, July 24, 1934, n.p.; Manchester *Guardian*, July 24, 1934, p. 8; "Police Get Dillinger," *The Age* (Melbourne), July 24, 1934, p. 8; "Dillinger Skotinn," Reykjavik *Morgunbladid*, July 24, 1934, p. 6.

12. "Barbarism?" *Volkischer Beobachter*, July 25, 1934, translated and submitted by William E. Dodd, American Embassy in Berlin, to U.S. State Department, July 30, 1934, in RG 59, Decimal File, 1930–1939, 811.108/1230, box 4806, National Archives and Records Administration (hereafter NARA), Department of State.

13. "Cummings Says Slaying of Dillinger Is 'Gratifying as Well as Reassuring,'" New York *Times*, July 23, 1934, p. 1; "'Delighted,' McNutt Says, When Told Dillinger's Bloody Trail Is Ended," Indianapolis *Star*, July 23, 1934, p. 1; Hal H. Smith, "Agents of Justice Who 'Got' Dillinger," New York *Times*, July 29, 1934, p. 2.

14. "Story of Purvis, Leader in Long Desperado Hunt," Chicago *Tribune*, July 23, 1934, p. 1; "Dillinger Trap Leader Admits Being 'Scared,'" Washington *Post*, July 24, 1934, p. 3; "Dillinger Death Brings Elation to Cummings," Chicago *Tribune*, July 23, 1934, p. 2; "Cummings Here; Praises Purvis' Drive on Crime," Chicago *Tribune*, July 24, 1934, p. 3; "Dillinger Trapped, Slain at Close Range," Indianapolis *Star*, July 23, 1934, p. 1; "Hunt for Aids of Dillinger Still Pursued," Washington *Post*, July 23, 1934, pp. 1–2.

15. "Inquest Justifies Dillinger's Death," New York Times, July 24, 1934, p. 3; "Jury Commends U.S. Agents for Killing Outlaw," Chicago *Tribune*, July 24, 1934, p. 2.

16. "Women Figured Prominently in Dillinger's Life," Zanesville (Ohio) *Times Recorder*, July 24, 1934, p. 1; "Clear Up Dillinger Mystery," Chicago *Tribune*, July 25,

1934, p. 1; fragment without title, Martinsville (Ind.) *Republican,* July 26, 1934, dateline Chicago, July 23, n.p., in Dillinger file, Mooresville Public Library; "Jealousy Set Dillinger Trap," Chicago *Tribune,* July 24, 1934, p. 1.

17. Ibid.; "Women Figured Prominently in Dillinger's Life," Zanesville (Ohio) *Times Recorder,* July 24, 1934, p. 1; "Clear Up Dillinger Mystery," Chicago *Tribune,* July 25, 1934, p. 1.

18. "Bloody Career of Killer Brought to an End," *Nevada State Journal,* July 23, 1934, pp. 3,6; "Dillinger Tipster Girl Guarded from Guns of Desperado's Aids," Washington *Post,* July 24, 1934, p. 1; "'Girl in Red Dress' Credited with Putting John Dillinger on Spot Hidden under Guard," Zanesville (Ohio) *Times Recorder,* July 24, 1934, p. 1; "Outlaw Trapped by Woman Hit by Jealousy, Claim," Oshkosh (Wisc.) *Northwestern,* July 24, 1934, p. 24; "Jealousy of Woman Suspected," *Nevada State Journal,* July 24, 1934, p. 1.

19. "Clear Up Dillinger Mystery," Chicago *Tribune,* July 25, 1934, p. 1; "Dillinger 'Broke,' Betrayed by Spies," New York *Times,* July 24, 1934, p. 1. Some of the newspaper reports are simply incredible. One *Times* story had Dillinger dying at the feet of a Mooresville woman he knew as a boy; coincidentally strolling Lincoln Avenue, she arrived just in time to hear Dillinger utter as he fell, "They've got me at last," then expire: "They've Got Me at Last," New York *Times,* July 24, 1934, p. 2.

20. "Dillinger's Weakness for Movies Leads to Sudden Death," *Nevada State Journal,* July 23, 1934, p. 1. Another widely reprinted story emphasized how the police staked out the movies: "Dillinger Under Observance for One Week Before Death at Hands of Law," Hamilton (Ohio) *Journal,* p. 1.

21. David Ruth, *Inventing the Public Enemy: The Gangster in American Culture* (Chicago: University of Chicago Press, 1996), is a fine discussion of the relationship between film, gangsters, the culture of consumption, and cultural style.

22. "Dillinger Dies," Chicago *Tribune,* July 23, 1934, p 1.

23. "Clear Up Dillinger Mystery," Chicago *Tribune,* July 25, 1934, p. 1; "Exit Dillinger," Washington *Post,* July 24, 1934, p. 8; "Dillinger's Death Pleases Agent's Widow," Washington *Post,* July 24, 1934, p. 3.

24. "Crime and Punishment," New York *Times,* July 24, 1934, p. 16; "Treachery in the Underworld," New York *Times,* July 25, 1934, p. 16; "Types of Gangs," New York *Times,* July 27, 1934, p. 16; "The End of Dillinger," Montana *Standard,* July 24, 1934, p. 4; "Up from Boyhood—or Down," Mansfield (Ohio) *News-Journal,* July 26, 1934, p. 4.

25. "'Girl in Red Dress' Credited with Putting John Dillinger on Spot Hidden under Guard," Zanesville (Ohio) *Times Recorder,* July 25, 1934, p. 1; "U.S. Manhunters Search for Last Dillinger Refuge," Oshkosh (Wisc.) *Northwestern,* July 24, 1934, p. 1; Robert Loughran, "Federal Agents Plan Drive on Dillinger Pals," Stevens Point (Wisc.) *Daily Journal,* July 24, 1934, p. 1; "Turn Heat on Remnants of Daring Gang," Zanesville (Ohio) *Signal,* July 24, 1934, p. 1; "Federal Agents Launch Hunt for New Enemy No. 1," Chicago *Tribune,* July 25, 1934, p. 2; "Last Hideout of Dillinger Searched," Elyria (Ohio) *Chronicle-Telegram,* July 26, 1934, p. 2; "5 of Dillinger's Gangsters Are Still at Large," Chicago *Tribune,* July 23, 1934, p. 3; "Rest of Gang Faces Finale," *Nevada State Journal,* July 24, 1934, p. 1; "Girl in Red Dress Said to have Led Dillinger to Death," Titusville (Pa.) *Herald,* July 24, 1934, p. 1.

26. "Undertaker Says Brain of Outlaw Had Been Taken," *Nevada State Journal,* August 2, 1934, p. 2; "Elder Dillinger Threatens Suit," Mansfield (Ohio) *News-Journal,* August 2, 1934, p. 1; "Terms Dillinger Autopsy Merely Routine Matter,"

Chicago *Tribune*, August 2, 1934, p. 6; "Dillinger's Body Will Be Exhumed," Frederick (Md.) *Post*, August 2, 1934, p. 1; "Decides He Won't Disinter Dillinger," Frederick (Md.) *Post*, August 3, 1934, p. 1; "Dillinger's Brain Is Destroyed, Says Doctor," Gettysburg (Penna.) *Times*, August 3, 1934, p. 5.

27. See Helmer's comment in G. Russell Girardin with William J. Helmer, *Dillinger: The Untold Story* (Bloomington: Indiana University Press, 1994), p. 312. For the missing autopsy report, see "Long-lost Report on Dillinger Is Found," Indianapolis *Star*, March 25, 1984, p. 1 (reprinted from the Chicago *Tribune*).

28. "Bandit Executed So Quickly," *Nevada State Journal*, July 23, p. 1; Gusinow's remarks are in "Jealousy Set Dillinger Trap," Chicago *Tribune*, July 24, 1934, p. 1; "Woman Witness to Dillinger 'Liquidation' Tells Simple Story of How It Was Done," Clearfield (Pa.) *Progress*, July 23, 1934, p. 1; l'Allemand's remarks can be found in "Witness Tells How Dillinger Went to His Death," Chicago *Tribune*, July 23, 1934, p. 3. L'Allemand, incidentally, was also featured prominently on newsreel footage.

29. Girardin, *Dillinger*, pp. 226, 308; Alston Purvis and Alex Tresniowski, *The Vendetta: FBI Hero Melvin Purvis' War against Crime and J. Edgar Hoover's War against Him* (New York: Public Affairs, 2005), p. 161; "Dillinger Cache Eludes Police," New York *Times*, July 26, 1934, p. 40; "Bandit Carries Photo of Indian Sweetheart," Lima (Ohio) *News*, July 23. 1934, p. 1; "Body of Arch Criminal on an Old Trail," Butte (Mont.) *Standard*, July 25, 1934, p. 1; "Face in Watch Identified," New York *Times*, July 24, 1934, p. 2; "Dillinger Watch Photo Not That of Ohio Woman," Chicago *Tribune*, July 25, 1934, p. 3; "'Girl in Red Dress' Credited with Putting John Dillinger on Spot Hidden under Guard," Zanesville (Ohio) *Times Recorder*, July 24, 1934, p. 1. On the anniversary of his death, Audrey told reporters that John often went about Chicago unarmed, but that he did wear a money belt that was missing and a ruby ring worth five hundred dollars, also never found; "Dillinger's Sister Recalls his Capture," Hammond (La.) *Times*, July 22, 1935, p 1. Dillinger's guns and bulletproof vest were found in Lake Michigan three days after his death; see S.P. Cowley memo to J. Edgar Hoover, July 25, 1934, Dillinger file, 62–29777–2985, FBI.

30. "Purvis Is Accused of Taking Credit in Dillinger Trap," Chicago *Tribune*, July 25, 1934, p. 2; "Jealousy Set Dillinger Trap," Chicago *Tribune*, July 24, 1934, p. 1. The Chicago *Herald and Examiner* wrote that one of Dillinger's chums gave Captain O'Neil of the East Chicago police the crucial news that for weeks Dillinger attended every new movie at the Biograph: Chicago *Herald and Examiner* cited in "Relentless Cop Spied on Bandit for Many Days," Newark (Ohio) *Advocate*, July 24, 1934, p. 2; "Clear Up Dillinger Mystery," Chicago *Tribune*, July 25, 1934, p. 1.

31. George Wright, "Indiana's Police Launch Quiz on Dillinger Death," Chicago *Tribune*, July 30, 1934, p. 3.

32. J. Edgar Hoover to E. A. Tamm, July 26, 1934, Dillinger file, 62–29777–2910, FBI; "Dillinger Case Suspect Killed in Loop Plunge," Chicago *Tribune*, July 27, 1934, p. 5; "Victim of Plunge Takes Dillinger Secret to Grave," Chicago *Tribune*, July 31, 1934, p. 6; "Dillinger's Host Ends Life by Leap," New York *Times*, July 27, 1934, p. 34. Purvis and Tresniowski, *The Vendetta*, pp. 170–71, quotes Doris Lockerman at length.

33. "The Death of Dillinger," Chicago *Tribune*, July 30, 1934, p. 12; J Edgar Hoover to the acting attorney general, July 31, 1934, RG 60, 95–57–8, box 14022, section 5, NARA, DOJ.

34. J. Edgar Hoover, memorandum for the acting attorney general, July 31, 1934, with appended message from *Tribune* city editor to Duffield, RG 60, 95–57–8, box 14022, section 3, NARA, DOJ.

35. Ibid. The idea that Sage and Zarkovich took Dillinger's money is plausible; we know that Sage got to Dillinger's personal property ahead of the authorities because the guns and clothes he kept in a locked closet in her building were recovered from Lake Michigan a few days after his death.

36. For example, an editorial in the Elyria (Ohio) *Chronicle-Telegram* titled "The Nation's War on Criminals," August 1, 1934, p. 10, reads like the editor worked from an FBI press release. The Bureau, according to the editorial, obtained 3,531 convictions the previous year, a 98.81 percent rate, and the feds also brought in 928 fugitives from justice. The lesson was clear: the law could not be defied successfully. Also see "Dillinger Relics Sought; Showmen Offer $100 to $1,000 for Momentos [*sic*] of Gangster," New York *Times*, July 24, 1934, p. 3; Robert T. Loughran, "U.S. Manhunters Search for Last Dillinger Refuge," Oshkosh (Wisc.) *Northwestern*, July 24, 1934, p. 1; "Girl Tricks Dillinger," Chicago *Daily News*, July 23, 1934, pp. 1, 4; "Throngs Fight for Glimpse of Dead Dillinger," Chicago *Tribune*, July 25, 1934, p. 2.

37. Fred Myers, "Throngs View Body of U.S.'s No. 1 Bad Man," Stevens Point (Wisc.) *Daily Journal*, July 24, 1934, p. 8; "Thousands File Slowly Past for View of Dillinger's Body," Oelwein (Iowa) *Daily Register*, July 24, 1934, p. 1.

38. "Crowd Storms Morgue to See Outlaw's Body," Chicago *Tribune*, July 23, 1934, p. 3. According to "Crowds of Home Town Folks See Dillinger Body," Chicago *Tribune*, July 25, 1934, p. 2, employees at the morgue estimated that fifteen thousand people came to view the corpse.

39. "Outlaw's Father to Go on Stage to Pay for Dillinger Funeral," Oshkosh (Wisc.) *Northwestern*, July 27, 1934, p. 4. Dillinger Senior defended his decision to go on the stage in a letter to an Indianapolis newspaper. He denied that he was capitalizing on John's misfortune; he barely covered John's funeral expenses when he and his family worked in an Indianapolis theater. A year later his barn burned down, leaving him without seed or tools; a traveling carnival offered him a few hundred dollars. "I don't think it is anything wrong. The newspapers capitalized a great deal more than I did. They charged John with things he never did, and kicked him down instead of giving him a square deal. I have friends all over the country and they advised me to go": "Dillinger Sr.'s Letter Defends Carnival Tour," Chicago *Tribune*, April 14, 1935, p. 22. Comment on the Dillinger show can be found in "The Dillinger 'Benefit,'" Montana *Standard*, August 1, 1934, p. 4; "The Nation's War on Criminals," Elyria (Ohio) *Chronicle-Telegram*, August 1, 1934, p. 10; "The Public as Censor," Elyria (Ohio) *Chronicle-Telegram*, August 7, 1934, p. 12; "The Dillinger Tour," Zanesville (Ohio) *Times-Recorder*, August 6, 1934, p. 4; "Ohio City Draws Line on Dillinger Troupe," Nevada *State Journal*, August 7, 1934, p. 1.

40. "Dillinger's 'Blood' on Sale in Chicago," Nevada *State Journal*, July 24, 1934, p. 1; "Showmen Scramble for Dillinger Mementoes," Oshkosh (Wisc.) *Northwestern*, July 24, 1934, p. 3; Carlton B. McCullock to Meredith Nicholson, August 2, 1934, p. 2, in Carlton B. McCullock papers, M 192, Indiana Historical Society.

41. "At the Observation Post: Photographs in Newspapers of John Dillinger's Bullet-Riddled Body Substantiate Charge That 'There Is No Aspect of Human Morbidity Which American Editors Will Not Exploit,'" *Literary Digest*, August 4, 1934, p. 11; "Gangsters Get Death Penalty for Murder," Chicago *Defender*, August 4, 1934, p. 3. One of the Black Dillingers, incidentally, was represented by a young attorney named Thurgood Marshall.

42. "Editorial Comments," *New Masses*, July 31, 1934, p. 5; Sender Garlin, "Change the World," *Daily Worker*, July 25, 1934, p. 5.

43. "Corpse of Outlaw Son Is Claimed by Parents in Chicago," Bismarck (N.D.) *Tribune,* July 24, 1934, p. 1; "Outlaw Death Closes Long Crime Career," Butte (Mont.) *Standard,* July 23, 1934, p. 1; "John Dillinger Legend Born of His Daring Deeds," Chicago *Tribune,* July 23, 1934, p. 2.

44. "Dillinger Blazed His Way," Washington *Post,* April 23, 1934, p. 2; "Arthur Brisbane," Newark (Ohio) *Advocate,* July 25, 1934, p. 4; "Death of Dillinger," Sheboygan (Wisc.) *Press,* July 23, 1934, p. 18; "Society 'Gets' Dillinger," Coshocton (Ohio) *Tribune,* July 23, 1934, p. 4; "The End of John Dillinger," Lima (Ohio) *News,* July 24, 1934, p. 6.

45. Joseph K. Shepard, "Dillinger Expected Such a Death: Sense of Humor Kept Him in Trouble," Indianapolis *Star,* July 24, 1934, p. 3.

46. Ibid.

47. Robert J. Casey, "Dillinger, the Country Boy Killer," Chicago *Daily News,* three-part series, July 25, 26, 27, 1934, pp. 5, 5, 9. Also see "John Dillinger Legend Born of His Daring Deeds," Chicago *Tribune,* July 23, 1934, p. 2. A year after Dillinger's death Matt Leach gave an interview in which he denied that Dillinger was attractive to women. "Dillinger had no sex appeal," the International News Service story quoted him as saying. "Now a man with sex appeal is one who is pursued by classy, ravishing, fancy blondes or redheads. Dillinger was pursued by federal 'G' men." Leach went on to denigrate the outlaw's girlfriends, one the married sister of Dillinger's fellow prisoner, one a "half-breed Indian girl," and one a brothel keeper: "Leach Scoffs at Dillinger's Sex Appeal," Hammond (Ind.) *Times,* October 5, 1935, p. 6.

48. "Dillinger Used Nun's Disguise, Hoover Recalls," Chicago *Tribune,* July 24, p. 2; "Dillinger Was Bankers' Guest, Hoover Claims," Frederick (Md.) *Post,* July 24, 1934, p. 1; "Varied Guises," Gettysburg (Penna.) *Times,* July 24, 1934, p. 2.

49. Hoover's use and manipulation of popular culture is the subject of Richard Gid Power's fascinating *G-Men: Hoover's FBI in American Popular Culture* (Carbondale: Southern Illinois University Press, 1983).

50. Sometimes Hoover's best skill was knowing when not to get in the way. A quarter of a million children enrolled in the Post Toasties Melvin Purvis Junior G-Men Clubs, which flourished after Purvis quit the Bureau. Purvis was paid tens of thousands of dollars for the use of his name, a comic strip featured his likeness ("Stick 'em up, Joe Barkus! . . . We've got you and your gang dead to rights this time!"), children were encouraged to take the club's pledge ("I pledge myself to obey the laws of my country. . . . I further pledge to keep myself strong and fit for all duties of the corps at all times"), and to send in cereal box tops and receive special rings, whistles, fingerprint kits, and badges: Purvis and Tresniowski, *The Vendetta,* pp. 283–84. Ray C. Tincher repeats the legend that Hoover kept Dillinger's penis in a jar, in *Inmate #13225: John Herbert Dillinger* (Baltimore: Publish America, 2007), p. v, in frontispiece titled "Triviality." The Bureau even opened its doors to public tours of its facilities; see, for example, Allen Dibble's glowing United Press report on the FBI's efficiency and sophistication, based on a two-hour visit shared with his fellow citizens: "Shooting Code of G-Men Calls for Quick Fire at the Stomach," Chillicothe (Mo.) *Constitution-Tribune,* September 25, 1937, p. 3. Another good example of the press carrying the FBI's message can be found in Marjorie Van de Water's syndicated story for *EveryWeek* Magazine, "Crime's Desperate Flight from the Fingerprint," in Lima (Ohio) *News,* June 21, 1936, n.p.

51. For all of the hype about scientific police work, it was, after all, not fingerprint or ballistics analysis that brought down Dillinger, but Martin Zarkovich's greed and Anna Sage's desire to avoid deportation.

52. For an excellent article on Hoover's influence on American popular culture, see Richard Gid Powers, "One G-Man's Family: Popular Entertainment Formulas and J. Edgar Hoover's F.B.I.," *American Quarterly* 30(4) Autumn, 1978, pp. 471–92. This article was the germ of his book, *G-Men: Hoover's FBI in American Popular Culture.*

53. Quoted in Girardin, *Dillinger*, pp. 308–9.

54. Of course the literature on the trickster and the picaresque is extensive, but see Paul Radin, *The Trickster: A Study in American Indian Mythology* (London: Routledge and Paul, 1955); Lawrence Levine, *Black Culture and Black Consciousness* (New York: Oxford University Press, 1977); and Alexander A. Parker, *Literature and the Delinquent: The Picaresque Novel in Spain and Europe.* (Edinburgh: Edinburgh University Press, 1967).

55. On social bandits, see Eric Hobsbawm, *Primitive Rebels: Studies in Archaic Forms of Social Movement During the Eighteenth and Nineteenth Centuries,* (New York, W. W. Norton, 1965). Also see Hobsbawm's *Bandits* (New York: Delacorte Press, 1969).

56. Paul Kooistra, *Criminals and Heroes: Structure, Power and Identity* (Bowling Green, Ohio: Bowling Green State University Press, 1988) makes the strongest case for Dillinger as part of a long tradition of rural American social bandits.

57. The history of consumerism has become a growth industry; start with Lizabeth Cohen's *A Consumer's Republic: The Politics of Mass Consumption in Postwar America* (New York: Alfred A. Knopf, 2003). Also see her *Making a New Deal: Industrial Workers in Chicago, 1919–1939* (New York: Cambridge University Press, 1990).

58. David Kennedy summarizes these wide-ranging responses to the Depression in his *Freedom from Fear: The American People in Depression and War, 1929–1945* (New York: Oxford University Press, 2001).

59. Lynn Dumenil, *The Modern Temper: American Culture and Society in the 1920s* (New York: Hill and Wang, 1995), pp. 76–97; Alan Brinkley, *Voices of Protest: Huey Long, Father Coughlin, and the Great Depression* (New York: Alfred A. Knopf, 1982).

60. For examples of FSA photographs, see Walker Evans, *Photographs for the Farm Security Administration, 1933–1938* (New York: Da Capo Press, 1978); Dorothea Lange, *An American Exodus: A Record of Human Erosion* (New York: Reynal and Hitchcock, 1939). Decades later, playing with the conventions of martyrdom, Dillinger scholars Rick Mattix and William Helmer founded, tongue-in-cheek, the "John Dillinger Died for You Society."

Chapter Seven

1. The discrepancy in eye color is better explained by the occlusion of the human cornea at death than by a cadaverous bait and switch. In fact the autopsy report described Dillinger's cornea as cloudy: "Long-lost Report on Dillinger Is Found," Indianapolis *Star*, March 25, 1984, p. 1. The FBI's Dillinger file contains a copy of the coroner's report and minutes of the inquest: 62–29777–2941–2943, FBI. Joe Pinkston reported that folks in Mooresville believed Dillinger was still alive as of the 1960s: Joe M. Pinkston, "Dillinger: Morgan County Youth Becomes Nation's Number One Desperado," *Hoosierland*, February 1963, pp. 24–26.

2. Robert Nash, *The Dillinger Dossier* (Highland Park, Ill.: December Press, 1983). Also see Ron Offen and Jay Robert Nash, *Dillinger: Dead or Alive?* (Chicago: H. Regnery, 1970). In the strained logic of conspiracy narratives one story even had Dillinger present at the assassination of President Kennedy; see Robert Shea and Robert Anton Wilson, *The Illuminatus Trilogy* (New York: Dell, 1983).

3. Riggs was no doubt influenced by Nash, *The Dillinger Dossier*. "Barber, Others Weren't Sure That Body in Coffin Was His," *Indianapolis Star*, July 24, 1983, pp. 1, 3F; see also Kay Severinsen, "Did John Dillinger Really Die?" Scottsdale (Ariz.) *Progress*, March 31, 1934, in Dillinger file, Mooresville Public Library (hereafter MPL).

4. The Discovery channel recently reprised the story with a documentary, *The Dillinger Conspiracy* (2006).

5. See "A List of Songs Concerning John Dillinger" (ms), Archive of Folk Song, Library of Congress (hereafter AFC.LC). The list has thirteen titles, a few of them with multiple copyrights. The Library of Congress also has two commercial recordings and one field recording.

6. Rieley Lausch and Cliff Grey, "John Dillinger," 1934, E pub. 43221, AFC.LC; Bob Miller, "Killer John Dillinger," New York, 1934, E unpub. 91430, AFC.LC. Miller's song is a partly typed, partly handwritten manuscript; he obviously rushed it to print because the accession date for "Killer John Dillinger" at the Library of Congress is July 24, 1934, just two days after the outlaw's death. The Frank Luther Trio probably recorded it within a month for Conqueror Records, #8385, Matrix # 15158–2; my thanks to A. Lanset for the recording. Another song in the vein of evil brought down is Buck Nation, "The End of Public Enemy #1," recorded February, 19, 1935, Decca MX #39372, Label #5075B.

7. On broadside ballads, see Leslie Shepard, *The Broadside Ballad: A Study in Origins and Meaning* (London: H. Jenkins, 1962).

8. Hershel K. Deckard, "The Life and Fate of John Dillinger," cie unpub. 92170; Forrest Herbert, "John Dillinger," 1934, E pub. 45965, both in AFC.LC. See "A List of Songs Concerning John Dillinger," 1.12/2: D 58, AFC.LC.

9. Wilf Carter, "The Life and Death of John Dillinger," Gordon V. Thompson, Limited, Toronto, 1936, E pub. 201930, AFC.LC; Dwight Butcher's recording of "John Dillinger," originally released 1934, rereleased on Certified Records, CR 1502, LP 1972, A.07, both AFC.LC.

10. Frank Carlisle and Al Arnstam, "The Death of John Dillinger," Hill Billy Publications, Milwaukee, 1934, E pub. 43804; "Dillinger's Doom," no author, E unpub. 91545 (both AFC.LC). Available on tape is Bill Cox, "The Gangster's Yodel," Melotone Recordings, 9/4/34, Label #13067, MX #15853.

11. Dorothy Hardy and H. Robinson Vaughan, "John Dillinger," Victoria, VA, E pub. 46203, AFC.LC.

12. Ibid. Also see Nelson Algren's magnificent *Chicago: City on the Make* (New York: Doubleday, 1951).

13. "Van Meter, Dillinger Gangster, Slain," *Chicago* Tribune, August 24, 1934, p. 1; "Van Meter, Dillinger Aide, Slain by Police," Salamanca (N.Y.) *Republican-Press*, August 24, 1934, p. 1; "Two Dillinger Bandits to Die, Third Draws Life in Prison," Helena (Mont.) *Daily Independent*, March 25, 1934, p. 1; "Dillinger Aid Slain in Break at Death House," Chicago *Tribune*, September 23, 1934, p. 1; "Go 'Head, Shoot Last Words of Dying Gunman," Zanesville (Ohio) *Times-Signal*, September 23, 1934, p. 1; "Pierpont to Live, Bullet Still in Back," Gettysburg (Pa.) *Times*, September 24,

1934, p. 3; "Pierpont Dies in Chair; Shot Dillinger Free," Chicago *Tribune*, October 17, 1934, p. 1; "Dillinger Gunner, Van Meter, Slain by St. Paul Police," New York *Times*, August 24, 1934, p. 1; "Dillinger Lawyer and Surgeons Held," New York *Times*, September 2, 1934, p. 6.

14. "2 Dillinger Doctors Confess," Chicago *Tribune*, September 2, 1934, p. 1; "Call Law Office a Dillinger Den," New York *Times*, September 5, 1934, p. 16; "Lawyer Called Payoff Man of Dillinger Gang," Chicago *Tribune*, September 7, 1934, p. 3; "U.S. Jury Indicts Piquett and 3 in Dillinger Plot," Chicago *Tribune*, September 7, 1934, p. 3; Philip Kinsley, "Swear Piquett Hid Dillinger," Chicago *Tribune*, January 10, 1935, p. 1; Philip Kinsley, "U.S. Jury Sets Piquett Free," January 15, 1935, p. 1; "Pequett [*sic*] Defense Opens; Battles Woman's Story," Chicago *Tribune*, June 23, 1935, p. 3; Philip Kinsley, "Jury Told How Piquett Walked into U.S. Trap," Chicago *Tribune*, June 22, 1935, p. 2; Philip Kinsley, "Lawyer Piquett Convicted," Chicago *Tribune*, June 26, 1935 p. 1; "Bar Group Votes Disbarment of Lawyer Piquett," October 2, 1935, p. 11. Justice Department documents can be found in RG 60, 95–57–8, box 14023, files 6 and 7, National Archives and Records Administration (hereafter NARA).

15. "George Nelson New U.S. Public Enemy No. 1," Chicago *Tribune*, August 5, 1934, p. 21; "Two Shot Down in Clash with Outlaw Nelson," Chicago *Tribune*, November 28, 1934, p. 1; "'Babe' Nelson Kills Agent in Pistol Battle," Gettysburg (Penna.) *Times*, November 28, 1934, p. 2; "'Baby Face' Nelson Kills 2 U.S. Agents in Illinois Battle," New York *Times*, November 28, 1934, p. 1; "Seventeen Bullet Wounds Are Found in Gangster's Body," Charleston (W.Va.) *Daily Mail*, November 28, 1934, p. 1; "Outlaw Nelson Found Dead from Slain Officers' Shots," New York *Times*, November 29, 1934, p. 1; "Federal Agents Tell Thrills of Nelson Battle," Chicago *Tribune*, March 20, 1935, p. 1. Also see the documents in RG 60, 95–57–8, section 2, file 2, box 14022, and files 6 and 8, box 14023, NARA, Department of Justice (hereafter DOJ); "Find Last Dillinger Aid Dead," Chicago *Tribune*, August 29, 1935, p. 1; Earl Aykroid, "Finding of Body Told by G-Men," Ironwood (Mich.) *Daily Globe*, August 29, 1935, p. 1.

16. "Policemen Who Found Dillinger Rewarded by Government," Gettysburg (Pa.) *Times*, October 5, 1934, p. 5; "Order Insurance Paid in Dillinger Suspect's Death," Chicago *Tribune*, March 15, 1935, p. 20; "Three Shot by U.S. Agents in Dillinger Fights Denied Pay," Chicago *Tribune*, October 14, 1934, p. 9. Also see the federal documents in RG 60, 95–57–8, Central files, classified subjects, correspondence, box 14022, files 6 and 7, NARA, DOJ; "Contend O'Neil Fired Shot Fatal to Dillinger," Sheboygan (Wisc.) *Press*, October 1, 1935, p. 9; "Old Dispute as to Who Shot Bandit J. Dillinger," Hammond (Ind.) *Times*, February 13, 1936, p. 1; "U.S. Agents Too Quick on Trigger, Lawyers Charge," Chicago *Tribune*, December 1, 1934, p. 9; "Dillinger About to Give Up As Guns Bark," Hammond (Ind.) *Times*, October 29, 1935, n.p.; "Purvis Quits G Men; 'Glad to Get Out,'" Chicago *Tribune*, July 13, 1935, p. 1; "Dillinger's Betrayer to Sail Monday," Syracuse (N.Y.) *Herald*, April 25, 1936, p. 2; "Not Keeping Faith," Miami (Fla.) *Herald*, n.d., n.p., in RG 60, 95–57–8, box 14023, file 8, NARA, DOJ.

17. Frank Cipriani, "Records Shed New Light on Dillinger Assassination," Chicago *Tribune*, July 21, 1935, pp. D7, 10. Also see the Independent News Service stories "Dillinger's Sister Recalls His Capture" and "Dillinger Was Killed Year Ago Tonight," both reprinted in Hammond (Ind.) *Times*, July 22, 1935, pp. 1, 11.

18. Ellen Paulsen, *Don't Call Us Molls: Women of the John Dillinger Gang* (Little Neck, NY: Clinton Cook Publishing Company, 2002), p. 403. The feds kept

after Billie for the money for twenty years. They finally closed the case in 1954. See letter from George E. Mackinnon to the Department of Justice, Criminal Division, dated December 20, 1954, advising them that the Office of Indian Affairs in the Department of the Interior had paid Billie's fine in full. For this and related documents, see RG 60, 95–57–8, box 1, NARA, DOJ.

19. I've not found a script or transcript of the program; for a description, see Larry Wolters, "News of the Radio Stations," Chicago *Tribune*, July 19, 1934, p. 18. Writing the Dillinger script launched a whole new career for Phillips Lord; the following year he began the enormously popular series *Gang Busters* for CBS, featuring the on-air voice of Colonel Norman Schwarzkopf, the man who solved the Lindbergh kidnapping case. In preparing the series Lord's staff had direct access to J. Edgar Hoover's office.

20. Jack Alexander, "Profiles: The Director—I," *New Yorker*, September 25, 1937, p. 20; J. Edgar Hoover, *Persons in Hiding* (Boston: Little, Brown, 1938), pp. 93, 303. Both quoted in William Beverly, *On the Lam: Narratives of Flight in J. Edgar Hoover's America* (Jackson: University of Mississippi Press, 2003), pp. 67–68.

21. I am especially indebted to Beverly's chapter about John Dillinger, "'This Sure Keeps a Fellow Moving': The Making of John Dillinger," in *On the Lam*, pp. 67–112.

22. "Chicagoland," Chicago *Tribune*, December 1, 1935, p. A8.

23. These are remarkably forgettable books. See Saul Cooper, *Dillinger* (New York: Hillman Books, 1959); Ovid Demaris, *Dillinger* (New York: Belmont Tower Books, 1961); Dean Fredericks, *John Dillinger* (New York: Pyramid Books, 1963); Sidney Stewart, *Young Dillinger* (New York: Belmont Books, 1965).

24. See, for example, Don Reeder, "Dillinger Shot Down 25 Years Ago," Pasco (Wash.) *Tri-City Herald*, July 22, 1959, p. 11. Ten years later newspapers gave the anniversary even less space, although Rex Redifer wrote an article in the Indianapolis *Star* capturing the likable qualities of the young Dillinger—charming, loyal, friendly, quick to smile, a youth bored by the farm, finding small adventure in girls, baseball, and fast cars—whose life was simply enveloped first by prison, then by the Great Depression: "Luck Ran Out for 'Johnnie Dillinger,'" July 23, 1969, p. 1, in Dillinger file, MPL.

25. Robert Cromie and Joe Pinkston, *Dillinger: A Short and Violent Life* (New York: McGraw Hill, 1962); John Toland, *The Dillinger Days* (New York: Random House, 1963).

26. *The Untouchables* ran from 1959 to 1963 on the American Broadcasting System; it is available on DVD from CBS Home Entertainment; *Dragnet* ran from 1951 to 1959 on the National Broadcasting Network; it is available on DVD from Alpha Home Entertainment.

27. *G-Men*, DVD, directed by William Keigley (1935; Burbank, Calif.: Warner Home Video, 2006); *Petrified Forest*, DVD, directed by Archie Mayo (1936; Burbank, Calif.: Warner Home Video, 2005).

28. *High Sierra*, DVD, directed by Raoul Walsh (1941; Burbank, Calif.: Warner Home Video, 2006).

29. *Dillinger*, DVD, directed by Max Nosseck (1945; Burbank, Calif.: Warner Home Video, 2005). Twenty years later, Terry O. Morse directed *Young Dillinger* for United Artists, a 1965 film starring Nick Adams as Dillinger and Mary Ann Mobley as Billie Frechette. You have to search hard for this movie. The Library of Congress film division has one reel of it; it is not on DVD; there were very few reviews.

30. *Bonnie and Clyde*, DVD, directed by Arthur Penn (1967; Burbank, Calif.: Warner Brothers/Seven Arts, 1999).

31. *Dillinger*, DVD, directed by John Milius (1973; Burbank, Calif.: MGM, 2000).

32. Ibid.

33. Ibid.

34. Ibid.

35. Ibid.

36. Ibid. Also worth viewing is *Dillinger and Capone*, DVD, directed by Jon Purdy (1995; New Concorde Studios, 2002).

37. Joseph Snurr to the director of Scientific Research Dept., May 15, 1974, and Laurel Overman, associate editor, *The Book of Lists*, to Western History curator, July 13, 1978, Smithsonian Institution, Dillinger Letters file (hereafter SIDL). All of the letters referred to here are from the Dillinger Letters file, kept by the Division of Medical Sciences. The file contains a few dozen letters in total, all from the early 1970s through early 1990s, plus office memoranda and clippings such as the article in *Playboy*. Judith Chelnick kindly allowed me access to the file.

38. Patsy Jo Masonhall, San Antonio, to Smithsonian Institute, September 5, 1974; Mr. W. E. Wright, Westwood, New Jersey, to Smithsonian Institute, March 28, 1973; Brian Gaston, Durham, North Carolina, to Smithsonian, March 4, 1975; Mrs. James Reynolds, North Chili, New York, to Office of the Secretary, Smithsonian Institution, January 29, 1992, all in SIDL.

39. Jack H. to Med. Sci., n.d.; Jeff Sacks, Washington, D.C., to Office of Exhibits, April 15, 1988; Linda Raffel, New Dorm, Alfred University, to Smithsonian, September 25, 1973; A. Rolff, Houston, to Smithsonian Institute of Medical Science, n.d.; Gary Simpson, Reese Hall, University of Tennessee, to Smithsonian, n.d.; "The regular customers of this Bar," to whom it may concern, December 24, 1974, all in SIDL. Also see Robert Zumstein, Evanston, Illinois, to Smithsonian Institute, August 29, 1973, SIDL.

40. James H. Griggs, Birmingham, Alabama, to Smithsonian Institute, May 18, 1973; Elizabeth Vieux, Jamaica Plain, Massachusetts, to curator, Smithsonian Institute, October 20, 1973; John R. Smith, Palm Beach, Florida, to unnamed correspondent, n.d., all in SIDL.

41. William J. Helmer, "A Quiz You Can't Refuse," *Playboy*, March, 1991, n.p., copy, SIDL. For an interesting discussion of human remains, real and fictive, in the National Museum of Health and Medicine of the Armed Forces Institute of Pathology, see Paul S. Sledzik and Lenore T. Barbian, "From Privates to Presidents: Past and Present Memoirs from the Anatomical Collections of the National Museum of Health and Medicine," in Emily Williams, ed., *Human Remains: Conservation, Retrieval, and Analysis*, proceedings of a conference held in Williamsburg Virginia, November 7–11, 1999, BAR International Series 934, 2001, n.p.

42. For example, in the early 1970s the Smithsonian's Division of Medical Sciences sent out memos to all who enquired about Dillinger that read in part, "The Smithsonian Institution does not have any part of the anatomy of John Dillinger. We have never had an exhibit on Dillinger, nor do we have anatomical specimens in our medical collection." Twenty years later the Smithsonian felt the need to send out another memo, which read, "The National Museum of American History does not have nor do we know of any other museum or institution that has any part of the anatomy of John Dillinger." SIDL.

43. Helmer discusses the legend and the 1930s cartoon in G. Russell Girardin with William J. Helmer, *Dillinger: The Untold Story* (Bloomington: Indiana University Press, 1994), p. 312. Hal Kirshbaum, "Legend—Personal," reported February 25, 1969, in U.C. Berkeley Folklore Archive, Department of Folklore, Kroeber Hall, Dillinger File; Ronald L. Baker, *Hoosier Folk Legends* (Bloomington: Indiana University Press, 1984), #181, "Why the Lady in Red Betrayed Dillinger," p. 161, and #182, "Dillinger's Long Penis in the Smithsonian," p. 162. The Internet is also packed with Dillinger lore.

44. Joseph Snurr to director of scientific research, May 15, 1974, SIDL.

45. Norman Mailer, "The White Negro: Superficial Reflections on the Hipster," *Dissent*, Fall 1957; Barbara Ehrenreich, *The Hearts of Men: American Dreams and the Flight from Commitment* (New York: Anchor Press/Doubleday, 1983), especially chapters 4–9; Michael Kimmel sketches the historical background of mid-twentieth century masculinity in *Manhood in America: A Cultural History* (New York: Free Press, 1996), pp. 223–90.

46. "Dillinger Defied Capture for Year," New York *Times*, July 23, 1934, p. 10; "Women Figured Prominently in Dillinger's Life," Zanesville (Ohio) *Times Recorder*, July 24, 1934, p. 1; "Clear Up Dillinger Mystery," Chicago *Tribune*, July 25, 1934, p. 1; "Jealousy Set Dillinger Trap," Chicago *Tribune*, July 24, 1934, p. 1; Martinsville (Ind.) *Republican*, no title, n.p., in Dillinger file, MPL.

47. Tincher reports the legend of J. Edgar Hoover keeping Dillinger's manhood in a jar on his desk in *Inmate #13225, John Herbert Dillinger*, p. v.

48. For the widely reprinted Associated Press story, see, for example, James Litke, "50th Anniversary of Death of Gangster John Dillinger," Clearfield (Pa.) *Progress*, July 23, 1984, p. 7.

49. Don Hayner, "Dillinger: 50 Years Later, the Legend Lives" Chicago *Sun Times*, July 22, 1984, pp. 16, 17; Anna Madrzyk, "Dillinger," Chicago *Sunday Herald* (published in Arlington Heights, a northern suburb), July 22, 1984, section 5, p. 8.

50. Anne Saker, "Town Can't Forget the Daring Dillinger," *USA Today*, January 2, 1991, p. 6A.

51. Michael Stewart, "Famous Gangster Catapults Greencastle into National Spotlight," *The DePauw*, April 24, 1987, p. 12. Other pieces from Greencastle, Indiana, can be found in a file kept by the Greencastle Public Library: Larry Gibbs, "Dillinger's Gang Came to Violent End within Months after Greencastle Robbery," Greencastle *Daily Banner*, September 13, 1969, n.p.; John J. Baughman, "Our Past, Their Present," *Greencastle Monthly*, March 2000, p. 7; Larry Gibbs, "50 Years Ago Sunday, John Dillinger Thrust Greencastle into National Headlines," Greencastle *Banner-Graphic*, October 20, 1983, n.p.; Bluffton-Richland, Ohio, Public Library, press release, August 10, 1998; "Footnote to the Dillinger Robbery of '33," Bluffton (Ohio) *News*, November 13, 1997, p. 2; "The Day John Dillinger Robbed Our Bank," Bluffton (Ohio) *News*, December 24, 1998, p. 26; James L. Kalleen III, "The John Dillinger Saga," *Indianapolis Home and Garden*, April 1979, p. 20; Brian Downes, "The Dillinger Trail," Chicago *Tribune*, March 13, 1994, pp. 1, 10, 11.

52. "Crown Point Studying Promotion of Dillinger," Bloomington (Ind.) *Herald Times*, November 12, 1993, p. C4. Just a few months before this story, the Fort Wayne *News Sentinel* ran a long story by Tanya Isch Caylor titled "An Awkward Claim to Fame" (April 3, 1993), which described how Crown Point residents still hesitated to talk about Dillinger's jailbreak or Sheriff Lillian Holley. Mooresville, Dillinger's hometown, still does not commemorate its most famous citizen. When the Dillinger

farmhouse came up for sale, local businessmen allegedly purchased it rather than see it made into a museum, and when a McDonald's restaurant decorated its walls with Dillinger memorabilia the volume of complaints forced management to take them all down. As recently as 2002 the town council rejected a new plan to hold a "Dillinger Days" festival and develop a local museum, claiming these would draw unwanted attention to Mooresville's connection to Dillinger. "He was a criminal bum, and he's dead, so let him stay that way," one councilman told a reporter. Randy Haymaker, "Fifty Years of the Correct Posture," Mooresville *Times*, July 25, 1984, p. 6, in Dillinger file, MPL; "Town Council Rejects Idea of 'Dillinger Days' Festival," Lafayette (Ind.) *Journal-Courier*, January 11, 2002, p. B5; "Town Snubs Dillinger," *New York Times*, January 11, 2002, p. A18.

53. "Wax Dillinger Moves on Down the Road," Indianapolis *Star*, January 27, 1993, p. E3; "Indiana Town Honors Gangster John Dillinger," Elyria (Ohio) *Chronicle-Telegram*, April 7, 1994, p. D7. After Pinkston's untimely death Lake County seized the opportunity to open its museum.

54. Rich Bird, "Dillinger Museum Hits Positive Note," Indianapolis *Star*, November 7, 1999, pp. K1–2; Summer Wood, "Punishment and Posterity," *ArtsIndiana*, Summer 2001, pp. 16–17; "Distant Relative of John Dillinger Fights for Rights to 'Public Enemy No. 1,'" Gettysburg (Pa.) *Times*, January 13, 2004, p. 8.

55. Kim Beck, "Smoke, Guns and Gangsters," *Tucson Guide Quarterly*, Winter 2002–2003, pp. 68–71; "Tucson Ready to Celebrate Dillinger Days," Tucson *Citizen*, January 17, 2004, p. 1; Laurel Allen, "City Week—Bang, You're History," Tucson *Weekly*, January 20, 2005, online edition; Janet Webb Farnsworth, "The Day Tucson Corralled Dillinger," *Arizona Highways*, January 8, 2006, online edition; Elana Acoba, "Going Gangbusters," Arizona *Daily Star*, January 19, 2006, online edition; Alexis Huicochea, "Police Shoot at Teen at Festivities," Arizona *Daily Star*, January 22, 2006, online edition. Since the 1970s the Tucson newspapers have run frequent stories about the Dillinger gang; see the thick Dillinger file at the Arizona Historical Society.

56. Stephen Kinzer, "Felonious and Urbane, Dillinger Still Charms," New York *Times*, July 25, 2004, p. 11. The Internet is filled with booking information, fan commentary, and more for Daz Dillinger and the Dillinger Escape Plan.

57. Mark Sufrin, "Dillinger: Public Enemy," *American History Illustrated*, February 10, 1970, pp. 34–43.

58. Jay Robert Nash, *The Dillinger Dossier*, (Highland Park, Ill.: December Press, 1983); G. Russell Girardin, with William J. Helmer, *Dillinger: The Untold Story* (Bloomington: Indiana University Press, 1994); Paul Maccabee, *John Dillinger Slept Here: A Crooks' Tour of Crime and Corruption in St Paul, 1920–1936* (St. Paul: Minnesota Historical Society Press, 1995); Claire Bond Potter, *War on Crime: Bandits, G-Men, and the Politics of Mass Culture* (New Brunswick, N.J.: Rutgers University Press, 1998); William Beverly, *On the Lam: Narratives of Flight in J. Edgar Hoover's America* (Oxford: University Press of Mississippi, 2008).

59. Ellen Poulsen, *Don't Call Us Molls: Women of the John Dillinger Gang* (Little Neck, N.Y.: Clinton Cook Publishing Co., 2002); Dary Matera, *John Dillinger: The Life and Death of America's First Celebrity Criminal* (New York: Carroll and Graf Publishers, 2004); Bryan Burrough, *Public Enemies: America's Greatest Crime Wave and the Birth of the FBI, 1933–1934* (New York: Penguin Press, 2004); Jeffrey S. King, *The Rise and Fall of the Dillinger Gang* (Nashville, Tenn.: Cumberland House Publishing, 2005); Alston Purvis with Alex Tresniowski, *The Vendetta: FBI Hero*

Melvin Purvis's War Against Crime, and J. Edgar Hoover's War Against Him (New York: Public Affairs, 2005). Also see Tony Stewart, *Dillinger, the Hidden Truth* (n.p., Xlibris Books, 2002); and Ray C. Tincher, *Inmate #13225, John Herbert Dillinger, Public Enemy #1* (Baltimore: Publishamerica, 2007).

60. Reginald Marsh's *The Death of Dillinger* is owned by the Phoenix Art Institute. The painting was reproduced in *Life*, March 11, 1940, pp. 70–71.

61. Todd Moore, *The Name Is Dillinger* (n.p.: Kangaroo Court Publishing, 1986), pp. 1, 13, 9, 12.

62. Jack Kelly, *Mad Dog* (New York: Atheneum, 1992), pp. 147, 242.

63. James Carlos Blake, *Handsome Harry* (New York: William Morrow, 2004). Also see Stephen King's poignant short story, "The Death of Jack Hamilton," *The New Yorker*, September 24, 2001, p. 76. Kurt Vonnegut invoked Dillinger on the very first page of his novel *Jailbird* (New York: Dial Press, 1979): "Crown Point is notorious for a jailbreak there by the bank robber John Dillinger, during the depths of the Great Depression. . . . Dillinger was the Robin Hood of my early youth. He is buried near my parents—and near my sister Alice, who admired him even more than I did—in Crown Hill Cemetery in Indianapolis. . . . Dillinger was summarily executed by agents of the Federal Bureau of Investigation. He was shot down in a public place, although he was not trying to escape or resist arrest. So there is nothing recent in my lack of respect for the F.B.I."

64. There are several biographies of Hoover; see Richard Gid Powers, *Secrecy and Power, The Life of J. Edgar Hoover* (New York: Free Press, 1986); Kenneth Ackerman, *Young J. Edgar: Hoover, the Red Scare, and the Assault on Civil Liberties* (New York: Da Capo Press, 2007); Curt Gentry, *J Edgar Hoover, the Man and the Secrets* (New York: Norton, 2001). Kelly, *Mad Dog*, p. 267. The powerful image of the outlaw on the open road, of course, is why Dillinger was so often compared to Jesse James. But see T. J. Stiles's excellent biography, *Jesse James: Last Rebel of the Civil War* (New York: Vintage, 2003), for a much different take on the Missouri bandit.

65. John Patterson, "On Film: The Bust Boom," *The Guardian*, September 26, 2008, online edition.

Index